The Definitive Guide to Jakarta Faces in Jakarta EE 10

Building Java-Based Enterprise Web Applications

Second Edition

Bauke Scholtz
Arjan Tijms

Apress®

The Definitive Guide to Jakarta Faces in Jakarta EE 10: Building Java-Based Enterprise Web Applications

Bauke Scholtz
Willemstad, Curaçao

Arjan Tijms
Amsterdam, Noord-Holland, The Netherlands

ISBN-13 (pbk): 978-1-4842-7309-8
https://doi.org/10.1007/978-1-4842-7310-4

ISBN-13 (electronic): 978-1-4842-7310-4

Managing Director, Apress Media LLC: Welmoed Spahr
Acquisitions Editor: Steve Anglin
Development Editor: Laura Berendson
Coordinating Editor: Mark Powers

Cover designed by eStudioCalamar

Cover image by Shutterstock (www.shutterstock.com)

Distributed to the book trade worldwide by Apress Media, LLC, 1 New York Plaza, New York, NY 10004, U.S.A. Phone 1-800-SPRINGER, fax (201) 348-4505, e-mail orders-ny@springer-sbm.com, or visit www.springeronline.com. Apress Media, LLC is a California LLC and the sole member (owner) is Springer Science + Business Media Finance Inc (SSBM Finance Inc). SSBM Finance Inc is a **Delaware** corporation.

For information on translations, please e-mail booktranslations@springernature.com; for reprint, paperback, or audio rights, please e-mail bookpermissions@springernature.com.

Apress titles may be purchased in bulk for academic, corporate, or promotional use. eBook versions and licenses are also available for most titles. For more information, reference our Print and eBook Bulk Sales web page at http://www.apress.com/bulk-sales.

Any source code or other supplementary material referenced by the author in this book is available to readers on GitHub. For more detailed information, please visit http://www.apress.com/source-code.

Printed on acid-free paper

Table of Contents

About the Authors

Bauke Scholtz is an Oracle Java Champion, a committer of the Jakarta Faces API and Mojarra projects, and the main creator of the Jakarta Faces helper library OmniFaces. He is on the Internet more commonly known as BalusC who is among the top users and contributors on Stack Overflow. Bauke has integrated several OmniFaces solutions into Jakarta Faces. He is a web application specialist and consults or has consulted for Virtua Inc, Mercury1 Limited, MyTutor, Nava Finance, LinkPizza, ZEEF, M4N/Zanox, ITCA, RDC, and clients from fintech, affiliate marketing, big data, social media, and more as part of his more than 20 years of experience. This book offers Bauke the opportunity to go into depth as to answering most frequently asked questions and correctly solving most commonly encountered problems while using Jakarta Faces.

Arjan Tijms works for Payara Services Ltd and is a Jakarta Faces (JSR 372) and Security API (JSR 375) Expert Group member. He is the co-creator of the popular OmniFaces library for Jakarta Faces that was a 2015 Duke's Choice Award winner and is the main creator of a set of tests for the Jakarta EE authentication SPI (JASPIC) that has been used by various Jakarta EE vendors. Arjan holds an MSc in Computer Science from the University of Leiden, the Netherlands. Writing about this topic was a natural choice for Arjan; he has already written much about it at his blog and would like to expand that by contributing to a book.

About the Technical Reviewer

Luqman Saeed is a Jakarta EE developer with Pedantic Devs. He has been in software development for close to a decade. He started with PHP and now does Jakarta EE full time. His goal on Udemy is to help you get productive with powerful, modern, intuitive, and easy-to-use Jakarta EE APIs. He will provide you with the best of vanilla, pure, and awesome Jakarta EE courses to help you master the skills needed to solve whatever development challenge you have at hand.

CHAPTER 1

History

This chapter describes the history of Jakarta Faces, starting from its early conception and ending where we are today at the moment of writing. We'll discuss how the Jakarta Faces API (application programming interface) itself evolved, which important events took place during that evolution, and who some of the people were that were involved in all of this.

This is in no way a complete description of the history, and the reader should take notice of the fact that many more events took place and many more people were involved than we were able to mention here.

In the Beginning...

Jakarta Faces goes back a long time. Its initial JSR, JSR 127, started in 2001. At that time, the Struts web framework was wildly popular, although it wasn't that long ago that it was released itself (around 2000). Despite Struts' popularity, a large number of other web frameworks were in use in the Java space, and new ones were popping up all the time. Jakarta Faces was conceived as an attempt to bring a standardized MVC (model-view-controller) web framework base into the overall Jakarta EE platform.

Controversies are quite common in the web framework space, and Jakarta Faces is no exception here. Right at the start of its inception, there was a big controversy where Apache opposed the creation of Jakarta Faces on the bases that Apache Struts already existed and a closed source alternative would have little value. Apache therefore voted against the creation of Jakarta Faces with the following comment:

> *This JSR conflicts with the Apache open source project Struts. Considering Sun's current position that JSRs may not be independently implemented under an open source license, we see little value in recreating a technology in a closed environment that is already available in an open environment.*

© Bauke Scholtz and Arjan Tijms 2022
B. Scholtz and A. Tijms, *The Definitive Guide to Jakarta Faces in Jakarta EE 10*,
https://doi.org/10.1007/978-1-4842-7310-4_1

To the extent that this JSR extends beyond Struts today, we would encourage the Sun developers proposing this JSR to join the Sun developers already leading Struts to create an open solution at Apache, something which when finished would be assured of being able to be implemented as open source.

Eventually the conflict was resolved when after about a year into the process, spec lead Amy Fowler (from Swing fame) was replaced by Craig McClanahan, the very father of the Struts project that Jakarta Faces was said to be competing with. The open source restriction was lifted as well, and the open source Jakarta Faces implementation, called MyFaces, was developed in parallel with the (then nameless) RI and hence the specification itself. MyFaces initially started as an LGPL licensed project at `http://sourceforge.net` in December 2002 and had an initial 0.1 release conforming to what was then called an "Early Access Specification" in January 2003.

Open source implementations are the most common implementations in Jakarta EE 8, and there's barely any EE specification at the time of this writing (2018) that's still implemented as closed source. In 2001, however, this was not just uncommon; it was actually not allowed for new JSRs. Allowing for an open source implementation was therefore quite a change, and the honor fell to Jakarta Faces to be the first of its kind for which this was allowed.

Despite the open source implementation being allowed, the actual development of the spec was still done in secret and behind closed doors. There was no public mailing list and no tracker (e.g., a JIRA instance) for the public to create issues or express wishes. Occasionally, interviews were being done, and in the fall of 2002, by then, former spec lead Amy Fowler did reveal quite a few details about Jakarta Faces, but largely the project was shrouded in mystery for the general public.

The team behind Jakarta Faces was, however, hard at work. The first email to the internal JSR 127 list was sent on August 17, 2001. As with most projects, the team spent the initial months on gathering requirements and looking at the existing competing products. A package name was chosen as well. The initial placeholder package, which was "`javax.servlet.ui`", now "`javax.faces`", was chosen as the package to use. The very first technical architecture to be considered was the component model. For a component-based MVC framework, this is obviously one of the most important aspects. During the last month of 2001 and the first two months of 2002, the team looked at what is now known as the Managed Bean (called "Object Manager" then). Managed beans with their scopes, names, and dependency injection are clearly another cornerstone of the Jakarta Faces framework. Events and the model behind it were being looked at as well during that time frame.

In the second quarter of 2002, two other cornerstones of Jakarta Faces were discussed: the Expression Language (inspired by Jakarta Tags), which is instrumental for the so-called bindings of beans from a template to backing code, and the factory finder, which allowed key parts of Jakarta Faces to be replaced and, although perhaps not fully realized at the time, may have contributed greatly to Jakarta Faces still being relevant some 16 years later.

It was in this same quarter that Craig McClanahan took over as spec lead, father of Struts and architect of Tomcat's Servlet container. Not long after the discussion about using Jakarta Pages started, a discussion, perhaps unbeknownst to the team at the time, that would, unfortunately, have a rather negative impact on Jakarta Faces later on. Around the end of the year 2002, Ed Burns, who like McClanahan had also worked on Tomcat before, joined the team as co-spec lead. Burns is the person who would eventually become the main spec lead of Jakarta Faces for well over a decade.

While the team continued to work on things like the aforementioned managed beans and the so-called value binding, which is the Java representation of the also aforementioned expression language binding, the first dark cloud appeared when in the spring of 2003, team member Hans Bergsten realized that there were very real and major issues with using Jakarta Pages as the templating language for Jakarta Faces. He brought these concerns to the team, but ultimately they weren't addressed and instead the following months were spent, among other things, on a variant of the value binding; it later on became clear that the method binding and the state saving mechanism were another of Jakarta Faces's less-than-ideal implementations.

Jakarta Faces 1.0 and its still nameless RI were eventually released on March 11, 2004—coincidentally, a mere two weeks before the release of another framework that's still strong today, Spring 1.0. MyFaces released its 1.0.0 alpha version only days later, on March 19. It's perhaps an interesting observation that Jakarta Faces went final with a full-fledged XML-based dependency injection (DI) framework just before Spring, which is largely known for its DI, went final.

Jakarta Faces 1.0 was generally well received; despite a rather crowded market with competitors such as Tapestry, WebObjects, Velocity, and Cocoon operating, not less than three books from writers such as Horst Caymann and Hans Bergsten appeared in the months after, and the eXo platform (a Digital Collaboration Platform) started using Jakarta Faces right away.

Hans Bergsten's earlier concerns, however, became painfully clear almost just as quickly; the Jakarta Pages technology is based on processing a template from start to end, immediately writing to the response as tags are encountered. Jakarta Faces, however, requires a phased approach where components need to be able to inspect and act on the component tree, which is built from the tags on the page, before starting to write anything to the response. This mismatch led to many strange issues, such as content disappearing or being rendered out of order.

Only three months after the introduction of Jakarta Faces, Hans Bergsten made a strong case of dropping Jakarta Pages in his legendary article "Improving Jakarta Faces by Dumping Jakarta Pages." There, Bergsten explains how ill-suited Jakarta Pages is for use as a template language in Jakarta Faces, but he also presents a glimmer of hope; because of Jakarta Faces's great support for extendibility, it's relatively easy to introduce alternative templating simply by replacing the so-called view handler, something which Jakarta Faces explicitly allows. It would, however, take five long years until Jakarta Faces would indeed ship with a more suitable view templating language, and even though Jakarta Pages had been essentially deprecated at that point, it's still present in Jakarta Faces at the time of writing.

The Adolescent Years

Back in 2004, another first befell Jakarta Faces; on June 28, Ed Burns announced that the source of the RI was released by Sun. This represented a major milestone as before that date, most technology in active use by Sun was closed source. Initially, the source was licensed under the somewhat exotic JRL, but later this would be changed to dual licenses, GPL with classpath exception and CDDL. At the same time as this announcement, the tradition was established that every new feature or bug fix should be accompanied by a test and that all existing tests should be executed before committing the change. Some 14 years later, there's a largely different set of people working on the RI source, and the project structure and code conventions have changed as well, but the test-driven tradition is still being uphold in its original form.

At that point, Ed Burns decided to focus more on the specification aspects of Jakarta Faces as the Jakarta Faces 1.2 spec work had started right away, and Jayashri Visvanathan, one of the early team members, took on the lead role concerning the implementation aspects, with Ryan Lubke, working as the TCK (testing) engineer.

Still only a few months old, a variety of component libraries for Jakarta Faces had already started to pop up, although all of them were commercial. Among those was the one from Oracle, ADF Faces. ADF Faces was put on Oracle's road map well before Jakarta Faces 1.0 went final, and the first early access release was presented on August 17, 2004. Its lead was Adam Winer, who represented Oracle in the team that created

Jakarta Faces 1.0. ADF Faces primarily contained a set of rich components, but also a dialog framework, and remarkably already featured partial page rendering (PPR), quite a bit ahead of the later crop of AJAX solutions. ADF Faces also contained a "for each" tag (af:forEach) that actually worked. Adam Winer explained in these early days that such tag is not quite trivial to build but promised that Oracle would contribute the knowledge back to Jakarta Faces itself.

The ADF Faces components originated mostly from the earlier User Interface XML (UIX) framework, of which Adam Winer was the lead architect as well. Earlier versions of UIX used the names "Cabo," "Baja," and "Marlin." UIX was a rich client framework for use in the browser. With Jakarta Faces sharing more than a few similarities to UIX and with its lead, Adam Winer, being part of the original Jakarta Faces team, it's perhaps not unreasonable to surmise that UIX influenced Jakarta Faces. Such similarities include the concept of components with separate renderers, Jakarta Pages tag handlers, and declarative options to compose a page and the ability to instantiate those same components programmatically in Java. There was even a conceptually similar data binding, although with a less elegant syntax. Instead of, say, value="#{user.age}", UIX would use data:value="age@user" but also required a kind of producer to be defined on each page to declare where "user" comes from and then nest the page's content within that declaration. By contrast, Jakarta Faces and EL have always used global definitions and left it up to the user to avoid name clashes.

One of the first, if not the first open source component library in 2004, was Matthias Unverzagt's OurFaces. As Jakarta Faces did not have its own resource API (application programming interface) at the time to serve up things like images, OurFaces required a Servlet to be added to web.xml, the so-called SkinServlet (ourfaces.common.webapp.SkinServlet). The significance of this is that it became a rather common thing for Jakarta Faces libraries in those days to ask their users: add something manually to web.xml before the component library can be used.

Most of the last months of 2004 and early months of 2005 were spent by the Jakarta Faces 1.2 expert group (EG) working on various Jakarta Pages and EL issues, such as the Jakarta Tags <c:forEach> support and the generation of IDs in Jakarta Pages, as well as on the dreaded "content interweaving" issue, which refers to the aforementioned content that appears at wrong places in the response when rendering.

While OurFaces may have been one of the first component libraries, it didn't last, and few will remember it or have even heard about it today. This is not quite the same for another framework that has its roots in early 2005, namely, Alexander Smirnov's Telamon framework, later renamed Ajax4jsf. This framework was one of the first of its kind that combined Jakarta Faces and the then new and fresh AJAX technology. The beauty of Ajax4Jsf was that it could add AJAX support to existing components, which weren't built with AJAX support in mind at all by enclosing them among others in the `<a4j:region>` tag. This technology was incorporated in the Exadel Visual Component Platform, which was released in March 2006 and would later be renamed RichFaces and would become one of the most memorable Jakarta Faces component libraries.

At around the same time Alexander Smirnov started work on what eventually would become RichFaces, a company called ICEsoft started working on a Jakarta Faces component library. ICEsoft had been in business for a couple of years and had been working on a product called ICEbrowser, a Java-based browser, and a product called ICEbrowser beans, which were "lightweight, configurable JavaBean components that can be rapidly integrated into Java client applications." During JavaOne 2005 of that year, on June 27, ICEsoft announced its component library for Jakarta Faces—ICEfaces. This was based on AJAX as well but incorporated AJAX directly into the components. ICEsoft called its specific technique "patent pending Direct-to-DOM," which basically meant that changes coming from the server were directly injected into the DOM tree structure of a web page. A final version wasn't available right away though, but an early access release was provided. This was closed source but cost-free.

Meanwhile, Jakarta Faces EG member Jacob Hookom, inspired by Hans Bergsten's concerns about the unsuitability of Jakarta Pages, grabbed the bull by the horns and started working himself on that alternative templating language envisioned by Bergsten. In August 2005, this work had progressed into a usable initial version. The name of this templating language? Facelets! It immediately took the Jakarta Faces world by storm. Kito Mann published the first part of a series of articles about it on JSFCentral the very first month, and Richard Hightower published the famous article "Facelets fits Jakarta Faces like a glove" several months later.

Oracle had not been sitting still either in 2005, and after about 16(!) early access releases, it announced in late 2005 at the JavaPolis conference in Antwerpen (nowadays called Devoxx) that ADF Faces would be donated to MyFaces and thus become open source.

In the first month of 2006, Jacob Hookom and Adam Winer contemplated the terrible implementation of Jakarta Faces's state save mechanism. This worked by first creating a component tree from a template and then, near the end of the request, blindly serializing the entire tree with all data that may have been put there during the request. During a postback, the tree is restored from this serialized form (hence the name of the phase "restore view"). This is a tremendous waste, as the majority of this information is already available in the template. Especially when doing AJAX requests with client-side state saving, this poses a very big burden, but it is also a problem when storing this state on the server as it massively increases Jakarta Faces's memory usage. One of the main reasons for doing state saving in such terrible way again has to do with that one decision: to support Jakarta Pages. With Jakarta Faces 1.2 about to go final, there was unfortunately no time left to fix this for version 1.2.

Even though it was clear at this point that Facelets was the future of Jakarta Faces, when Jakarta Faces 1.2 was eventually released in May 2006, it still contained only Jakarta Pages. Not all was bad though. Thanks to a cooperation between the Jakarta Faces and Jakarta Pages EGs, a revision of Jakarta Pages was released, Jakarta Pages 2.1, which was much better aligned with the demands of Jakarta Faces. On top of that, Jakarta Pages's expression language and Jakarta Faces's expression language were merged. The result was UEL (Unified Expression Language). A very practical advantage of UEL is that Jakarta Faces components no longer have to convert Strings manually into expressions but directly receive a `ValueExpression` from the templating language. Both Jakarta Pages 2.1 and Jakarta Faces 1.2 became part of Jakarta EE 5, which was released at the same time.

On June 13, 2006, the MyFaces community announced that the donated project would have its name changed to Trinidad. ADF Faces kept existing at Oracle, though, but was based on Trinidad with some extra features (such as support for Portals, JSR 227, etc.). Just 2 weeks prior to that, on May 31, 2006, ICEsoft announced its free, although still closed source, community edition. A few months later, on November 14, 2006, ICEsoft would fully open source ICEfaces under the MPL license. RichFaces, still closed source at that point and being sold by Exadel, would not stay behind for long though, and some 4 months later, on March 29, 2007, Exadel announced a partnership with Red Hat that made RichFaces available under an open source license and available and supported via its JBoss group.

On to Maturity

On May 22, 2007, the specification work for Jakarta Faces 2.0 began. The scope was hugely ambitious and promised not only to fix many of the issues that people had been complaining about but also to introduce quite a bunch of new features. Mentioned among the many goals in the JSR was a particularly interesting one when looking at the bigger picture—extracting the managed bean facility from Jakarta Faces and making it available for the entire platform.

During the fall of 2007, the community was polled for a name for the Jakarta Faces RI. Four names rose to the top, but as is often the case, none of these names could be approved by Sun's legal department. Eventually, Mojarra was proposed, and perhaps to the surprise of some, this one did pass legal's scrutiny. Ryan Lubke, one of the main Jakarta Faces committers then, made the official announcement on December 5, 2007.

A little under a year later, on October 29, 2008, Çağatay Çivici started a new library, PrimeFaces as a new start after his older YUI4JSF Jakarta Faces component library. The name derives from Çağatay's nickname, which is Optimus Prime, the courageous leader of the heroic autobots in the fictional Transformers universe. Çivici had been involved with Jakarta Faces development for a long time; right after graduation for his bachelor's degree at the university, he started working on a military project that used Jakarta Faces. At the time, this was the closed source Sun version, but Çivici was more interested in MyFaces, since it was already open source. After he provided several patches to this project, he was invited as a committer. Çivici worked for Spring Source for a time while he lived in the UK, working on the Web Flow and Jakarta Faces integration. Ultimately, Spring Source didn't go through with that, after which Çivici worked for Visa, located in Reading, United Kingdom. Many pieces of PrimeFaces were coded by Çivici on his commute from London to Reading.

PrimeFaces was initially based on Jakarta Faces 1.x, but with Jakarta Faces 2.x looming and the project still young, it would soon after switch to Jakarta Faces 2.x.

On July 1, 2009, the long-awaited Jakarta Faces 2.0 finally arrived. Jakarta Faces 2.0 indeed fixed nearly every problem that the industry had with Jakarta Faces; finally, Facelets was included as the default view templating language. Jakarta Pages was effectively deprecated. The state saving concerns that Hookom and Winer brought forward more than 3 years earlier were addressed as well; from then on, Jakarta Faces only saved delta state (state changes), and in restore view, the component tree was reloaded from the template, instead of actually restored.

Another big concern brought forward by the Jakarta Faces community over the years, Jakarta Faces's over-the-top emphasis on postbacks, was addressed too; GET requests became a first-class citizen in Jakarta Faces 2.0. A well-known usability problem with Jakarta Faces, sometimes called "The Trap," was that for a number of operations, the data involved needed to be the same during both the original request and the postback. This is not entirely trivial to guarantee in Jakarta Faces 1.x. Jakarta Faces 2.0 introduced the so-called view scope for this, which elegantly solved the problem. The creation of custom components, yet another problem area of Jakarta Faces 1.x, was made much simpler as well. Jakarta Faces 2.0 also introduced core support for AJAX, modeled after the way Ajax4Jsf worked, a resource API, system events, and quite a few other things.

One of Jakarta Faces 2.0's goals, making its managed bean facility usable outside Jakarta Faces, was implicitly reached by the CDI spec, which was introduced together with Jakarta Faces 2.0 in Jakarta EE 6. The CDI spec itself has a long history too, but one of its defining characteristics is that CDI Beans are strongly based on Jakarta Faces Managed Beans and are essentially a super set of those.

Altogether the impact of all those fixes and new features was such that it split the community essentially in two; those who had used Jakarta Faces 1.x and never looked at it again and those who switched to Jakarta Faces 2.x or, specifically, the ones who started using Jakarta Faces with 2.0 and never saw 1.x. This often led to heated debates, with the 1.x side arguing that Jakarta Faces is horrible and the 2.x side not understanding at all why that would be the case. Even at the time of this writing, which is almost 9 years after Jakarta Faces 2.0 was released, and a longer period than Jakarta Faces 1.x ever existed, these sentiments still remain to some degree.

Despite the many things that Jakarta Faces 2.0 did right, there was one missed opportunity; even though CDI was now available and superseded Jakarta Faces's Managed Beans, Jakarta Faces chose not to deprecate its managed bean facility right away. Even worse, it introduced an annotation-based alternative to the XML-based system Jakarta Faces 1.x used to define managed beans. With CDI already out there having annotations like `javax.enterprise.context.RequestScoped`, simultaneously introducing a `javax.faces.bean.RequestScoped` annotation that did exactly the same thing seems debatable as best. The EG seemed to be aware of this conflict, as a warning was put in place that these new annotations would possibly be superseded by platform functionality before long.

On December 23, Cay Horstmann raised his concerns about this very unwanted situation in an article titled "Is @`javax.faces.bean.ManagedBean` Dead on Arrival?" The response was quite clear; people, including Jakarta EE book writer Antonio Goncalves, asked for this huge mistake that Jakarta Faces 2.0 had made to be corrected as soon as possible and to deprecate `javax.faces.bean.ManagedBean` right away in the upcoming Jakarta Faces 2.1 maintenance release which was called for, among other things, to rectify another mistake (namely, the problem Jakarta Faces 2.0 introduced that in addition to a custom `ResourceResolver`, it was also necessary to provide a custom `ExternalContext`, which was very unclear). Why `javax.faces.bean.ManagedBean` indeed wasn't deprecated in the Jakarta Faces 2.1 MR remains a mystery to this day.

While applications written against the Jakarta Faces 1.x APIs would mostly run unchanged on Jakarta Faces 2.0, or only needed a few small changes, the component libraries had a much harder time. Specifically, the platform-provided AJAX support meant that the existing component libraries would have to forego their own AJAX implementations and rebase on the standard APIs. Clearly, that was no small feat, and it took a long time for component libraries to migrate, with some never really making the switch at all.

Here, PrimeFaces was clearly at an advantage. Being a relatively new library without much legacy, it could switch with much ease, while RichFaces and ICEfaces struggled a lot. For a year, PrimeFaces was really the only component library available for Jakarta Faces 2. PrimeFaces' ascension in popularity started right after Jakarta Faces 2.0 was released, which was also the exact same time that both ICEfaces and RichFaces seemed to become less popular. Although it must be noted that hard statistics are difficult to obtain and contain many facets (downloads, deployments, books, questions asked, available jobs, taking different industries into account, etc.), somewhere around 2012, PrimeFaces had seemingly become the more popular Jakarta Faces component library.

A year earlier, in March 2011, a German software developer working for Samhammer AG named Thomas Andraschko started a project that provided several add-ons for PrimeFaces, called PrimeFaces Extensions. Andraschko would later play a very important role in Jakarta Faces.

In the beginning of that same year, February 19, 2012, Arjan Tijms and Bauke Scholtz (by coincidence also the authors of this book) started the OmniFaces library for Jakarta Faces. The goal of OmniFaces was to be a utility library for Jakarta Faces, essentially what Apache Commons and Google Guava are to Java SE. Tijms and Scholtz had worked on a Jakarta Faces-based website together and found that they both had a collection of private Jakarta Faces utilities that they reused for different projects and also that a great number of similar utilities were essentially rewritten again and again for many Jakarta Faces projects and were partially floating around in places like forum messages and blog posts. OmniFaces was set up in particular not to compete component libraries like PrimeFaces but to work together with those. Hence, visual-oriented components were largely out of scope for OmniFaces.

In 2012, the specification process for Jakarta Faces 2.2 was also in full swing. Jakarta Faces 2.2 was eventually released on May 21, the next year. Jakarta Faces 2.2 specifically came up with a formal version of the alternative mode in which Facelets could operate; instead of putting component tags on a view, plain HTML was put on it, with a special ID linking the tag to a component. Such a mode is generally speaking somewhat less interesting to Jakarta Faces developers but appeals specifically to web designers who can more easily use plain HTML tools for such views. Jakarta Faces 2.2 also introduced a CDI-compatible @ViewScoped annotation, which removed one of the last reasons to still use the Jakarta Faces managed bean facility in Jakarta Faces 2.1, namely, that in that version, @ViewScoped only worked on those beans. Jakarta Faces 2.2 also introduced two new big features, Faces Flow and Resource Contracts, but these seem to have seen little uptake in practice.

On January 2013, Çağatay Çivici announced that Thomas Andraschko had joined the PrimeFaces team as a committer. Not long after, Andraschko would become the community lead for PrimeFaces and one of the top committers for that project.

Just prior to the start of Jakarta Faces 2.3, on July 20, 2014, RichFaces lead Brian Leathem announced on his blog that RichFaces 5, the next-generation version of RichFaces, would be canceled. Instead, RichFaces would "pursue a path of stability over innovation," which means that JBoss will make RichFaces 4.x compatible with Jakarta Faces 2.2 and port back a few things that were in development for RichFaces 5. While the post was somewhat optimistic, it strongly looked like the writing was on the wall for RichFaces.

On August 26, 2014, the specification work for Jakarta Faces 2.3 started. A new co-spec lead was introduced—Manfred Riem, who up to then had been working mostly on the implementation side of Mojarra, doing such things as migrating hundreds of the tests for which Jakarta Faces is famous away from the ancient and retired Cactus framework to a more modern Maven-based one and making sure the gazillions of open Mojarra issues were reduced to a manageable number. Jakarta Faces 2.3 started off with a perhaps somewhat remarkable message that Oracle had only a few resources available. During the specification process, those few resources dropped to a number that few would have expected—absolutely zero. Basically, after JavaOne 2015, nearly all of the spec leads just vanished, and most specs as a result abruptly ground to a halt. Josh Juneau reported about this in his famous study, "Jakarta EE 8, What Is the Current Status: Case Study for Completed Work Since Late 2015," which undeniably makes it clear by showing graphs of emails, commits, and issues resolved that Oracle had just walked away.

The openness of the Jakarta Faces and its RI Mojarra were fortunately such that the specification work and implementation thereof in Mojarra can largely be carried on by the other EG members, which indeed happens.

Also helping the Jakarta Faces 2.3 efforts and Mojarra was Andraschko, who, in addition to a PrimeFaces committer, had also become a MyFaces committer in July 2015. Andraschko donated a standardized version of the PrimeFaces search expression feature to Jakarta Faces 2.3 and Mojarra.

Meanwhile on February 12, 2016, Red Hat announced that RichFaces would be end of lived (EOL) later that year, namely, in June 2016. One of the most popular Jakarta Faces component libraries at some point, often named something like "One of the big three," effectively was no more. On June 20, 2016, the last real commit to the project was done, "RF-14279: update JSDoc." Two days later, Red Hat released RichFaces 4.5.17, and the GitHub repos were put into archived (read only) mode. Brian Leathem, who is still a Jakarta Faces 2.3 EG member, announced a few days later on February 18 that he would no longer be doing any Jakarta Faces-related work.

Rejuvenation

In late 2016, the Jakarta Faces spec leads briefly returned, but with the message that the spec must be completed in only a few weeks, so the (somewhat) lengthy finalization process could start. On March 28, 2017, Jakarta Faces 2.3 was then eventually released, bringing with it the start of replacing Jakarta Faces native artifacts with CDI versions and finally something which should have happened years ago: the deprecation of the Jakarta Faces managed bean facility in favor of using CDI beans. Other features are support for WebSocket using the Jakarta EE WebSocket APIs donated by OmniFaces, the introspection of available view resources in the system, and the abovementioned search expression framework donated by PrimeFaces.

Following the somewhat turbulent development of the Jakarta Faces 2.3 spec is the even more turbulent announcement by Oracle in 2017 that Jakarta EE, thus including Jakarta Faces, would be transferred to the Eclipse Foundation. Oracle would stop leading the specs it owned before, which again includes Jakarta Faces. This would mean that Mojarra would be re-licensed, and Jakarta Faces would be evolved by a new process with different leads.

The transition from Oracle to Eclipse was done in several steps. A new top-level project called Eclipse Enterprise for Java (EE4J) was created, and a snapshot of the Jakarta Faces 2.3 branch was scrubbed (legally speaking) and moved to a new GitHub repository at http:// github.com/eclipse-ee4j. Only Jakarta Faces 2.3 (and associated Mojarra 2.3) was moved, meaning Jakarta Faces 2.2 and earlier remained at their Oracle locations. This specifically meant the commit history wasn't transferred. After this first step of the transfer, a new release of the API was done in January 2019 as *jakarta.faces:jakarta.faces-api:2.3.1*, which was mostly identical to the existing *javax.faces:javax.faces-api:2.3*. The license of both the API and the Mojarra implementation was changed to the Eclipse Public License 2.0. Arjan Tijms became the next project lead. Previous spec leads Ed Burns and Manfred Riem shortly after left Oracle to work at Microsoft. Riem, however, would stay involved with Jakarta Faces.

The next step in the transfer process involved creating a new certification process and a new specification license. The JCP process was replaced by the Jakarta EE Specification Process (JESP), and the new specification license became the Eclipse Foundation Technology Compatibility Kit License (EFTL).

Early in 2019, Tijms went to the Javaland conference in Germany, where he met up with Ivar Grimstad, the Jakarta EE Developer Advocate at the Eclipse Foundation. In the warm sun of the German afternoon, the two discussed a new naming scheme for the Jakarta EE specifications. New names were required, as the deal between Oracle and the Eclipse Foundation included an agreement to not use a number of names previously used by Oracle, such as Jakarta EE, Jakarta Faces, JavaServer Faces, and Jakarta Pages. Tijms proposed a simpler naming scheme, essentially abolishing as much of the various "filler words" (such as "service," "api," and "architecture") in the names, making cryptic abbreviations (like, indeed, Jakarta Faces) necessary. Ivar agreed with this, and in the following months, this naming scheme was introduced; code, documentations, and specifications were painstakingly combed through to find and replace occurrences of the old names with the new names. For Jakarta Faces, the name became "Faces," a logical choice, since from day one the package name had actually been *javax.faces.**, not *javax.jsf.**. The artifact id also had been "faces" for a long time.

Later that year, in September 2019, the Faces 2.3.2 API was released as part of Jakarta EE 8. This API was again largely the same as the Jakarta Faces 2.3.1 API but now had all terms replaced by the new ones, and it was certified using the new JESP process.

That same month, during the JakartaOne Livestream 2019, Tijms, from his hotel in Jakarta, Indonesia, presented some of the ideas for the next version of Faces, in a presentation called "What's Coming to Jakarta Faces?" In it, Tijms mentioned that central for that release would be the removal of deprecated items, such as the Faces native expression language that was deprecated in 2005, Jakarta Server Pages support that was deprecated in 2009, the Faces native Managed Beans (deprecated in 2016), and more. With regard to features, Tijms mentioned extensionless views by default and a new life cycle phase to make things for which the view action is now used on an empty page easier to use.

After this second step was completed, the third step started. This involved changing the namespace of all Jakarta EE APIs, which of course included Faces, from javax.* to jakarta.*. This was needed since per the JCP rules, packages are only allowed to be modified per the JCP process. As Jakarta EE was no longer following that process, the package had to be changed. Tijms and other committers worked hard the following months to change the package names in the source code and documentation, which eventually resulted in the release of Faces 3.0 in October 2020 as part of Jakarta EE 9. Due to time constraints, the original plan of certifying Jakarta EE 9 (and therefore Faces 3.0) for JDK 11 compatibility had to be dropped.

Shortly after the release of Faces 3.0, Tijms kicks off the work for Faces 4.0 with a mail to the faces-dev list titled "Starting Jakarta Faces 4.0." The mail reiterates some of the plans from the earlier presentation but adds several API enhancements proposed earlier by Thomas Andraschko.

On October 23, 2020, Arjan Tijms sets the version of the Mojarra branch to 4.0.0-SNAPSHOT, marking the start of Faces 4.0. A few days later, on October 27, 2020, a historical commit is done by Tijms: "Remove Jakarta Pages support." That one technical decision, which in 2003 was strongly criticized by Hans Bergsten and that indeed as Bergsten predicted would bring so much pain to Faces, is finally undone. Again a few days later, on November 1, 2020, the native managed bean system of Faces also bites the dust. CDI beans from that moment on are the only designated bean type for Faces.

Early 2021, Tijms, Andraschko, and Scholtz discuss how to go forward with the proposed changes, and the next months see a flurry of new issues being created and commits done in both the Mojarra and MyFaces projects to implement several of those proposed new features.

Simultaneously, the Jakarta EE TCK is updated to support JDK 11, which eventually results in a Jakarta EE 9.1 release in May 2021. As both the Faces API and the Mojarra 3.0 implementation are already JDK 11 compatible, no new releases were required for those.

The following table shows the timeline and the differences between the various versions released:

Date	Maven coordinates	Build from	Certified	Javadoc	Java package	TCK level	API level
2017, Mar	javax. faces:javax. faces-api:2.3	github/ javaee	Jakarta EE 8	Jakarta EE terms	javax. faces	JDK 8	JDK 8
2019, Jan	**jakarta**. faces:**jakarta**. faces-api:2.3.1	github/**eclipse- ee4j**	Jakarta EE 8	Jakarta EE terms	javax. faces	JDK 8	JDK 8
2019, Sep	**jakarta**. faces:**jakarta**. faces-api:2.3.2	github/**eclipse- ee4j**	**Jakarta EE 8**	**Jakarta EE** terms	javax. faces	JDK 8	JDK 8

Date	Maven coordinates	Build from	Certified	Javadoc	Java package	TCK level	API level
2020, Oct	*jakarta. faces:jakarta. faces-api:3.0*	*github/**eclipse- ee4j***	*Jakarta EE 9*	*Jakarta EE* terms	*Jakarta. faces*	*JDK8*	*JDK 8*
2021, May	*jakarta. faces:jakarta. faces-api:3.0*	*github/**eclipse- ee4j***	*Jakarta EE 9.1*	*Jakarta EE* terms	*Jakarta. faces*	*JDK11*	*JDK 8*

On August 21, 2021, Çağatay Çivici presents the latest state of Faces in a presentation for the Turkish edition of the JakartaOne Livestream. His presentation is aptly titled "Jakarta Faces 4.0." At the moment of writing, the release review for Faces 4.0 is planned to start at around May 15, 2022.

CHAPTER 2

From Zero to Hello World

In this chapter, you will learn how to set up a Jakarta Faces development environment with the Eclipse IDE (integrated development environment), the Maven dependency management system, the WildFly application server and the H2 database from scratch.

Installing Java SE JDK

You probably already know that Java SE is available as JRE for end users and as JDK for software developers. Eclipse itself does not strictly require a JDK as Eclipse has its own compiler. Jakarta Faces being a software library does not require a JDK to run either. WildFly, however, does require a JDK to run, primarily in order to be able to compile Jakarta Pages files, even though Jakarta Pages (formerly known as Jakarta Pages, Java Server Pages) has, since Jakarta Faces 2.0, been deprecated as view technology for Jakarta Faces.

Therefore, you need to make sure that you already have a JDK installed as per Oracle's instructions. At the time of writing, the latest available Java SE version is 17, but as Jakarta EE 10 was designed for Java SE 11, you could get away with a minimum version of Java SE 11. Installation instructions depend on the platform being used (Windows, Linux, or MacOS). You can find detailed Java SE 17 JDK installation instructions here: `https://docs.oracle.com/en/java/javase/17/install/overview-jdk-installation.html`

The most important parts are that the `PATH` environment variable must cover the `/bin` folder containing the Java executables (e.g., "`/path/to/jdk/bin`") and that the `JAVA_HOME` environment variable is set to the JDK root folder (e.g., "`/path/to/jdk`"). This is not strictly required by Jakarta Faces itself, but Eclipse and WildFly need this. Eclipse as being an integrated development environment will need the `PATH` in order to find the Java executables. WildFly as being a Jakarta EE application server will need the `JAVA_HOME` in order to find the JDK tools.

17

© Bauke Scholtz and Arjan Tijms 2022
B. Scholtz and A. Tijms, *The Definitive Guide to Jakarta Faces in Jakarta EE 10*,
https://doi.org/10.1007/978-1-4842-7310-4_2

What About Jakarta EE?

Jakarta Faces itself is part of Jakarta EE. Jakarta EE is basically an abstract specification of which the so-called application servers represent the concrete implementations. Examples of those application servers are Eclipse GlassFish, Red Hat WildFly, Apache TomEE, and IBM WebSphere Liberty. You can find them all at the Jakarta EE Compatible Products page: `https://jakarta.ee/compatibility/`. It is exactly those application servers that actually provide among others Jakarta Faces, Jakarta Expression Language (EL), Jakarta Tags (formerly known as Jakarta Tags), Jakarta Contexts and Dependency Injection (CDI), Jakarta Enterprise Beans (formerly known as Jakarta Enterprise Beans, Enterprise Java Beans), Jakarta Persistence, Jakarta Servlet, Jakarta WebSocket, Jakarta JSON Processing, and many more APIs (application programming interfaces) of the box.

There also exist so-called servlet containers that provide basically *only* the Jakarta Servlet, Jakarta Pages, Jakarta Expression Language, Jakarta WebSocket, and Jakarta Security out of the box, such as Apache Tomcat and Eclipse Jetty. Therefore, it would require some additional work to manually install and configure, among others, Jakarta Faces, Jakarta Tags, Jakarta Contexts and Dependency Injection, Jakarta Enterprise Beans, Jakarta Persistence, Jakarta JSON Processing, and/or many other missing APIs from the Jakarta EE platform on such a servlet container. It is not even trivial in the case of Jakarta Enterprise Beans as it requires modifying the servlet container's internals. That is, by the way, exactly why Apache TomEE exists. It's a Jakarta EE application server built on top of the bare-bones Tomcat servlet container engine.

So you do not need to download and install "Jakarta EE" as a whole. Basically downloading any Jakarta EE application server to your choice is sufficient. We're going to pick Red Hat WildFly for this book.

Installing WildFly

WildFly is an open source Jakarta EE application server from Red Hat. You can download it from `https://wildfly.org/downloads`. Make sure you choose the "Jakarta EE 10 Full & Web Distribution" and not, for example, the "Servlet-Only Distribution" or "Preview Distribution," as they have other purposes. Installing is basically a matter of unzipping the downloaded file and putting it somewhere in your home folder. We'll leave it there until we have Eclipse up and running so that we can then integrate WildFly in Eclipse and let Eclipse manage the WildFly application server.

Installing Eclipse

Eclipse is an open source IDE written in Java. You can download it from `https://eclipse.org`. It is basically like notepad but then with thousands if not millions of extra features, such as automatically compiling class files, building a WAR (Web Application Archive) file with them, and deploying it to an application server without the need to manually fiddle around with `javac` and others in a command console.

Eclipse is available in a lot of flavors, even for C/C++ and PHP. As we're going to develop with Jakarta EE (Enterprise Edition), we need the one saying "Eclipse IDE for **Enterprise** Java and Web developers," importantly the one with "Enterprise" in its name. The one without it doesn't contain the mandatory plug-ins for developing Jakarta EE web applications. Here is the main download page: `https://www.eclipse .org/downloads/packages/`. Also here, installing is basically a matter of unzipping the downloaded file and putting it somewhere in your home folder.

In Windows and Linux, you'll find the `eclipse.ini` configuration file in the unzipped folder. In MacOS, this configuration file is located in `Eclipse.app/Contents/ Eclipse`. Open this file for editing. We want to increase the allocated memory for Eclipse. At the bottom of `eclipse.ini`, you'll find the following lines:

```
-Xms256m
-Xmx2048m
```

This sets, respectively, the initial and maximum memory size pool which Eclipse may use. This is a bit too low when you want to develop a bit of a decent Jakarta EE application. Let's at least double both the values.

```
-Xms512m
-Xmx4g
```

Watch out that you don't declare more than the available physical memory in the Xmx setting. When the actual memory usage exceeds the available physical memory, then it will continue into virtual memory, usually in flavor of a swap file on disk. This will greatly decrease performance and result in major hiccups and slowdowns.

Now you can start Eclipse by executing the `eclipse` executable in the unzipped folder. You will be asked to select a directory as workspace. This is the directory where Eclipse will save all workspace projects and metadata.

After that, Eclipse will show a welcome screen. This is not interesting for now. You can click the *Hide* button on the right top to close the welcome screen. Untick if necessary "Always show Welcome at start up" on the bottom right. After that, you will enter the workbench. By default, it looks like the screenshot in Figure 2-1.

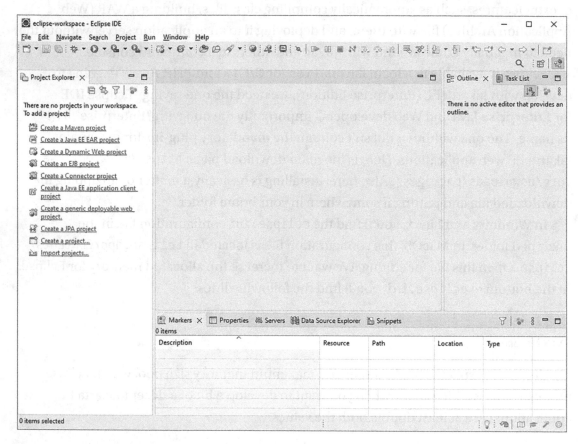

Figure 2-1. *Eclipse workbench*

Configuring Eclipse

Before we can start writing code, we would like to fine-tune Eclipse a bit so that we don't eventually end up in trouble or with annoyances. Eclipse has an enormous amount of settings, and some of its default values should not have been the default values. You can verify and configure the settings via *Window* ➤ *Preferences*.

- *General* ➤ *Workspace* ➤ *Text file encoding* must be set to **UTF-8**. Particularly in Windows, this might otherwise default to the proprietary encoding CP-1252 that supports only 255 different characters and does not support any characters beyond the Latin range. When reading and saving Unicode files with CP-1252, you risk seeing unintelligible sequences of characters. This is also called "mojibake."[1]

- *General* ➤ *Workspace* ➤ *New text file line delimiter* must be set to **Unix**. It will work just fine on Windows as well. This will particularly keep version control systems happy. Otherwise, developers pulling code on different operating systems might face confusing conflicts or diffs caused by different line endings.

- *General* ➤ *Editors* ➤ *Text editors* ➤ *Spelling* should preferably be **disabled**. This will save you from a potentially big annoyance because it unnecessarily also spellchecks technical entries in XML configuration files such as `faces-config.xml` and `web.xml`, causing confusing warnings in those files such as "`*.xhtml` is not correctly spelled."

- *Java* ➤ *Installed JREs* must be set to the **JDK** (actually the same as you've configured in `JAVA_HOME` environment variable) and thus not the JRE. This setting will normally also be used to execute the integrated application server that usually requires the JDK.

- *Java* ➤ *Compiler* ➤ *Compiler compliance level* must be set to at least **11**. This is the minimum required Java version for Jakarta EE 10. You can of course also pick a higher version. For example, **17** will work just fine.

Integrating Application Server in Eclipse

We need to familiarize Eclipse with any installed application server so that you can seamlessly deploy, run, and debug web projects from within Eclipse. In order to integrate a new application server in Eclipse, first check the bottom section of the workbench with several tabs representing several *Views* (you can add new ones via *Window* ➤ *Show View*). Click the *Servers* tab to open the servers view (see Figure 2-2).

---

[1] https://en.wikipedia.org/wiki/Mojibake

21

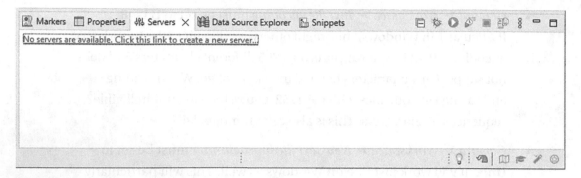

Figure 2-2. *Servers view of Eclipse workbench*

Click the link that literally says "No servers are available. Click this link to create a new server...." It'll show the *New Server* wizard, displaying a list of available server types. From the list, select *Red Hat Boss JBoss Middleware* ➤ *JBoss AS, WildFly, & EAP Server Tools* (see Figure 2-3).

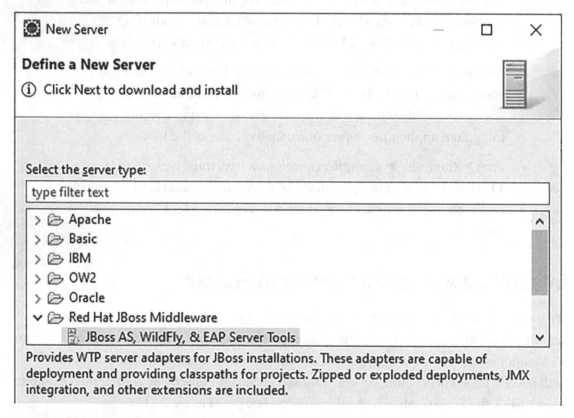

Figure 2-3. *Selecting JBoss AS, WildFly, & EAP Server Tools in New Server wizard*

After clicking *Next*, it will download the plug-in in the background and request you to accept the license agreement before installing the plug-in. This plug-in is mandatory in order to manage any JBoss server from inside the workbench. This will allow you to add and remove Eclipse projects to the deployments folder, as well as starting and stopping the server, and running the server in debug mode.

Let it finish downloading and installing the plug-in in the background. Confirm any possible warning of "unsigned software" with *Install Anyway*. This is okay in this specific case. Finally, it will request you to restart Eclipse. Take action accordingly.

Once returned into the workspace, click the same link in the *Servers* view again. You'll now see *JBoss Community* ➤ *WildFly* options for several WildFly versions. Select the version matching the one you downloaded. Or if you have downloaded a newer version, then the latest available version of the server plug-in will generally also work just fine (see Figure 2-4).

Figure 2-4. *Select the WildFly version matching the downloaded one*

Advance to the next step. Just leave this screen default (see Figure 2-5).

Figure 2-5. *Create a new Server Adapter, and just leave this screen default*

Advance once more to the next step. Here, you should point the *Home Directory* field to the folder of the WildFly installation, where you have unzipped it after downloading (see Figure 2-6). And you should adjust the *Execution Environment* to the desired Java version. Pick a minimum of JavaSE-11. This is the minimum required Java version for Jakarta EE 10. You can of course also pick a higher version. For example, **JavaSE-17** will work just fine on current WildFly versions.

Figure 2-6. *Specifying WildFly location in New Server wizard*

Complete the remainder of the *New Server* wizard with default settings. You don't need to edit any other fields. The newly added server will now appear in the *Servers* view (see Figure 2-7).

Figure 2-7. *The WildFly server in Servers view*

Creating New Project in Eclipse

We're now ready to create a new project for our Jakarta Faces application in Eclipse. This can be done via the left section of the workbench that by default shows only one tab representing the *Project Explorer* view (also here, you can add new views via *Window* ➤ *Show View*). Right-click anywhere in this view and select *New* ➤ *Project*. It'll show the *New Project* wizard that may have a bit too many options.

Eclipse, being an IDE for many different project tasks, offers a bewildering amount of different project types from which to choose. For a Jakarta EE-based application that is going to be deployed as a simple WAR file, there are basically two project types that we could choose from: *Web* ➤ *Dynamic Web Project* and *Maven* ➤ *Maven Project*.

The difference is that the first is an Eclipse native project that really only works on Eclipse, while the latter is a universal type of project that can be built by any IDE other than Eclipse, as well as easily on the command line and by various CI servers such as GitHub Actions, CircleCI, and Jenkins. For this reason, the Maven project type is really the only viable choice (see Figure 2-8).

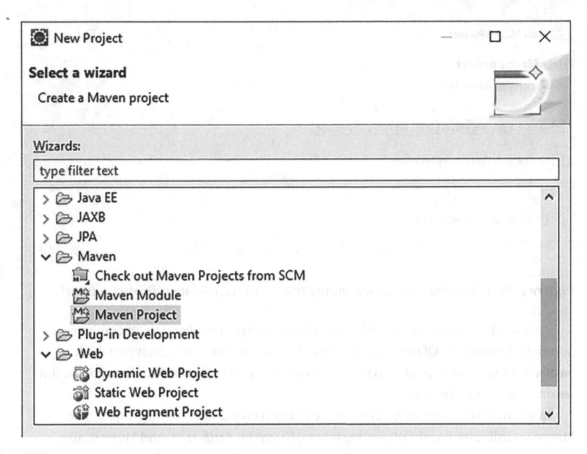

Figure 2-8. *Selecting Maven Project in New Project wizard (note the Dynamic Web Project as another but nonviable option)*

In the next step, make sure that the option *Create a simple project (skip archetype selection)* is checked (see Figure 2-9).

Figure 2-9. *Checking "Create a simple project" in New Maven Project wizard*

This will let us start with a really empty Maven project so that we can configure and populate it ourselves. Of course, you could also choose from an archetype, which is basically a template project with several already-prepared files and configurations. But we don't need any for now.

In the next step, we can specify our own Maven coordinates of the project. The Maven coordinates consist of, among others, *Group Id*, *Artifact Id,* and *Version*, also known as GAV in the Maven world. The *Group Id* usually matches the root package name you're going to use, such as com.example. The *Artifact Id* usually represents the project name you're going to use. For simplicity and in order to be consistent in the rest of the book, we'll use project. The *Version* can be kept default at 0.0.1-SNAPSHOT. Finally, the *Packaging* **must** be set to war (Web Application Archive). This will, during the build, produce a WAR file instead of a JAR file (see Figure 2-10).

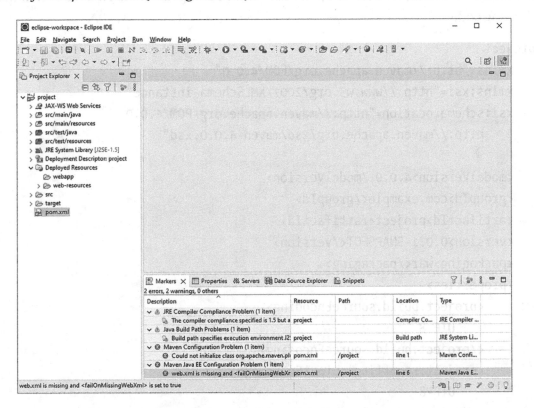

Figure 2-10. *Filling out the Maven GAV in New Maven Project wizard*

Complete the remainder of the *New Maven Project* wizard. You don't need to edit any other fields. Once you've finished the wizard, you'll get to see the project structure in the *Project Explorer* view (see Figure 2-11).

Figure 2-11. *The newly created Maven project in Eclipse*

Unfortunately, the Eclipse-generated `pom.xml`, which is the main indicator of the project being a Maven project and containing its configuration, is less than ideal. It's not current anymore, even when generated by the latest Eclipse version at the time of writing, the 2021-12 (December 2021).

You can already see that by the `pom.xml` file that is marked with an alarming red cross and two error messages in the *Markers* view. Any project that has at least one such red cross cannot be built and won't be deployable. One of the error messages literally says "web.xml is missing and <failOnMissingWebXml> is set to true." In other words, Maven somehow thinks that it's still a pre-Jakarta EE 6 project, when this was indeed disallowed. Another error message says "Could not initialize class org.apache.maven.plugin.war.util. WebappStructureSerializer". This is basically caused by incompatibility of the default Maven WAR plug-in version with Java 17. This can be solved by downgrading Java to a lower version, but this can also be solved by explicitly setting the default Maven WAR plug-in version to a higher version.

In order to solve this problem and to catch up the Eclipse-generated `pom.xml` with the current standards, we need to open `pom.xml` for editing and adjust it as shown in the following code:

```
<project
    xmlns="http://maven.apache.org/POM/4.0.0"
    xmlns:xsi="http://www.w3.org/2001/XMLSchema-instance"
    xsi:schemaLocation="http://maven.apache.org/POM/4.0.0
        http://maven.apache.org/xsd/maven-4.0.0.xsd"
>
    <modelVersion>4.0.0</modelVersion>
    <groupId>com.example</groupId>
    <artifactId>project</artifactId>
    <version>0.0.1-SNAPSHOT</version>
    <packaging>war</packaging>
    <properties>
        <project.build.sourceEncoding>
            UTF-8
        </project.build.sourceEncoding>
        <project.reporting.outputEncoding>
            UTF-8
        </project.reporting.outputEncoding>
```

```
            <maven.compiler.source>17</maven.compiler.source>
            <maven.compiler.target>17</maven.compiler.target>
            <failOnMissingWebXml>false</failOnMissingWebXml>
        </properties>
        <dependencies>
            <dependency>
                <groupId>jakarta.platform</groupId>
                <artifactId>jakarta.jakartaee-api</artifactId>
                <version>10.0.0</version>
                <scope>provided</scope>
            </dependency>
        </dependencies>
        <build>
            <plugins>
                <plugin>
                    <artifactId>maven-war-plugin</artifactId>
                    <version>3.3.2</version>
                </plugin>
            </plugins>
        </build>
</project>
```

Once you save this file and right-click on the project and choose *Maven* ➤ *Update Project... ➤ OK*, then Eclipse will automatically sort it out by itself and clear out the alarming red cross on the project. This *Update Project* action will also sort out the two pending warnings: "The compiler compliance specified is 1.5 but a JRE 17 is used" and "Build path specifies execution environment J2SE-1.5. There are no JREs installed in the workspace that are strictly compatible with this environment" based on the updated pom.xml. Now that looks much better. We'll briefly go through the most important settings here.

- Packaging **war**: This indicates the project is a "web" project and that the project's contents will be assembled into a web archive.

- Encoding **UTF-8**: This sets the encoding that the source files are in and with which the (reporting) output files should be generated. This makes the build repeatable, as it otherwise would default to the system default encoding (again, a rather bad default).

31

- Compiler **17**: This sets both the version of Java used in the `.java` source files and the byte code output in the `.class` files. Without setting this, Maven defaults to the oldest version possible and sometimes even a lower version than that.

- `failOnMissingWebXml` **false**: Older versions of Jakarta EE required the `/WEB-INF/web.xml` to be present. Even though this has not been required anymore since Jakarta EE 6, which was released in 2009, Maven still checks for this file to be present. Setting this to `false` prevents this unnecessary check.

- Dependency **jakarta.platform:jakarta.jakartaee-api:10.0.0 provided**: This declares a dependency on the Jakarta EE 10 API and makes sure all the Jakarta EE types like `FacesServlet`, `@Named`, and `@Entity` are known to the compiler. This dependency is set to `provided`" because those types are already provided by the target runtime, which is in our case WildFly. This dependency will then only be used to compile the source code against, and the associated JAR files won't be included in the generated WAR file. You need to make absolutely sure that any compile time dependency that is already provided by the target runtime is set to `provided`; otherwise, it will eventually end up in the generated WAR file, and you may run into class loading trouble wherein duplicate different versioned libraries are conflicting with one another. In case you're actually not targeting a full-fledged Jakarta EE server but a bare-bones servlet container such as Tomcat, then you would need to adjust the dependencies as instructed in the README of Mojarra,[2] one of the available Faces implementations and actually the one used under the cover of WildFly.

- Plug-in **maven-war-plugin:3.3.2**: This basically overrides the Eclipse built-in default version of the Maven WAR plug-in. This entry is *not* necessary if you're not facing the error message "Could not initialize class WebappStructureSerializer" in your Eclipse version.

The next step is basically to instruct Eclipse to generate the deployment descriptor files. Right-click the project in *Project Explorer* view and choose *Properties* and then open

---

[2] https://github.com/eclipse-ee4j/mojarra#readme

the *Project Facets* section. Update the Servlet API version and add the Jakarta Faces and Jakarta Persistence facets. The Servlet API is represented by the "Dynamic Web Module" entry. This needs to be set to version 6.0, which matches the Jakarta EE 10 specification. Further, the "Jakarta Faces" and "Jakarta Persistence" entries need to be selected and set to versions 4.0 and 3.1, respectively, matching the Jakarta EE 10 specification (see Figure 2-12). While at it, you also need to double-check if the version of the Java facet is indeed 17 or whatever version is set in pom.xml. This value is supposed to be automatically updated via the *Update Project* action.

Figure 2-12. *The Project Facets section of the project properties with "JavaServer Faces" (Jakarta Faces) and "Jakarta Persistence" (Jakarta Persistence) facets enabled (note that the Jakarta Servlet API version is represented by "Dynamic Web Module" and that the versions in the screenshot are at the time of writing unfortunately outdated)*

Unfortunately, in the latest available Eclipse version at the time of writing this chapter, the version 2021-12 (December 2021), these versions weren't available yet in the drop-downs. The highest available versions are Servlet 5.0, Faces 2.3, and Persistence 2.2.

This is not a big problem. Its only influence is on the available code generators and wizards. We can always manually adjust the Eclipse-generated `web.xml`, `faces-config.xml`, and `persistence.xml` files afterward to match the Jakarta EE 10–compatible versions.

As you can see in the yellow warning bar near the bottom, Eclipse only requires further configuration. This concerns the newly selected Jakarta Faces and Jakarta Persistence facets. When clicking the link, we get to see the *Modify Faceted Project* wizard (see Figure 2-13).

Figure 2-13. *The Jakarta Persistence Facet configuration*

The first step of the *Modify Faceted Project* wizard allows us to configure the Jakarta Persistence facet. We need to make sure that Eclipse is being instructed that the Jakarta Persistence implementation is already provided by the target runtime and thus Eclipse doesn't need to include any libraries. This can be achieved by choosing the "Disable Library Configuration" option in the *Jakarta Persistence implementation* field. As we're going to use the WildFly-provided Hibernate as the actual Jakarta Persistence implementation, which supports automatically discovering of `@Entity` annotated classes, we'd like to instruct Eclipse to do the same. So choose the "Discover annotated classes automatically" option in *Persistent class management* field. Otherwise, Eclipse would automatically add entities to the `persistence.xml` when going through the entity code generation wizard or show warnings when we create one manually and don't add it to the `persistence.xml`.

Note that configuring a database connection (for Eclipse's built-in data explorer) is not necessary for now as we're going to use an embedded database.

In the next step of the *Modify Faceted Project* wizard, we can configure the Jakarta Faces capabilities (see Figure 2-14). Also here, we need to make sure that Eclipse is being instructed that the Jakarta Faces implementation is already provided by the target runtime and thus Eclipse doesn't need to include any libraries. This can be achieved by choosing the "Disable Library Configuration" option in the *Jakarta Faces Implementation Library* field.

Figure 2-14. *The Jakarta Faces Capabilities configuration*

Further, we need to rename the servlet name of the FacesServlet to match the fictive instance variable name: facesServlet. Last but not least, we need to change the URL mapping pattern from the Jurassic /faces/* to the modern *.xhtml.

Actually, the entire registration of the FacesServlet in web.xml is, since Jakarta Faces version 2.2, not strictly necessary anymore; you could even uncheck the *Configure Jakarta Faces servlet in deployment descriptor* option and rely on the default auto-registered mappings of /faces/*, *.faces, *.jsf, and *.xhtml. However, as this allows end users and even search bots to open the very same Jakarta Faces page by different URLs and thus causes confusion among end users and potential duplicate content penalties among search bots, we'd better restrict to only one explicitly configured URL pattern of *.xhtml.

Now, finish and apply all the wizards and dialogs. Unfortunately, the Jakarta Persistence plug-in of the current Eclipse version only puts the generated `persistence.xml` in the wrong place. It's seemingly not being aware of the project being a Maven project, and the plug-in blindly puts the generated `persistence.xml` file in the `src/main/java/META-INF` folder as if it were a plain vanilla project. This is wrong. You need to manually move it into `src/main/resources/META-INF` to conform to the rules of a Maven project. Figure 2-15 shows us how the workbench looks now.

Figure 2-15.   *Correctly configured Jakarta EE 10 Maven project in Eclipse*

Adjusting Deployment Descriptors

We only need to adjust all the deployment descriptors to catch up to the actually used Servlet, Faces, Persistence, and CDI versions. This is normally done by adjusting the root element of the deployment descriptor XML file to set the desired XML schemas and the version.

You can find all Jakarta EE 10 XML schemas at https://jakarta.ee/xml/ns/jakartaee/, which is an actual web page. You can open the deployment descriptor XML file for editing by double-clicking it in the Eclipse project explorer and then selecting the *Source* tab in the editor. The correct root element declarations for Jakarta EE 10–compatible deployment descriptors are thus as follows.

1. **src/main/webapp/WEB-INF/web.xml** for Servlet 6.0:

```xml
<?xml version="1.0" encoding="UTF-8"?>
<web-app
    xmlns="https://jakarta.ee/xml/ns/jakartaee"
    xmlns:xsi="http://www.w3.org/2001/XMLSchema-instance"
    xsi:schemaLocation="https://jakarta.ee/xml/ns/jakartaee
        https://jakarta.ee/xml/ns/jakartaee/web-app_6_0.xsd"
    version="6.0"
>
    <!-- Servlet configuration here. -->
</web-app>
```

Make sure that the jakarta.faces.webapp.FacesServlet as we created in the *Modify Faceted Project* wizard is indeed there and that it's indeed mapped on a URL pattern of *.xhtml.

2. **src/main/webapp/WEB-INF/faces-config.xml** for Faces 4.0:

```xml
<?xml version="1.0" encoding="UTF-8"?>
<faces-config
    xmlns="https://jakarta.ee/xml/ns/jakartaee"
    xmlns:xsi="http://www.w3.org/2001/XMLSchema-instance"
    xsi:schemaLocation="https://jakarta.ee/xml/ns/jakartaee
        https://jakarta.ee/xml/ns/jakartaee/web-facesconfig_4_0.xsd"
    version="4.0"
>
    <!-- Faces configuration here. -->
</faces-config>
```

As of now, it's indeed empty.

3. **src/main/resources/META-INF/persistence.xml** for
   Persistence 3.1:

```xml
<?xml version="1.0" encoding="UTF-8"?>
<persistence
    xmlns="https://jakarta.ee/xml/ns/persistence"
    xmlns:xsi="http://www.w3.org/2001/XMLSchema-instance"
    xsi:schemaLocation="https://jakarta.ee/xml/ns/persistence
        https://jakarta.ee/xml/ns/persistence/persistence_3_1.xsd"
    version="3.1"
>
    <!-- Persistence configuration here. -->
</persistence>
```

As of now, it indeed only contains the default persistence unit.
We'll reconfigure it later on. Only the currently available Jakarta
Persistence plug-in of Eclipse might show an error on this like
"The persistence.xml file does not have recognized content." You
could ignore this by disabling the Jakarta Persistence validator
in the project's properties, but you can also just step back to the
originally generated persistence.xml file for the time being.

4. **src/main/webapp/WEB-INF/beans.xml** for CDI 4.0

Finally, for the sake of completeness, we need to create one more deployment
descriptor file, the one for CDI 4.0. This isn't automatically generated as it's not required.
CDI is by default always enabled in any Jakarta EE–compatible web application. It's even
mandatory for the functioning of Jakarta Faces.

Right-click the /WEB-INF folder of the project and choose *New* ➤ *File*. Give it the
name *beans.xml*. Populate the new file as follows:

```xml
<?xml version="1.0" encoding="UTF-8"?>
<beans
    xmlns="https://jakarta.ee/xml/ns/jakartaee"
    xmlns:xsi="http://www.w3.org/2001/XMLSchema-instance"
    xsi:schemaLocation="https://jakarta.ee/xml/ns/jakartaee
```

```
        https://jakarta.ee/xml/ns/jakartaee/beans_4_0.xsd"
    version="4.0" bean-discovery-mode="annotated"
>
    <!-- CDI configuration here. -->
</beans>
```

Note that the `bean-discovery-mode` is set to `annotated`. This is the default value. The other value is `all`. This is slightly more intrusive and expensive as it will consider **any** Java class as a potential CDI bean.

Configuring Jakarta Faces

Jakarta Faces has a lot of settings available that can be configured via `<context-param>` entries in `web.xml`. The default configuration is okay to start with, but there's one peculiar setting that we really want to set right from the beginning on. It's the setting that instructs Jakarta Faces whether to interpret empty string submitted values as `null` in the model. Due to the nature of HTML and Jakarta Servlets, empty input fields will by default be set as empty strings in the model. This is more than often undesirable, and we'd rather like to keep them `null`. This is very significant as to validation constraints such as `@NotNull` in Jakarta Bean Validation and `NOT NULL` in relational databases.

This setting can be achieved by adding the following section to the `web.xml`:

```
<context-param>
    <param-name>
        jakarta.faces.INTERPRET_EMPTY_STRING_SUBMITTED_VALUES_AS_NULL
    </param-name>
    <param-value>true</param-value>
</context-param>
```

Creating the Backing Bean Class

With the project now correctly configured, we can start with developing the actual MVC application. The *Controller* part of MVC is already configured as `FacesServlet` in `web.xml`. The *Model* part of MVC is what we're going to create now. It's basically just a simple Java class that is by Jakarta Faces convention called a *Backing Bean* since it "backs" a *View*.

Right-click the `src/main/java` folder of the project and choose *New ➤ Class*. The *New Java Class* wizard will now appear (see Figure 2-16). In this wizard, set the *Package* to `com.example.project.view`, and set the *Name* to `HelloWorld`. The rest of the fields can be kept default or empty.

Figure 2-16. *New Java Class wizard in Eclipse*

The class editor will now open with the newly created backing bean class. We'll modify it to add CDI `@Named` and `@RequestScoped` annotations on the class so that it becomes a CDI managed bean. And we need to add two properties, `input` and `output`, and accompany the `input` property with a getter and setter pair, the `output` property with only a getter, so that these can be referenced from the view. Finally, we'll add a `submit()` action method that prepares the `output` property based on the `input` property so that this can be invoked from the view.

As a hint, in Eclipse after entering the properties, you can right-click anywhere in the class editor and choose *Source ➤ Generate Getters and Setters* to have the IDE to generate them. In its entirety, the edited backing bean class should look as follows:

```
package com.example.project.view;

import jakarta.enterprise.context.RequestScoped;
import jakarta.inject.Named;
```

```
@Named @RequestScoped
public class HelloWorld {

    private String input;
    private String output;

    public void submit() {
        output = "Hello World! You have typed: " + input;
    }

    public String getInput() {
        return input;
    }

    public void setInput(String input) {
        this.input = input;
    }

    public String getOutput() {
        return output;
    }
}
```

We'll briefly go through the annotations that are used here.

- **@Named**: This gives the bean a name, which is primarily used to reference it via EL in the view. Without any attributes, this name defaults to the simple class name with the first letter in lowercase, thus "helloWorld" here. It will be available by #{helloWorld} in EL. This can be used in Jakarta Faces pages.

- **@RequestScoped**: This gives the bean a scope, which means the same instance of the bean is used throughout the given life span. In the case of @RequestScoped, that life span is the duration of an HTTP request. When the scope ends, then the bean is automatically destroyed. You can read more about scopes in Chapter 8.

Creating the Facelets File

Next, we'll create the *View* part of MVC. It's basically just an XHTML file that is by Jakarta Faces interpreted as a *Facelets file* or just "Facelet." When the FacesServlet is invoked with a URL matching the path of this Facelets file, then Jakarta Faces will ultimately parse it and generate the HTML markup that is sent to the browser as a response to the request. With help of EL, it can reference a bean property and invoke a bean action.

Right-click the webapp folder of the project and choose *New* ➤ *File* (see Figure 2-17). Give it the name hello.xhtml.

Figure 2-17. Create New File wizard in Eclipse

The HTML editor will now open with the newly created Facelets file. It's initially empty. Fill it with the following content:

```
<!DOCTYPE html>
<html lang="en"
    xmlns:f="jakarta.faces.core"
    xmlns:h="jakarta.faces.html"
>
    <h:head>
        <title>Hello World</title>
    </h:head>
    <h:body>
        <h1>Hello World</h1>
        <h:form>
            <h:outputLabel for="input" value="Input" />
            <h:inputText id="input" value="#{helloWorld.input}" />
            <h:commandButton value="Submit"
                action="#{helloWorld.submit}">
                <f:ajax execute="@form" render=":output" />
            </h:commandButton>
        </h:form>
        <h:outputText id="output" value="#{helloWorld.output}" />
    </h:body>
</html>
```

We'll briefly go through the Jakarta Faces–specific XHTML tags that are used here.

- **<h:head>**: This generates the HTML <head> element. It gives Jakarta Faces the opportunity to automatically include any necessary JavaScript files, such as the one containing the necessary logic for <f:ajax>.

- **<h:body>**: This generates the HTML <body> element. You can also use a plain HTML <body> in this specific Facelet, but then it doesn't give any other Jakarta Faces tag the opportunity to automatically include any necessary JavaScript in the end of the HTML <body>.

- **`<h:form>`**: This generates the HTML `<form>` element. Jakarta Faces will automatically include the so-called view state in a hidden input field within the form.

- **`<h:outputLabel>`**: This generates the HTML `<label>` element. You can also use a plain HTML `<label>` in this specific Facelet, but then you'd have to manually take care of figuring out the actual ID of the target input element.

- **`<h:inputText>`**: This generates the HTML `<input type="text">` element. Jakarta Faces will automatically get and set the value in the bean property specified in the `value` attribute.

- **`<h:commandButton>`**: This generates the HTML `<input type="submit">`. Jakarta Faces will automatically invoke the bean method specified in the `action` attribute.

- **`<f:ajax>`**: This generates the necessary JavaScript code to enable Ajax behavior of the tag it is being nested in, in this case, the `<h:commandButton>`. You can also do as good without it, but then the form submit won't be performed asynchronously. The `execute` attribute of `@form` indicates that the entire `<h:form>` where it is sitting in must be processed on submit, and the `render` attribute of `:output` indicates that the tag identified by `id="output"` must be automatically updated on completion of the Ajax submit.

- **`<h:outputText>`**: This generates the HTML `<span>` element. This is the one being updated on completion of the Ajax submit. It will merely print the bean property specified in the `value` attribute.

Those Jakarta Faces–specific XHTML tags are also called *Jakarta Faces Components*. There will be more on Facelets files and Jakarta Faces components in the upcoming chapters. Note that you can also perfectly embed plain vanilla HTML in a Facelets file. Jakarta Faces components should only be used when the functionality requires so or is more easily achievable with them.

Deploying the Project

In the *Servers* view, right-click the WildFly server entry and choose *Add and Remove*. It will show the *Add and Remove* wizard (see Figure 2-18) that gives you the opportunity to add and remove WAR projects to the server. Do so for our newly created project and finish the wizard.

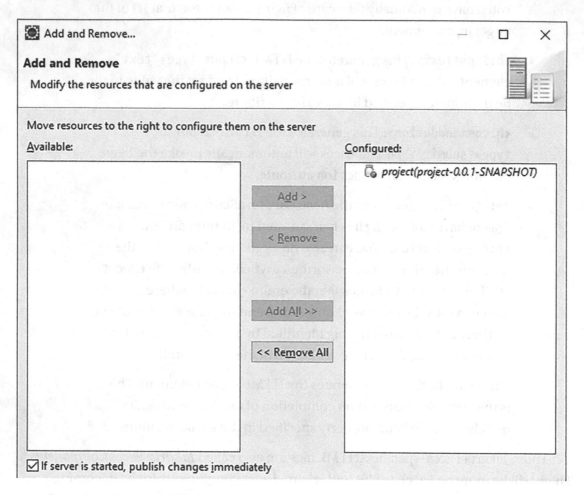

Figure 2-18. *The Add and Remove wizard wherein the project has been deployed to the server by moving it to the right*

Now start the WildFly server. You can do so by selecting it and then clicking the green arrow icon whose tool tip says "Start the server." You can, of course, also use the bug icon whose tool tip says "Start the server in debug mode." The *Console* view will briefly show the server startup log. Wait until the server starts up and has, in the *Servers* view, gained the status *Started* (see Figure 2-19).

Figure 2-19. *The WildFly server in Servers view with the status Started (note that the Console view is highlighted as it has unread server logs)*

Now, open a tab in your favorite web browser (see Figure 2-20) and enter the address `http://localhost:8080/project-0.0.1-SNAPSHOT/hello.xhtml` in order to open the newly created Jakarta Faces page.

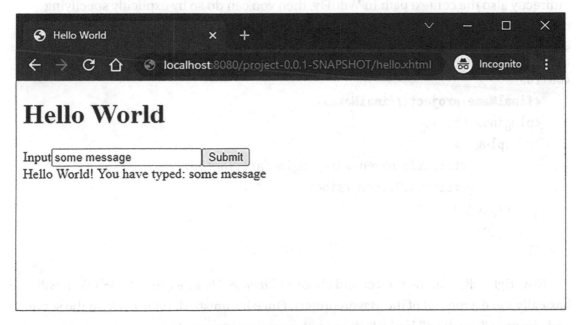

Figure 2-20. *The Hello World page in Chrome browser wherein the input field is filled with the text "some message" and the submit button has been pressed*

Coming back to the URL, the "localhost:8080" part is by convention the default domain of any Jakarta EE server that is running in development mode. The same address is also used by, among others, GlassFish and TomEE. The "/project-0.0.1-SNAPSHOT" part in URL is in case of WildFly by default inferred from the file name of the Maven-generated WAR file, which you can find in the /standalone/deployments folder of the WildFly installation. This part in URL is in Jakarta Servlet terms called the "context path" and obtainable by HttpServletRequest#getContextPath() and in Jakarta Faces delegated by ExternalContext#getRequestContextPath().

If you have a hard time in figuring out the actually used context path, then you can usually find it in the server logs. The exact logger line is, however, dependent on the server being used. In case of WildFly, it'll be the line identified by WFLYUT0021. Open the *Console* view in Eclipse, press Ctrl+F and search for WFLYUT0021. It'll show the following line:

```
WFLYUT0021: Registered web context: '/project-0.0.1-SNAPSHOT' for server
'default-server'
```

In case you want to adjust the file name of the Maven-generated WAR file, and thus indirectly also the context path in WildFly, then you can do so by explicitly specifying the so-called final name of the build in pom.xml via a new <finalName> entry in <build> section as follows:

```
<build>
    <finalName>project</finalName>
    <plugins>
        <plugin>
            <artifactId>maven-war-plugin</artifactId>
            <version>3.3.2</version>
        </plugin>
    </plugins>
</build>
```

Now right-click on the project and choose *Maven* ➤ *Update Project...* ➤ *OK*. It will basically force a rebuild of the Maven project. Once it's finished, right-click on the server and choose *Clean*. It will basically force a clean redeployment. If you have paid close attention to the server logs, then the WFLYUT0021 line should now say

```
WFLYUT0021: Registered web context: '/project' for server 'default-server'
```

Now you can use the URL http://localhost:8080/project/hello.xhtml to access the same page (Figure 2-21).

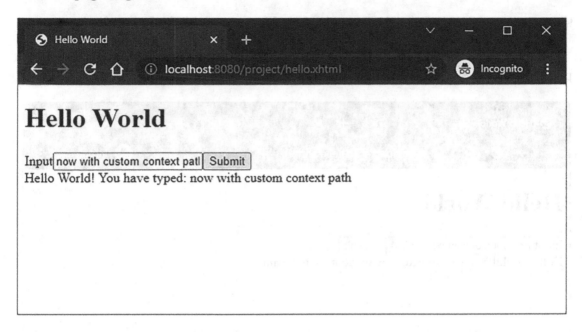

Figure 2-21. *The web application is now using a custom context path*

The context path part can also be set to simply "/". The deployed web application will then end up in the domain root. How to do that depends on the server being used. In case of WildFly, you'll need to create the JBoss-specific jboss-web.xml as follows:

src/main/webapp/WEB-INF/jboss-web.xml:

```
<?xml version="1.0" encoding="UTF-8"?>
<!DOCTYPE jboss-web PUBLIC
    "-//JBoss//DTD JBOSS 5.0//EN"
    "http://www.jboss.org/j2ee/dtd/jboss-web_5_0.dtd"
>
<jboss-web>
    <context-root>/</context-root>
</jboss-web>
```

Right-click on the server and choose *Clean*. The WFLYUT0021 line in the server logs should now say

```
WFLYUT0021: Registered web context: '/' for server 'default-server'
```

Now you can use the URL http://localhost:8080/hello.xhtml to access the same page (Figure 2-22).

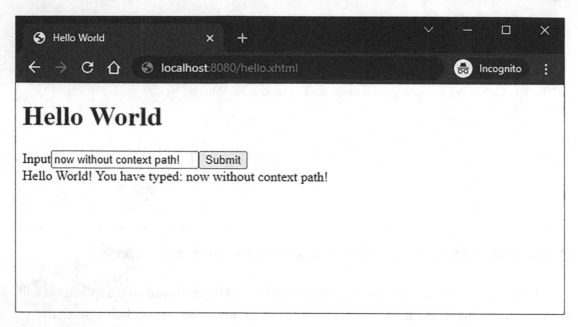

Figure 2-22. *The web application is now deployed without context path*

We can get a step further by making use of the new Faces 4.0–introduced "automatic extensionless mapping" feature so that we do not anymore need to specify the .xhtml extension in the URL. This can be achieved by adding the following entry to the web.xml:

```
<context-param>
    <param-name>
        jakarta.faces.AUTOMATIC_EXTENSIONLESS_MAPPING
    </param-name>
    <param-value>true</param-value>
</context-param>
```

This will basically instruct Jakarta Faces to automatically map the FacesServlet to the extensionless variant of the URL as well, allowing you to open the page via `http://localhost:8080/hello` (Figure 2-23).

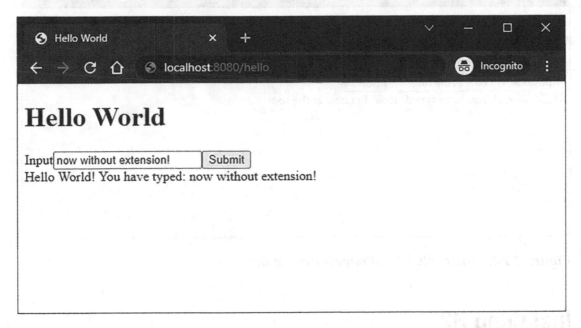

Figure 2-23. *The web application is now extensionless*

We can get yet another step further by making `hello.xhtml` the default landing file so that this also doesn't need to be specified in the URL. This can be achieved by adding the following entry to the `web.xml`:

```
<welcome-file-list>
    <welcome-file>hello.xhtml</welcome-file>
</welcome-file-list>
```

This will basically instruct the server to use the specified file within the folder as default resource when any folder is requested. So if, for example, the "/" folder is requested, then it'll search for a "/hello.xhtml" file and transparently serve it back. The same applies when the "/foo" folder is requested, the server will then search for a "/foo/hello.xhtml" file and serve it (or else return a 404 "Not found" when absent).

Now, save the `web.xml` and clean the server. Coming back to the web browser, you'll notice that the web page is now also accessible by just `http://localhost:8080` (see Figure 2-24).

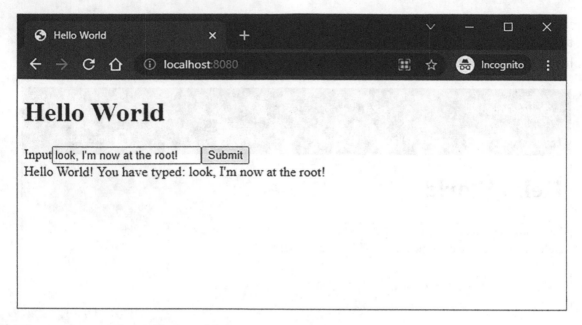

Figure 2-24. *The Hello World page is now at the root*

Installing H2

H2[3] is an in-memory SQL database. It's an embedded database useful for quickly modeling and testing Jakarta Persistence entities, certainly in combination with autogenerated SQL tables based on Jakarta Persistence entities. Adding H2 to your web application project is a matter of adding the following dependency to the `<dependencies>` section of the `pom.xml`:

```
<dependency>
    <groupId>com.h2database</groupId>
    <artifactId>h2</artifactId>
    <version>2.1.210</version>
</dependency>
```

That's basically it. The JDBC (Java Database Connectivity) driver is also provided by this dependency.

---

[3] https://h2database.com

Configuring DataSource

In order to be able to interact with an SQL database, we need to configure a so-called data source in the web application project. This can be done by adding the following section to the web.xml:

```
<data-source>
    <name>java:global/DataSourceName</name>
    <class-name>org.h2.jdbcx.JdbcDataSource</class-name>
    <url>jdbc:h2:mem:test;MODE=LEGACY;DB_CLOSE_DELAY=-1</url>
</data-source>
```

The <name> of the data source represents the JNDI (Java Naming and Directory Interface) name. The "java:global/" part is mandatory. The "DataSourceName" part is free to your choice. It's the one that ultimately needs to be registered in the persistence.xml later on. The <class-name> represents the fully qualified name of the javax.sql.DataSource implementation of the JDBC driver being used. The <url> represents the JDBC driver–specific URL format. The syntax is dependent on the JDBC driver being used. For an in-memory H2 database with a database name of "test", that's thus jdbc:h2:mem:test. The H2-specific MODE=LEGACY path parameter is basically a work around for Hibernate incompatibility with SQL "IDENTITY" type, you could try removing this part in a newer Hibernate version. The H2-specific DB_CLOSE_DELAY=-1 path parameter basically instructs its JDBC driver not to automatically shut down the database when it hasn't been accessed for some time, even though the application server is still running.

After configuring the data source, a concrete instance of the javax.sql.DataSource can now be injected in any servlet container managed artifact such as a servlet or filter as follows:

```
@Resource
private DataSource dataSource;
```

You could get an SQL connection from it via DataSource#getConnection() for the plain old JDBC work. However, as we're going to use pure Jakarta EE, it's better to use Jakarta EE's own Jakarta Persistence for this instead.

Configuring Jakarta Persistence

In order to familiarize Jakarta Persistence with the newly added data source, we need to edit the persistence unit entry in the persistence.xml as follows:

```
<persistence-unit name="PersistenceUnitName" transaction-type="JTA">
    <jta-data-source>java:global/DataSourceName</jta-data-source>
    <properties>
        <property
            name="jakarta.persistence.schema-generation.database.action"
            value="drop-and-create" />
    </properties>
</persistence-unit>
```

You see, the data source is identified by its JNDI name which we configured earlier in web.xml. You'll also notice a Jakarta Persistence–specific property jakarta.persistence.schema-generation.database.action with a value of "drop-and-create" which basically means that the web application should automatically drop and create all SQL tables based on Jakarta Persistence entities. This is, of course, only useful for prototyping purposes, as we're going to do with this project in the rest of the book. For real-world applications, you'd better pick either "create" or "none" (which is the default). Or better yet, a real data base server such as PostgreSQL instead of an in-memory database.

The transaction type being set to "JTA" basically means that the application server itself should automatically manage database transactions. This way, every method invocation on a Jakarta Enterprise Beans service class from its client (usually, a Jakarta Faces backing bean class) transparently starts a new transaction, and when the service method returns to the client (usually, the calling backing bean), then the transaction is automatically committed and flushed. And any runtime exception from a service method automatically rolls back the transaction.

Creating the Jakarta Persistence Entity

Now we're going to create a Jakarta Persistence entity. Basically, it's a JavaBean class that represents a single record of a database table. Each bean property is mapped to a particular column of the database table. Normally, Jakarta Persistence entities are modeled against existing database tables. But as you've read in the previous section,

"Configuring Jakarta Persistence," about the persistence.xml, it's also possible to do it the other way round: database tables are generated based on Jakarta Persistence entities.

Right-click the src/main/java folder of the project and choose *New* ➤ *Jakarta Persistence Entity*. In the wizard, set the *Package* to com.example.project.model and set the *Class name* to Message. The rest of the fields can be kept default or empty (see Figure 2-25). Click *Finish*.

Figure 2-25. *The New Jakarta Persistence Entity wizard in Eclipse*

Modify the new entity class as follows:

```
package com.example.project.model;

import java.io.Serializable;
import jakarta.persistence.Column;
import jakarta.persistence.Entity;
import jakarta.persistence.GeneratedValue;
import jakarta.persistence.GenerationType;
import jakarta.persistence.Id;
import jakarta.persistence.Lob;
import jakarta.validation.constraints.NotNull;
```

```
@Entity
public class Message implements Serializable {

    private static final long serialVersionUID = 1L;

    @Id @GeneratedValue(strategy=GenerationType.IDENTITY)
    private Long id;

    @Column(nullable = false) @Lob
    private @NotNull String text;

    // Add/generate getters and setters.
}
```

As a reminder, you can let Eclipse generate getters and setters by right-clicking anywhere in the class editor and choosing *Source* ➤ *Generate Getters and Setters*. We'll briefly go through the annotations that are used here.

- **@Entity**: This marks the bean as a Jakarta Persistence entity so that the Jakarta Persistence implementation will automatically collect database-related metadata based on all its properties.

- **@Id @GeneratedValue(strategy=IDENTITY)**: This marks a property to be mapped to an SQL database column of SQL "IDENTITY" type. In MySQL terms, that's the equivalent of "AUTO_INCREMENT". In PostgreSQL terms, that's the equivalent of "BIGSERIAL".

- **@Column**: This marks a property to be mapped to a regular SQL database column. The actual SQL database column type depends on the Java type being used. In case of a Java String, without the additional @Lob annotation, that's by default a VARCHAR(255) whose length can be manipulated by @Column(length=n). With the @Lob annotation, however, the SQL database column type becomes by default TEXT.

- **@Lob**: This marks a String property to be mapped to an SQL database column of type TEXT instead of a limited VARCHAR.

- **@NotNull**: This is actually not part of Jakarta Persistence but of "Jakarta Bean Validation." To the point, it ensures that the bean property is being validated never to be null when submitting a Jakarta Faces form and when persisting the Jakarta Persistence entity (see also Chapter 5). Also note that this basically replicates the @Column(nullable=false), but that's only because Jakarta Persistence doesn't consider any Jakarta Bean Validation annotations as valid SQL database metadata in order to generate appropriate SQL tables.

Creating the Jakarta Enterprise Beans Service

Next, we need to create a Jakarta Enterprise Beans service class in order to be able to save an instance of the aforementioned Jakarta Persistence entity in the database and to obtain a list of Jakarta Persistence entities, among others.

Right-click the src/main/java folder of the project and choose *New ➤ Class*. In the wizard, set the *Package* to com.example.project.service and set the *Name* to MessageService (see Figure 2-26). The rest of the fields can be kept default or empty.

Figure 2-26. *The New Java Class wizard in Eclipse*

Modify the new service class as follows:

```
package com.example.project.service;

import java.util.List;
import com.example.project.model.Message;
import jakarta.ejb.Stateless;
import jakarta.persistence.EntityManager;
import jakarta.persistence.PersistenceContext;

@Stateless
public class MessageService {

    @PersistenceContext
    private EntityManager entityManager;

    public void create(Message message) {
        entityManager.persist(message);
    }

    public List<Message> list() {
        return entityManager
            .createQuery("FROM Message m", Message.class)
            .getResultList();
    }
}
```

That's basically it. Let's briefly go through the annotations.

- **@Stateless**: This marks the bean as a stateless Jakarta Enterprise Beans service so that the application server knows whether it should pool them and when to start and stop database transactions. The alternative annotations are @Stateful and @Singleton. Note that a @Stateless does not mean that the container will make sure that the class itself is stateless. You as developer are still responsible to ensure that the class doesn't contain any shared and mutable instance variables. Otherwise, you'd better mark it as either @Stateful or @Singleton, depending on its purpose.

- **@PersistenceContext**: This basically injects the Jakarta Persistence entity manager from the persistence unit as configured in the project's persistence.xml. The entity manager is, in turn, responsible for mapping all Jakarta Persistence entities against an SQL database. It will, under the covers, do all the hard JDBC work.

Adjusting the Hello World

Now we're going to adjust the earlier created HelloWorld backing bean in order to save the messages in the database and display all of them in a table.

```java
package com.example.project.view;

import java.util.List;
import com.example.project.model.Message;
import com.example.project.service.MessageService;
import jakarta.annotation.PostConstruct;
import jakarta.enterprise.context.RequestScoped;
import jakarta.inject.Inject;
import jakarta.inject.Named;

@Named @RequestScoped
public class HelloWorld {

    private Message message = new Message();
    private List<Message> messages;

    @Inject
    private MessageService messageService;

    @PostConstruct
    public void init() {
        messages = messageService.list();
    }

    public void submit() {
        messageService.create(message);
        messages.add(message);
    }
```

```
    public Message getMessage() {
        return message;
    }

    public List<Message> getMessages() {
        return messages;
    }
}
```

Note that you don't need setters for message and messages. We're going to use the getters and setters of the Message entity itself.

Finally, adjust the <h:body> of hello.xhtml as follows:

```
<h1>Hello World</h1>
<h:form>
    <h:outputLabel for="input" value="Input" />
    <h:inputText id="input" value="#{helloWorld.message.text}" />
    <h:commandButton value="Submit"
        action="#{helloWorld.submit}">
        <f:ajax execute="@form" render=":table" />
    </h:commandButton>
</h:form>
<h:dataTable id="table" value="#{helloWorld.messages}" var="message">
    <h:column>#{message.id}</h:column>
    <h:column>#{message.text}</h:column>
</h:dataTable>
```

Now, restart the server, reload the page in your favorite web browser, and create some messages (see Figure 2-27).

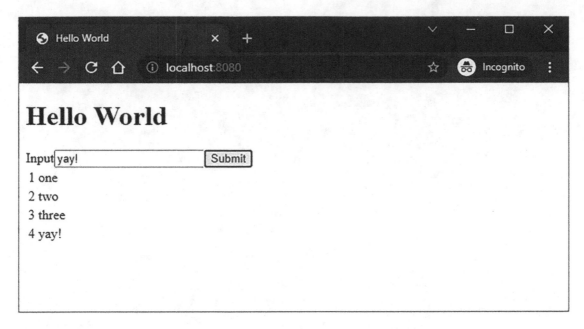

Figure 2-27. *The Hello World using Jakarta Faces, Jakarta CDI, Jakarta Enterprise Beans, and Jakarta Persistence*

CHAPTER 3

Components

Jakarta Faces is a component-based MVC (model-view-controller) framework. In essencè, Jakarta Faces parses the view definition into a "component tree." The root of this tree is represented by the "view root" instance associated with the current instance of the faces context.

```
UIComponent tree = FacesContext.getCurrentInstance().getViewRoot();
```

The view is usually defined using XHTML+XML markup in a Facelets file. XML is a markup language that is very suitable for defining a tree hierarchy using a minimum of code. The component tree can also be created and manipulated using Java code in a Java class, but this generally ends up in very verbose code in order to declare value or method expressions and to correlate parents and children with one another. It's much better to use tag handlers such as Jakarta Tags (formerly known as Jakarta Tags, Jakarta Pages Standard Tag Library) to manipulate the component tree using just XML.

The component tree basically defines how Jakarta Faces should consume the HTTP request in order to apply request values coming from input components, convert and validate them, update the managed bean model values, and invoke the managed bean action. It also defines how Jakarta Faces should produce the HTTP response by generating the necessary HTML output using renderers tied to the components whose attributes can in turn reference managed bean properties. In other words, the component tree defines how the phases of the Jakarta Faces life cycle should be processed. The diagram in Figure 3-1 shows how an HTTP postback request is usually being processed by Jakarta Faces.

© Bauke Scholtz and Arjan Tijms 2022
B. Scholtz and A. Tijms, *The Definitive Guide to Jakarta Faces in Jakarta EE 10*,
https://doi.org/10.1007/978-1-4842-7310-4_3

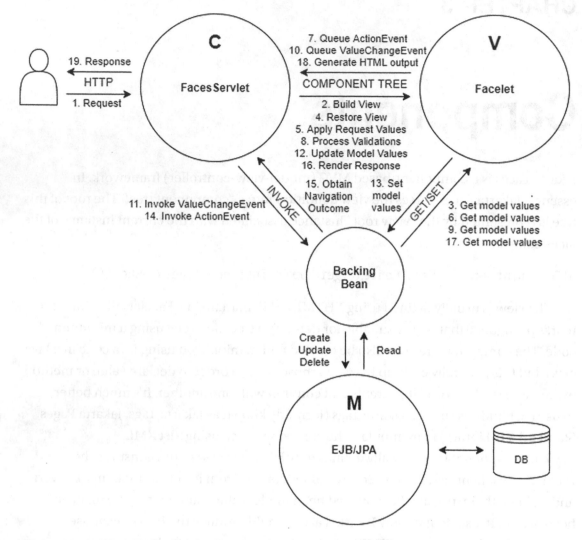

Figure 3-1. How Jakarta Faces processes the HTTP postback request within the MVC architecture (the numbers represent the ordering)

The following is a brief description of each step:

1. End user sends an HTTP request using a URL that matches the mapping of the FacesServlet, and thus the FacesServlet gets invoked.

2. The FacesServlet will build the component tree based on the Facelets file identified by the HTTP request path.

3. The component tree will, if necessary, get the current model values from the backing bean during building the view. Any attribute of a Facelets template tag and a Jakarta Tags core tag and only the "id" and "binding" attributes of a Jakarta Faces component will get executed.

4. The FacesServlet will restore the Jakarta Faces view state on the component tree.

5. The FacesServlet will let the component tree apply the HTTP request parameters, and the input components will store them as "submitted value."

6. The input and command components will, if necessary, get the current model values from the backing bean during consulting their "rendered", "disabled", and "readonly" attributes in order to check whether they are allowed to apply the request parameters.

7. The command components will queue the ActionEvent when it detects, based on HTTP request parameters, that the HTML representation of the command component was being invoked in the client side.

8. The FacesServlet will let the component tree process all registered converters and validators on the submitted values, and the input components will store the newly converted and validated value as "local value."

9. The input components will get the old model value from the backing bean and compare them with the new value.

10. If the new value is different from the old model value, then the input component will queue the ValueChangeEvent.

11. When all conversion and validation are finished, then the FacesServlet will invoke the listener methods of any queued ValueChangeEvent on the backing bean.

12. The FacesServlet will let the component tree update all model values.

13. The input components will set the new model values in the backing bean.

14. The `FacesServlet` will invoke the listener methods of any queued `ActionEvent` on the backing bean.

15. The final action method of the backing bean will, if necessary, return a non-`null` `String` outcome referring the target view.

16. The `FacesServlet` will let the component tree render the HTTP response.

17. The component tree will, if necessary, get the current model values from the backing bean during generating the HTML output. Practically any attribute of a Facelets component and a Jakarta Faces component that is involved in generating the HTML output will get executed.

18. The component tree will write the HTML output to the HTTP response.

19. The `FacesServlet` will return the HTTP response to the end user.

This is different from a request-based MVC framework wherein the developer needs to write more boilerplate code in the "controller" class associated with the view in order to define which request parameters need to be applied and/or how they should be converted and validated before populating the entity. The developer also often needs to manually populate the entity by manually invoking a bunch of getters and setters before passing the entity to the service layer while invoking the action. This all is unnecessary in a component-based MVC framework like Jakarta Faces.

It should be noted that the backing bean has a rather unique position in the MVC paradigm. It can act as a Model, a View, and a Controller, depending on the point of view. This is detailed in Chapter 8.

Standard HTML Components

The default Jakarta Faces implementation already provides an extensive set of components for authoring HTML pages with the help of the Facelets view technology. Those HTML components are available under the `jakarta.faces.html` XML namespace URI (Uniform Resource Identifier) that should be assigned to the "h" XML namespace prefix.

```
xmlns:h="jakarta.faces.html"
```

The most important HTML components that should always be present in your Jakarta Faces page are the `<h:head>` and `<h:body>`. Without them, Jakarta Faces won't be able to auto-include any script or stylesheet resources associated with a particular component.

For example, the `<h:commandButton>`, which generates an HTML submit button, can optionally contain Ajax functionality via a `<f:ajax>` tag. This Ajax functionality requires the `faces.js` script file to be included in the HTML document. The renderer of that component will automatically take care of that, but that would only work properly if the `<h:head>` is present.

The `<h:body>` is not necessary for the Ajax functionality, but there may exist components that need to add a script to the end of the HTML body in order to perform initialization during page load, such as the `<f:websocket>` that needs to create a new `window.WebSocket` instance in JavaScript. In other words, the most minimal and HTML5-valid Jakarta Faces view definition would look as follows:

```
<!DOCTYPE html>
<html lang="en" xmlns:h="jakarta.faces.html">
    <h:head>
        <title>Title</title>
    </h:head>
    <h:body>
        ...
    </h:body>
</html>
```

The generated HTML response, as you can inspect by right-clicking *View page source* in the average web browser, should look as follows:

```
<!DOCTYPE html>
<html lang="en">
    <head>
        <title>Title</title>
    </head>
```

```
    <body>
        ...
    </body>
</html>
```

You see, Jakarta Faces basically replaces all components in the view definition by their generated HTML output. As discussed previously, Jakarta Faces provides an extensive set of standard HTML components. Table 3-1 provides an overview.

Table 3-1. *Standard HTML Components Provided by Jakarta Faces*

Component tag	Component superclass	Value type	HTML output	Since
<h:body>	UIOutput	-	<body>	2.0
<h:button>	UIOutcomeTarget	String	<button onclick=window. location>	2.0
<h:column>	UIColumn	-	<td> (for h:dataTable)	1.0
<h:commandButton>	UICommand	String	<input type=submit>	1.0
<h:commandLink>	UICommand	String	<a onclick=form.submit()>	1.0
<h:commandScript>	UICommand	-	<script> (function to submit a form)	2.3
<h:dataTable>	UIData	Object[ ]	<table> (dynamic)	1.0
<h:doctype>	UIOutput	-	<!DOCTYPE>	2.0
<h:form>	UIForm	-	<form method=post>	1.0
<h:graphicImage>	UIGraphic	-	<img src>	1.0
<h:head>	UIOutput	-	<head>	2.0
<h:inputFile>	UIInput	Part	<input type=file>	2.2
<h:inputHidden>	UIInput	Object	<input type=hidden>	1.0
<h:inputSecret>	UIInput	Object	<input type=password>	1.0
<h:inputText>	UIInput	Object	<input type=text>	1.0
<h:inputTextarea>	UIInput	Object	<textarea>	1.0
<h:link>	UIOutcomeTarget	String	<a href>	2.0

(continued)

Table 3-1. (*continued*)

Component tag	Component superclass	Value type	HTML output	Since
<h:message>	UIMessage	-	<span> (if necessary)	1.0
<h:messages>	UIMessages	-	<ul>	1.0
<h:messages layout=table>	UIMessages	-	<table>	1.0
<h:outputFormat>	UIOutput	Object	<span> (if necessary)	1.0
<h:outputLabel>	UIOutput	String	<label>	1.0
<h:outputText>	UIOutput	Object	<span> (if necessary)	1.0
<h:outputScript>	UIOutput	-	<script>	2.0
<h:outputStylesheet>	UIOutput	-	<link rel=stylesheet>	2.0
<h:panelGrid>	UIPanel	-	<table> (static)	1.0
<h:panelGroup>	UIPanel	-	<span>	1.0
<h:panelGroup layout=block>	UIPanel	-	<div>	1.2
<h:selectBooleanCheckbox>	UIInput	Boolean	<input type=checkbox>	1.0
<h:selectManyCheckbox>	UIInput	Object[ ]	<table><input type=checkbox>*	1.0
<h:selectManyCheckbox layout=list>	UIInput	Object[]	<ul><li><input type=checkbox>*	4.0
<h:selectManyListbox>	UIInput	Object[ ]	<select multiple size=n><option>*	1.0
<h:selectManyMenu>	UIInput	Object[ ]	<select multiple size=1><option>*	1.0
<h:selectOneListbox>	UIInput	Object	<select size=n><option>*	1.0
<h:selectOneMenu>	UIInput	Object	<select size=1><option>*	1.0
<h:selectOneRadio>	UIInput	Object	<table><input type=radio>*	1.0
<h:selectOneRadio layout=list>	UIInput	Object	<ul><li><input type=radio>*	4.0
<h:selectOneRadio group>	UIInput	Object	<input type=radio name=group>	2.3

The "Component superclass" column specifies the most important `UIComponent` superclass which the component extends from. You must interpret the specified class to be from the `jakarta.faces.component` package.

The "Value type" column specifies the supported type of the model value behind the component's `value` attribute, if it has any. If the value type is `String`, then it means that only the model value's `toString()` outcome will be used as value of the component, generally in components which would render it as some sort of label. If it's `Object`, it means that it supports any kind of value, generally in components which would render it as text or parse it as input value, if necessary with help of an implicit or explicit `Converter`. If the value type is `Object[]`, it means that it requires an array or collection of objects as model value, generally in data and multiselection input components, if necessary with an implicit or explicit `Converter`.

There are two specialized input components: the `<h:inputFile>`, which binds the uploaded file to a `jakarta.servlet.http.Part` property and doesn't support outputting it—for security reasons—and the `<h:selectBooleanCheckbox>`, which binds the checked value to a `boolean` property. These two input components don't support a `Converter` and therefore don't support any other model value type.

The "HTML output" column specifies the minimum generated HTML output. If the HTML output says "if necessary," then it means that the specified HTML element is only emitted when the component has any attribute specified that requires being outputted as an HTML element attribute, such as `id`, `styleClass`, and `onclick`. That is, a component can have attributes that don't end up in the generated HTML output at all, such as `binding`, `rendered`, and `converter`. If a component can have multiple HTML element representations, then that's usually controlled by the `layout` attribute as you can see with `<h:messages>` and `<h:panelGroup>`. If the HTML output contains "*" (an asterisk), then it means that the component may emit zero or more of the specified nested HTML elements.

The "Since" column indicates the first Jakarta Faces version the HTML component was available in. At the time this book was written, the following Jakarta Faces versions were available: 1.0 (March 2004), 1.1 (May 2004), 1.2 (May 2006), 2.0 (July 2009), 2.1 (November 2010), 2.2 (March 2013), 2.3 (March 2017), 2.0 (October 2020), and 4.0 (May 2022).

The individual HTML components are detailed in Chapter 4 and in Chapter 6.

Standard Core Tags

Next to the standard HTML components, Jakarta Faces also provides a set of "core" tags. Those are essentially "helper" tags that allow you to declaratively configure one or more target HTML components by either nesting in them or wrapping around them. Those core tags are available under the XML namespace URI of `jakarta.faces.core` which should be assigned to the "`f`" XML namespace prefix.

```
xmlns:f="jakarta.faces.core"
```

Technically, those tags are intended to be reusable on non-HTML components. Jakarta Faces also offers the possibility of attaching a different render kit to the component tree that doesn't generate HTML output but a different markup, hence the different XML namespace. Table 3-2 provides an overview.

Table 3-2. Standard Core Tags Provided by Jakarta Faces

Core tag	Creates/handles	Target component	Since
<f:actionListener>	jakarta.faces.event.ActionListener	ActionSource	1.0
<f:ajax>	jakarta.faces.component.behavior.AjaxBehavior	ClientBehaviorHolder(s)	2.0
<f:attribute>	UIComponent#getAttributes()	UIComponent	1.0
<f:attributes>	UIComponent#getAttributes()	UIComponent	2.2
<f:convertDateTime>	jakarta.faces.convert.DateTimeConverter	(Editable)ValueHolder	1.0
<f:convertNumber>	jakarta.faces.convert.NumberConverter	(Editable)ValueHolder	1.0
<f:converter>	jakarta.faces.convert.Converter	(Editable)ValueHolder	1.0
<f:event>	jakarta.faces.event.ComponentSystemEvent	UIComponent	2.0
<f:facet>	UIComponent#getFacets()	UIComponent	1.0
<f:importConstants>	jakarta.faces.component.UIImportConstants	UIViewRoot (metadata)	2.3
<f:loadBundle>	java.util.ResourceBundle	UIViewRoot	1.0
<f:metadata>	jakarta.faces.view.ViewMetadata	UIViewRoot	2.0
<f:param>	jakarta.faces.component.UIParameter	UIComponent	1.0
<f:passthroughAttribute>	UIComponent#getPassthroughAttributes()	UIComponent	2.2
<f:passthroughAttributes>	UIComponent#getPassthroughAttributes()	UIComponent	2.2
<f:phaseListener>	jakarta.faces.event.PhaseListener	UIViewRoot	1.0
<f:selectItem>	jakarta.faces.component.UISelectItem	UISelectOne/UISelectMany	1.0
<f:selectItems>	jakarta.faces.component.UISelectItems	UISelectOne/UISelectMany	1.0

Table 3-2. (*continued*)

Core tag	Creates/handles	Target component	Since
`<f:setPropertyActionListener>`	jakarta.faces.event.ActionListener	ActionSource	1.0
`<f:subview>`	jakarta.faces.component.NamingContainer	UIComponents	1.0
`<f:validateBean>`	jakarta.faces.validator.BeanValidator	UIForm	2.0
`<f:validateDoubleRange>`	jakarta.faces.validator.DoubleRangeValidator	EditableValueHolder	1.0
`<f:validateLength>`	jakarta.faces.validator.LengthValidator	EditableValueHolder	1.0
`<f:validateLongRange>`	jakarta.faces.validator.LongRangeValidator	EditableValueHolder	1.0
`<f:validateRegex>`	jakarta.faces.validator.RegexValidator	EditableValueHolder	2.0
`<f:validateRequired>`	jakarta.faces.validator.RequiredValidator	EditableValueHolder	2.0
`<f:validateWholeBean>`	jakarta.faces.validator.BeanValidator	UIForm	2.3
`<f:validator>`	jakarta.faces.validator.Validator	EditableValueHolder	1.0
`<f:valueChangeListener>`	jakarta.faces.event.ValueChangeListener	EditableValueHolder	1.0
`<f:view>`	jakarta.faces.component.UIViewRoot	UIComponents	1.0
`<f:viewAction>`	jakarta.faces.component.UIViewAction	UIViewRoot (metadata)	2.2
`<f:viewParam>`	jakarta.faces.component.UIViewParameter	UIViewRoot (metadata)	2.0
`<f:websocket>`	jakarta.faces.component.UIWebsocket	UIViewRoot (body resource)	2.3

The "Creates/handles" column specifies the thing which the core tag creates or handles on the specified target component.

The "Target component" column specifies the target component superclass or interface supported by the core tag. You must interpret the specified superclass or interface to be from the `jakarta.faces.component` package. If the target component is optionally pluralized as in `UIComponent(s)`, then it means that the core tag can either be nested in the target component or wrapped in one or more target components. If the target component is explicitly pluralized as in `UIComponents`, then it means that the core tag can only wrap one or more target components and thus not be nested.

As to target component interfaces, the `ActionSource` interface is implemented by `UICommand` components. The `ClientBehaviorHolder` interface is implemented by `UIForm`, `UIInput`, `UICommand`, `UIData`, `UIOutput`, `UIPanel`, and `UIOutcomeTarget` components. The `ValueHolder` interface is implemented by `UIOutput` and `UIInput` components. The `EditableValueHolder` interface is implemented by `UIInput` components. Based on Table 3-1, you should be able to derive the actual HTML components from them.

The "Since" column indicates the first Jakarta Faces version the core tag was available in. At the time this book was written, the following Jakarta Faces versions were available: 1.0 (March 2004), 1.1 (May 2004), 1.2 (May 2006), 2.0 (July 2009), 2.1 (November 2010), 2.2 (March 2013), 2.3 (March 2017), 2.0 (October 2020), and 4.0 (May 2022).

Most of the individual core tags are detailed in separate chapters.

Life Cycle

Jakarta Faces has a very well-defined life cycle. It is broken down into six phases. Each of those phases runs the HTTP request through the component tree, performs operations on it, and fires component system events. A brief description was already given in the introduction of this chapter, along with a diagram (Figure 3-1). The following sections describe each individual phase of the Jakarta Faces life cycle.

Restore View Phase (First Phase)

First, create the `UIViewRoot` instance and set its properties such as `locale` from any `<f:view>` tag. The component tree is at that moment usually empty. Only when the current request is a postback request, or when the view has a `<f:metadata>` with children, then build the full component tree based on the view definition. Basically, a specific `UIComponent` subclass will be instantiated based on the component tag defined in the view and populated with all attributes defined in the view, and then `UIComponent#setParent()` will be invoked, passing the actual parent component.

The `UIComponent#setParent()` method will first check if there isn't already an existing parent, and if so, then it will fire the `PreRemoveFromViewEvent` on the old parent. Then, when the new parent has been set, and thus the current component has become part of the component tree, it will fire the `PostAddToViewEvent` with the current component.

If the current request is a postback request, then it will restore the "view state" identified by the `jakarta.faces.ViewState` request parameter into the freshly built component tree. After that, the `PostRestoreStateEvent` is explicitly fired for each component in the tree, even when the component tree has actually not been restored. In other words, even when it's not a postback request, that event is fired. You'd better reinterpret that event as "PostRestoreViewPhase". In case when you're, during the `PostRestoreStateEvent`, actually interested in whether it's a postback request or not, then you should consult the `FacesContext#isPostback()` as well.

By the end of the restore view phase, if the component tree is still empty, then the life cycle will immediately advance to the render response phase (sixth phase), hereby skipping any phase in between.

Apply Request Values Phase (Second Phase)

The `UIComponent#processDecodes()` method will be invoked on the `UIViewRoot`. The `processDecodes()` method will first invoke the `processDecodes()` method on each child and facet and then invoke `UIComponent#decode()` on itself. Finally, the `UIViewRoot#broadCastEvents()` will be invoked to fire any `FacesEvent` queued for the current phase. The default Jakarta Faces API (application programming interface) doesn't offer such events for the apply request values phase, but developers can create and queue their own.

The default implementation of the decode() method will delegate to the Renderer#decode() method. In the decode() method of either the component or the renderer, the implementation has the opportunity to extract the submitted value from the HTTP request parameter and set it as an internal property. From the standard HTML component set, the only components that do that are the HTML form–based components deriving from UIForm, UIInput, and UICommand. The UIForm component will invoke UIForm#setSubmitted() with true. The UIInput component will invoke UIInput#setSubmittedValue() with the HTTP request parameter value. The UICommand component will queue the ActionEvent for the invoke application phase (fifth phase).

Process Validations Phase (Third Phase)

The UIComponent#processValidators() will be invoked on the UIViewRoot. The processValidators() method will basically first fire the PreValidateEvent for the current component, then invoke processValidators() on each child and facet, and then invoke the PostValidateEvent for the current component. Finally, the UIViewRoot#broadCastEvents() will be invoked to fire any FacesEvent queued for the current phase, which is usually an instance of ValueChangeEvent.

From the standard HTML component set, only UIInput components behave differently here. Right before calling processValidators() on each child and facet, they will first invoke UIInput#validate() on itself. If there's a submitted value set during the apply request values phase (second phase), then they will first invoke Converter#getAsObject() on any attached Converter. When it doesn't throw ConverterException, then they will invoke Validator#validate() on every single attached Validator instance, regardless of whether any of them has thrown a ValidatorException.

When no ConverterException or ValidatorException was thrown, then UIInput#setValue() will be invoked with the converted and validated value, and the UIInput#isLocalValueSet() flag will return true and UIInput#setSubmittedValue() will be invoked with null.

When any ConverterException or ValidatorException was thrown, then UIInput#setValid() will be invoked with false, and the message of the exception will be added to the faces context via FacesContext#addMessage(). Finally, when UIInput#isValid() returns false, then FacesContext#setValidationFailed() will be invoked with true.

By the end of the phase, when `FacesContext#isValidationFailed()` returns `true`, then the life cycle will immediately advance to the render response phase (sixth phase), hereby skipping any phase in between.

Update Model Values Phase (Fourth Phase)

The `UIComponent#processUpdates()` method will be invoked on the `UIViewRoot`. The `processUpdates()` method will in turn invoke the `processUpdates()` method on each child and facet. Finally, the `UIViewRoot#broadCastEvents()` will be invoked to fire any `FacesEvent` queued for the current phase. The default Jakarta Faces API doesn't offer such events for the update model values phase, but developers can create and queue their own.

Also during this phase, from the standard HTML component set, only `UIInput` components have additional functionality here. After calling `processUpdates()` on each child and facet, they will invoke `UIInput#updateModel()` on itself. When both the `UIInput#isValid()` and `UIInput#isLocalValueSet()` return `true`, then they will invoke the setter method behind the `value` attribute with `getLocalValue()` as argument and immediately invoke `UIInput#setValue()` with `null` and clear out the `UIInput#isLocalValueSet()` flag by letting it return `false`.

When a `RuntimeException` is thrown here, usually caused by a bug in the setter method itself, then it will invoke `UIInput#setValid()` with `false` and queue the `UpdateModelException`, and the life cycle will immediately advance to the render response phase (sixth phase), hereby skipping any phase in between.

Invoke Application Phase (Fifth Phase)

The `UIViewRoot#processApplication()` method will be invoked. This method will in turn invoke the `UIViewRoot#broadCastEvents()` to fire any `FacesEvent` queued for the current phase, which is usually an instance of `AjaxBehaviorEvent` or `ActionEvent`. Note that the `processApplication()` method is only defined on the `UIViewRoot` class and does not traverse the component tree.

Render Response Phase (Sixth Phase)

When the component tree is still empty, i.e., when the HTTP request is not a postback request, or when the view has no `<f:metadata>` with children, or when the developer has in the meanwhile explicitly invoked `FacesContext#setViewRoot()` with its own instance, then build the full component tree based on the view definition. When the component tree is present, first, fire the `PreRenderViewEvent` for the `UIViewRoot`, then invoke `UIComponent#encodeAll()` on the `UIViewRoot`, and finally fire the `PostRenderViewEvent` for the `UIViewRoot`.

The `UIComponent#encodeAll()` method of each component will basically first invoke its own `encodeBegin()` method. Then, if the `getRendersChildren()` method returns `true`, the component will invoke its own `encodeChildren()` method, else it will invoke `encodeAll()` on each child. Finally, the component will invoke its own `encodeEnd()` method. This all happens only if `UIComponent#isRendered()` returns `true`–that is, when the `rendered` attribute of the component tag doesn't evaluate to `false`.

The default implementation of the `encodeBegin()` method will first fire the `PreRenderComponentEvent` for the current component and then delegate to `Renderer#encodeBegin()`. The default implementation of the `encodeChildren()` method will delegate to `Renderer#encodeChildren()`. The default implementation of the `encodeEnd()` method will delegate to `Renderer#encodeEnd()`. If the component has no renderer attached, that is, when `UIComponent#getRendererType()` returns `null`, then no HTML output will be rendered to the response.

In the `encodeBegin()` method, the component or the renderer implementation has the opportunity to write the opening HTML element and all of its attributes to the response. In the `encodeChildren()` method, the component or the renderer implementation has the opportunity to decorate or override the rendering of the children if necessary. In the `encodeEnd()` method, the component or the renderer implementation has the opportunity to write the closing HTML tag. Writing to the response happens with the response writer as available by `FacesContext#getResponseWriter()`.

For any mentioned `XxxEvent` class that has been fired in any phase, if any listener method throws `jakarta.faces.event.AbortProcessingException`,[1] then the currently running phase will be immediately aborted, and the life cycle will immediately advance to the render response phase (sixth phase), hereby skipping any phase in between.

---

[1] https://jakarta.ee/specifications/platform/10/apidocs/jakarta/faces/event/
AbortProcessingException.html

Ajax Life Cycle

The life cycle is almost identical during Ajax requests. Only the second, third, fourth, and sixth phases are slightly different. The `processDecodes()`, `processValidators()`, and `processUpdates()` methods will only be invoked on the `UIViewRoot` itself and any component covered by the component search expression specified in `<f:ajax execute>`. And the `encodeAll()` method will only be invoked on the `UIViewRoot` itself and any component covered by the component search expression specified in `<f:ajax render>`. Read more on search expressions in Chapter 12.

Note thus that there would be no difference in the Ajax life cycle when the component search expression contains the "@all" keyword. It would unnecessarily process and encode the entire component tree. In other words, use "@all" with care. There are no sensible real-world use cases for `<f:ajax execute="@all">`. On the HTML side, it's not possible to submit multiple forms at once. Only the enclosing form is submitted. The biggest value is thus `<f:ajax execute="@form">`. However, there is one sensible real-world use case for a `<f:ajax render="@all">`, namely, rendering a full error page in case an exception is thrown during an Ajax request. Even then, this can better be programmatically triggered via `PartialViewContext#setRenderAll()`. For more details, see Chapter 9.

View Build Time

The "view build time" is not tied to a particular phase of the Jakarta Faces life cycle. The view build time is that moment when the physical `UIViewRoot` instance will be populated with all of its children based on the view definition.

When Jakarta Faces is about to create a `UIComponent` instance based on the view definition, then it will first check whether the getter method behind the `binding` attribute, if any, returns a concrete `UIComponent` instance. If so, then continue using it instead, or else create the `UIComponent` instance based on the "component type" associated with it and then invoke the setter behind the `binding` attribute, if any, with it. If the `id` attribute is specified, then `UIComponent#setId()` will be invoked with it. Finally, `UIComponent#setParent()` will be invoked with the parent component, and then the component instance becomes physically part of the component tree. This tree will exist until the end of the render response phase (sixth phase). Then it becomes eligible for the garbage collector, along with the released faces context instance.

Effectively, `UIComponent` instances are thus request scoped. The `binding` attribute can refer a managed bean property, but as `UIComponent` instances are inherently request scoped, the target managed bean must be request scoped and may not be in a broader scope. This won't be checked by the Jakarta Faces API, so you as being a Jakarta Faces developer should make absolutely sure that you don't reference a broader scoped managed bean in the `binding` attribute of any component.

When the `binding` attribute of any component incorrectly references a managed bean in a broader scope than the request scope, then you're not only basically saving the entire component tree in the HTTP session in case the bean is view or session scoped, but you're also essentially sharing the entire component tree across multiple HTTP requests that are concurrently accessing the very same managed bean instance. Very inefficient and thus dangerous.

The view build time can technically happen during any phase of the Jakarta Faces life cycle. Generally, that's the restore view phase (first phase), particularly during a postback request, or when the view has `<f:metadata>` with children. It can also happen during the render response phase (sixth phase), particularly during a GET request when the view has no `<f:metadata>` with children, or when a non-redirect navigation has taken place during a postback. It will also happen when the developer programmatically invokes `ViewDeclarationLanguage#buildView()`, which can be implicitly done via, among others, `ViewHandler#createView()` as shown in the following example of an action method that forces Jakarta Faces to fully rebuild the current view from scratch:

```
public void rebuildCurrentView() {
    FacesContext context = FacesContext.getCurrentInstance();
    UIViewRoot currentView = context.getViewRoot();
    String viewId = currentView.getViewId();
    ViewHandler viewHandler = context.getApplication.getViewHandler();
    UIViewRoot newView = viewHandler.createView(context, viewId);
    context.setViewRoot(newView);
}
```

Do note that the view state is not per definition during the view build time restored into the component tree. The view state is only restored into the component tree during the restore view phase (first phase), and that happens after the `FacesServlet` has executed the view build time by itself. In other words, the `rebuildCurrentView()` method shown before does not restore the current view state into the newly created component tree. Programmatically restoring the view state is generally not recommended when programmatically rebuilding the view as above, as in a real-world Jakarta Faces application, the sole reason to rebuild the current view is usually to get rid of any changes caused by the persistent view state and/or to forcibly reexecute any Jakarta Tags based on the freshly changed values in the managed bean.

View Render Time

The "view render time" is also not tied to a particular phase of the Jakarta Faces life cycle. The view render time is that moment when UIComponent#encodeAll() of a particular component is invoked.

True, it's by default always executed on the UIViewRoot during the render response phase (sixth phase) by the FacesServlet itself, but this doesn't stop you from programmatically invoking it during a different phase, such as the invoke application phase (fifth phase), for example, in order to obtain the generated HTML output of an arbitrary component as a String variable.

View State

As explained in the section "View Build Time," the UIComponent instances resembling the component tree are inherently request scoped. They are created during the view build time, and they are destroyed right after the render response phase (sixth phase). Any changes to properties of the UIComponent instances, which are not referenced by an EL (Expression Language) expression and are different from their default values, will be saved as "view state." In other words, the "view state" is very definitely not the same as the "component tree." Moreover, if the entire component tree itself would be saved in the view state, then this would result in not only an unnecessarily bloated view state but also corrupted application behavior as UIComponent instances are inherently not thread safe and may therefore absolutely not be shared across multiple HTTP requests.

Saving the view state usually happens during the view render time. Therein, Jakarta Faces will write out the view state to a jakarta.faces.ViewState hidden input field of the generated HTML representation of every Jakarta Faces form. When the Jakarta Faces "state saving method" setting has the default value "server," then the hidden input value represents a unique identifier referring the serialized view state object that is stored in the HTTP session. When the Jakarta Faces "state saving method" setting is explicitly set to "client" using the following web.xml context parameter, then the hidden input value itself represents the encrypted form of the serialized view state object.

```
<context-param>
    <param-name>jakarta.faces.STATE_SAVING_METHOD</param-name>
    <param-value>client</param-value>
</context-param>
<env-entry>
    <env-entry-name>faces/ClientSideSecretKey</env-entry-name>
    <env-entry-type>java.lang.String</env-entry-type>
    <env-entry-value>[AES key in Base64 format]</env-entry-value>
</env-entry>
```

Note that explicitly specifying the faces/ClientSideSecretKey environment entry with a fixed AES (Advanced Encryption Standard) key is mandatory in case you're running the Jakarta Faces application on a cluster of servers ("cloud"), or when you'd like the view state still to be valid after a server restart. You can generate a Base64-encoded AES key yourself using the following plain Java snippet:

```
KeyGenerator keyGen = KeyGenerator.getInstance("AES");
keyGen.init(256); // Or 128 in case you don't have JCE.
byte[] rawKey = keyGen.generateKey().getEncoded();
String key = Base64.getEncoder().encodeToString(rawKey);
System.out.println(key); // Prints AES key in Base64 format.
```

The standard Jakarta Faces form, as represented by <h:form>, submits by default using the POST method to the very same HTTP request URI as where the Jakarta Faces page containing the form is being requested. In other words, when you request a Jakarta Faces page by http://example.com/project/page.xhtml, then it will submit to the very same http://example.com/project/page.xhtml URI. This is in web development terms known as "postback." When Jakarta Faces needs to process an incoming postback request, then the restore view phase (first phase) will, after the view build time, extract the view state from the jakarta.faces.ViewState HTTP request parameter and restore all changed properties into the newly created UIComponent instances of the current request so that the component tree ultimately reflects exactly the same state as it had during the view render time of the previous request.

On an average Jakarta Faces web application, the major part of the saved view state is represented by internal properties of `UIComponent` instances implementing the `jakarta.faces.component.EditableValueHolder` interface,[2] which covers all `UIInput` components such as `<h:inputText>`. When submitting a Jakarta Faces form fails with a conversion or validation error, then all changed "is valid?" states and "local value" states, which can be either the submitted string value or the already-converted and validated value, will for all involved `UIInput` components be saved in the view state. This has the major advantage that the developer doesn't need to worry about manually keeping track of them in order to re-present the submitted form with all valid and invalid values preserved to the website user while keeping the model (the managed bean properties) completely free of those values. This is a major usability advantage for both the Jakarta Faces developer and the website user.

The minority of the saved view state is represented by programmatic changes to the component tree hierarchy, or to component attributes. Among others, any programmatic changes to `readonly`, `disabled`, and `rendered` attributes are tracked in the view state so that a hacker doesn't have any chance to spoof the request in such a way that those attributes flip to the wrong side so that the hacker could do potentially hazardous things. This is a major security advantage.

View Scope

The Servlet API, which Jakarta Faces, among others, is built on top of, offers three well-defined scopes: the request scope, the session scope, and the application scope. Basically, the request scope is established by storing the object of interest as an attribute of the `HttpServletRequest`. Equivalently, the session scope is established by storing the object of interest as an attribute of the `HttpSession`, and the application scope is established by storing the object of interest as an attribute of the `ServletContext`.

Jakarta Faces adds one more scope to this, the view scope. This must not be confused with the component tree itself. The component tree (the physical `UIViewRoot` instance) is created and destroyed during the very same HTTP request and is therefore clearly request scoped. The view scope must also not be confused with the view state, although they are closely related.

---

[2] `https://jakarta.ee/specifications/platform/10/apidocs/jakarta/faces/component/EditableValueHolder.html`

When the end user fires a postback request on a Jakarta Faces form, and the application doesn't perform any kind of navigation (i.e., the action method returns `null` or `void`), then the view state identifier will stay the same, and the lifetime of the view scope will be prolonged to the next postback request, until the application performs an explicit navigation, or when the HTTP session expires. You can establish the view scope by storing the object of interest as an entry of `UIViewRoot#getViewMap()`. This is exactly where Jakarta Faces stores its `@ViewScoped` managed beans. No, this map is not in turn stored in the view state, not even when the Jakarta Faces state saving method is explicitly set to "client." The entire view scope is stored in the HTTP session, separate from the view state. Only the view scope identifier is stored in the view state. Only the changed attributes of the `UIViewRoot` instance are stored in the view state.

Phase Events

The `jakarta.faces.event.PhaseListener` interface[3] can be used to listen on any phase of the Jakarta Faces life cycle. This interface defines three methods: `getPhaseId()`, which should return the phase you're interested in; `beforePhase()`, which will be invoked right before the specified phase is executed; and `afterPhase()`, which will be invoked right after the specified phase is executed. In the `beforePhase()` and `afterPhase()` methods, you thus have the opportunity to run some code before or after the phase specified by `getPhaseId()`.

The `jakarta.faces.event.PhaseId` class[4] defines a set of public constants. It still dates from Jakarta Faces 1.0 that was released only a few months before Java 1.5 and hence was too late in the game in order to become a real enum. The following are the constants with their ordinal values:

- `PhaseId.ANY_PHASE` (0)

- `PhaseId.RESTORE_VIEW` (1)

- `PhaseId.APPLY_REQUEST_VALUES` (2)

- `PhaseId.PROCESS_VALIDATIONS` (3)

- `PhaseId.UPDATE_MODEL_VALUES` (4)

---

[3] https://jakarta.ee/specifications/platform/10/apidocs/jakarta/faces/event/PhaseListener.html

[4] https://jakarta.ee/specifications/platform/10/apidocs/jakarta/faces/event/PhaseId.html

- PhaseId.INVOKE_APPLICATION (5)

- PhaseId.RENDER_RESPONSE (6)

Phase listener instances can be registered in various ways. Declaratively, they can be registered application-wide via the `faces-config.xml`:

```
<lifecycle>
    <phase-listener>com.example.project.YourListener</phase-listener>
</lifecycle>
```

or view-wide via a `<f:phaseListener>` tag enclosed in the `<f:view>`:

```
<f:view>
    <f:phaseListener type="com.example.project.YourListener" />
    ...
</f:view>
```

Programmatically, they can be added and removed application-wide via the `addPhaseListener()` and `removePhaseListener()` methods of the currently used `jakarta.faces.lifecycle.Lifecycle` instance.[5]

```
FacesContext context = FacesContext.getCurrentInstance();
Lifecycle lifecycle = context.getLifecycle();
lifecycle.addPhaseListener(new YourListener());
```

And they can be added and removed view-wide via the `addPhaseListener()` and `removePhaseListener()` methods of `UIViewRoot`.

```
FacesContext context = FacesContext.getCurrentInstance();
UIViewRoot viewRoot = context.getViewRoot();
viewRoot.addPhaseListener(new YourListener());
```

A concrete example of a `PhaseListener` is given in the section "Custom Component System Events."

---

[5] https://jakarta.ee/specifications/platform/10/apidocs/jakarta/faces/lifecycle/Lifecycle.html

Component System Events

As noted in the section "Life Cycle," a bunch of component system events are fired during the Jakarta Faces life cycle. They extend from the abstract class `jakarta.faces. event.ComponentSystemEvent`.[6] In summary, those are

- `PreRemoveFromViewEvent`: Fired when a component is about to be removed from the component tree.

- `PostAddToViewEvent`: Fired when a component has been added to the component tree.

- `PostRestoreStateEvent` (read: "`PostRestoreViewEvent`"): Fired for each component when the restore view phase ends. Note that this event is only fired for `UIViewRoot` when the view build time hasn't yet taken place during this phase. If the view build time has taken place during this phase, then this event is fired for any component in the tree.

- `PreValidateEvent`: Fired when a component is about to process its converter and validators, also when there are actually none.

- `PostValidateEvent`: Fired when a component is finished processing its converter and validators, also when there are actually none.

- `PreRenderViewEvent`: Fired when the `UIViewRoot` is about to write HTML output to the HTTP response. Note that this is the latest possible safe moment to change the destination of the HTTP response, or to programmatically manipulate the component tree. When doing so after this moment, there's no guarantee that any programmatic changes to the response or the component tree will take place as intended because by then the response may already be committed, or the view state may already be saved.

- `PreRenderComponentEvent`: Fired when a component is about to write its HTML output to the HTTP response.

---

[6]`https://jakarta.ee/specifications/platform/10/apidocs/jakarta/faces/event/ ComponentSystemEvent.html`

- **PostRenderViewEvent**: Fired when the `UIViewRoot` is finished writing the HTML output to the HTTP response. Note that this event is new since Jakarta Faces 2.3. All others are from Jakarta Faces 2.0.

There are two more component system events that were left unmentioned in the section "Life Cycle."

- **PostConstructViewMapEvent**: Fired when the `UIViewRoot` has just started the view scope

- **PreDestroyViewMapEvent**: Fired when the `UIViewRoot` is about to destroy the view scope

These two are not strictly tied to the six-phase component-based life cycle and can happen basically any time during the life cycle. The `PostConstructViewMapEvent` is fired when the application invokes `UIViewRoot#getViewMap()` for the first time. By default, this happens only when the first `@ViewScoped` managed bean of the current view state has been created. The `PreDestroyViewMapEvent` is fired when the application invokes `Map#clear()` on the `UIViewRoot#getViewMap()`, which usually only happens when `FacesContext#setViewRoot()` is invoked while there is already an existing instance set. This will end the view scope and destroy any active `@ViewScoped` managed bean. Normally, this happens only when the action method has returned a non-`null` navigation outcome.

You can listen on any of those component system events using the `jakarta.faces.event.ComponentSystemEventListener` interface.[7] In the Jakarta Faces API, the `UIComponent` class itself already implements `ComponentSystemEventListener`. This interface provides a `processEvent()` method with a `ComponentSystemEvent` argument that in turn has a `getComponent()` method returning the concrete `UIComponent` instance the event was fired on. The default implementation of `UIComponent#processEvent()` basically checks if the given `ComponentSystemEvent` argument is an instance of `PostRestoreStateEvent` and if the `binding` attribute is specified, and if so, then invoke the setter method behind the `binding` attribute with the component instance itself as argument.

---

[7]`https://jakarta.ee/specifications/platform/10/apidocs/jakarta/faces/event/ComponentSystemEventListener.html`

There are three ways to subscribe listeners to those component system events. The first is to declaratively use the `<f:event>` tag in the view. This can be attached to any component tag. One example that you'll see in relatively a lot of Jakarta Faces 2.0/2.1 targeted resources is the following:

```
<f:metadata>
    <f:viewParam name="id" value="#{bean.id}" />
    <f:event type="preRenderView" listener="#{bean.onload()}" />
</f:metadata>
```

wherein the `onload()` method is often implemented as follows:

```
public void onload() {
    FacesContext context = FacesContext.getCurrentInstance();

    if (!context.isPostback() && !context.isValidationFailed()) {
        // ...
    }
}
```

Note that the `<f:event listener="#{bean.onload}">` by default expects a method with `ComponentSystemEvent` argument, but if you don't need it, then it can be omitted for brevity, and the method expression should be parenthesized as in `<f:event listener="#{bean.onload()}">`, although the EL implementation being used may be forgiving in this.

The usage of `<f:event type="preRenderView">` as shown before is in essence a work-around in order to be able to simulate the invoke application phase during a GET request based on model values set by the `<f:viewParam>`. This was needed because the `@PostConstruct` was unsuitable as it was invoked directly after bean's construction but far before the model values were set by the `<f:viewParam>`. Since Jakarta Faces 2.2 with its new `<f:viewAction>`, this `<f:event>` trick is not needed anymore:

```
<f:metadata>
    <f:viewParam name="id" value="#{bean.id}" />
    <f:viewAction action="#{bean.onload}" />
</f:metadata>
```

wherein the onload() method is just implemented as follows:

```
public void onload() {
    // ...
}
```

Another real-world example of <f:event> is to have a @PostConstruct-like behavior in the backing component of a composite component wherein you can safely perform any necessary initialization based on its attributes.

```
<cc:interface componentType="someComposite">
    ...
</cc:interface>
<cc:implementation>
    <f:event type="postAddToView" listener="#{cc.init()}" />
    ...
    #{cc.someInitializedValue}
</cc:implementation>
```

and wherein the init() method of the SomeComposite class looks as follows:

```
private Object someInitializedValue; // +getter

public void init() {
    Map<String, Object> attributes = getAttributes();
    someInitializedValue = initializeItBasedOn(attributes);
}
```

The second way to subscribe listeners to component system events is to programmatically use UIComponent#subscribeToEvent() in Java code. This allows you to conditionally subscribe a component system event listener on an existing component. It is important to keep in mind that a component system event listener is saved in the view state. In other words, it's restored in the component instance during the restore view phase of the subsequent postback request. Keep this in mind when using UIComponent#subscribeToEvent(); otherwise, you may end up subscribing the very same listener multiple times. This can be avoided by at least correctly implementing equals() method and the Serializable interface.

This all makes it a little complicated to correctly register a component system event listener programmatically for a specific component. If it's an existing component, you'd better use <f:event> instead, or if it's a custom component, you'd better use @ListenerFor annotation instead, which is actually the third way. Below is a kickoff example of correctly registering a component system event listener programmatically, provided that YourListener class has its equals() and hashCode() methods correctly implemented and that it implements Serializable or Externalizable or jakarta.faces.component.StateHolder so that it can be saved correctly in view state.

```
Class<PreRenderViewEvent> event = PreRenderViewEvent.class;
ComponentSystemEventListener listener = new YourListener();
component.subscribeToEvent(event, listener);
```

As previously stated, the third way to subscribe listeners to component system events is declaratively to use the @ListenerFor annotation. You can put this annotation only on a UIComponent or Renderer class. You can't put this annotation on a backing bean class. For that, you should use <f:event> instead. The @ListenerFor annotation takes the target event(s) as value. The concrete ComponentSystemEventListener instance is the UIComponent instance itself. If the annotation is declared on a Renderer class, then the target component is the UIComponent instance whose UIComponent#getRendererType() refers the particular Renderer class. The following example shows it for a custom component YourComponent:

```
@FacesComponent("project.YourComponent")
@ListenerFor(systemEventClass=PostAddToViewEvent.class)
public class YourComponent extends UIComponentBase {

    @Override
    public void processEvent(ComponentSystemEvent event) {
        if (event instanceof PostAddToViewEvent) {
            // ...
        }
        else {
            super.processEvent(event);
        }
    }
    // ...
}
```

Yes, that instanceof check is necessary. As noted in the section "Life Cycle," the PostRestoreStateEvent is by default explicitly fired for any component in the tree. The super.processEvent(event) call is necessary in case this component has the binding attribute specified because the default UIComponent#processEvent() implementation calls during PostRestoreStateEvent the setter method behind the binding attribute.

Custom Component System Events

You can create your own ComponentSystemEvent types. Basically all you need to do is to extend from the ComponentSystemEvent abstract class and declare the @NamedEvent annotation on it and finally invoke Application#publishEvent() at the desired moment.

Imagine that you want to create a custom component system event that is fired before the invoke application phase (fifth phase), a PreInvokeApplicationEvent. You can then create the custom event as follows:

```
@NamedEvent(shortName="preInvokeApplication")
public class PreInvokeApplicationEvent extends ComponentSystemEvent {
    public PreInvokeApplicationEvent(UIComponent component) {
        super(component);
    }
}
```

And here's how you can use a custom PhaseListener to publish it.

```
public class PreInvokeApplicationListener implements PhaseListener {

    @Override
    public PhaseId getPhaseId() {
        return PhaseId.INVOKE_APPLICATION;
    }

    @Override
    public void beforePhase(PhaseEvent event) {
        FacesContext context = FacesContext.getCurrentInstance();
        context.getApplication().publishEvent(context,
            PreInvokeApplicationEvent.class, context.getViewRoot());
    }
```

```
    @Override
    public void afterPhase(PhaseEvent event) {
        // NOOP.
    }
}
```

After registering this phase listener in `faces-config.xml`, you can use `<f:event>` or `@ListenerFor` to listen on this event. One real-world example would be nested in the `<f:view>` or a master template, or in a particular `<h:form>`, so that you don't need to copy/paste the very same `<f:actionListener>` over multiple `UICommand` components in template clients or forms, or even the very same `<f:viewAction>` over multiple template clients.

```
<f:event type="preInvokeApplication"
         listener="#{bean.prepareInvokeApplication}" />
```

Jakarta Tags

If you have ever developed with Jakarta Pages, then you'll most likely have stumbled upon Jakarta Tags. In Facelets, however, only a limited subset of Jakarta Tags is reincarnated. They are `<c:if>`, `<c:choose><c:when><c:otherwise>`, `<c:forEach>`, `<c:set>`, and `<c:catch>`. Essentially, the tag names are identical to those from Jakarta Pages, but the implementations are completely rewritten for Facelets. Those Jakarta Tags are available under the `jakarta.tags.core` XML namespace URI which should be assigned to the "`c`" XML namespace prefix.

```
xmlns:c="jakarta.tags.core"
```

Jakarta Tags have a different life cycle than Jakarta Faces standard HTML components. Jakarta Tags already run directly during the view build time while Jakarta Faces is busy building the component tree based on the view definition. Jakarta Tags don't physically end up as components in the Jakarta Faces component tree. In other words, you can use Jakarta Tags to control the flow of building of the Jakarta Faces component tree.

When developing Jakarta Faces pages with Jakarta Tags, the most important thing to keep in mind is thus that they don't participate in the Jakarta Faces life cycle. In the following, I have demonstrated the most important behavioral differences between a tag of Jakarta Tags and its counterpart in either Jakarta Faces or Facelets.

`<c:forEach>` versus `<ui:repeat>`

The following is a `<c:forEach>` example iterating over a `List<Item>` with three instances of an example `Item` entity having `id` and `value` properties:

```
<c:forEach items="#{bean.items}" var="item">
    <h:outputText id="item_#{item.id}" value="#{item.value}" />
</c:forEach>
```

During the view build time, the preceding markup using `<c:forEach>` creates three physically separate `HtmlOutputText` instances in the Jakarta Faces component tree, roughly represented as follows:

```
<h:outputText id="item_1" value="#{bean.items[0].value}" />
<h:outputText id="item_2" value="#{bean.items[1].value}" />
<h:outputText id="item_3" value="#{bean.items[2].value}" />
```

In turn, they individually generate their HTML output during view render time, as follows:

```
<span id="item_1">one</span>
<span id="item_2">two</span>
<span id="item_3">three</span>
```

Do note that the `id` attribute of a Jakarta Faces component is also evaluated during the view build time and thus you need to manually ensure the uniqueness of the resulting component ID the above demonstrated way. Otherwise, Jakarta Faces will throw an `IllegalStateException` with a message that goes like this: "Duplicate component ID found in view." The only other Jakarta Faces component attribute that is also evaluated during the view build time is the `binding` attribute. If you absolutely need to bind a component generated by Jakarta Tags to a backing bean property, which would be a rare real-world use case, then you should be specifying a unique array index, collection index, or map key. The following is an example provided that `#{bean.components}` refers an already-prepared `UIComponent[]`, `List<UIComponent>`, or `Map<Long, UIComponent>` property:

```
<c:forEach items="#{bean.items}" var="item">
    <h:outputText binding="#{bean.components[item.id]}"
        id="item_#{item.id}" value="#{item.value}" />
</c:forEach>
```

The Facelets counterpart of the `<c:forEach>` is the `<ui:repeat>`. This is in essence a `UIComponent`. In other words, the `<ui:repeat>` itself also ends up in the Jakarta Faces component tree during the view build time. It also runs during the view render time, but it doesn't generate any HTML output by itself. It basically reexecutes the HTML output generation of its children during every iteration round against the currently iterated item as `var` attribute.

```
<ui:repeat id="items" value="#{bean.items}" var="item">
    <h:outputText id="item" value="#{item.value}" />
</ui:repeat>
```

During the view build time, the aforementioned ends up exactly as is in the Jakarta Faces component tree: a single `UIRepeat` instance with one nested `HtmlOutputText` instance, whereas the `<c:forEach>` example creates here three `HtmlOutputText` instances. Then, during the view render time, the very same `<h:outputText>` component is being *reused* to generate its HTML output based on current iteration round.

```
<span id="items:0:item">one</span>
<span id="items:1:item">two</span>
<span id="items:2:item">three</span>
```

Do note that the `<ui:repeat>` as being an instance of the `NamingContainer` interface already ensured the uniqueness of the client ID based on the iteration index. It's technically also not possible to reference its `var` attribute in the `id` attribute of any child component as the `var` attribute is only set during the view render time while the `id` attribute is already set during the view build time.

`<c:if>`/`<c:choose>` versus rendered

Imagine that we have a custom tag file input.xhtml that contains the following Facelets markup conditionally adding different tags using a <c:choose> (a more elaborate example can be found in the section "Tag Files" in Chapter 7):

```
<c:choose>
    <c:when test="#{type eq 'password'}">
        <h:inputSecret id="#{id}" label="#{label}" value="#{value}" />
    </c:when>
    <c:when test="#{type eq 'textarea'}">
        <h:inputTextarea id="#{id}" label="#{label}" value="#{value}" />
    </c:when>
    <c:otherwise>
        <h:inputText id="#{id}" label="#{label}" value="#{value}"
            a:type="#{type}">
        </h:inputText>
    </c:otherwise>
</c:choose>
```

When it's declared in the view definition as follows:

```
<t:input type="email" id="email" label="Email" value="#{bean.email}" />
```

then this will only create the <h:inputText> component in the component tree, roughly represented as follows:

```
<h:inputText id="email" label="Email" value="#{bean.email}"
    a:type="email">
</h:inputText>
```

When using the rendered attribute instead of <c:choose> as follows:

```
<h:inputSecret id="#{id}_password" rendered="#{type eq 'password'}"
    label="#{label}" value="#{value}">
</h:inputSecret>
<h:inputTextarea id="#{id}_textarea" rendered="#{type eq 'textarea'}"
    label="#{label}" value="#{value}">
</h:inputTextarea>
```

```
<h:inputText id="#{id}_text"
    rendered="#{type ne 'password' and type ne 'textarea'}"
    label="#{label}" value="#{value}">
</h:inputText>
```

then they would all end up in the component tree roughly as follows:

```
<h:inputSecret id="email_password" rendered="#{type eq 'password'}"
    label="Email" value="#{bean.email}">
</h:inputSecret>
<h:inputTextarea id="email_textarea" rendered="#{type eq 'textarea'}"
    label="Email" value="#{bean.email}">
</h:inputTextarea>
<h:inputText id="email_text"
    rendered="#{type ne 'password' and type ne 'textarea'}"
    label="Email" value="#{bean.email}">
</h:inputText>
```

You see, this will thus end up in an unnecessarily bloated component tree with a lot of unused components when you have many of `<t:input>` custom tags. It's therefore much better to use `<c:choose>` instead of `rendered` attribute here, particularly when the `type` attribute is actually static (i.e., it does not ever change, at least during the view scope).

`<c:set>` versus `<ui:param>`

They are not interchangeable. The `<c:set>` can be used anywhere in a Facelets file, and it sets a variable in the EL scope, which is accessible only after the tag location during the view build time, but anywhere else in the view during the view render time. The `<ui:param>` should only be nested in `<ui:include>`, `<ui:decorate template>`, or `<ui:composition template>`, and it sets a variable in the EL scope of the Facelets template, which is accessible only in the template itself. Older Jakarta Faces versions had bugs whereby the `<ui:param>` variable was also available outside the Facelets template in question. This should never be relied upon.

The `<c:set>` without a `scope` attribute will behave like an alias. It does not cache the result of the EL expression in any scope. Its primary purpose is to be able to have a shortcut to a relatively long EL expression that is repeated several times in the same Facelets file. It can thus be used perfectly well inside iterating Jakarta Faces components:

```
<ui:repeat value="#{bean.products}" var="product">
    <c:set var="price" value="#{product.price}" />
    #{price}
</ui:repeat>
```

It's only not suitable for calculating the sum in a loop. The following construct will never work:

```
<c:set var="total" value="#{0}" />
<ui:repeat value="#{bean.products}" var="product">
    <c:set var="total" value="#{total = total + product.price}" />
    #{product.price}
</ui:repeat>
Total price: #{total}
```

For that, use EL 3.0 stream API instead.

```
<ui:repeat value="#{bean.products}" var="product">
    #{product.price}
</ui:repeat>
Total price: #{bean.products.stream().map(product->product.price).sum()}
```

However, when you set the scope attribute with one of allowable values, request, view, session, or application, then it will be evaluated immediately during the view build time and stored in the specified scope.

```
<c:set var="DEV"
    value="#{facesContext.application.projectStage eq 'Development'}"
    scope="application" />
```

This will be evaluated only once during the first time this view is being built, and the value will in this example be available as an EL variable #{DEV} throughout the entire application. You'd best declare such <c:set> somewhere on top of the master template file that is used by every single Facelets file in the entire application. Note that the EL variable is capitalized to conform to Java naming conventions for constants.

CAVEATS

Using Jakarta Tags will only lead to unexpected results when a Jakarta Tags attribute references an EL variable that is not available during Jakarta Faces view build time. Examples of such EL variables are those defined by `var` attribute of iterating components such as `<h:dataTable>` and `<ui:repeat>` and those set in model by `<f:viewParam>`, `<f:viewAction>`, and `<f:event type="preRenderView">`.

In a nutshell, use Jakarta Tags only to control the flow of Jakarta Faces component tree building and use Jakarta Faces UI components only to control the flow of HTML output generation. In Jakarta Tags, do not rely on EL variables that are not available during view build time.

Manipulating the Component Tree

This can be done declaratively using Jakarta Tags as well as programmatically using Java code. The Jakarta Tags approach has already been elaborated in the previous section. It's also possible to use Java code instead. As a precaution, this generally ends up in very verbose and hard-to-maintain code. Tree-based hierarchies in code are best readable and maintainable when using a hierarchical markup language such as XML. Facelets itself is already XML based. Jakarta Tags is also XML based and therefore seamlessly integrates in a Facelets file. Jakarta Tags is therefore the recommended approach to dynamically manipulate the component tree, rather than Java code.

The Javadoc of `jakarta.faces.component.UIComponent`[8] specifies when you could safely manipulate the component tree:

> *Dynamically modifying the component tree can happen at any time, during and after restoring the view, but not during state saving and needs to function properly with respect to rendering and state saving.*

In other words, the earliest moment when you can guaranteedly safely modify the component tree is during the `PostAddToViewEvent`, and the latest moment when you can guaranteedly safely modify the component tree is during the `PreRenderViewEvent`.

---

[8] `https://jakarta.ee/specifications/platform/10/apidocs/jakarta/faces/component/UIComponent.html`

Any moment in between is thus also possible. Before the `PostAddToViewEvent`, there's not necessarily a means of a concrete `UIViewRoot` instance. After the `PreRenderViewEvent`, there's a risk that the view state is already saved, and you'd rather not get trapped here because the view state is the one that contains all the information about any dynamic changes to the component tree. In other words, manipulating the component tree during the render response phase (sixth phase) is a bad idea.

When you intend to manipulate the building of the component tree by means of adding new components based on a Java model that is at least view scoped, then listen on the `PostAddToViewEvent` of the parent component of interest. When you intend to manipulate an already-built component tree by means of adding, moving, or removing components, then listen on the `PreRenderViewEvent` of the `UIViewRoot`.

The following example programmatically populates a dynamic form based on a Java model during the `PostAddToViewEvent`:

```
<h:form id="dynamicFormId">
    <f:event type="postAddToView" listener="#{dynamicForm.populate}" />
</h:form>
```

wherein the #{dynamicForm} looks something like the following:

```
@Named @RequestScoped
public class DynamicForm {

    private transient UIForm form;
    private Map<String, Object> values = new HashMap<>();

    @Inject
    private FieldService fieldService;

    public void populate(ComponentSystemEvent event) {
        form = (UIForm) event.getComponent();
        List<Field> fields = fieldService.list(form.getId());
        fields.forEach(field -> field.populate(this));
    }

    public void createOutputLabel(Field field) {
        HtmlOutputLabel label = new HtmlOutputLabel();
        label.setId(field.getName() + "_l");
        label.setFor(field.getName());
```

```
        label.setValue(field.getLabel());
        form.getChildren().add(label);
    }

    public void createInputText(Field field) {
        HtmlInputText text = new HtmlInputText();
        text.setId(field.getName()); // Explicit ID is required!
        text.setLabel(field.getLabel());
        text.setValueExpression("value", createValueExpression(field));
        form.getChildren().add(text);
    }

    public void createMessage(Field field) {
        HtmlMessage message = new HtmlMessage();
        message.setId(field.getName() + "_m");
        message.setFor(field.getName());
        form.getChildren().add(message);
    }

    public static ValueExpression createValueExpression(Field field) {
        String el = "#{dynamicForm.values['" + field.getName() + "']}"
        FacesContext context = FacesContext.getCurrentInstance();
        ELContext elContext = context.getELContext();
        return context.getApplication().getExpressionFactory()
            .createValueExpression(elContext, el, Object.class);
    }

    public Map<String, Object> getValues() {
        return values;
    }
}
```

and wherein the abstract class Field represents your custom model of a form field
with at least type, name, and label properties and the concrete implementation of a
TextField#populate() looks something like the following:

```
public void populate(DynamicFormBean form) {
    form.createOutputLabel(this);
    form.createInputText(this);
    form.createMessage(this);
}
```

Note the naming pattern of concrete UIComponent classes. For HTML components, they follow exactly the convention "Html[TagName]". For the <h:inputText>, that's thus HtmlInputText and so on. The preceding Java example will basically create the following XML representation:

```
<h:outputLabel id="name_l" for="name" value="Label" />
<h:inputText id="name" value="#{dynamicForm.values['name']}" />
<h:message id="name_m" for="name" />
```

It only does that quite verbosely. Essentially, you're here reinventing the job of Facelets. There's really nothing which is impossible using XML and only possible in Java. As long as you understand how you can use Jakarta Tags for this:

```
<h:form id="dynamicFormId">
    <c:forEach items="#{dynamicForm.fields}" var="field">
        <t:field type="#{field.type}"
            id="#{field.name}" label="#{field.label}"
            value="#{dynamicForm.values[field.name]}">
        </t:field>
    </c:forEach>
</h:form>
```

wherein the #{dynamicForm} instead looks something like the following:

```
@Named @RequestScoped
public class DynamicForm {

    private List<Field> fields;
    private Map<String, Object> values = new HashMap<>();

    @Inject
    public FieldService fieldService;
```

```
    public List<Field> getFields() {
        if (fields = null) {
            FacesContext context = FacesContext.getCurrentInstance();
            UIComponent form = UIComponent.getCurrentComponent(context);
            fields = fieldService.list(form.getId());
        }
        return fields;
    }

    public Map<String, Object> getValues() {
        return values;
    }
}
```

You see, there is no need to mess with manually creating and populating UIComponent instances. Facelets does that all for you based on simple XML. The <t:field> custom tag can be found in the section "Tag Files" in Chapter 7.

CHAPTER 4

Form Components

These are the most important components of the standard Jakarta Faces component set. Without them, Jakarta Faces wouldn't have been very useful in the first place. When using plain HTML elements instead of Jakarta Faces form components, you'd end up polluting the controller class with code to manually apply, convert, and validate submitted values; to update the model with those values; and to figure out the action method to be invoked. That's exactly the hard work Jakarta Faces should take off your hands as being a component-based MVC (model-view-controller) framework for HTML form-based web applications.

Input, Select, and Command Components

All input components extend from the UIInput superclass. All selection components extend from a subclass thereof, which can be UISelectBoolean, UISelectOne, or UISelectMany (see Chapter 3, Table 3-1, for a comprehensive list of standard Jakarta Faces components). All input and select components implement the EditableValueHolder interface that allows attaching a Converter, Validator, and ValueChangeListener. All command components extend from the UICommand superclass and implement the ActionSource interface that allows defining one or more managed bean methods which should be invoked during the invoke application phase (fifth phase). They can have only one "action" method and multiple "action listener" methods.

HTML requires all input, select, and command elements to be nested in a form element. The standard Jakarta Faces component set offers only one such component, the <h:form>, which is from the UIForm superclass. You could also use a plain HTML <form> element, but that wouldn't automatically include the mandatory jakarta.faces. ViewState hidden input field in the form that represents the Jakarta Faces view state.

© Bauke Scholtz and Arjan Tijms 2022
B. Scholtz and A. Tijms, *The Definitive Guide to Jakarta Faces in Jakarta EE 10*,
https://doi.org/10.1007/978-1-4842-7310-4_4

The renderer of the <h:form> is the one responsible for automatically including it in every generated HTML representation of the Jakarta Faces form. Without any jakarta.faces.ViewState HTTP request parameter, Jakarta Faces won't recognize the request as a valid postback request. In other words, the FacesContext.getCurrent Instance().isPostback() would return false, and then Jakarta Faces wouldn't even process the submitted values, let alone invoke the action method. A plain HTML <form> element in a Jakarta Faces page is only useful for GET requests in combination with <f:viewParam> tags which should take care of processing the GET request parameters as submitted values. This will be detailed later in the section "GET Forms."

All command components have an action attribute that can be bound to a managed bean method. This method will be invoked during the invoke application phase (fifth phase), as long as there's no conversion or validation error. Conversion and validation are in detail covered in Chapter 5, so we'll skip detailing this step in this chapter.

Text-Based Input Components

All text-based input components have a value attribute that can be bound to a managed bean property. The getter of this property will, during the view render time, be consulted to retrieve and display any preset value. And the setter of this property will, during the update model values phase (fourth phase) of the postback request, be invoked with the submitted and already converted and validated value, if applicable. The following is a basic usage example that demonstrates all text-based input components.

Facelets file /test.xhtml:

```
<h:form>
    <h:inputText value="#{bean.text}" />
    <h:inputSecret value="#{bean.password}" />
    <h:inputTextarea value="#{bean.message}" />
    <h:inputHidden value="#{bean.hidden}" />
    <h:commandButton value="Submit" action="#{bean.submit}" />
</h:form>
```

Backing bean class com.example.project.view.Bean:

```
@Named @RequestScoped
public class Bean {
```

```
    private String text;
    private String password;
    private String message;
    private String hidden;

    public void submit() {
        System.out.println("Form has been submitted!");
        System.out.println("text: " + text);
        System.out.println("password: " + password);
        System.out.println("message: " + message);
        System.out.println("hidden: " + hidden);
    }

    // Add/generate getters and setters for every property here.
}
```

Generated HTML output:

```
<form id="j_idt4" name="j_idt4" method="post"
    action="/project/test.xhtml"
    enctype="application/x-www-form-urlencoded">
    <input type="hidden" name="j_idt4" value="j_idt4" />
    <input type="text" name="j_idt4:j_idt5" />
    <input type="password" name="j_idt4:j_idt6" />
    <textarea name="j_idt4:j_idt7"></textarea>
    <input type="hidden" name="j_idt4:j_idt8" />
    <input type="submit" name="j_idt4:j_idt9" value="Submit" />
    <input type="hidden" name="jakarta.faces.ViewState"
        id="j_id1:jakarta.faces.ViewState:0"
        value="-4091383829147627416:3884402765892734278"
        autocomplete="off" />
</form>
```

Rendering in Chrome browser (with newlines added):

```
some text

••••••••

some message
with a newline

Submit
```

You'll notice several things in the generated HTML output. Undoubtedly, the first thing noticeable is that Jakarta Faces has also automatically generated the id and name attributes of the form and input HTML elements, all with a j_id prefix that is defined by the public API (application programming interface) constant UIViewRoot.UNIQUE_ID_PREFIX. The "t" coming thereafter basically stands for "tree," and the number coming thereafter basically represents the position of the component in the component tree. This is thus prone to be changed whenever you add, remove, or move around components in the Facelets file. This is thus also subject to headaches when QA (quality assurance) needs to write integration tests for the web application wherein more than often the HTML element IDs need to be used.

Jakarta Faces will use an autogenerated ID when it's mandatory for the functionality in order to have an id and/or a name attribute in the generated HTML output. The id attribute is mandatory in order to be able to find the HTML element by any JavaScript code that can also be autogenerated by Jakarta Faces, such as functions responsible for the Ajax works. As this makes the generated HTML code rather hard to read and, frankly, ugly, we'd like to just explicitly specify the value of the id attribute of any Jakarta Faces form, input, select, and command component. This way, Jakarta Faces will just use it for the id and name attributes of the generated HTML elements instead of using an autogenerated one.

Now, let's rewrite the Facelets file /test.xhtml for that. A good practice is to let the ID attribute of the input component match exactly the bean property name and the ID attribute of the command component match exactly the bean method name. This would end up in more self-documenting code and generated HTML output.

```
<h:form id="form">
    <h:inputText id="text" value="#{bean.text}" />
    <h:inputSecret id="password" value="#{bean.password}" />
```

```
    <h:inputTextarea id="message" value="#{bean.message}" />
    <h:inputHidden id="hidden" value="#{bean.hidden}" />
    <h:commandButton id="submit" value="Submit"
        action="#{bean.submit}" />
</h:form>
```

Now, the generated HTML output looks as follows:

```
<form id="form" name="form" method="post" action="/project/test.xhtml"
    enctype="application/x-www-form-urlencoded">
    <input type="hidden" name="form" value="form" />
    <input id="form:text" type="text" name="form:text" />
    <input id="form:password" type="password" name="form:password" />
    <textarea id="form:message" name="form:message"></textarea>
    <input id="form:hidden" type="hidden" name="form:hidden" />
    <input id="form:submit" type="submit" name="form:submit"
        value="Submit" />
    <input type="hidden" name="jakarta.faces.ViewState"
        id="j_id1:jakarta.faces.ViewState:0"
        value="2090058036319432427:3588175615710022056"
        autocomplete="off" />
</form>
```

That's already clearer. Note that when you explicitly set a component ID, then it will always end up in the generated HTML output. The generated HTML element ID, then, represents the "client ID" that may be different from the component ID, depending on its parents. If the component has any parent that is an instance of the `NamingContainer` interface, then the ID of the `NamingContainer` parent will be prepended to the client ID of the component. From the standard Jakarta Faces HTML component set, only the `<h:form>` and `<h:dataTable>` are instances of `NamingContainer`. Others are `<ui:repeat>` from the Facelets tags and `<f:subview>` from the Jakarta Faces core tags.

If you look closer at the generated HTML output, there's only one generated ID left. It's the one of the view state hidden input field, which is always `j_id1`. It represents the ID of the `UIViewRoot` instance, which by default cannot be set from a Facelets file on. When using Jakarta Faces in Portlet-based web applications instead of Servlet-based web applications, it is overridable, and it would represent the unique name of the Portlet.

In a Portlet-based web application, it is possible to have multiple Portlet views in a single Jakarta Faces page. In other words, a single Jakarta Faces page in a Portlet-based web application can have multiple UIViewRoot instances.

Coming back to the generated HTML output, the name attribute of the HTML input element is mandatory for HTML in order to be able to send the submitted values as request parameters via HTTP. It will become the request parameter name. In any decent web browser, you can inspect the request parameters in the "Network" section of the web developer's toolset, which is accessible by pressing F12 in the web browser. Figure 4-1 shows how Chrome presents the postback request after submitting the form with some values filled out, as you can see in the "Payload" section of the figure.

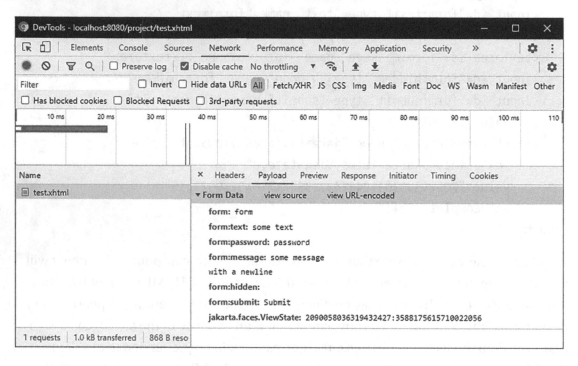

Figure 4-1. *Chrome Developer Tools—Network—Payload*

As you can see in the generated HTML output and in the form data, there are two additional hidden input fields. The hidden input field with the name representing the ID of the <h:form> will signal Jakarta Faces which form exactly was submitted during the postback request. Because a single HTML document can have multiple form elements, this way Jakarta Faces can, during the apply request values phase (second phase), determine whether the current form component was actually submitted. It will cause the UIForm#isSubmitted() of the form component to return true. The hidden input field with the name `jakarta.faces.ViewState` represents the unique identifier referring the serialized view state object that is stored in the session. The `autocomplete="off"` on the view state hidden input field is, by the way, not a technical requirement but just a work-around against some browsers overriding it with the last known value when the back button is pressed, which may not be the correct value per se. These two hidden input fields are automatically included by the renderer associated with the `UIForm` component.

Our example hidden input field as generated by the `<h:inputHidden>` tag has an empty value. It's effectively useless in this form. Such a hidden input field is generally only useful when its value is being set by some JavaScript code which you'd like to capture in the managed bean. There's generally no point to "transferring" managed bean properties from one to the next request using hidden input fields. Instead, such properties should be assigned to a managed bean that is declared to be in a broader scope than the request scope, such as the view, flow, or session scope. This saves the effort of hassling with hidden input fields. The bean scopes will be detailed in Chapter 8.

The other request parameters visible in the form data should speak for themselves if you're familiar with basic HTML. They represent the name/value pairs of the involved input elements. You should be able to determine which values were actually entered in the form prior to submitting. Jakarta Faces will also be able to do the same. It will traverse the component tree and use the "client ID" of the component as request parameter name to obtain the value from the request parameter map. Basically, the following code will under the hood be executed for each input component during the apply request values phase (second phase). This happens in the `UIInput#decode()` method.

```
FacesContext context = FacesContext.getCurrentInstance();
ExternalContext externalContext = context.getExternalContext();
Map<String, String> formData = externalContext.getRequestParameterMap();
String clientId = component.getClientId(context);
String submittedValue = formData.get(clientId);
component.setSubmittedValue(submittedValue);
```

And during the same phase, the following code is basically executed for each command component in the `decode` method of the renderer associated with the command component:

```
if (formData.get(clientId) != null) {
    component.queueEvent(new ActionEvent(context, component));
}
```

During the process validations phase (third phase), Jakarta Faces will first convert the submitted value to a "local value" using any explicit converter registered on the component or any implicit converter associated with the type of the "local value." Then it will validate the "local value" using all validators registered on the component, if any. If conversion and validation were executed without errors, then the "local value" will be set as actual value of the component, and the submitted value will be cleared out. This all happens in the UIInput#validate() method whose core logic is shown in the following code snippet in a (very!) simplified form:

```
String submittedValue = component.getSubmittedValue();

try {
    Object localValue = component.getConvertedValue(submittedValue);

    for (Validator validator : component.getValidators()) {
        validator.validate(context, component, localValue);
    }

    component.setValue(localValue);
    component.setSubmittedValue(null);
}
catch (ConverterException | ValidatorException e) {
    context.addMessage(clientId, e.getFacesMessage());
    context.validationFailed(); // Skips phases 4 and 5.
    component.setValid(false);
}
```

When there are no conversion or validation errors and the FacesContext#isVal idationFailed() thus returns false, then Jakarta Faces will advance to the update model values phase (fourth phase). During this phase, the "local value" of the input components will ultimately be set as managed bean properties associated with the value attribute of the input components. This will happen in the UIInput#updateModel() method that is simplified as follows:

```
ValueExpression el = component.getValueExpression("value");

if (el != null) {
    Object localValue = component.getValue();
```

```
    el.setValue(context.getELContext(), localValue);
    component.setValue(null);
}
```

The el variable basically represents the Expression Language (EL) statement as defined in the value attribute, which is, in case of our <h:inputText> example, thus #{bean.text}. The ValueExpression#setValue() will basically trigger the setter method behind this expression with the component's value. So effectively it will execute bean.setText(component.getValue()).

Once all model values have been updated, Jakarta Faces will advance to the invoke application phase (fifth phase). Any ActionEvent that is, during the apply request values phase (second phase), queued in a command component will be broadcasted. It will ultimately invoke all methods associated with the command component. In the case of our <h:commandButton> example, which has #{bean.submit} defined as an action attribute, it will invoke the Bean#submit() method. Finally, Jakarta Faces will advance to the last phase, the render response phase (sixth phase), generating the HTML output and thereby invoking the getter methods in order to obtain the model values to be embedded in the HTML output.

File-Based Input Component

There is only one file-based input component. That's the <h:inputFile>. It has only one additional requirement on the <h:form> it is being placed in; its enctype attribute has to be explicitly set to multipart/form-data to conform the HTML specification. This has no effect on other input components; they will continue to work just fine. It's just that the default form encoding application/x-www-form-urlencoded doesn't support embedding binary data. The multipart/form-data encoding supports this, but it is only slightly more verbose. Every request parameter value is preceded by a boundary line, a Content-Disposition header with the request parameter name, a Content-Type header with the content type of the value, and two newlines. It is very inefficient compared to the default encoding wherein the URL-encoded request parameter name/value pairs are just concatenated by the & character, but it's actually the only reliable way to be able to embed files in an HTTP POST request without inducing ambiguity, particularly when uploading text files whose content in turn coincidentally resembles URL-encoded request parameter name/value pairs.

The value attribute of the <h:inputFile> must be bound to a bean property of the jakarta.servlet.http.Part interface.

Facelets file /test.xhtml:

```
<h:form id="form" enctype="multipart/form-data">
    <h:inputFile id="file" value="#{bean.file}" />
    <h:commandButton id="submit" value="Submit"
        action="#{bean.submit}" />
</h:form>
```

Backing bean class com.example.project.view.Bean:

```
@Named @RequestScoped
public class Bean {

    private Part file;

    public void submit() throws IOException {
        System.out.println("Form has been submitted!");
        System.out.println("file: " + file);

        if (file != null) {
            System.out.println("name: " + file.getSubmittedFileName());
            System.out.println("type: " + file.getContentType());
            System.out.println("size: " + file.getSize());
            InputStream content = file.getInputStream();
            // Write content to disk or DB.
        }
    }

    // Add/generate getters and setters for every property here.
}
```

Generated HTML output:

```
<form id="form" name="form" method="post" action="/project/test.xhtml"
    enctype="multipart/form-data">
    <input type="hidden" name="form" value="form" />
    <input id="form:file" type="file" name="form:file" />
    <input id="form:submit" type="submit" name="form:submit"
```

```
        value="Submit" />
    <input type="hidden" name="jakarta.faces.ViewState"
        id="j_id1:jakarta.faces.ViewState:0"
        value="6034213708100805615:8835868421785849982"
        autocomplete="off" />
</form>
```

Rendering in Chrome browser (with newlines added):

| Choose File | No file chosen |

| Submit |

The request processing life cycle is the same as for text-based input components, except for the apply request values phase (second phase). Instead of extracting the submitted file as a request parameter in the UIInput#decode() method, the submitted file is being extracted as a request part in the renderer associated with the file input component. The default implementation basically looks as follows:

```
FacesContext context = FacesContext.getCurrentInstance();
ExternalContext ec = context.getExternalContext();
HttpServletRequest request = (HttpServletRequest) ec.getRequest();
String clientId = component.getClientId(context);
Part submittedValue = request.getPart(clientId);
component.setSubmittedValue(submittedValue);
```

Selection Components

Jakarta Faces offers a bunch of selection components of the UISelectBoolean, UISelectOne, and UISelectMany component families that all extend from UIInput. Except for the UISelectBoolean, they all expect the available items for selection to be provided via <f:selectItem> or <f:selectItems> tags nested in the selection component. The value attribute of a UISelectBoolean component can only be bound to a bean property of boolean or Boolean type and doesn't support a converter, while other components support a converter. The value attribute of a UISelectOne component has to be bound to a single-value property such as String, and the value attribute of a UISelectMany component can only be bound to a multivalue property such as Collection<String> or String[].

In real-world HTML-based web applications, the `<h:selectOneListbox>` (single-select list box) and `<h:selectManyMenu>` (multiselect drop-down) aren't terribly useful. Generally, the `<h:selectOneMenu>` (single-select drop-down) and `<h:selectManyListBox>` (multiselect list box) are preferred as they are more user-friendly. The following is a basic usage example that demonstrates all selection components except for the aforementioned least useful ones. In case you want to use them anyway, just follow the demonstrated approach with a different tag name.

Facelets file `/test.xhtml`:

```
<h:form id="form">
    <h:selectBooleanCheckbox id="checked" value="#{bean.checked}" />
    <h:selectOneMenu id="oneMenu" value="#{bean.oneMenu}">
        <f:selectItems value="#{bean.availableItems}" />
    </h:selectOneMenu>
    <h:selectOneRadio id="oneRadio" value="#{bean.oneRadio}">
        <f:selectItems value="#{bean.availableItems}" />
    </h:selectOneRadio>
    <h:selectManyListbox id="manyListbox" value="#{bean.manyListbox}">
        <f:selectItems value="#{bean.availableItems}" />
    </h:selectManyListbox>
    <h:selectManyCheckbox id="manyCheckbox" value="#{bean.manyCheckbox}">
        <f:selectItems value="#{bean.availableItems}" />
    </h:selectManyCheckbox>
    <h:commandButton id="submit" value="Submit"
        action="#{bean.submit}" />
</h:form>
```

Backing bean class `com.example.project.view.Bean`:

```
@Named @RequestScoped
public class Bean {

    private boolean checked;
    private String oneMenu;
    private String oneRadio;
    private List<String> manyListbox;
    private List<String> manyCheckbox;
    private List<String> availableItems;
```

```
@PostConstruct
public void init() {
    availableItems = Arrays.asList("one", "two", "three");
}

public void submit() {
    System.out.println("Form has been submitted!");
    System.out.println("checked: " + checked);
    System.out.println("oneMenu: " + oneMenu);
    System.out.println("oneRadio: " + oneRadio);
    System.out.println("manyListbox: " + manyListbox);
    System.out.println("manyCheckbox: " + manyCheckbox);
}

// Add/generate getters and setters for every property here.
// Note that availableItems property doesn't need a setter.
}
```

Generated HTML output:

```
<form id="form" name="form" method="post" action="/project/test.xhtml"
    enctype="application/x-www-form-urlencoded">
    <input type="hidden" name="form" value="form" />
    <input id="form:checked" type="checkbox" name="form:checked" />
    <select id="form:oneMenu" name="form:oneMenu" size="1">
        <option value="one">one</option>
        <option value="two">two</option>
        <option value="three">three</option>
    </select>
    <table id="form:oneRadio">
        <tr>
            <td>
                <input id="form:oneRadio:0" type="radio"
                    name="form:oneRadio" value="one" />
                <label for="form:oneRadio:0"> one</label>
            </td>
            <td>
```

```
            <input id="form:oneRadio:1" type="radio"
                name="form:oneRadio" value="two" />
            <label for="form:oneRadio:1"> two</label>
        </td>
        <td>
            <input id="form:oneRadio:2" type="radio"
                name="form:oneRadio" value="three" />
            <label for="form:oneRadio:2"> three</label>
        </td>
    </tr>
</table>
<select id="form:manyListbox" name="form:manyListbox"
    multiple="multiple" size="3">
    <option value="one">one</option>
    <option value="two">two</option>
    <option value="three">three</option>
</select>
<table id="form:manyCheckbox">
    <tr>
        <td>
            <input id="form:manyCheckbox:0" type="checkbox"
                name="form:manyCheckbox" value="one" />
            <label for="form:manyCheckbox:0"> one</label>
        </td>
        <td>
            <input id="form:manyCheckbox:1" type="checkbox"
                name="form:manyCheckbox" value="two" />
            <label for="form:manyCheckbox:1"> two</label>
        </td>
        <td>
            <input id="form:manyCheckbox:2" type="checkbox"
                name="form:manyCheckbox" value="three" />
            <label for="form:manyCheckbox:2"> three</label>
        </td>
    </tr>
```

```
        </table>
        <input id="form:submit" type="submit" name="form:submit"
            value="Submit" />
        <input type="hidden" name="jakarta.faces.ViewState"
            id="j_id1:jakarta.faces.ViewState:0"
            value="403461711995663039:117935361680169981"
            autocomplete="off" />
</form>
```

Rendering in Chrome browser (with newlines added):

In the generated HTML output, you'll immediately notice that `<h:selectOneRadio>` and `<h:selectManyCheckbox>` generate an HTML table around the inputs. Such a markup is indeed frowned upon since Web 2.0. Since Jakarta Faces 4.0, you can let them generate an HTML list instead by explicitly setting the layout attribute to list as follows:

```
<h:selectOneRadio ... layout="list">
    ...
</h:selectOneRadio>
<h:selectManyCheckbox ... layout="list">
    ...
</h:selectManyCheckbox>
```

In case you want full control over the generated HTML markup, then you could, instead of the <h:selectManyCheckbox>, use a bunch of <h:selectBooleanCheckbox> components in the desired HTML markup that are bound against a slightly adjusted model.

Facelets file /test.xhtml:

```
<h:form id="form">
    <ul>
        <ui:repeat id="many" value="#{bean.availableItems}" var="item">
            <li>
                <h:selectBooleanCheckbox id="checkbox"
                    value="#{bean.manyCheckboxMap[item]}" />
                <h:outputLabel for="checkbox" value="#{item}" />
            </li>
        </ui:repeat>
    </ul>
    <h:commandButton id="submit" value="Submit"
        actionListener="#{bean.collectCheckedValues}"
        action="#{bean.submit}" />
</h:form>
```

Backing bean class com.example.project.view.Bean:

```
@Named @RequestScoped
public class Bean {

    private List<String> manyCheckbox;
    private List<String> availableItems;
    private Map<String, Boolean> manyCheckboxMap = new LinkedHashMap<>();

    @PostConstruct
    public void init() {
        availableItems = Arrays.asList("one", "two", "three");
    }

    public void collectCheckedValues() {
        manyCheckbox = manyCheckboxMap.entrySet().stream()
            .filter(e -> e.getValue())
```

```
            .map(Map.Entry::getKey)
            .collect(Collectors.toList());
    }

    public void submit() {
        System.out.println("Form has been submitted!");
        System.out.println("manyCheckbox: " + manyCheckbox);
    }

    // Add/generate getters for availableItems and manyCheckboxMap.
    // Note that setters are not necessary for them.
}
```

Generated HTML output:

```
<form id="form" name="form" method="post" action="/project/test.xhtml"
    enctype="application/x-www-form-urlencoded">
    <input type="hidden" name="form" value="form" />
    <ul>
        <li>
            <input id="form:many:0:checkbox" type="checkbox"
                name="form:many:0:checkbox" />
            <label for="form:many:0:checkbox">one</label>
        </li>
        <li>
            <input id="form:many:1:checkbox" type="checkbox"
                name="form:many:1:checkbox" />
            <label for="form:many:1:checkbox">two</label>
        </li>
        <li>
            <input id="form:many:2:checkbox" type="checkbox"
                name="form:many:2:checkbox" />
            <label for="form:many:2:checkbox">three</label>
        </li>
    </ul>
    <input id="form:submit" type="submit" name="form:submit"
        value="Submit" />
```

```
    <input type="hidden" name="jakarta.faces.ViewState"
        id="j_id1:jakarta.faces.ViewState:0"
        value="-2278907496447873737:-4769857814543424434"
        autocomplete="off" />
</form>
```

Rendering in Chrome browser:

- ☐ one
- ☐ two
- ☐ three

Submit

The bullets of the <ul> can of course be hidden by setting the CSS (Cascading Style Sheets) list-style-type property to none. Note that the actionListener attribute of the <h:commandButton> always runs before the action attribute. The same approach was not possible for <h:selectOneRadio> for a long time. There's no such component as <h:radioButton> or anything like that. Solutions were sought in third-party component libraries such as PrimeFaces. Since Jakarta Faces 2.2, this could be tricked with the new "pass-through elements" and "pass-through attributes" feature on plain HTML <input type="radio"> elements.[1] Only since Jakarta Faces 2.3 has it been natively possible with the help of the new group attribute that basically represents the same as the name attribute of the plain HTML <input type="radio"> element.

Facelets file /test.xhtml:

```
<h:form id="form">
    <ul>
        <ui:repeat id="one" value="#{bean.availableItems}" var="item">
            <li>
                <h:selectOneRadio id="radio" group="groupName"
                    value="#{bean.oneRadio}">
                    <f:selectItem itemValue="#{item}" />
                </h:selectOneRadio>
                <h:outputLabel for="radio" value="#{item}" />
```

---

[1]https://balusc.omnifaces.org/2015/10/custom-layout-with-hselectoneradio-in.html

```
        </li>
      </ui:repeat>
   </ul>
   <h:commandButton id="submit" value="Submit"
      action="#{bean.submit}" />
</h:form>
```

Backing bean class com.example.project.view.Bean:

```java
@Named @RequestScoped
public class Bean {

    private String oneRadio;
    private List<String> availableItems;

    @PostConstruct
    public void init() {
        availableItems = Arrays.asList("one", "two", "three");
    }

    public void submit() {
        System.out.println("Form has been submitted!");
        System.out.println("oneRadio: " + oneRadio);
    }

    // Add/generate getters and setters for every property here.
    // Note that availableItems property doesn't need a setter.
}
```

Generated HTML output:

```html
<form id="form" name="form" method="post" action="/project/test.xhtml"
    enctype="application/x-www-form-urlencoded">
    <input type="hidden" name="form" value="form" />
    <ul>
        <li>
            <input type="radio" id="form:one:0:radio"
                name="form:groupName" value="form:one:0:radio:one" />
            <label for="form:one:0:radio">one</label>
```

```
        </li>
        <li>
            <input type="radio" id="form:one:1:radio"
                name="form:groupName" value="form:one:1:radio:two" />
            <label for="form:one:1:radio">two</label>
        </li>
        <li>
            <input type="radio" id="form:one:2:radio"
                name="form:groupName" value="form:one:2:radio:three" />
            <label for="form:one:2:radio">three</label>
        </li>
    </ul>
    <input id="form:submit" type="submit" name="form:submit"
        value="Submit" />
    <input type="hidden" name="jakarta.faces.ViewState"
        id="j_id1:jakarta.faces.ViewState:0"
        value="3336433674711048358:164229014603307903"
        autocomplete="off" />
</form>
```

Rendering in Chrome browser:

- ○ one
- ○ two
- ○ three

Submit

Technically, the `<h:selectManyCheckbox>` could support the group attribute too, but this hasn't yet been implemented.

SelectItem Tags

Providing available items for UISelectOne and UISelectMany components can be done in several ways. As demonstrated in the previous section, you can use the <f:selectItem> and <f:selectItems> tags nested in the selection component for this. You can use the <f:selectItem> tag to define the available items entirely on the view side. The following is an example using <h:selectOneMenu>, but you can use it the same way in any other UISelectOne and UISelectMany component:

```
<h:selectOneMenu id="selectedItem" value="#{bean.selectedItem}">
    <f:selectItem itemValue="#{null}" itemLabel="-- select one --" />
    <f:selectItem itemValue="one" itemLabel="First item" />
    <f:selectItem itemValue="two" itemLabel="Second item" />
    <f:selectItem itemValue="three" itemLabel="Third item" />
</h:selectOneMenu>
```

Note that a select item with value of #{null} can be used to represent the default selection in case the bean property associated with selection component's value attribute is null. If you have consulted the tag documentation of <f:selectItem>, then you'll perhaps have noticed the noSelectionOption attribute and have thought that it was intended to represent a "no selection option." Actually, this isn't true. In spite of the attribute name, it does not represent a "no selection option." A better attribute name would have been hideWhenOtherOptionIsSelected, and even then it works only when the parent selection component has explicitly a hideNoSelectionOption="true" attribute set like the one that follows:

```
<h:selectOneMenu id="selectedItem" value="#{bean.selectedItem}"
    hideNoSelectionOption="true">
    <f:selectItem itemValue="#{null}" itemLabel="-- select one --"
        noSelectionOption="true" />
    <f:selectItem itemValue="one" itemLabel="First item" />
    <f:selectItem itemValue="two" itemLabel="Second item" />
    <f:selectItem itemValue="three" itemLabel="Third item" />
</h:selectOneMenu>
```

123

So hideWhenOtherOptionIsSelectedAndHideNoSelectionOptionIsTrue would ultimately have been the most self-explanatory attribute name. Unfortunately, this wasn't very well thought out when the noSelectionOption was implemented in Jakarta Faces 1.2. Requiring two attributes for this attribute to function shouldn't have been necessary. The primary purpose of this attribute pair is to prevent the website user from being able to reselect the "no selection option" when the component has already a non-null value. For example, by having it prepared in a @PostConstruct method, or by re-rendering the component after a form submit with a non-null value.

That said, the itemValue attribute of the <f:selectItem> represents the value that will be set as bean property when the form is submitted, as well as the value that will be preselected from any non-null bean property when the HTML output is to be generated. The itemLabel attribute represents the label that will be displayed to the website user. When the itemLabel attribute is absent, then Jakarta Faces will default to itemValue. Note that the label is in no way submitted back to the server. That is, in the generated HTML output, the <option> label is not part of the <option> value.

You can use the <f:selectItems> tag to reference a Collection, Map, or array of available items in the backing bean. You can even mix this with <f:selectItem> tags.

```
<h:selectOneMenu id="selectedItem" value="#{bean.selectedItem}">
    <f:selectItem itemValue="#{null}" itemLabel="-- select one --" />
    <f:selectItems value="#{bean.availableItems}" />
</h:selectOneMenu>
```

They will be rendered in the same order as they are declared in the view. Only when you use an unordered Collection or Map implementation as value, such as HashSet or HashMap, then the order of items provided by <f:selectItems> will be undefined. It's therefore better to use an ordered Collection or Map implementation, such as TreeSet, ArrayList, TreeMap, or LinkedHashMap.

When populating the available items as a Map, then keep in mind that the map key represents the item label and that the map value represents the item value. You'd perhaps intuitively expect it to be the other way around, but this was a technical limitation. That is, on the Java side, the map key enforces uniqueness, while the map value doesn't. And on the HTML side, the option label is supposed to be unique, while the option value doesn't need to be unique.

The following is how you can populate such a map:

```
private Map<String, String> availableItems;

@PostConstruct
public void init() {
    availableItems = new LinkedHashMap<>();
    availableItems.put("First item", "one");
    availableItems.put("Second item", "two");
    availableItems.put("Third item", "three");
}

// Add/generate getter. Note that a setter is unnecessary.
```

As said, you can also use a `TreeMap` or `HashMap` instead of `LinkedHashMap`, but then the item labels will become, respectively, automatically sorted or unsorted, regardless of the insertion order.

In case you'd really like to swap the map keys and values around on the view side, then you can always do so by manually assigning the map entry value as an item label and the map entry key as an item value. You can do that with the help of the `var` attribute of the `<f:selectItems>` by which you can declare the EL variable name of the currently iterated item. This can, in turn, be accessed in the `itemValue` and `itemLabel` attributes of the same tag. When you pass `Map#entrySet()` to the `value` attribute of the `<f:selectItems>`, then each iterated item will represent a `Map.Entry` instance. This has, in turn, `getKey()` and `getValue()` methods that are thus perfectly usable as EL properties.

```
<f:selectItems value="#{bean.availableItems.entrySet()}" var="entry"
    itemValue="#{entry.key}" itemLabel="#{entry.value}">
</f:selectItems>
```

This also works when using a `Collection` or array as available items. You don't explicitly need to first convert it to a `Set` (more specifically, `Iterable`), as demonstrated previously. This is particularly useful when you have a `Collection` or an array of complex objects as available items, such as model entities.

Model entity representing a "country":

```
public class Country {

    private Long id;
    private String code;
    private String name;

    // Add/generate getters and setters.
}
```

Backing bean:

```
@Named @RequestScoped
public class Bean {

    private String countryCode;
    private List<Country> availableCountries;

    @Inject
    private CountryService countryService;

    @PostConstruct
    public void init() {
        availableCountries = countryService.list();
    }

    // Add/generate getters and setters.
    // Note that a setter is unnecessary for availableCountries.
}
```

View:

```
<h:selectOneMenu id="countryCode" value="#{bean.countryCode}">
    <f:selectItem itemValue="#{null}" itemLabel="-- select one --" />
    <f:selectItems value="#{bean.availableCountries}" var="country">
        itemValue="#{country.code}" itemLabel="#{country.name}">
    </f:selectItems>
</h:selectOneMenu>
```

Note that any persistence framework–specific annotations, such as `@Entity` and `@Id` of Jakarta Persistence and the actual implementation of `CountryService`, are omitted in the previous example for clarity. Those are irrelevant to any front-end framework, such as Jakarta Faces.

With the previous construct, the value as obtained from `Country#getCode()` will end up as value of the generated HTML `<option>` element. Now, when the form is submitted, it will become the submitted value of the selection component, which will in turn invoke the setter method behind the `#{bean.countryCode}` property with exactly that value. Of course, you can also use the whole `Country` object as the property value of the selection component, but that would require a converter that can convert between the complex object and a unique string suitable to be embedded in HTML output and to be sent as an HTTP request parameter. You can read more in Chapter 5.

SelectItem Groups

In case you'd like to group a bunch of options under a common label, then you can use the `<f:selectItemGroup>` and `<f:selectItemGroups>` tags nested in the selection component for this. The following is a kickoff example:

```
<h:selectOneMenu id="selectedItem" value="#{bean.selectedItem}">
    <f:selectItemGroup itemLabel="Group 1">
        <f:selectItem itemValue="1-1" itemLabel="Group 1 Label 1" />
        <f:selectItem itemValue="1-2" itemLabel="Group 1 Label 2" />
        <f:selectItem itemValue="1-3" itemLabel="Group 1 Label 3" />
    </f:selectItemGroup>
    <f:selectItemGroup itemLabel="Group 2">
        <f:selectItem itemValue="2-1" itemLabel="Group 2 Label 1" />
        <f:selectItem itemValue="2-2" itemLabel="Group 2 Label 2" />
        <f:selectItem itemValue="2-3" itemLabel="Group 2 Label 3" />
    </f:selectItemGroup>
</h:selectOneMenu>
```

The `<h:selectOneMenu>` will render each group as HTML `<optgroup>`:

The `<h:selectOneRadio layout="pageDirection">` will render it as a nested table:

The `<h:selectManyListbox>` will render each group as HTML `<optgroup>`:

Group 1
  Group 1 Label 1
  Group 1 Label 2
  Group 1 Label 3
Group 2
  Group 2 Label 1
  Group 2 Label 2
  Group 2 Label 3

The `<h:selectManyCheckbox layout="pageDirection">` will render it as a nested table:

Group 1
  ☐ Group 1 Label 1
  ☐ Group 1 Label 2
  ☐ Group 1 Label 3
Group 2
  ☐ Group 2 Label 1
  ☐ Group 2 Label 2
  ☐ Group 2 Label 3

Note the importance of the `layout="pageDirection"` attribute in `<h:selectOneRadio>` and `<h:selectManyCheckbox>`. This will look much better than the default of `layout="lineDirection"` which would render everything in a big single table row.

You can use the `<f:selectItemGroups>` tag to reference a `Collection`, `Map`, or array of available item groups in the backing bean. You can even mix this with `<f:selectItems>` tags. The following is an example that iterates over a `List<Category>` property whereby the `Category` entity has in turn a `List<Product>` property:

```
<h:selectOneMenu id="selectedProduct" value="#{bean.selectedProduct}">
    <f:selectItemGroups value="#{bean.categories}" var="category"
        itemLabel="#{category.name}">
        <f:selectItems value="#{category.products}" var="product"
            itemValue="#{product.id}" itemLabel="#{product.name}">
        </f:selectItems>
    <f:selectItemGroups>
</h:selectOneMenu>
```

Label and Message Components

In an average well-designed form, input elements are usually accompanied with a label element and a message element targeting the input field. In HTML, labels are represented by the `<label>` element. In Jakarta Faces, you can use the `<h:outputLabel>` component to generate an HTML `<label>` element. HTML does not have a dedicated element to represent a message. In Jakarta Faces, the `<h:message>` component generates an HTML `<span>` element, and the `<h:messages>` component generates either a `<ul>` element or a `<table>` element, depending on the value of the `layout` attribute.

The label element has various SEO (search engine optimization) and usability advantages. It tells in text about the associated input element. Screen readers, like those used by people with visual disabilities, will find the label and tell its contents by sound. Search bots will find the label and index the associated input element with the label as keyword. And the label will focus and activate the associated input element when being clicked itself. Text-based input elements will then show the text cursor. Check box and radio button input elements will then be toggled. List box and drop-down input elements will then be focused. File input elements will then open the browse dialog. Submit buttons will then be invoked.

The message element is usually used to display any conversion and validation error messages coming from the server side. This way, the end user is informed about the state of the form and can act accordingly, usually by correcting the input values. You can also use it to display warning or informal messages.

In Jakarta Faces, the `<h:outputLabel>`, `<h:message>`, and `<h:messages>` components have a `for` attribute wherein you normally define the ID of the associated input component. The following is an example in the flavor of a login form:

```
<h:form id="login">
    <fieldset>
        <legend>Login</legend>
        <section>
            <h:outputLabel for="email" value="Email address" />
            <h:inputText id="email" value="#{login.email}"
                required="true" />
            <h:message id="m_email" for="email" />
        </section>
        <section>
            <h:outputLabel for="password" value="Password" />
            <h:inputSecret id="password" value="#{login.password}"
                required="true" />
            <h:message id="m_password" for="password" />
        </section>
        <footer>
            <h:commandButton id="submit" value="Login"
                action="#{login.submit}" />
        </footer>
    </fieldset>
</h:form>
```

You can actually use any arbitrary component search expression in the `for` attribute. For the `<h:outputLabel>` component, this doesn't make much sense. For the `<h:message>` and `<h:messages>` components, referring the ID of a non-input component would only make sense when you want to programmatically add a faces message from the managed bean on. But you would then need to know the client ID of the target component.

```
<h:form id="login">
    ...
            <h:commandButton id="submit" value="Login"
                action="#{login.submit}" />
            <h:message id="m_submit" for="submit" />
    ...
</h:form>
```

The preceding <h:commandButton> will generate a client ID of "login:submit" in the HTML output. You can then programmatically add a faces message as follows:

```
public String submit() {
    try {
        yourAuthenticator.authenticate(email, password);
        return "/user/home.xhtml?faces-redirect=true";
    }
    catch (YourAuthenticationException e) {
        FacesContext context = FacesContext.getCurrentInstance();
        FacesMessage message = new FacesMessage("Authentication failed");
        context.addMessage("login:submit", message);
        return null;
    }
}
```

A better practice, however, is to add the faces message as a global message by passing null as the client ID.

```
        context.addMessage(null, message);
```

Such a message will then only end up in a <h:messages globalOnly="true">.

```
            <h:commandButton id="submit" value="Login"
                action="#{login.submit}" />
            <h:messages id="messages" globalOnly="true"
                rendered="#{component.namingContainer.submitted}" />
```

Note the logic in the rendered attribute of the messages component. It will thus only be rendered when the submitted property of the NamingContainer parent evaluates to true. In this specific case, it's consulting the UIForm#isSubmitted(). This is very useful in case you have multiple non-Ajax forms, each with its own global messages component, and/or in case you have a "catch-all" `<h:messages redisplay="false">` component somewhere near the bottom of the Jakarta Faces page, which is then using CSS fixed positioned on top. Otherwise, the same global message would unintentionally show up over there as well.

This message-rendering logic is not necessary in Ajax forms as you could just fine-tune the message rendering by simply explicitly specifying the message(s) component(s) in the `render` attribute of `<f:ajax>`. Moreover, the `UIForm#isSubmitted()` would unexpectedly return `false` when the `execute` attribute of the `<f:ajax>` does not explicitly target the form as in `execute="@form"`.

Command Components

You'll have noticed examples of the `<h:commandButton>` in the previous sections about input and select components. This thus generates an HTML `<input type="submit">` element, which is the HTML way to send all input values of the `<form>` element it is sitting in to the server. On the server side, this component is also capable of invoking one or more Java methods, which are usually defined in the `action` or `actionListener` attribute, or via a `<f:actionListener>` tag nested in the command component. You'll also have read that the action listener method always runs before the method associated with the `action` attribute.

You can use the `<f:actionListener>` tag to register one or more additional action listeners on the very same command component. All those action listeners are invoked in the same order as they're declared in the view and attached to the component. The target method can be declared in three ways on the `<f:actionListener>` tag. One way is via the `type` attribute, and the other two ways are via the `binding` attribute.

```
<h:commandButton ...>
    <f:actionListener type="com.example.project.SomeActionListener" />
    <f:actionListener binding="#{beanImplementingActionListener}" />
    <f:actionListener binding="#{bean.someActionListenerMethod()}" />
<h:commandButton>
```

The `type` attribute in the first way must basically represent the fully qualified name of the class implementing the `ActionListener` interface.

```
package com.example.project;

import jakarta.faces.event.ActionListener;
import jakarta.faces.event.ActionEvent;

public class SomeActionListener implements ActionListener {

    @Override
    public void processAction(ActionEvent event) {
        // ...
    }
}
```

The binding attribute in the second way must basically reference a managed bean instance implementing the ActionListener interface.

```
@Named @RequestScoped
public class BeanImplementingActionListener implements ActionListener {

    @Override
    public void processAction(ActionEvent event) {
        // ...
    }
}
```

And the binding attribute in the third way can basically reference any arbitrary managed bean method that is declared void.

```
@Named @RequestScoped
public class Bean {

    public void someActionListenerMethod() {
        // ...
    }
}
```

Note that the third way is more or less undocumented. It has only been possible since the introduction of EL 2.2 (2009), wherein developers could start explicitly declaring method expressions by simply adding the parenthesis, if necessary with arguments. Coincidentally, the `binding` attribute of the `<f:actionListener>` could deal with them. Under the hood, the `binding` attribute is treated as a `ValueExpression`. When invoking `ValueExpression#getValue()` on it, the logic expected to obtain a managed bean instance implementing the `ActionListener` interface. However, instead of a getter method, a void method was invoked and returned nothing that is in turn interpreted as `null`. So the logic continued silently as if there was simply no bean instance available.

The action listeners have an additional feature on top of the `action` attribute. When a `jakarta.faces.event.AbortProcessingException` is explicitly thrown from an action listener, then Jakarta Faces will swallow the exception and abort processing the invoke application phase (fifth phase) and immediately advance to the render response phase (sixth phase). All remaining action listeners and the action method, if any, will be skipped. The swallowed exception won't end up in any error response. Given this fact, and the fact that action listeners are always invoked before the action method, you could (ab)use it to perform some conversion and validation based on already-updated model values before the action method is invoked.

```
public void someActionListenerMethod() {
    try {
        convertOrValidate(this);
    }
    catch (SomeConversionOrValidationException e) {
        FacesContext context = FacesContext.getCurrentInstance()
        context.addMessage(null, new FacesMessage(e.getMessage()));
        throw new AbortProcessingException(e);
    }
}

public void someActionMethod() {
    // Won't be invoked when AbortProcessingException is thrown.
}
```

I'm saying "(ab)use" because it is essentially the responsibility of a normal `Converter` or `Validator` implementation to perform such task so that the model values are not polluted with invalid values. However, for a long time in Jakarta Faces, it was not possible to perform conversion or validation based on multiple fields. Hence, developers started using the action (listener) methods for this task, which is essentially a violation of the Jakarta Faces life cycle.

Only in Jakarta Faces 2.3, a new `<f:validateWholeBean>` tag was introduced to perform validation on multiple fields. You can read more about this in Chapter 5. So this leaves only one reasonable real-world use case open for action listener methods: performing conversion based on one or more model values. One example has already been demonstrated in the section "Selection Components" (the case of using multiple `<h:selectBooleanCheckbox>` in `<ui:repeat>` to work around the fact that the `<h:selectManyCheckbox>` generates an HTML table). Another example would be invoking an external web service with the supplied model values and obtaining its result as a "converted" value. The action method should then still be used to execute business service logic. When the action method itself throws an exception, then it won't be swallowed, but the request will end up as an HTTP 500 error response. You can find more about this in Chapter 9.

Apart from the `<h:commandButton>`, Jakarta Faces offers two more command components: the `<h:commandLink>` and the `<h:commandScript>`. The `<h:commandLink>` has basically an identical life cycle as the `<h:commandButton>`, except that it generates an HTML `<a>` element that submits the enclosed form with the help of JavaScript. Everywhere where you use `<h:commandButton>`, it could be substituted with `<h:commandLink>`:

```
<h:form id="form">
    ...
    <h:commandLink id="submit" value="Submit" action="#{bean.submit}" />
</h:form>
```

whereby the generated HTML output looks as follows:

```
<script type="text/javascript"
    src="/project/jakarta.faces.resource/faces.js.xhtml?ln=jakarta.faces">
</script>
<form id="form" name="form" method="post" action="/project/test.xhtml"
    enctype="application/x-www-form-urlencoded">
    <input type="hidden" name="form" value="form" />
    ...
    <a id="form:submit" href="#" onclick="
```

```
    mojarra.cljs(
        document.getElementById('form'),
        {'form:submit':'form:submit'},
        ''
    ); return false;">Submit</a>
  <input type="hidden" name="jakarta.faces.ViewState"
      id="j_id1:jakarta.faces.ViewState:0"
      value="-6936791897896630173:-5064219023156239099"
      autocomplete="off" />
</form>
```

And the rendering in Chrome browser:

<u>Submit</u>

In the generated HTML output, you'll notice that it auto-includes the `faces.js` JavaScript file. This contains, among other things, the `window.faces` object and the Jakarta Faces implementation–specific helper functions that are, in case of the Mojarra implementation, put in the `window.mojarra` object. In plain HTML, there's no way to submit a `<form>` using an `<a>` element. Hence, some JavaScript had to be thrown into the game.

In Mojarra's specific case, the `mojarra.cljs()` function will be invoked with the parent form as the first argument, the command component's client ID as a request parameter name and value as the second argument, and the `target` attribute of the `<h:commandLink>` as the third argument, if any. The `mojarra.cljs()` function will in turn create `<input type="hidden">` elements for each name/value pair provided as the second argument and add them to the form provided as the first argument, making sure that those parameters end up a postback request. Then it will create an invisible `<input type="submit">` button, add it to the form, and invoke the `click()` function on it, as if you would be using a regular submit button. Finally, it will remove all of those dynamically created elements from the form.

This function is actually also used by the `<h:commandButton>`, but only when you need to pass additional HTTP request parameters via one or more `<f:param>` tags nested in the command component.

```
<h:form id="form">
    ...
```

```
    <h:commandButton id="submit" value="Submit" action="#{bean.submit}">
        <f:param name="id" value="#{otherBean.id}" />
    </h:commandButton>
</h:form>
```

Generated HTML output:

```
<script type="text/javascript"
    src="/project/jakarta.faces.resource/faces.js.xhtml?ln=jakarta.faces">
</script>
<form id="form" name="form" method="post" action="/project/test.xhtml"
    enctype="application/x-www-form-urlencoded">
    <input type="hidden" name="form" value="form" />
    <input id="form:submit" type="submit" name="form:submit"
        value="Submit" onclick="mojarra.cljs(
            document.getElementById('form'),
            {'form:submit':'form:submit','id':'42'},
            '');return false" />
    <input type="hidden" name="jakarta.faces.ViewState"
        id="j_id1:jakarta.faces.ViewState:0"
        value="8868114377399390021:6102567809374231851"
        autocomplete="off" />
</form>
```

Rendering in Chrome browser:

Submit

You can obtain the additional HTTP request parameters in the managed bean via
@Inject @ManagedProperty.

```
@Inject @ManagedProperty("#{param.id}")
private Integer id;

public void submit() {
    System.out.println("Submitted ID: " + id);
}
```

There's another way of passing parameters around via command components, that is, by simply passing them as an action method argument:

```
<h:form id="form">
    ...
    <h:commandButton id="submit" value="Submit"
        action="#{bean.submit(otherBean.id)}">
    </h:commandButton>
</h:form>
```

whereby the modified action method looks as follows:

```
public void submit(Integer id) {
    System.out.println("Submitted ID: " + id);
}
```

In case of the <h:commandButton>, this won't generate any JavaScript, and it thus looks identical as when you aren't using any action method arguments. This thus also means that the #{otherBean.id} value isn't passed via HTML source code back to the server as an HTTP request parameter. This in turn means that it's only evaluated during the postback request when Jakarta Faces is about to invoke the action method. This in turn means that the #{otherBean.id} must at least be @ViewScoped in order to be still available in the postback request. In other words, this method argument passing approach is definitely not exchangeable with the <f:param> tag approach whereby both beans can be just @RequestScoped for this to work.

The last command component offered by the standard Jakarta Faces component set is the <h:commandScript>. This is available since Jakarta Faces 2.3. It allows you to invoke a managed bean action method by just calling a named JavaScript function from your own script. The postback request will always be performed via Ajax.

```
<h:form id="form">
    <h:commandScript id="submit" name="invokeBeanSubmit"
        action="#{bean.submit}">
    </h:commandScript>
</h:form>
```

Generated HTML output:

```
<script type="text/javascript"
    src="/project/jakarta.faces.resource/faces.js.xhtml?ln=jakarta.faces">
</script>
<form id="form" name="form" method="post" action="/project/test.xhtml"
    enctype="application/x-www-form-urlencoded">
    <input type="hidden" name="form" value="form" />
    <span id="form:submit">
        <script type="text/javascript">
            var invokeBeanSubmit = function(o) {
                var o = (typeof o==='object') && o ? o : {};
                mojarra.ab('form:submit',null,'action',0,0,{'params':o});
            }
        </script>
    </span>
    <input type="hidden" name="jakarta.faces.ViewState"
        id="j_id1:jakarta.faces.ViewState:0"
        value="3568384626727188032:3956762118801488231"
        autocomplete="off" />
</form>
```

It has no visible HTML rendering in web browsers. In the generated script, you'll see that it has generated a function variable with the same name as specified in the name attribute. In this example, it's indeed in the global scope. As this is considered poor practice in the JavaScript context ("global namespace pollution"), you'd better provide a namespaced function name. This only pre-requires that you've already declared your own namespace somewhere before in the HTML document, usually via a JavaScript file in the <head> element. The following example simplifies it with an inline script:

```
<h:head>
    ...
    <script>var mynamespace = mynamespace || {};</script>
</h:head>
<h:body>
    <h:form id="form">
        <h:commandScript id="submit" name="mynamespace.invokeBeanSubmit"
```

```
            action="#{bean.submit}">
        </h:commandScript>
    </h:form>
</h:body>
```

Coming back to the generated function variable, you'll also see that it accepts an object argument and passes it through as "params" property of the last object argument of the Mojarra-specific `mojarra.ab()` function. That helper function will in turn prepare and invoke the `faces.ajax.request()` function of the standard Jakarta Faces JavaScript API. In other words, you can pass JavaScript variables to a managed bean action method this way. They are injectable via `@ManagedProperty` the same way as if you were using `<f:param>`. The following example demonstrates the JavaScript call with hard-coded variables in a JavaScript object, but you can of course obtain those variables from anywhere else in JavaScript context:

```
var params = {
    id: 42,
    name: "John Doe",
    email: "john.doe@example.com"
};

invokeBeanSubmit(params);
```

Backing bean class:

```
@Inject @ManagedProperty("#{param.id}")
private Integer id;

@Inject @ManagedProperty("#{param.name}")
private String name;

@Inject @ManagedProperty("#{param.email}")
private String email;

public void submit() {
    System.out.println("Submitted ID: " + id);
    System.out.println("Submitted name: " + name);
    System.out.println("Submitted email: " + email);
}
```

The <h:commandScript> can also be used to defer the partial rendering of an HTML document to the window load event. To achieve this, simply set the autorun attribute to true and specify the client ID of the target component in the render attribute. The following example loads and renders a data table only when the page has finished loading in the client side:

```
<h:panelGroup layout="block" id="lazyPersonsPanel">
    <h:dataTable rendered="#{not empty bean.lazyPersons}"
        value="#{bean.lazyPersons}" var="person">
        <h:column>#{person.id}</h:column>
        <h:column>#{person.name}</h:column>
        <h:column>#{person.email}</h:column>
    </h:dataTable>
</h:panelGroup>
<h:form id="form">
    <h:commandScript id="loadLazyPersons" name="loadLazyPersons"
        autorun="true" action="#{bean.loadLazyPersons}"
        render=":lazyPersonsPanel">
    </h:commandScript>
</h:form>
```

whereby the backing bean looks as follows:

```
@Named @RequestScoped
public class Bean {

    private List<Person> lazyPersons;

    @Inject
    private PersonService personService;

    public void loadLazyPersons() {
        lazyPersons = personService.list();
    }

    public List<Person> getLazyPersons() {
        return lazyPersons;
    }
}
```

141

and the `Person` entity looks as follows:

```
public class Person {

    private Long id;
    private String name;
    private String email;

    // Add/generate getters and setters.
}
```

Note that any persistence framework–specific annotations, such as `@Entity` and `@Id` of Jakarta Persistence and the actual implementation of `PersonService`, are omitted in the previous example for clarity. Those are, namely, irrelevant to any front-end framework, such as Jakarta Faces.

It may speak for itself that `<h:commandScript>` is only useful in order to be able to invoke a Jakarta Faces managed bean action method using native JavaScript, generally during a specific HTML DOM (Document Object Model) event, and that both `<h:commandLink>` and `<h:commandButton>` seem to do exactly the same thing; only the visual presentation is different; the one renders a link and the other renders a button. The user experience (UX) consensus is that a button must be used to submit a form and that a link must be used to navigate to another page or to jump to another section in the same page. Using a link to submit a form is therefore not always considered the best practice. It's only useful when you'd like to submit an HTML form using an icon or image. The following example shows how a command link can be used on a Font Awesome icon:

```
<h:commandLink id="delete" action="#{bean.delete}">
    <i class="fa fa-trash" />
</h:commandLink>
```

For all other cases, use a normal button.

Navigation

Sometimes, you'd like to navigate to a different Jakarta Faces page when a certain form has been successfully submitted, for example, from the login page to the user home page, as demonstrated in the section "Label and Message Components," or from the detail page back to the master page.

Historically, navigation targets must be defined separately in `<navigation-rule>` entries in the `faces-config.xml` which then does the job based on the `String` return value from the action method of command components. This approach turns out to be quite cumbersome in the long term and not terribly useful for HTML-based web applications. This idea was more or less derived from desktop-oriented applications. Hence, Jakarta Faces 2.0 introduced the "Implicit navigation" feature, which allows you to define the navigation target directly in the `String` return value itself.

In other words, instead of the following action method:

```
public String someActionMethod() {
    // ...
    return "someOutcome";
}
```

and the following `faces-config.xml` entry:

```
<navigation-rule>
    <navigation-case>
        <from-outcome>someOutcome</from-outcome>
        <to-view-id>/otherview.xhtml</to-view-id>
    </navigation-case>
</navigation-rule>
```

you could just do as follows in the action method:

```
public String someActionMethod() {
    // ...
    return "/otherview.xhtml";
}
```

You could even leave out the default suffix of the view technology you're using.

```
public String someActionMethod() {
```

```
    // ...
    return "/otherview";
}
```

You can force a redirect by appending a faces-redirect=true query parameter.

```
public String someActionMethod() {
    // ...
    return "/otherview?faces-redirect=true";
}
```

Returning `null` would return to the very same view from where the form was submitted. In other words, the end user would stay in the same page. It is cleaner, however, to declare the action method as `void`.

```
public void someActionMethod() {
    // ...
}
```

Coming back to the redirect approach, this is also known as "Post-Redirect-Get" pattern[2] and makes a major difference with regard to bookmarkability and avoiding double submits. Without a redirect after a POST request on a Jakarta Faces form, the URL (uniform resource locator) in the web browser's address bar wouldn't change to the URL of the target page but would just stay the same. That's caused by the nature of the "postback": submitting the form back to the very same URL from which the page with the form was served. In other words, actually the URL as specified in `action` attribute of the HTML `<form>` is being displayed in browser's address bar. When Jakarta Faces is instructed to navigate to a different view without a redirect, then it will basically build and render the target page directly to the response of the current postback request without changing the URL in browser's address bar to the URL of the target page.

This approach has disadvantages. One is that refreshing the page in the web browser would cause the POST request to be reexecuted and thus perform a so-called double submit. This would potentially pollute the data store in the back end with duplicate entries, particularly if the involved relational table doesn't have proper unique constraints defined. Another disadvantage is that the target page isn't bookmarkable. The URL currently visible in the browser's address bar basically represents the previous

---

[2] https://en.wikipedia.org/wiki/Post/Redirect/Get

page. You won't get the currently shown target page back by bookmarking, copy/pasting, and/or sharing the URL and then opening it in a new browser window.

When Jakarta Faces is instead instructed to navigate to a different view with a redirect, then it will basically return a very small HTTP response with a status code of 302 and a `Location` header whose value represents the URL of the target page. When the web browser retrieves such an HTTP response, then it will immediately fire a brand-new GET request on the URL specified in the `Location` header. This URL is ultimately reflected in the web browser's address bar and becomes thus bookmarkable. Also, refreshing the page would only refresh the GET request and therefore not cause a double submit.

Ajaxifying Components

As you have noticed in the `<h:commandScript>` example in the section "Command Components," Jakarta Faces is capable of firing Ajax requests and performing partial rendering as well. This capability was introduced in Jakarta Faces 2.0 for the first time with the `<f:ajax>` tag. This tag can be nested in any component implementing `ClientBehaviorHolder` interface, or it can be wrapped around a group of components implementing this interface. In the standard Jakarta Faces component set, almost all HTML components implement `ClientBehaviorHolder` as well. If you consult the `ClientBehaviorHolder` Javadoc,[3] then you'll find the following list:

All Known Implementing Classes:

```
HtmlBody, HtmlCommandButton, HtmlCommandLink, HtmlDataTable, HtmlForm,
HtmlGraphicImage, HtmlInputFile, HtmlInputSecret, HtmlInputText,
HtmlInputTextarea, HtmlOutcomeTargetButton, HtmlOutcomeTargetLink,
HtmlOutputLabel, HtmlOutputLink, HtmlPanelGrid, HtmlPanelGroup,
HtmlSelectBooleanCheckbox, HtmlSelectManyCheckbox, HtmlSelectManyListbox,
HtmlSelectManyMenu, HtmlSelectOneListbox, HtmlSelectOneMenu,
HtmlSelectOneRadio, UIWebsocket
```

Those are thus the `<h:body>`, `<h:commandButton>`, `<h:commandLink>`, `<h:dataTable>`, `<h:form>`, `<h:graphicImage>`, `<h:inputFile>`, `<h:inputSecret>`, `<h:inputText>`, `<h:inputTextarea>`, `<h:button>`, `<h:link>`, `<h:outputLabel>`,

---

[3] https://jakarta.ee/specifications/platform/10/apidocs/jakarta/faces/component/
behavior/ClientBehaviorHolder.html

`<h:outputLink>`, `<h:panelGrid>`, `<h:panelGroup>`, `<h:selectBooleanCheckbox>`, `<h:selectManyCheckbox>`, `<h:selectManyListbox>`, `<h:selectManyMenu>`, `<h:selectOneListbox>`, `<h:selectOneMenu>`, `<h:selectOneRadio>`, and `<f:websocket>`.

You'll see that all visible input, select, and command components are covered as well.

A requirement of the `<f:ajax>` is that the `ClientBehaviorHolder` component is nested in `<h:form>` and that `<h:head>` is being used in the template. The `<h:form>` basically enables JavaScript to perform a postback request with the right Jakarta Faces view state associated. The `<h:head>` basically enables `<f:ajax>` to automatically include the necessary `faces.js` JavaScript file that contains, among others, the mandatory `faces.ajax.request()` function.

Here's an example:

```
<h:head id="head">
    <title>f:ajax demo</title>
</h:head>
<h:body>
    <h:form id="form">
        <h:inputText id="text" value="#{bean.text}">
            <f:ajax />
        </h:inputText>
        <h:commandButton id="submit" value="Submit"
            action="#{bean.submit}">
            <f:ajax execute="@form" />
        </h:commandButton>
    </h:form>
</h:body>
```

Generated HTML output:

```
<head id="head">
    <title>f:ajax demo</title>
    <script type="text/javascript"
     src="/project/jakarta.faces.resource/faces.js.xhtml?ln=jakarta.faces">
    </script>
</head>
<body>
```

```
<form id="form" name="form" method="post"
    action="/project/test.xhtml"
    enctype="application/x-www-form-urlencoded">
    <input type="hidden" name="form" value="form" />
    <input id="form:text" type="text" name="form:text"
        onchange="mojarra.ab(this,event,'valueChange',0,0)" />
    <input id="form:submit" type="submit" name="form:submit"
        value="Submit" onclick="mojarra.ab(
            this,event,'action','@form',0);return false;" />
    <input type="hidden" name="jakarta.faces.ViewState"
        id="j_id1:jakarta.faces.ViewState:0"
        value="6345708413515990903:-8460061657159853996"
        autocomplete="off" />
</form>
</body>
```

Rendering in Chrome browser (with newlines added) is identical as without Ajax:

[   ]

[Submit]

In the generated HTML output, you'll see that the faces.js JavaScript file containing the necessary Jakarta Faces Ajax API is auto-included in the HTML head. You'll also notice that <f:ajax> has generated in <h:inputText> an additional onchange attribute and in <h:commandButton> an additional onclick attribute, both defining some Jakarta Faces implementation–specific JavaScript code responsible for performing the Ajax request.

Jakarta Faces specifies two internal Ajax event types: valueChange and action. Those are the default event types in case <f:ajax> doesn't have the event attribute specified. When <f:ajax> is attached to a component implementing the EditableValueHolder interface, then the default event type becomes valueChange. For components implementing the ActionSource interface, this is action. For all other ClientBehaviorHolder components, the default event is click. The actual generated HTML DOM event type for those internal event types depends on the component and the associated renderer.

In case of text input components and drop-down and list box selection components, the default HTML DOM event type for `<f:ajax>` is `"change"`. In case of check box and radio button selection components and command components, this is `"click"`. You can see this in the generated HTML output, which can be overridden by explicitly specifying the event attribute on the `<f:ajax>` tag.

```
<h:inputText ...>
    <f:ajax event="blur" />
</h:inputText>
```

The preceding example will generate the JavaScript code in the `onblur` attribute instead of the `onclick` attribute. The supported values for the event attribute depend on the target `ClientBehaviorHolder` component. They can be found in the VDL documentation of the component of interest. All `on[event]` attributes are defined over there. When you remove the "on" prefix on them, then you have a list of supported event types. For example, the VDL documentation of `<h:inputText>`[4] indicates that the following event types are supported:

> `blur`, `change`, `click`, `dblclick`, `focus`, `keydown`, `keypress`, `keyup`,
> `mousedown`, `mousemove`, `mouseout`, `mouseover`, `mouseup`, `select`

When the desired DOM event type occurs on the client side and triggers the associated Jakarta Faces implementation–specific JavaScript code defined in the `on[event]` attribute, then ultimately the `faces.ajax.request()` function of the standard Jakarta Faces JavaScript API will be invoked. It will prepare a bunch of predefined postback parameters of which `jakarta.faces.source` and `jakarta.faces.behavior.event` are the most important ones. The former specifies the client ID of the source component, essentially the value of `this.id` in JavaScript context. The latter specifies the event type, essentially the value of `event.type` in JavaScript context. You'll have guessed that they are derived from the first two arguments passed to the Mojarra-specific `mojarra.ab()` function as visible in the generated HTML output.

Once fired, the Ajax request will run through the Jakarta Faces life cycle almost the same way as a non-Ajax request. The restore view phase (first phase), process validations phase (third phase), update model values phase (fourth phase), and invoke application phase (fifth phase) are identical. The apply request values phase (second phase) is slightly different. It will only decode the components that are covered by the execute

---

[4]`https://jakarta.ee/specifications/faces/4.0/vdldoc/facelets/h/inputText.html`

attribute of the <f:ajax> tag, which defaults to @this ("the current component"). The render response phase (sixth phase) is completely different. Instead of generating a whole HTML document, it generates a special XML document that contains only the generated HTML output of components that are covered by the render attribute of the <f:ajax> tag, which defaults to @none ("no one component").

The execute and render attributes of the <f:ajax> tag accept a space-separated collection of component search expressions. This can represent a client ID relative to the closest NamingContainer parent, or an absolute client ID that is always relative to the UIViewRoot, or standard or custom search keywords, or chained combinations thereof. See Chapter 12 for an in-depth explanation of them. For now, we only need to know about three standard search keywords: @this, @form, and @none. As its name suggests, the @form keyword refers to the closest parent component of the UIForm type, such as <h:form>.

During the apply request values phase (second phase) of the Ajax request, Jakarta Faces will, for each component covered by the execute attribute of the <f:ajax> tag in addition to the default decode process, also check if the jakarta.faces.source request parameter equals the client ID of the current component. If so, then Jakarta Faces will queue the AjaxBehaviorEvent for the invoke application phase (fifth phase). Under the hood of queueing the AjaxBehaviorEvent, it boils down to the following logic:

```
FacesContext context = FacesContext.getCurrentInstance();
ExternalContext externalContext = context.getExternalContext();
Map<String, String> formData = externalContext.getRequestParameterMap();

String clientId = component.getClientId(context);
String source = formData.get("jakarta.faces.source");
String event = formData.get("jakarta.faces.behavior.event");

if (clientId.equals(source)) {
    component.getClientBehaviors().get(event)
        .forEach(clientBehavior -> component.queueEvent(
            new AjaxBehaviorEvent(context, component, clientBehavior)));
}
```

Here, the ClientBehavior basically represents the definition of the <f:ajax> tag. Based on this logic, you will conclude that you can have multiple <f:ajax> tags attached in the very same component, even on same event types. The advantage is that you can, if necessary, register multiple Ajax behavior listeners on the very same event type.

```
<h:inputText id="foo" ...>
    <f:ajax listener="#{bean.onchangeFoo}" />
    <f:ajax listener="#{otherBean.onchangeFoo}" />
</h:inputText>
```

Those Ajax behavior listener methods will thus be invoked during the invoke application phase (fifth phase); of course, only when there's no conversion or validation error during the process validations phase (third phase). In case of command components, those Ajax behavior listener methods will always be invoked *before* the action listener methods and the action method. Regardless of the target component, the Ajax behavior listener method must be a `public void` method that can optionally take the `AjaxBehaviorEvent` argument.

```
public void onchangeFoo(AjaxBehaviorEvent event) {
    // ...
}
```

This gives you, in input and select components, the opportunity to perform some business task on a specific Ajax event. Most occurring real-world examples involve preparing a bean property that in turn gets rendered in another component. Think of cascading drop-down menus wherein the available items of the child drop-down menu depend on the selected item of the parent drop-down.

In command components, the `<f:ajax listener>` isn't terribly useful. You already have the possibility to perform the business task in action listener and/or action method. You can just continue using them even when having `<f:ajax>` attached.

During the render response phase (sixth phase) of the Ajax request, Jakarta Faces will, for each component covered by the `render` attribute of the `<f:ajax>` tag, generate an XML `<update>` element in the Ajax response that contains the generated HTML output of only the particular component and all of its children, if any. The `faces.ajax.response()` function of the standard Jakarta Faces JavaScript API, which is by the `faces.ajax.request()` registered as Ajax callback function, will extract the `id` attribute of the `<update>` element, which represents the client ID of the target component, and obtain via JavaScript's `document.getElementById()` the concrete HTML element and replace it in the HTML DOM tree with the contents of the `<update>` element.

The following is an example of a form with one required input field having a message attached and a command button that explicitly targets the message component:

```
<h:form id="form">
    <h:inputText id="text" value="#{bean.text}" required="true" />
    <h:message id="m_text" for="text" />
    <br />
    <h:commandButton id="submit" value="Submit" action="#{bean.submit}">
        <f:ajax execute="@form" render="m_text" />
    </h:commandButton>
</h:form>
```

Figure 4-2 shows how Chrome presents the Ajax response after submitting the form with the input field not filled out. It's a big one-liner, so it's scrolled a bit so it starts at the <update> element of interest. It contains the generated HTML output of the <h:message id="m_text"> component.

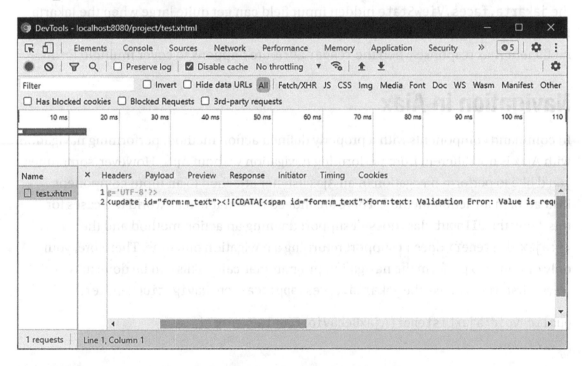

Figure 4-2. *Chrome Developer Tools—Network—Response*

If you scroll further in the XML response, then you'll also notice an `<update id="j_id1:jakarta.faces.ViewState:0">` element containing the value of the `jakarta.faces.ViewState` hidden input element. This is important for Jakarta Faces in order to maintain the view state across Ajax requests. When the `render` attribute happens to cover a `UIForm` component, then the `jakarta.faces.ViewState` hidden input element currently in the HTML document will basically be completely wiped out during the replacement of the element in the HTML DOM tree with contents of the `<update>` element of the Ajax response.

Any missing `jakarta.faces.ViewState` hidden input element will ultimately be appended to every `<form method="post">` of the current `UIViewRoot`, and the value of any existing `jakarta.faces.ViewState` hidden input element will be updated with the new value. This approach is actually by design for two reasons: (1) because the view state value could change across Ajax requests and therefore the existing forms currently in the HTML document have to be updated to catch up this change, just in case those forms are not covered by the `render` attribute, and (2) because the value of the `jakarta.faces.ViewState` hidden input field can get quite large when the Jakarta Faces state saving method is explicitly set to "`client`" and thus otherwise produce an inefficient Ajax response when the `render` attribute happens to cover multiple forms.

Navigation in Ajax

In command components with a properly defined action method, performing navigation with Ajax is not different from performing navigation without Ajax. However, sometimes, you'd like to perform navigation in an Ajax listener attached to an input component instead of in an action method. There are indeed reasonable real-world use cases for this. Only the `UIInput` class doesn't support defining an action method and the `<f:ajax listener>` doesn't support returning a navigation outcome. Therefore, your only option is to perform the navigation programmatically. This can be done in two ways. First way is to use the `jakarta.faces.application.NavigationHandler`.[5]

```
public void ajaxListener(AjaxBehaviorEvent event) {
    // ...

    String outcome = "/otherview?faces-redirect=true";
```

---

[5]https://jakarta.ee/specifications/platform/10/apidocs/jakarta/faces/application/
NavigationHandler.html

```
    FacesContext context = FacesContext.getCurrentInstance();
    Application application = context.getApplication();
    NavigationHandler handler = application.getNavigationHandler();
    handler.handleNavigation(context, null, outcome);
}
```

Second way is to use the `jakarta.faces.context.ExternalContext#redirect()`.[6]

```
public void ajaxListener(AjaxBehaviorEvent event) throws IOException {
    // ...

    String path = "/otherview.xhtml";
    FacesContext context = FacesContext.getCurrentInstance();
    ExternalContext externalContext = context.getExternalContext();
    String uri = externalContext.getRequestContextPath() + path;
    externalContext.redirect(uri);
}
```

There are several differences. Most importantly, the `NavigationHandler` can deal with implicit navigation outcome values, but `ExternalContext#redirect()` can only deal with actual paths and requires manual prefixing of the request context path when it concerns a web application resource. However, it can take basically any URI, such as an external URL as in `externalContext.redirect("https://example.com")`, whereas the `NavigationHandler` can't deal with them.

GET Forms

Jakarta Faces has no concept of "GET forms," but you can just use plain HTML for this. Jakarta Faces supports processing GET request parameters and invoking managed bean actions on GET requests. For this, the `<f:viewParam>` and `<f:viewAction>` tags can be used. They must be placed in a `<f:metadata>` tag that in turn can only be declared in the top-level page. So when using templating, it must be declared in the template client, and you can't declare it in the master template. In other words, the `<f:metadata>` tag cannot be shared across template clients.

---

[6]https://jakarta.ee/specifications/platform/10/apidocs/jakarta/faces/context/
ExternalContext.html#redirect-java.lang.String

Technically, the location of the `<f:metadata>` tag in the view doesn't matter, as long as it's in the top-level page. Most self-documenting would be to put it in the very top of the view, directly after the root tag.

```
<!DOCTYPE html>
<html lang="en"
    xmlns:f="jakarta.faces.core"
    xmlns:h="jakarta.faces.html"
>
    <f:metadata>
        ...
    </f:metadata>
    <h:head>
        ...
    </h:head>
    <h:body>
        ...
    </h:body>
</html>
```

When using templating, give it its own template definition.

```
<ui:composition template="/WEB-INF/templates/layout.xhtml"
    xmlns:f="jakarta.faces.core "
    xmlns:h="jakarta.faces.html"
>
    <ui:define name="metadata">
        <f:metadata>
            ...
        </f:metadata>
    </ui:define>
    <ui:define name="content">
        ...
    </ui:define>
</ui:composition>
```

No, you can't put the `<f:metadata>` tag in the master template and keep the `<f:viewParam>` and `<f:viewAction>` tags in the template client. This is a technical limitation. The best you can do is to create a custom `<f:event>` type that runs after the invoke application phase (fifth phase) and then declare it in the master template. An example is given in the section "Custom Component System Events" in Chapter 3.

The `<f:viewParam>` tag is backed by the `UIViewParameter` component that in turn extends from `UIInput` superclass. This means that it behaves almost exactly like `<h:inputText>`, but then for GET parameters. The subtle differences are found in the process validations phase (third phase). By default, an empty parameter would skip any custom validators and Jakarta Bean Validation. For example, the `@NotNull` Jakarta Bean Validation annotation will only work when the context parameter `jakarta.faces.INTERPRET_EMPTY_STRING_SUBMITTED_VALUES_AS_NULL` is explicitly set to `true` in `web.xml`. The other difference is in the render response phase (sixth phase). Basically, it renders absolutely nothing.

The `<f:viewAction>` tag is backed by the `UIViewAction` component that in turn implements the `ActionSource` interface. This means that it behaves almost exactly like `<h:commandButton>`, but then for GET requests. Of course, you could also use a `@PostConstruct` annotated method on a `@ViewScoped` managed bean for performing logic on GET requests, but the problem is that it would run directly after the managed bean instance is created, when any `<f:viewParam>` hasn't even had a chance to run. The `<f:viewAction>` will be invoked during the invoke application phase (fifth phase), after the model values are updated. It even supports returning a `String` representing a navigation outcome, which will then behave as a redirect. The following is an example of a search form:

Facelets file `/search.xhtml`:

```
<f:metadata>
    <f:viewParam id="query" name="query" value="#{search.query}" />
    <f:viewAction action="#{search.onload}" />
</f:metadata>
<h:body>
    <form>
        <label for="query">Query</label>
        <input type="text" name="query"
            value="#{empty search.query ? param.query : search.query}">
        </input>
```

```
        <input type="submit" value="Search" />
        <h:message for="query" />
    </form>
    <h:dataTable id="results" rendered="#{not empty search.results}"
        value="#{search.results}" var="result">
        <h:column>#{result.name}</h:column>
        <h:column>#{result.description}</h:column>
    </h:dataTable>
</h:body>
```

Backing bean class com.example.project.view.Search:

```
@Named @RequestScoped
public class Search {

    private String query;
    private List<Result> results;

    @Inject
    private SearchService searchService;

    public void onload() {
        results = searchService.listResults(query);
    }

    // Add/generate getters and setters here.
    // Note that results doesn't need a setter.
}
```

In the Facelets file, there are a couple of things to notice apart from the plain HTML form approach. The value attribute of the text input displays #{param.query} when #{search.query} is empty, because the submitted value would otherwise not show up at all when there's a conversion or validation error on <f:viewParam>. The #{param} is actually an implicit EL object referring the request parameter map. The #{param.query} basically prints the value of the request parameter with the name "query". Please note that this construct of the value attribute utilizing the ternary operator #{x ? y : z} is invalid for Jakarta Faces input components. It would throw a jakarta.el.PropertyNotWritableException during the update model values phase (fourth phase). Moreover, it is basically already doing the very same logic under the hood of the UIInput class.

The `<h:message>` can be attached to a `<f:viewParam>` as well. In this specific construct, however, it's not really used. Only when you add a converter or a validator to `<f:viewParam>`, for example, by `<f:viewParam ... required="true">`, then you would see the error message in `<h:message>`, and then the `<f:viewAction>` won't be invoked.

Now, when you open the page and submit the form, the submitted value will appear as a query string in the URL as in `/search.xhtml?query=submitted%20value`. This is bookmarkable and reexecutable every time you open the URL.

Stateless Forms

State saving is particularly helpful in dynamically manipulated forms that use Ajax to conditionally render parts of the form, such as cascading drop-down menus and secondary input fields. Jakarta Faces remembers the state of the form across Ajax postbacks on the same view. Generally, it is those forms where you absolutely need a view-scoped managed bean instead of a request-scoped managed bean.

When your website has "public" and "private" sections, you'd like to postpone the HTTP session creation as much as possible until the end user has actually logged in. This way robots won't trigger the unnecessary creation of the HTTP session. However, if you have a standard Jakarta Faces login form in the public section, then the HTTP session would already be created by just accessing that page. This is an unnecessary cost in terms of server memory if the form has basically no dynamic state of its own and is already tied to a request-scoped managed bean. You could consider using client-side state saving instead, but this will affect the entire website, and it has a cost in terms of network bandwidth and CPU (central procession unit) power. True, the cost is negligible if you have state-of-the-art hardware, but it's not negligible if you have a lot of visitors and/or relatively poor hardware.

In case of static forms tied to a request-scoped bean, such as a simple two-field login form that can theoretically safely be entirely cleared out on every postback, then the view state doesn't necessarily need to be saved. This can be achieved by setting the `transient` attribute of `<f:view>` to `true`.

```
<f:view transient="true">
    <h:form id="login">
        ...
    </h:form>
</f:view>
```

This way, Jakarta Faces won't create any view state, and the `jakarta.faces.ViewState` hidden input field will receive a fixed value of "`stateless`". Note that this affects the entire view and that there's no way to toggle this for only a specific form. Jakarta Faces currently does not support configuring the state saving method on a per-form basis. Also, statelessness has an additional disadvantage in that it's theoretically easier to perform a CSRF (cross site request forgery) attack if there's an open XSS hole. See also the section "Cross-Site Request Forgery Protection" in Chapter 13. Fortunately, with Jakarta Faces, it's already very hard to accidentally introduce an XSS hole in first place. The only way to get an XSS hole is to explicitly use `<h:outputText escape="false">` to redisplay user-controlled data.

CHAPTER 5

Conversion and Validation

At its core, Jakarta Faces as an HTML form–based MVC (model-view-controller) framework basically needs to convert between Java objects (entities, beans, value objects, data transfer objects, and whatnot) and character sequences (strings) all the time. The HTTP request is basically broken down into plain vanilla strings representing headers and parameters, not into Java objects. The HTTP response is basically written as one big sequence of characters representing HTML or XML, not as some sort of serialized form of a Java object. However, the average Java model behind a Jakarta Faces page doesn't necessarily contain String properties everywhere. That would defeat the strong typed nature of Java. This is where converters come into the picture: converting between objects in model and strings in view.

Before updating the model values with freshly submitted and, if necessary, converted values, you would of course also like to validate whether they conform to the business rules of the web application and, if necessary, present end users an informative error message so that they can fix any errors themselves. Usually, the business rules are already very well defined in the data store, such as a relational database management system. A decently designed database table already has strict constraints on the data type, maximum size, nullability, and uniqueness. You as a front-end developer should make absolutely sure that the submitted and converted values can be inserted in the database without errors.

If, for example, the email address column is constrained as a unique and nonnullable column with a maximum size of 254 characters, then you should make sure that the submitted value is validated as such before inserting it in the database. Otherwise, the database insert would throw some SQL exception that is generally cumbersome to break down into detailed information in order to tell the end user about the exact mistake. This is where validators come into the picture: validating submitted (and converted) values before updating the model.

© Bauke Scholtz and Arjan Tijms 2022
B. Scholtz and A. Tijms, *The Definitive Guide to Jakarta Faces in Jakarta EE 10*,
https://doi.org/10.1007/978-1-4842-7310-4_5

Standard Converters

Jakarta Faces has, from the beginning, provided a bunch of standard converters out the box. Most of them even do their job fully transparently based on the Java type of the model property. They are all available in the `jakarta.faces.convert` package,[1] and they all implement the `Converter<T>` interface. Table 5-1 provides an overview of them.

Table 5-1. *Standard Converters Provided by Jakarta Faces*

Converter class	Converter ID	Converter tag	Value type	Since
BigDecimalConverter	jakarta.faces.BigDecimal	n/a	java.math.BigDecimal	1.0
BigIntegerConverter	jakarta.faces.BigInteger	n/a	java.math.BigInteger	1.0
BooleanConverter	jakarta.faces.Boolean	n/a	boolean/java.lang.Boolean	1.0
ByteConverter	jakarta.faces.Byte	n/a	byte/java.lang.Byte	1.0
CharacterConverter	jakarta.faces.Character	n/a	char/java.lang.Character	1.0
DateTimeConverter	jakarta.faces.DateTime	<f:convertDateTime>	java.util.Date	1.0
			java.time.LocalDate	2.3
			java.time.LocalTime	2.3
			java.time.OffsetTime	2.3
			java.time.LocalDateTime	2.3
			java.time.OffsetDateTime	2.3
			java.time.ZonedDateTime	2.3
DoubleConverter	jakarta.faces.Double	n/a	double/java.lang.Double	1.0
EnumConverter	jakarta.faces.Enum	n/a	enum/java.lang.Enum	1.0
FloatConverter	jakarta.faces.Float	n/a	float/java.lang.Float	1.0
IntegerConverter	jakarta.faces.Integer	n/a	int/java.lang.Integer	1.0
LongConverter	jakarta.faces.Long	n/a	long/java.lang.Long	1.0
NumberConverter	jakarta.faces.Number	<f:convertNumber>	java.lang.Number	1.0
ShortConverter	jakarta.faces.Short	n/a	short/java.lang.Short	1.0

---

[1]https://jakarta.ee/specifications/platform/10/apidocs/jakarta/faces/convert/
package-summary.html

The "Converter ID" column basically specifies the converter identifier as you could specify in the `converter` attribute of any `ValueHolder` component, or in the `converterId` attribute of any nested `<f:converter>` tag in order to activate the specific converter. All `UIOutput` and `UIInput` components implement the `ValueHolder` interface. The converters that say "n/a" in the "Converter tag" column are implicit converters. In other words, you can just bind the `value` attribute of any `ValueHolder` component to any bean property of type `BigDecimal`, `BigInteger`, `boolean/Boolean`, `byte/Byte`, `char/Character`, `double/Double`, `enum/Enum`, `float/Float`, `int/Integer`, `long/Long`, and `short/Short` and have Jakarta Faces to automatically convert it without any additional configuration. Only `<f:convertDateTime>` and `<f:convertNumber>` require explicit registration because the desired conversion algorithm isn't necessarily obvious from the model value alone.

In all `ValueHolder` components, the converter will be invoked during the render response phase (sixth phase), converting the non-`String`-based model value to a `String` suitable for embedding in HTML. And in `EditableValueHolder` components, the converter will also be invoked during the process validations phase (third phase), converting the submitted `String` request parameter to the non-`String`-based model value. The `EditableValueHolder` interface extends the `ValueHolder` interface and is implemented by all `UIInput` components.

However, implicit conversion doesn't work on bean properties where those value types are actually parameterized. Imagine that you have a `List<Integer>` in the model and you'd like to be able to edit it as follows:

```
<ui:repeat value="#{bean.integers}" varStatus="loop">
    <h:inputText value="#{bean.integers[loop.index]}" />
</ui:repeat>
```

Then, after submitting, you would end up with unconverted `String` values in the list and get baffled by class cast exceptions when attempting to iterate over the list. The reason is that the EL (Expression Language) API (application programming interface), which is responsible for processing those #{ . . . } things that are, behind the scenes, represented by `jakarta.el.ValueExpression` instances, is in its current version not capable of detecting the parameterized type of a generic collection and just returns `Object.class` on `ValueExpression#getType()`. Jakarta Faces can't do much about that limitation of EL. All you can do is explicitly specify the desired converter by its "Converter ID" on the input component.

```
<ui:repeat value="#{bean.integers}" varStatus="loop">
    <h:inputText value="#{bean.integers[loop.index]}"
        converter="jakarta.faces.Integer">
    </h:inputText>
</ui:repeat>
```

An alternative is to replace the List<Integer> by Integer[] or even int[]. EL will then be able to recognize the value expression as an integer type, and hence, Jakarta Faces will be able to locate the desired converter for it. However, using plain arrays instead of collections in the model are a "no-no" these days.

Coming back to the explicit standard converters <f:convertNumber> and <f:convertDateTime>, those can also be nested in any ValueHolder component. The difference between the <f:convertNumber> tag and the implicit number-based converters is that the tags allow more fine-grained setting of conversion options, such as the number type or pattern, the amount of integer and/or fraction digits, whether grouping is used, and the locale.

<f:convertNumber>

The <f:convertNumber>[2] uses under the hood java.text.NumberFormat.[3] The type attribute specifies which java.text.NumberFormat instance will be obtained and defaults to number. Other allowable values are currency and percent. In other words, the following tags:

```
<f:convertNumber type="number" />
<f:convertNumber type="currency" />
<f:convertNumber type="percent" />
```

will under the hood obtain the NumberFormat instance as follows:

```
NumberFormat numberFormat = NumberFormat.getNumberInstance(locale);
NumberFormat currencyFormat = NumberFormat.getCurrencyInstance(locale);
NumberFormat percentFormat = NumberFormat.getPercentInstance(locale);
```

---

[2] https://jakarta.ee/specifications/faces/4.0/vdldoc/f/convertNumber.html
[3] https://docs.oracle.com/en/java/javase/15/docs/api/java.base/java/text/NumberFormat.html

where the `locale` argument can be specified by the `locale` attribute of the
`<f:convertNumber>` tag and defaults to `UIViewRoot#getLocale()`, which in turn can
be specified by the `locale` attribute of `<f:view>`. In other words, those instances will
automatically apply the standard number format pattern based on the number type and
the specified locale. The following example:

```
<f:view locale="pt_BR">
    ...
    <h:outputText value="#{product.price}">
        <f:convertNumber type="currency" locale="en_US" />
    </h:outputText>
</f:view>
```

will not format the price (a `BigDecimal` property) as `R$ 12,34` (Brazilian real), but
instead as `$12.34` (US dollar). Note that the `locale` attribute of the `<f:convertNumber>`
tag does not necessarily need to be specified as a supported locale in `faces-config.xml`.
Also noted should be that the `value` attribute doesn't necessarily need to refer a
`BigDecimal`; any other `java.lang.Number` type is also supported, but for prices, we'd of
course like to store the value in a `BigDecimal` instead of, for example, a `Double` or `Float`
to avoid arithmetic errors due to the floating nature of floating-point numbers.[4]

In case you need to change the standard number format pattern for some reason–for
example, because you're working on a banking application that stores financial data with
five fractions–and you'd like to present the full value in some back-end admin screen so
that humans can, if necessary, verify them, then you can use the `pattern` attribute of the
`<f:convertNumber>` tag to override the standard number format pattern to conform to
the rules of `java.text.DecimalFormat`.[5]

```
<f:convertNumber pattern="¤ #,##0.00000" locale="pt_BR" />
```

Note that when the `pattern` attribute is specified, the `type` attribute is ignored. The
"currency sign" pattern character "¤" specifies where the actual currency symbol must
be inserted. The actual currency symbol depends on the specified locale. The "comma"
pattern character "," specifies when the grouping separator must be inserted, which is
relative to the decimal separator or the end of the value. The actual inserted grouping

---

[4] https://floating-point-gui.de
[5] https://docs.oracle.com/en/java/javase/15/docs/api/java.base/java/text/
DecimalFormat.html

separator symbol is coincidentally also a comma in US dollar format but is a period in Brazilian real format. The "period" pattern character "." specifies the location of the decimal separator. The actual inserted decimal separator symbol is coincidentally also a period in US dollar format but is a comma in Brazilian real format. The "optional digit" pattern character "#" is in this pattern merely used to indicate when the grouping separator symbol should be inserted and won't show anything when the actual digit is absent. The "required digit" pattern character "0" specifies the minimum format that will show zero when the actual digit is absent. The following is an exercise code that should give insight into how `<f:convertNumber>` works under the hood:

```
Locale locale = new Locale("pt", "BR");
DecimalFormatSymbols symbols = new DecimalFormatSymbols(locale);
System.out.println("Currency symbol: " + symbols.getCurrencySymbol());
System.out.println("Grouping symbol: " + symbols.getGroupingSeparator());
System.out.println("Decimal symbol: " + symbols.getDecimalSeparator());

DecimalFormat formatter = new DecimalFormat("¤ #,##0.00000", symbols);
System.out.println(formatter.format(new BigDecimal("12.34")));
System.out.println(formatter.format(new BigDecimal(".1234")));
System.out.println(formatter.format(new BigDecimal("1234")));
System.out.println(formatter.format(new BigDecimal("1234567.1234567")));
```

The output should look as follows:

```
Currency symbol: R$
Grouping symbol: .
Decimal symbol: ,
R$ 12,34000
R$ 0,12340
R$ 1.234,00000
R$ 1.234.567,12346
```

The `<f:convertNumber>` will also render exactly those values. Apart from the `pattern` attribute, you can also fine-grain the `type` attribute with additional attributes such as `currencySymbol`, `integerOnly`, `groupingUsed`, `minIntegerDigits`, `maxIntegerDigits`, `minFractionDigits`, and `maxFractionDigits`. You can basically achieve the same formatting pattern "¤ #,##0.00000" as follows:

```
<f:convertNumber type="currency" locale="pt_BR"
    minFractionDigits="5" maxFractionDigits="5" />
```

This is actually more readable and more convenient in case you have a hard time getting out the currency sign placeholder from your keyboard. The `pattern` attribute is rarely more useful than fine-graining the `type` attribute with additional attributes.

In case you're using `<f:convertNumber>` in a `UIInput` component and thus require the end user to enter the value, then you should keep in mind that currency and percent types explicitly require the end user to enter the currency or percent symbol in the input field as well. For the currency input, you can easily disable this by specifying an empty string as a currency symbol so that you can put it outside the input component.

```
<span class="currency">
    <span class="symbol">$</span>
    <h:inputText ...>
        <f:convertNumber type="currency" currencySymbol="" />
    </h:inputText>
</span>
```

For the percent type, this is, unfortunately, not possible. The end user really has to explicitly enter the percent symbol in the input field as well.

<f:convertDateTime>

The `<f:convertDateTime>`[6] uses under the hood `java.text.DateFormat`[7] and, since Jakarta Faces 2.3, also `java.time.formatter.DateTimeFormatter`.[8] In other words, you can use basically any kind of date for this. Also, this tag has a `type` attribute that must actually correspond to the actual type of the model value. Historically, it was not possible to programmatically detect the desired type based on a `java.util.Date` instance. This has changed since the new `java.time` API that offers distinct classes for each date time type. However, in order to be able to reuse the existing `<f:convertDateTime>` API for the new `java.time` API, new types had to be added. Table 5-2 provides an overview.

---

[6]https://jakarta.ee/specifications/faces/4.0/vdldoc/f/convertDateTime.html

[7]https://docs.oracle.com/en/java/javase/15/docs/api/java.base/java/text/DateFormat.html

[8]https://docs.oracle.com/en/java/javase/15/docs/api/java.base/java/time/format/DateTimeFormatter.html

Table 5-2. `<f:convertDateTime type>` *Supported Values*

Tag attribute	Value type	Actual formatter	Since
date (default)	java.util.Date (with zero time)	DateFormat#getDateInstance()	1.0
time	java.util.Date (with zero date)	DateFormat#getTimeInstance()	1.0
both	java.util.Date	DateFormat#getDateTimeInstance()	1.0
localDate	java.time.LocalDate	DateTimeFormatter#ofLocalizedDate()	2.3
localTime	java.time.LocalTime	DateTimeFormatter#ofLocalizedTime()	2.3
localDateTime	java.time.LocalDateTime	DateTimeFormatter#ofLocalizedDateTime()	2.3
offsetTime	java.time.OffsetTime	DateTimeFormatter#ISO_OFFSET_TIME	2.3
offsetDateTime	java.time.OffsetDateTime	DateTimeFormatter#ISO_OFFSET_DATE_TIME	2.3
zonedDateTime	java.time.ZonedDateTime	DateTimeFormatter#ISO_ZONED_DATE_TIME	2.3

Along with the `type` attribute, you should preferably also specify the `pattern` attribute, particularly when requesting the end user to enter a value of the `java.util.Date` or `java.time.LocalXxx` type via a `UIInput` component, because the actual pattern may vary in a not so self-documenting way across various locales. The `java.time.OffSetXxx` and `ZonedDateTime` types don't have that problem because they default to the universal ISO 8601 format.[9]

The `pattern` attribute of `<f:convertDateTime>` follows, for `java.util.Date`, the same rules as specified in the `java.text.SimpleDateFormat` Javadoc,[10] and for the `java.time` API, the same rules as specified in `java.time.format.DateTimeFormatter` Javadoc.[11] They are for the most part the same, but the `java.time` format supports more patterns. For both APIs, the "day of month" pattern character is "d", the "month of year" pattern character is "M", the "year" pattern character is "y", the "24h hour" pattern

---

[9] https://en.wikipedia.org/wiki/ISO_8601

[10] https://docs.oracle.com/en/java/javase/15/docs/api/java.base/java/text/SimpleDateFormat.html

[11] https://docs.oracle.com/en/java/javase/15/docs/api/java.base/java/time/format/DateTimeFormatter.html

character is "H", the "minute" pattern is "m", and the "second" pattern is "s". The ISO 8601 date format is "yyyy-MM-dd", and the ISO 8601 time format is "HH:mm:ss". The offset and zoned times require an additional offset after the time part, which is represented by the ISO 8601 time zone pattern character "X". Examples of valid values are "+01:00" for CET (Central European Time), "-03:00" for BRT (Brasilia Time), and "+5:30" for IST (Indian Standard Time). As before, the offset and zoned date and time need to be separated by the "T" character instead of a space. The following is an overview of all possible <f:convertDateTime> types whereby the localized ones have an explicitly specified pattern:

```
<h:form id="form">
    <h:inputText id="date" value="#{bean.date}">
        <f:convertDateTime type="date" pattern="yyyy-MM-dd" />
    </h:inputText>
    <h:inputText id="time" value="#{bean.time}">
        <f:convertDateTime type="time" pattern="HH:mm:ss" />
    </h:inputText>
    <h:inputText id="both" value="#{bean.both}">
        <f:convertDateTime type="both" pattern="yyyy-MM-dd HH:mm:ss" />
    </h:inputText>
    <h:inputText id="localDate" value="#{bean.localDate}">
        <f:convertDateTime type="localDate" pattern="yyyy-MM-dd" />
    </h:inputText>
    <h:inputText id="localTime" value="#{bean.localTime}">
        <f:convertDateTime type="localTime" pattern="HH:mm:ss" />
    </h:inputText>
    <h:inputText id="localDateTime" value="#{bean.localDateTime}">
        <f:convertDateTime type="localDateTime"
            pattern="yyyy-MM-dd HH:mm:ss">
        </f:convertDateTime>
    </h:inputText>
    <h:inputText id="offsetTime" value="#{bean.offsetTime}">
        <f:convertDateTime type="offsetTime" />
    </h:inputText>
```

```
<h:inputText id="offsetDateTime" value="#{bean.offsetDateTime}">
    <f:convertDateTime type="offsetDateTime" />
</h:inputText>
<h:inputText id="zonedDateTime" value="#{bean.zonedDateTime}">
    <f:convertDateTime type="zonedDateTime" />
</h:inputText>
<h:commandButton value="submit" action="#{bean.submit}" />
<h:messages showSummary="false" showDetail="true"/>
</h:form>
```

Note that <h:messages> is here reconfigured to show the detail instead of just the summary, because the detail message of a date time conversion error includes in standard Jakarta Faces an example value that is more useful for the end user in order to understand the required format. The following is what the associated backing bean looks like:

```
@Named @RequestScoped
public class Bean {

    private Date date;
    private Date time;
    private Date both;
    private LocalDate localDate;
    private LocalTime localTime;
    private LocalDateTime localDateTime;
    private OffsetTime offsetTime;
    private OffsetDateTime offsetDateTime;
    private ZonedDateTime zonedDateTime;

    public void submit() {
        System.out.println("date: " + date);
        System.out.println("time: " + time);
        System.out.println("both: " + both);
        System.out.println("localDate: " + localDate);
        System.out.println("localTime: " + localTime);
        System.out.println("localDateTime: " + localDateTime);
```

```
        System.out.println("offsetTime: " + offsetTime);
        System.out.println("offsetDateTime: " + offsetDateTime);
        System.out.println("zonedDateTime: " + zonedDateTime);
    }

    // Add/generate getters and setters.
}
```

Now that HTML5 has been out for some time and more and more browsers support the new HTML5 date and time inputs, you'd better activate it by default because it comes with a very useful built-in date picker. The web browser may show the date pattern in the date picker in a localized format, but it will always submit the value in ISO 8601 format. This is thus very useful. The HTML5 date and time inputs can be activated by setting the type attribute of the input text field to "date",[12] "time",[13] or "datetime-local"[14]. The following are some examples:

```
<h:form id="form">
    <h:inputText id="localDate" type="date" value="#{bean.localDate}">
        <f:convertDateTime type="localDate" pattern="yyyy-MM-dd" />
    </h:inputText>
    <h:inputText id="localTime" type="time" value="#{bean.localTime}">
        <f:convertDateTime type="localTime" pattern="HH:mm" />
    </h:inputText>
    <h:inputText id="localDateTime" type="datetime-local"
        value="#{bean.localDateTime}">
        <f:convertDateTime type="localDateTime"
            pattern="yyyy-MM-dd'T'HH:mm">
        </f:convertDateTime>
    </h:inputText>
    <h:commandButton value="submit" action="#{bean.submit}" />
    <h:messages showSummary="false" showDetail="true"/>
</h:form>
```

---

[12] https://developer.mozilla.org/en-US/docs/Web/HTML/Element/input/date
[13] https://developer.mozilla.org/en-US/docs/Web/HTML/Element/input/time
[14] https://developer.mozilla.org/en-US/docs/Web/HTML/Element/input/datetime-local

The following is how they're rendered in Chrome browser (with newlines added):

Standard Validators

When the submitted value is successfully converted during the process validations phase (third phase), then Jakarta Faces will immediately advance to perform validation on the converted value. Jakarta Faces already provides a handful of standard validators out of the box. They are all available in the `jakarta.faces.validator` package,[15] and they all implement the `Validator<T>` interface. Table 5-3 provides an overview of them.

---

[15] https://jakarta.ee/specifications/platform/10/apidocs/jakarta/faces/validator/
package-summary.html

Table 5-3. *Standard Validators Provided by Jakarta Faces*

Validator class	Validator ID	Validator tag	Value type	Since
LongRangeValidator	jakarta.faces.LongRange	<f:validateLongRange>	java.lang.Number	1.0
DoubleRangeValidator	jakarta.faces.DoubleRange	<f:validateDoubleRange>	java.lang.Number	1.0
LengthValidator	jakarta.faces.Length	<f:validateLength>	java.lang.Object	1.0
RegexValidator	jakarta.faces.RegularExpression	<f:validateRegex>	java.lang.String	2.0
RequiredValidator	jakarta.faces.Required	<f:validateRequired>	java.lang.Object	2.0
BeanValidator	jakarta.faces.Bean	<f:validateBean>	java.lang.Object	2.0
n/a	n/a	<f:validateWholeBean>	java.lang.Object	2.3

The "Validator ID" column basically specifies the validator identifier as you could specify in the `validator` attribute of any `EditableValueHolder` component, or in the `validatorId` attribute of any nested `<f:validator>` tag in order to activate the specific validator. In contrary to the converter, a single `EditableValueHolder` component can have multiple validators attached. They will all be executed regardless of each other's outcome.

<f:validateLongRange>/<f:validateDoubleRange>

These two validators allow you to specify a minimum and/or a maximum allowed number value for an input component tied to a `java.lang.Number`-based property. Those can be specified with the `minimum` and `maximum` attributes.

```
<h:inputText value="#{bean.quantity}">
    <f:validateLongRange minimum="1" maximum="10" />
</h:inputText>
```

This is, via pass-through attributes, also combinable with the HTML5 input types "number" (spinner) and "range" (slider), which in turn require `min`, `max`, and optionally `step` as pass-through attributes. In this example, `#{bean.quantity}` is just an `Integer`, and `#{bean.volume}` is a `BigDecimal`.

```
<h:inputText value="#{bean.quantity}"
    type="number" a:min="1" a:max="10">
    <f:validateLongRange minimum="1" maximum="10" />
</h:inputText>
<h:inputText value="#{bean.volume}"
    type="range" a:min="1" a:max="10" a:step="0.1">
    <f:validateLongRange minimum="1" maximum="10" />
</h:inputText>
```

Do note that you can just use `<f:validateLongRange>` on a `BigDecimal` property. It doesn't care about the actual `java.lang.Number` type of the property being a `Long` or not, but only the specified `minimum` and `maximum` attributes being a `Long`. In case you want to specify a fractional-based number as minimum and/or maximum, then use `<f:validateDoubleRange>` instead.

```
<h:inputText value="#{bean.volume}"
    type="range" a:min="0.1" a:max="10.0" a:step="0.1">
    <f:validateDoubleRange minimum="0.1" maximum="10.0" />
</h:inputText>
```

<f:validateLength>/<f:validateRegex>

These two validators are primarily designed for java.lang.String-based properties. The <f:validateLength> will first convert the submitted value to string by calling Object#toString() on it and then validate the result of String#length() based on the specified minimum and/or maximum attributes. The <f:validateRegex> will first cast the submitted value to String and then check if String#matches() returns true for the specified pattern attribute. In other words, it doesn't accept any other property type than java.lang.String. Imagine that you want to validate a value to be always three digits; then there are thus three possible ways:

```
<h:inputText value="#{bean.someStringOrInteger}" maxlength="3">
    <f:validateLength minimum="3" maximum="3" />
</h:inputText>
```

```
<h:inputText value="#{bean.someString}" maxlength="3">
    <f:validateRegex pattern="[0-9]{3}" />
</h:inputText>
```

```
<h:inputText value="#{bean.someInteger}" maxlength="3">
    <f:validateLongRange minimum="100" maximum="999" />
</h:inputText>
```

The maxlength="3" attribute is just there so that the end user can't enter more than three characters on the client side anyway. Storing numbers as strings is plain nonsense, so the second way is scratched. That leaves us with the first or third way. Technically, it does not really matter which one you pick. The first way is arguably more self-documenting because you actually want to validate the length, not the range.

Coming back to the <f:validateRegex>, the pattern attribute follows exactly the same regular expression rules as specified in java.util.regex.Pattern.[16] However, there's one potential caveat: the necessary amount of escape backslashes depends on the currently used EL implementation. In Oracle's EL implementation (com.sun. el.*), you need two backslashes, exactly as in a regular Java String, but in Apache's EL implementation (org.apache.el.*), you must use one backslash; otherwise, it will error out, or it won't match as you'd expect. As of now, Payara, WildFly, Liberty, and WebLogic use Oracle's EL implementation, and TomEE and Tomcat use Apache's EL implementation. In other words, the following example will work on servers using Oracle EL, but won't work on servers using Apache EL.

```
<h:inputText value="#{bean.someString}" maxlength="3">
    <f:validateRegex pattern="\\d{3}" />
</h:inputText>
```

When using Apache EL, you need pattern="\d{3}" instead. On the other hand, the regular expression pattern \d actually means "any digit" and thus matches not only the Latin digits but also the Hebrew, Cyrillic, Arabic, Chinese, etc. If that was not your intent, then you'd better use the [0-9] pattern.

<f:validateRequired>

This is a slightly odd beast. That is, all UIInput components already have a required attribute offering exactly the desired functionality. Why would you then use a whole <f:validateRequired> tag instead? It was added in Jakarta Faces 2.0 specifically for "Composite Components" (more on this later, in Chapter 7). More to the point, in some composite component compositions, the template client is given the opportunity to attach converters and validators to a specific EditableValueHolder interface exposed by the composite component, which in turn references one or more UIInput components enclosed in the composite component implementation. The following is an example of such a composite component:

---

[16] https://docs.oracle.com/en/java/javase/15/docs/api/java.base/java/util/regex/ Pattern.html

```
<cc:interface>
    ...
    <cc:editableValueHolder
        name="inputs" targets="input1 input3">
    </cc:editableValueHolder>
</cc:interface>
<cc:implementation>
    ...
    <h:inputText id="input1" ... />
    <h:inputText id="input2" ... />
    <h:inputText id="input3" ... />
    ...
</cc:implementation>
```

And the following is an example of the template client using this composite component:

```
<my:compositeComponent ...>
    <f:validateRequired for="inputs" />
</my:compositeComponent>
```

As you might have guessed, the for attribute must exactly match the name attribute of exposed <cc:editableValueHolder>, and this validator will basically target the enclosed input components identified by input1 and input3 (and thus not input2) and thus effectively make them required="true". This for attribute is, by the way, also present on all other converter and validator tags.

<f:validateBean>/<f:validateWholeBean>

When used, these two tags have a required dependency on the Jakarta Bean Validation API (application programming interface), previously more commonly known as "JSR 303" and "Jakarta Bean Validation." Like Jakarta Faces, Jakarta Bean Validation is part of the Jakarta EE API, already included in any Jakarta EE application server. In Tomcat and other servlet containers, you'd need to install it separately. In Java code, Jakarta Bean Validation is represented by annotations and interfaces of the jakarta.validation.*

package, such as @NotNull, @Size, @Pattern, and ConstraintValidator. Currently, the most popular implementation is Hibernate Validator.[17]

Jakarta Faces automatically detects the presence of Jakarta Bean Validation and will in such a case transparently process all Jakarta Bean Validation constraints during the end of the process validations phase (third phase), regardless of the outcome of Jakarta Faces' own validators. If desired, this can be disabled application-wide with the following context parameter in web.xml:

```
<context-param>
    <param-name>
        jakarta.faces.validator.DISABLE_DEFAULT_BEAN_VALIDATOR
    </param-name>
    <param-value>true</param-value>
</context-param>
```

Or if this is a little too rough, then you can fine-grain it with the help of the <f:validateBean> tag wrapping a group of UIInput components, or nested in them. When the disabled attribute of the <f:validateBean> tag is set to true, then any Jakarta Bean Validation will be disabled on the target UIInput components. The following code will disable any Jakarta Bean Validation only on the parent UIInput component.

```
<h:inputText ...>
    <f:validateBean disabled="true" />
</h:inputText>
```

And the following code will disable any Jakarta Bean Validation only on UIInput components identified by input3, input4, and input5:

```
<h:inputText id="input1" ... />
<h:inputText id="input2" ... />
<f:validateBean disabled="true">
    <h:inputText id="input3" ... />
    <h:inputText id="input4" ... />
    <h:inputText id="input5" ... />
<f:validateBean>
```

---

[17] https://hibernate.org/validator/

It is important to keep in mind that this will only disable Jakarta Faces–managed Jakarta Bean Validation and thus not, for example, Jakarta Persistence–managed Jakarta Bean Validation. So if you happen to use Jakarta Persistence to persist your entities that are filled out by Jakarta Faces components with Jakarta Bean Validation disabled, then Jakarta Persistence would still perform Jakarta Bean Validation on its behalf, fully independently from Jakarta Faces. In case you want to disable Jakarta Bean Validation on the Jakarta Persistence side as well, then you need to set the property `jakarta.persistence.validation.mode` to `NONE` in `persistence.xml` (see also the `jakarta.persistence.ValidationMode` Javadoc).[18]

```
<property name="jakarta.persistence.validation.mode">NONE</property>
```

With the `validationGroups` attribute of the `<f:validateBean>` tag, you can, if necessary, declare one or more validation groups. In such a case, only the Jakarta Bean Validation constraints that are registered on the same group will be processed. Imagine the following model:

```
@NotNull
private String value1;

@NotNull(groups=NotNull.class)
private String value2;

@NotNull(groups={NotNull.class, Default.class})
private String value3;
```

Note that the `groups` attribute of any Jakarta Bean Validation constraint must reference an interface, but it may be any one you want. For simplicity, in the preceding example, we're just reusing the `jakarta.validation.constraints.NotNull` interface as a group identifier. The common practice is, however, to create your own marker interface for the desired group.

---

[18] https://jakarta.ee/specifications/platform/10/apidocs/jakarta/persistence/ValidationMode.html

Also not unimportant is that the @NotNull would only work when you've configured Jakarta Faces to interpret empty string submitted values as null; otherwise, it would pollute the model with empty strings instead of nulls and cause the @NotNull not to be able to do its job because an empty string is not null. As a reminder, the web.xml context parameter of interest is as follows:

```
<context-param>
    <param-name>
        jakarta.faces.INTERPRET_EMPTY_STRING_SUBMITTED_VALUES_AS_NULL
    </param-name>
    <param-value>true</param-value>
</context-param>
```

Now, when submitting an empty form while having those three model properties referenced in the following input components, without any <f:validateBean> on them:

```
<h:inputText value="#{bean.value1}" />
<h:inputText value="#{bean.value2}" />
<h:inputText value="#{bean.value3}" />
```

then you will receive a validation error on Jakarta Bean Validation constraints belonging to the jakarta.validation.groups.Default group, which are thus the groupless value1 and the explicitly grouped value3. The value2 won't be validated by Jakarta Bean Validation as it doesn't have the default group explicitly declared.

And when submitting an empty form while having a <f:validateBean> tag with the validationGroups attribute set to NotNull.class:

```
<f:validateBean validationGroups="jakarta.validation.constraints.NotNull">
    <h:inputText value="#{bean.value1}" />
    <h:inputText value="#{bean.value2}" />
    <h:inputText value="#{bean.value3}" />
</f:validateBean>
```

then you will receive a validation error on Jakarta Bean Validation constraints belonging to the jakarta.validation.constraints.NotNull group, which are thus the value2 and value3, which explicitly have this group declared. The groupless value1 won't be validated by Jakarta Bean Validation as it only implies the default group.

Finally, when submitting an empty form while having a `<f:validateBean>` tag with the both groups specified in `validationGroups` attribute as a comma separated string:

```
<f:validateBean validationGroups="jakarta.validation.groups.Default,
                              jakarta.validation.constraints.NotNull">
    <h:inputText value="#{bean.value1}" />
    <h:inputText value="#{bean.value2}" />
    <h:inputText value="#{bean.value3}" />
</f:validateBean>
```

then you will receive a validation error on all inputs because they all match at least one of the specified groups. In real-world applications, however, this grouping feature has very little use. It's only really useful when the grouped fields can be validated at the same time by the same validator. With Jakarta Bean Validation, the only way to achieve that is to put a custom `Constraint` annotation on the bean class itself, get an instance of that bean with the values populated, and then pass it to the custom `ConstraintValidator` associated with the custom `Constraint` annotation. Imagine a "period" entity having a "start date" property which should always be before the "end date" property. It would look something like the following:

```
@PeriodConstraint
public class Period implements Serializable {

    @NotNull
    private LocalDate startDate;

    @NotNull
    private LocalDate endDate;

    // Add/generate getters and setters.
}
```

with the following custom constraint annotation:

```
@Constraint(validatedBy=PeriodValidator.class)
@Target(TYPE)
@Retention(RUNTIME)
```

```java
public @interface PeriodConstraint {
    String message() default "Start date must be before end date";
    Class<?>[] groups() default {};
    Class<?>[] payload() default {};
}
```

and the following custom constraint validator:

```java
public class PeriodValidator
    implements ConstraintValidator<PeriodConstraint, Period>
{
    @Override
    public boolean isValid
        (Period period, ConstraintValidatorContext context)
    {
        return period.getStartDate().isBefore(period.getEndDate());
    }
}
```

You see, Jakarta Bean Validation expects that the model values are already present in the given bean instance while performing the actual validation. In the Jakarta Faces perspective, this means that the model values must be updated before processing the validations. However, this doesn't fit into the Jakarta Faces life cycle wherein the model values are only updated after the validations are successfully processed. Essentially, Jakarta Faces would need to clone the bean instance, populate it with the desired model values, invoke Jakarta Bean Validation on the cloned bean instance, collect any validation errors, and then discard the cloned bean instance.

This is exactly what the `<f:validateWholeBean>` tag, introduced with Jakarta Faces 2.3, is doing under the hood. The following is an example form wherein this code is being used:

```html
<h:form>
    <h:inputText type="date" value="#{booking.period.startDate}">
        <f:convertDateTime type="localDate" pattern="yyyy-MM-dd" />
    </h:inputText>
    <h:inputText type="date" value="#{booking.period.endDate}">
        <f:convertDateTime type="localDate" pattern="yyyy-MM-dd" />
    </h:inputText>
```

```
    <h:commandButton value="Submit" />
    <h:messages />
    <f:validateWholeBean value="#{booking.period}" />
</h:form>
```

with this backing bean:

```
@Named @ViewScoped
public class Booking implements Serializable {
    private Period period = new Period();

    // Add/generate getter.
}
```

Do note that the `<f:validateWholeBean>` tag is explicitly placed as the last child of the parent `<h:form>`, which ensures that the validation is performed as the last thing after all individual input components in the same form. This is as per the specification; the Jakarta Faces implementation may throw a runtime exception when the tag is misplaced.

Immediate Attribute

The `EditableValueHolder`, `ActionSource`, and `AjaxBehavior` interfaces also specify an `immediate` property that basically maps to the `immediate` attribute of all `UIInput` and `UICommand` components and the `<f:ajax>` tag. When set to `true` on an `EditableValueHolder` component, then anything that normally takes place during the process validations phase (third phase) as well as the update model values phase (fourth phase) will instead be performed during the apply request values phase (second phase). When conversion or validation fails on them, then the life cycle will also skip the process validations phase (third phase). When set to `true` on an `ActionSource` component or `AjaxBehavior` tag, then anything that normally takes place during the invoke application phase (fifth phase) will instead be performed during the apply request values phase (second phase) and then only if conversion and validation haven't failed.

Historically, this attribute was mainly used to be able to perform an "inner" action on the form, usually to load a child input component depending on the submitted value of the parent input component, without being blocked by conversion or validation errors coming from other input components in the same form. A common use case was populating a child drop-down on the change of a parent drop-down without risking that the required attribute of the child drop-down blocks the submit.

```
<h:selectOneMenu value="#{bean.country}" required="true" immediate="true"
    onchange="submit()" valueChangeListener="#{bean.loadCities}">
    <f:selectItems value="#{bean.countries}" />
</h:selectOneMenu>
<h:selectOneMenu value="#{bean.city}" required="true">
    <f:selectItems value="#{bean.cities}" />
</h:selectOneMenu>
```

This approach obviously predates the Web 2.0 era wherein you'd just use Ajax for this. Understand that the immediate attribute has essentially become useless for this purpose since the introduction of <f:ajax> in Jakarta Faces 2.0. Exactly the same use case can be achieved in a much cleaner way as follows:

```
<h:selectOneMenu value="#{bean.country}" required="true">
    <f:selectItems value="#{bean.countries}" />
    <f:ajax listener="#{bean.loadCities}" render="city" />
</h:selectOneMenu>
<h:selectOneMenu id="city" value="#{bean.city}" required="true">
    <f:selectItems value="#{bean.cities}" />
</h:selectOneMenu>
```

As you learned in Chapter 4, the execute attribute of <f:ajax> already defaults to @this, so it's just omitted. This also means that all other EditableValueHolder components in the same form won't be processed and thus won't cause #{bean. loadCities} ever to be blocked by conversion or validation errors coming from other inputs.

These days, with the Ajax magic and all, the immediate attribute has thus lost its main use case. Jakarta Faces could do as well without it. Due to its historic use case, many starters may mistake its primary purpose to be "skip all validation." This is, however, not true. For that, you'd need to fine-tune the execute attribute of <f:ajax> in such a way that it only covers the input components that really need to be validated. In case you want to actually "skip all validation" while submitting the entire form, then you'd best use Jakarta Bean Validation constraints instead (the @NotNull and friends) and simply have <f:validateBean disabled="true"> wrapping the entire form.

Custom Converters

From the beginning, Jakarta Faces has supported custom converters. The main use case is to be able to convert a nonstandard model value, such as a persistence entity specific to the web application. The less common use case is to extend an existing standard converter and set some commonly used defaults in its constructor so that you can get away with less code in the view definition in order to declare the desired standard converter configuration on the component.

Imagine that you want to be able to create master-detail pages on your persistence entities wherein you'd like to pass the ID of the entity around as a request parameter from the master page to the detail page. The following is an example data table in the master page /products/list.xhtml based on a fictive Product entity:

```
<h:dataTable value="#{listProducts.products}" var="product">
    <h:column>#{product.id}</h:column>
    <h:column>#{product.name}</h:column>
    <h:column>#{product.description}</h:column>
    <h:column>
        <h:link value="Edit" outcome="edit">
            <f:param name="id" value="#{product.id}" />
        </h:link>
    </h:column>
</h:dataTable>
```

Note the last column of the table. It generates a link to the detail page /products/edit.xhtml whereby the ID of the entity is passed as a GET request parameter as in /product.xhtml?id=42. In the detail page, you can use <f:viewParam> to set the GET request parameter in the backing bean.

```
<f:metadata>
    <f:viewParam name="id" value="#{editProduct.product}"
        required="true" requiredMessage="Bad request">
    </f:viewParam>
</f:metadata>
...
```

```
<h:form>
    <h1>Edit product #{editProduct.product.id}</h1>
    <h:inputText value="#{editProduct.product.name}" />
    <h:inputText value="#{editProduct.product.description}" />
    ...
</h:form>
```

However, there's one small problem: the GET request parameter is in Java perspective basically a `String` representing the product ID, while the `product` property of the `EditProduct` backing bean actually expects a whole `Product` entity identified by the passed-in ID.

```
@Named @ViewScoped
public class EditProduct implements Serializable {

    private Product product;

    // Getter+setter.
}
```

For exactly this conversion step, a custom converter has to be created, which is capable of converting between a `String` representing the product ID and an `Object` representing the `Product` entity. Jakarta Faces offers the `jakarta.faces.convert.Converter` interface[19] to get started. The following is a concrete example of such a `ProductConverter`:

```
@FacesConverter(forClass=Product.class, managed=true)
public class ProductConverter implements Converter<Product> {

    @Inject
    private ProductService productService;

    @Override
    public String getAsString
        (FacesContext context, UIComponent component, Product product)
```

---

[19] https://jakarta.ee/specifications/platform/10/apidocs/jakarta/faces/convert/Converter.html

```
{
    if (product == null) {
        return "";
    }

    if (product.getId() != null) {
        return product.getId().toString();
    }
    else {
        throw new ConverterException(
            new FacesMessage("Invalid product ID"), e);
    }
}

@Override
public Product getAsObject
    (FacesContext context, UIComponent component, String id)
{
    if (id == null || id.isEmpty()) {
        return null;
    }

    try {
        return productService.getById(Long.valueOf(id));
    }
    catch (NumberFormatException e) {
        throw new ConverterException(
            new FacesMessage("Invalid product ID"), e);
    }
}
}
```

There are several important things to note here in the @FacesConverter annotation. First, the forClass attribute basically specifies the target entity type for which this converter should automatically run during the process validations phase (third phase) and the render response phase (sixth phase). This way, you don't need to explicitly register the converter in the view. In case you wanted to do so, then you'd replace the `forClass` attribute by the `value` attribute specifying the unique identifier of the converter, for example:

```
@FacesConverter(value="project.ProductConverter", managed=true)
```

Then you can specify exactly that converter ID in the `converter` attribute of any `ValueHolder` component, or in the `converterId` attribute of any nested `<f:converter>` tag.

```
<f:viewParam name="id" value="#{editProduct.product}"
    converter="project.ProductConverter"
    required="true" requiredMessage="Bad request">
</f:viewParam>
```

But this is thus not necessary when you just keep using the `forClass` attribute. Note that you can't specify both. It's the one or the other where the `value` attribute takes precedence over the `forClass` attribute. So if you specify both, then the `forClass` attribute is essentially ignored. We don't want to have that as it's much more powerful for this particular purpose of transparently converting whole entities.

The second thing to note in the annotation is the `managed` attribute. This is new since Jakarta Faces 2.3. Essentially, this manages the converter instance in the CDI context. Setting the `managed` attribute to `true` is mandatory in order to get dependency injection to work in the converter. Previously, this was worked around by making the converter itself a managed bean.[20]

If you have worked with Jakarta Faces converters before, you'll also notice the interface now finally being parameterized. The interface predates Java 1.5 and was hence not parameterized from the beginning. With a `Converter<T>`, the `getAsObject()` now returns a `T` instead of `Object`, and the `getAsString()` now takes a `T` as value argument instead of `Object`. This saves unnecessary `instanceof` checks and/or casts.

Note that Jakarta Faces' own standard converters that predate Jakarta Faces 2.3 (currently, basically all of them thus) are frozen in time and cannot take advantage of this as they would otherwise no longer be backward compatible. In other words, they are still raw types. That is, there's a small but not unavoidable chance that someone is programmatically using Jakarta Faces converters in plain Java code instead of letting

---

[20] https://stackoverflow.com/q/7665673/157882

Jakarta Faces deal with them. That plain Java code would no longer compile if the standard converters were parameterized. It's essentially the same reason that the `Map#get()` explicitly takes `Object` instead of `K` as argument. Further, there's a yet smaller but still not unavoidable chance that someone has created a custom converter that extends a standard converter but also explicitly redeclares the interface. Something like the following:

```
public class ExtendedNumberConverter
    extends NumberConverter implements Converter
{
    // ...
}
```

Such an obscure converter would no longer compile if `NumberConverter` was parameterized in some way. Even if we parameterize `NumberConverter` as a `Converter<Object>`, the compiler would error on `ExtendedNumberConverter` as follows and hence break backward compatibility:

> *The interface Converter cannot be implemented more than once with different arguments: Converter<Object> and Converter*

Coming back to our `ProductConverter` implementation, in the `getAsString()`, you'll notice that the converter explicitly returns an empty string when the model value is `null`. This is as per the Javadoc.[21] The technical reason is that Jakarta Faces won't render the associated HTML attribute when the evaluated value is `null`. In general, this is not a big problem. The fewer unused attributes in the generated HTML output, the better it is. Only, this won't work as expected for the `<option>` of a `<select>` element. If the custom converter would return `null` instead of an empty string, then the `<option>` element would be rendered without any `value` attribute and thus fall back to submitting its text content instead. Awkward indeed, but this is literally specified in the HTML specification.[22] In other words, if you have a converter that incorrectly returns `null` instead of an empty string, and you have a drop-down list with the associated entities along with a default option as follows:

---

[21] https://jakarta.ee/specifications/platform/10/apidocs/jakarta/faces/convert/Converter.html

[22] https://html.spec.whatwg.org/multipage/form-elements.html#attr-option-value

187

```
<h:selectOneMenu value="#{bean.product}">
    <f:selectItem itemValue="#{null}" itemLabel="Please select ..." />
    <f:selectItems value="#{bean.products}"
        var="product" itemLabel="#{product.name}">
    </f:selectItems>
</h:selectOneMenu>
```

then the web browser would, during submitting the default option, send the literal string "Please select ..." to the server instead of an empty string. This would cause a NumberFormatException in ProductConverter#getAsObject() while we intend to return null here. The correct solution is thus to let the getAsString() return an empty string in case the model value is null.

In case you have more persistence entities for which you need a Jakarta Faces converter, and you want to avoid repeating essentially the same ProductConverter logic for all other persistence entities, then you can create a generic Jakarta Faces converter for them. This works the best if all your persistence entities extend from the same base class wherein the getId() is defined.

```
@MappedSuperClass
public abstract class BaseEntity implements Serializable {

    @Id @GeneratedValue(strategy=IDENTITY)
    private Long id;

    public Long getId() {
        return id;
    }
}
```

And if you have a base entity service for all of them:

```
@Stateless
public class BaseEntityService {

    @PersistenceContext
    private EntityManager entityManager;
```

```
@TransactionAttribute(SUPPORTS)
public <E extends BaseEntity> E getById(Class<E> type, Long id) {
    return entityManager.find(type, id);
}
}
```

the generic converter can then look as follows:

```
@FacesConverter(forClass=BaseEntity.class, managed=true)
public class BaseEntityConverter implements Converter<BaseEntity> {

    @Inject
    private BaseEntityService baseEntityService;

    @Override
    public String getAsString
        (FacesContext context, UIComponent component, BaseEntity entity)
    {
        if (entity == null) {
            return "";
        }

        if (entity.getId() != null) {
            return entity.getId().toString();
        }
        else {
            throw new ConverterException(
                new FacesMessage("Invalid entity ID"), e);
        }
    }

    @Override
    public BaseEntity getAsObject
        (FacesContext context, UIComponent component, String id)
    {
        if (id == null || id.isEmpty()) {
            return null;
        }
```

```
        ValueExpression value = component.getValueExpression("value");
        Class<? extends BaseEntity> type = (Class<? extends BaseEntity>)
            value.getType(context.getELContext());

        try {
            return baseEntityService.getById(type, Long.valueOf(id));
        }
        catch (NumberFormatException e) {
            throw new ConverterException(
                new FacesMessage("Invalid entity ID"), e);
        }
    }
}
```

The key here is thus the ValueExpression#getType() call. This returns the actual type of the property behind the EL expression associated with the component's value attribute. In case of <f:viewParam value="#{editProduct.product}">, this would thus return Product.class, which fits Class<? extends BaseEntity>.

Coming back to the less common use case of a custom converter, extending a standard converter, imagine that you have a <f:convertDateTime> configuration that is repeated everywhere in your web application:

```
<f:convertDateTime type="localDate" pattern="yyyy-MM-dd" />
```

And you'd like to replace it with something like the following:

```
<t:convertLocalDate />
```

Then one way is to just extend it, set the defaults in the constructor, and register it in the *.taglib.xml file, and that's it. The following is what such a LocalDateConverter can look like:

```
@FacesConverter("project.ConvertLocalDate")
public class LocalDateConverter extends DateTimeConverter {

    public LocalDateConverter() {
        setType("localDate");
        setPattern("yyyy-MM-dd");
    }
}
```

190

And here's the /WEB-INF/example.taglib.xml entry.

```
<tag>
    <tag-name>convertLocalDate</tag-name>
    <converter>
        <converter-id>project.ConvertLocalDate</converter-id>
    </converter>
</tag>
```

Alternatively, you can also make it an implicit converter by getting rid of the converter ID and making it a forClass converter.

```
@FacesConverter(forClass=LocalDate.class)
```

This way, you don't even need any <t:convertLocalDate> tag. Don't forget to remove the <tag> entry in example.taglib.xml. They cannot be used simultaneously. If you need such case, for example, because you want to be able to change the LocalDate pattern, create another subclass.

You can even have a forClass converter for java.lang.String typed properties. This is very useful when you want to have an automatic application-wide string-trimming strategy which should prevent the model from being polluted with leading or trailing whitespace on user-submitted values. The following is how such a converter can look like:

```
@FacesConverter(forClass=String.class)
public class TrimConverter implements Converter<String> {

    @Override
    public String getAsString
        (FacesContext context, UIComponent component, String modelValue)
    {
        return modelValue == null ? "" : modelValue;
    }

    @Override
    public String getAsObject(FacesContext context,
        UIComponent component, String submittedValue)
```

```
    {
        if (submittedValue == null || submittedValue.isEmpty()) {
            return null;
        }

        String trimmed = submittedValue.trim();
        return trimmed.isEmpty() ? null : trimmed;
    }
}
```

Last but not least, when you need to provide whole entities as SelectItem values of a selection component as below (see also Chapter 4), along with a custom converter for Country.class:

```
<h:selectOneMenu value="#{bean.country}">
    <f:selectItem itemValue="#{null}" itemLabel="-- select one --" />
    <f:selectItems value="#{bean.availableCountries}" var="country">
        itemValue="#{country}" itemLabel="#{country.name}"
    </f:selectItems>
</h:selectOneMenu>
```

where the associated backing bean properties are declared as follows:

```
private Country country;
private List<Country> availableCountries;
```

then you need to keep in mind that the entity has its equals() and hashCode() properly implemented. Otherwise, Jakarta Faces may throw a confusing validation error when submitting the form.

Validation Error: Value is not valid

This may happen when the bean is request scoped instead of view scoped and thus recreates the list of available countries during every postback. As part of safeguard against tampered requests, Jakarta Faces will reiterate over the available options in order to validate if the selected option is indeed among them. Jakarta Faces will use the Object#equals() method to test the selected option against each available option. If this hasn't returned true for any of the available options, then the abovementioned validation error will be thrown.

Continuing with the BaseEntity example, here's how you'd best implement its equals() and hashCode() methods.

```
@Override
public boolean equals(Object other) {
    if (getId() != null
        && getClass().isInstance(other)
        && other.getClass().isInstance(this))
    {
        return getId().equals(((BaseEntity) other).getId());
    }
    else {
        return (other == this);
    }
}

@Override
public int hashCode() {
    if (getId() != null) {
        return Objects.hash(getId());
    }
    else {
        return super.hashCode();
    }
}
```

Note the bidirectional Class#isInstance() test in the equals() method. This is done instead of getClass() == other.getClass() because that would return false when your persistence framework uses proxies, such as Hibernate.

Custom Validators

Also, validators can be customized in Jakarta Faces from the beginning. As almost every basic use case is already covered by standard Jakarta Faces validators and even Jakarta Bean Validation constraints, such as length, range, and pattern validation, the most common use case left to a custom Jakarta Faces validator is validating the data integrity by testing the submitted value against database-based constraints. Generally, those concern unique constraints.

A good real-world example is validating during email-based sign-up or while changing the email address in the user account management page if the specified email address is not already in use. Particularly, the value change event can't be tested with a Jakarta Bean Validation constraint in a simple way because Jakarta Bean Validation doesn't offer any opportunity to compare the old value with the new value without reobtaining the entity from the database. In a Jakarta Faces validator, you can simply get the old value via the UIComponent argument. To start, implement the jakarta.faces.validator.Validator interface[23] accordingly.

```
@FacesValidator(value="project.UniqueEmailValidator", managed=true)
public class UniqueEmailValidator implements Validator<String> {

    @Inject
    private UserService userService;

    @Override
    public void validate
        (FacesContext context, UIComponent component, String email)
            throws ValidatorException
    {
        if (email == null || email.isEmpty()) {
            return; // Let @NotNull or required=true handle this.
        }

        String oldEmail = (String) ((UIInput) component).getValue();

        if (!email.equals(oldEmail) && userService.exist(email)) {
            throw new ValidatorException(
                new FacesMessage("Email already in use"));
        }
    }
}
```

---

[23] https://jakarta.ee/specifications/platform/10/apidocs/jakarta/faces/validator/Validator.html

The old value can simply be obtained from UIInput#getValue() that basically returns the current value attribute of the UIInput component. In order to get it to run, specify exactly the declared validator ID in the validator attribute of any EditableValueHolder component, or the validatorId attribute of any nested <f:validator> tag.

```
<h:inputText value="#{signup.user.email}"
    validator="project.UniqueEmailValidator">
</h:inputText>
```

When looking at the UniqueEmailValidator class, you'll notice that the annotation and the interface also got the same Jakarta Faces 2.3 changes as the converter. Like the @FacesConverter, the @FacesValidator annotation, since Jakarta Faces 2.3, also got a new managed attribute that should enable dependency injection in the validator implementation. And like the Converter<T>, the Validator<T> also got parameterized whereby the validate() method now takes a T instead of Object as a value argument.

You also need to make sure that your validators are implemented in such a way that they skip validation when the value argument is null or empty. Historically, in Jakarta Faces 1.x, the validate() method would always be skipped when the value argument is null. However, this has changed since the integration of Jakarta Bean Validation in Jakarta Faces 2.0, thereby breaking backward compatibility on existing Jakarta Faces 1.x–based custom validators. This breaking change could be turned off by explicitly setting the following web.xml context parameter:

```
<context-param>
    <param-name>jakarta.faces.VALIDATE_EMPTY_FIELDS</param-name>
    <param-value>false</param-value>
</context-param>
```

The disadvantage of this is that the @NotNull of Jakarta Bean Validation won't be triggered by Jakarta Faces and you'd basically need to repeat this constraint for all Jakarta Faces input components by explicitly setting their required attribute to true. You'd better not do this and just keep performing the null and empty check in your custom validator. Having validation constraints at a single place in the model with the help of Jakarta Bean Validation is more DRY (Don't Repeat Yourself) than repeating the validation constraints across different layers using the very same model.

Coming back to the use case of validating the uniqueness of the submitted value, of course, you could also skip this and insert the data anyway and catch any constraint violation exception coming from the persistence layer and display a faces message accordingly. However, this doesn't go well with the current trend of immediate feedback directly after changing the input field in the user interface.

In this specific use case of validating a unique email address during sign-up, however, there may be another reason not to give away too much detail about the uniqueness of the specified email address: security. In such a case, you'd best let the sign-up complete exactly the same way as if it was successful whereby you tell the user to check the mailbox but behind the scenes actually send a different email to the target recipient, rather than an activation email, preferably not more than once daily. The email would be similar to the following:

> *Dear user,*
>
> *It looks like you or someone else tried to sign up on our website using your email address* foo@example.com *while it is already associated with an existing account. Perhaps you actually wanted to log in or to reset your password? If it actually wasn't you, please let us know by replying to this email and we'll investigate this.*
>
> *Sincerely, Example Company*

Finally, you might also want to consider invalidating or deduplicating emails that contain the "+" character in the username part, followed by a sequence of characters, representing an email alias. For a lot of email providers, notably Gmail, email addresses foo@gmail.com and foo+bar@gmail.com refer to exactly the same email account, thereby basically allowing the end user to create a nearly unlimited amount of accounts.

Custom Constraints

While not part of the Jakarta Faces, for the sake of completeness, we'd like to show another example of a custom Jakarta Bean Validation constraint. An earlier example was already given in the section about `<f:validateWholeBean>`. The Jakarta Bean Validation API already offers a lot of existing constraints out of the box which you can find in the `jakarta.validation.constraints` package.[24]

---

[24] https://jakarta.ee/specifications/platform/10/apidocs/jakarta/validation/
constraints/package-summary.html

Most common use cases for a custom Jakarta Bean Validation constraint are related to localized patterns. Think of phone numbers, zip codes, bank account numbers, and passwords. Of course, most of those could be done with just a `@Pattern`, but this may end up in less self-documenting code, particularly if the desired pattern is relatively complex.

The following is an example of a custom @Phone constraint which should match as many as possible internationally known phone numbers:

```
@Constraint(validatedBy=PhoneValidator.class)
@Target(FIELD)
@Retention(RUNTIME)
public @interface Phone {
    String message() default "Invalid phone number";
    Class<?>[] groups() default {};
    Class<?>[] payload() default {};
}
```

And here's the associated PhoneValidator:

```
public class PhoneValidator
    implements ConstraintValidator<Phone, String>
{
    private static final Pattern SPECIAL_CHARS =
        Pattern.compile("[\\s().+-]|ext", Pattern.CASE_INSENSITIVE);
    private static final Pattern DIGITS =
        Pattern.compile("[0-9]{7,15}");

    @Override
    public boolean isValid
        (String phone, ConstraintValidatorContext context)
    {
        if (phone == null || phone.isEmpty()) {
            return true; // Let @NotNull/@NotEmpty handle this.
        }

        return isValid(phone);
    }
```

```
    public static boolean isValid(String phone) {
        String digits = SPECIAL_CHARS.matcher(phone).replaceAll("");
        return DIGITS.matcher(digits).matches();
    }
}
```

In order to activate it, simply annotate the associated entity property.

```
@Phone
private String phone;
```

This will be triggered on both the Jakarta Faces and Jakarta Persistence sides: in Jakarta Faces, during the process validations phase (third phase); in Jakarta Persistence, during the persist and merge. As noted in the `<f:validateBean>`/`<f:validateWholeBean>` section, it can be disabled on both sides.

Custom Messages

Conversion and validation error messages coming from Jakarta Faces as well as Jakarta Bean Validation are fully customizable. Application-wide, they can be customized by supplying a properties file that specifies the desired message as the value of a predefined key. You can find predefined keys for Jakarta Faces conversion and validation messages in Chapter 2.5.2.4, "Localized Application Messages," of the Jakarta Faces 4.0 specification.[25] You can find predefined keys for Jakarta Bean Validation messages in Appendix B, "Standard ResourceBundle Messages," of the Jakarta Bean Validation 3.0 specification.[26] For Jakarta Faces, the fully qualified name of the properties file must be registered as `<message-bundle>` in `faces-config.xml`. For Jakarta Bean Validation, the exact fully qualified name of the properties file is `ValidationMessages`.

As an example, we're going to modify the default message of the Jakarta Faces `required="true"` validation and the Jakarta Bean Validation `@NotNull` constraint.

main/java/resources/com/example/project/i18n/messages.properties
```
jakarta.faces.component.UIInput.REQUIRED = {0} is required.
```

---

[25] https://jakarta.ee/specifications/faces/4.0/jakarta-faces-4.0.pdf
[26] https://jakarta.ee/specifications/bean-validation/3.0/
jakarta-bean-validation-spec-3.0.html#standard-resolver-messages

```
jakarta.faces.validator.BeanValidator.MESSAGE = {1} {0}
```

main/java/resources/ValidationMessages.properties

```
jakarta.validation.constraints.NotNull.message = is required.
```

Note the absence of the label placeholder in the Jakarta Bean Validation message. Instead, the {1} of the `jakarta.faces.validator.BeanValidator.MESSAGE` represents the `label` associated with the Jakarta Faces component, and {0} represents the Jakarta Bean Validation message. The custom Jakarta Bean Validation message bundle file is already automatically picked up. The custom Jakarta Faces message bundle file needs to be explicitly registered in the `faces-config.xml` first.

```
<application>
    <message-bundle>com.example.project.i18n.messages</message-bundle>
</application>
```

With those properties files in place, the following input components will thus show exactly the same validation error message:

```
<h:inputText id="field" label="First input"
    value="#{bean.field}" required="true">
</h:inputText>
<h:message for="field" />

<h:inputText id="notNullField" label="Second input"
    value="#{bean.notNullField}">
</h:inputText>
<h:message for="notNullField" />
```

In case you want to fine-grain the message on a per-component basis, you can use the `converterMessage`, `validatorMessage`, and/or `requiredMessage` attribute of the `UIInput` component. The `converterMessage` will be displayed on any conversion error.

```
<h:inputText value="#{bean.localDate}"
    converterMessage="Please enter date in pattern YYYY-MM-DD.">
    <f:convertLocalDate type="localDate" pattern="yyyy-MM-dd" />
</h:inputText>
```

The `validatorMessage` will be displayed on any validation error, as well as those triggered by Jakarta Bean Validation.

```
<h:inputText value="#{bean.dutchZipCode}" required="true"
    validatorMessage="Please enter zip code in pattern 1234AB.">
    <f:validateRegex pattern="[0-9]{4}[A-Z]{2}" />
</h:inputText>
```

Note that this won't be shown when `required="true"` isn't satisfied. For that, you need to use `requiredMessage` instead.

```
<h:inputText value="#{bean.dutchZipCode}" required="true"
    requiredMessage="Please enter zip code."
    validatorMessage="Please enter zip code in pattern 1234AB.">
    <f:validateRegex pattern="[0-9]{4}[A-Z]{2}" />
</h:inputText>
```

Note that this won't be shown for any Jakarta Bean Validation @NotNull. You should then use `validatorMessage` instead.

CHAPTER 6

Output Components

Technically, the input components as described in Chapter 4 are also output components. They are not only capable of processing any submitted input values but they are also capable of outputting the model value during the render response phase (sixth phase). This is also visible in the Jakarta Faces API (application programming interface): the UIInput superclass extends from the UIOutput superclass.

There are also a bunch of components that merely output their model value or even just an HTML element. Those are the pure output components. They don't participate in all phases of the Jakarta Faces life cycle. Sometimes, they participate during the restore view phase (first phase), in case they are dynamically created or manipulated, but the majority of their job is executed during the render response phase (sixth phase), while generating the HTML output. During the other phases, they don't do many additional tasks.

Document-Based Output Components

These components are `<h:doctype>`, `<h:head>`, and `<h:body>`. Note that there's no such component as `<h:html>`. The `<h:doctype>` is arguably the least used HTML component of the entire standard Jakarta Faces HTML component set. You could get away with just a plain `<!DOCTYPE html>` element. The `<h:doctype>` is only useful when you want to have a pure XML representation of the `<!DOCTYPE>` element, which is generally only the case when you need to store entire Jakarta Faces views as part of another XML structure of some higher-level abstract layer around Jakarta Faces.

The `<h:head>` and `<h:body>` tags are the most important tags in Jakarta Faces. While generating the `<head>` and `<body>` elements of the HTML document doesn't require any special logic, those tags are mandatory for the proper automatic handling of JavaScript and CSS (Cascading Style Sheets) resource dependencies, also introduced in Jakarta Faces 2.0.

© Bauke Scholtz and Arjan Tijms 2022
B. Scholtz and A. Tijms, *The Definitive Guide to Jakarta Faces in Jakarta EE 10*,
https://doi.org/10.1007/978-1-4842-7310-4_6

The `<h:head>` and `<h:body>` allow Jakarta Faces to automatically relocate JavaScript and CSS resource dependencies to the right places in the component tree so that they ultimately end up in the right place in the generated HTML output. From the standard Jakarta Faces component set, only the `<h:commandLink>`, `<h:commandScript>`, `<f:ajax>`, and `<f:websocket>` utilize this facility. They all require the `faces.js` JavaScript file being included in the final HTML document. During the view build time, they will basically use `UIViewRoot#addComponentResource()`[1] to register the component resource dependency at the specified target component, which can be either `<h:head>` or `<h:body>`. During the view render time, the renderer associated with the `<h:head>` and `<h:body>` component will obtain all so far registered component resource dependencies by `UIViewRoot#g etComponentResources()`[2] and generate the appropriate `<link rel="stylesheet">` and `<script>` elements with a URL (uniform resource locator) referring the associated resource dependency.

As shown in the section "Standard HTML Components" in Chapter 3, the following code is what the most minimal and HTML5-valid Jakarta Faces page looks like:

```
<!DOCTYPE html>
<html lang="en" xmlns:h="jakarta.faces.html">
    <h:head>
        <title>Title</title>
    </h:head>
    <h:body>
        ...
    </h:body>
</html>
```

---

[1]https://jakarta.ee/specifications/platform/10/apidocs/jakarta/faces/component/
UIViewRoot.html#addComponentResource-jakarta.faces.context.FacesContext-jakarta.
faces.component.UIComponent-java.lang.String

[2]https://jakarta.ee/specifications/platform/10/apidocs/jakarta/faces/component/
UIViewRoot.html#getComponentResources-jakarta.faces.context.FacesContext-java.
lang.String

Text-Based Output Components

These components are `<h:outputText>`, `<h:outputFormat>`, `<h:outputLabel>`, and `<h:outputLink>`. They all extend from the UIOutput superclass and have a `value` attribute that can be bound to a managed bean property. During the view render time, the getter will be consulted to retrieve and display any preset value. These components will never invoke the setter method, and therefore, it could be safely left out of the managed bean class in order to reduce unused code.

Historically, in Jakarta Faces 1.x on Jakarta Pages, a `<h:outputText>` was mandatory in order to output a bean property as text. Jakarta Pages didn't support Jakarta Faces-style EL (Expression Language) #{...} in template text. Facelets supported Jakarta Faces–style EL #{...} in template text, and hence, bean properties could be outputted directly in Facelets without the need for a whole component. In other words, the following codes are equivalent in Facelets.

Using `<h:outputText>`:

```
<p>Welcome, <h:outputText value="#{user.name}" />!</p>
```

And using EL in template text:

```
<p>Welcome, #{user.name}!</p>
```

It doesn't need explanation that the latter code snippet is terser and readable. The `<h:outputText>` has, however, not become useless in Facelets. It's still useful for the following purposes:

- Disabling implicit HTML escaping

- Attaching an explicit converter

- Referencing in `<f:ajax render>`

Jakarta Faces has implicit HTML escaping everywhere. Anything outputted to the HTML response is checked on the HTML special characters "<", ">", "&", and optionally also """ when outputted within an attribute of an HTML element. Those HTML special characters will be replaced by "<", ">", "&", and """, respectively. The web browser will then not interpret those characters as part of the generated HTML output but as plain text and, ultimately, will present them as literal characters to the end user.

Imagine that a user chooses `<script>alert('xss')</script>` as a username, and it's emitted via `#{user.name}` through either one of the previously shown code snippets; then Jakarta Faces will render it as follows in the generated HTML output:

```
<p>Welcome, &lt;script&gt;alert('xss')&lt;/script&gt;!</p>
```

And the web browser will display it literally as "Welcome, <script>alert('xss')</script>!" instead of only "Welcome, !" along with a JavaScript alert with the text "xss" whereby the user-controlled JavaScript is unintentionally actually executed. The end user being able to execute arbitrary JavaScript code is dangerous. It would allow the malicious user to execute specific code that transfers information about session cookies to an external host when someone else logs in and views a page wherein the username of the malicious user is being rendered this way. (See also the section "Cross-Site Scripting Protection" in Chapter 13.)

On the other hand, there may also be cases whereby you'd like to embed safe HTML code in the generated HTML output. Most common use cases are related to posting messages for other users on a website, whereby a limited subset of formatting is allowed, such as bold, italics, links, lists, and headings. Generally, those are to be entered in a text area element using a predefined human-friendly markup format, such as Markdown, or the lesser known Wikicode, or the ancient BBCode.

```
<h:inputTextarea value="#{message.text}" />
```

The aforementioned markup formats are all capable of parsing the raw text with the markup and converting it to safe HTML code whereby any malicious HTML code is already escaped or stripped out. The raw text is at least always saved in the database for the record, and the resulting safe HTML code, along with the version of the parser used, can also be saved in the database for performance so that the parser doesn't need to be unnecessarily reexecuted for the same piece of raw text.

Given that we're going to use Markdown with CommonMark[3] and having the following `Markdown` interface:

```java
private interface Markdown {
    public String getText();
    public void setHtml(String html);
    public String getVersion();
    public void setVersion(String version);
}
```

---

[3] https://github.com/atlassian/commonmark-java

and the following MarkdownListener entity listener:

```java
public class MarkdownListener {
    private static final Parser PARSER = Parser.builder().build();
    private static final HtmlRenderer RENDERER =
        HtmlRenderer.builder().escapeHtml(true).build();
    private static final String VERSION = getCommonMarkVersion();

    @PrePersist
    public void parseMarkdown(Markdown markdown) {
        String html = RENDERER.render(PARSER.parse(markdown.getText()));
        markdown.setHtml(html);
        markdown.setVersion(VERSION);
    }

    @PreUpdate
    public void parseMarkdownIfNecessary(Markdown markdown) {
        if (markdown.getVersion() == null) {
            parseMarkdown(markdown);
        }
    }

    @PostLoad
    public void updateMarkdownIfNecessary(Markdown markdown) {
        if (!VERSION.equals(markdown.getVersion())) {
            parseMarkdown(markdown);
        }
    }

    private static String getCommonMarkVersion() {
        try {
            Properties properties = new Properties();
            properties.load(Parser.class.getResourceAsStream(
                "/META-INF/maven/com.atlassian.commonmark"
                    + "/commonmark/pom.properties"));
            return properties.getProperty("version");
        }
```

```
        catch (IOException e) {
            throw new UncheckedIOException(e);
        }
    }
}
```

then the Message entity implementing the Markdown interface and registered with the MarkdownListener entity listener can look as follows:

```
@Entity @EntityListeners(MarkdownListener.class)
public class Message implements Markdown, Serializable {

    @Id @GeneratedValue(strategy=IDENTITY)
    private Long id;

    @Column(nullable = false) @Lob
    private @NotNull String text;

    @Column(nullable = false) @Lob
    private String html;

    @Column(nullable = false, length = 8)
    private String version;

    @Override
    public void setText(String text) {
        if (!text.equals(this.text)) {
            this.text = text;
            setVersion(null); // Trigger for MarkdownListener @PreUpdate.
        }
    }

    // Add/generate remaining getters and setters.
}
```

Finally, in order to present the safe HTML code to the end user, you can use <h:outputText> with the escape attribute set to false, whereby you thus instruct Jakarta Faces that it doesn't need to implicitly HTML-escape the value.

```
<h:outputText value="#{message.html}" escape="false" />
```

Next to implicit HTML escaping, Jakarta Faces also supports implicit conversion. For any property type that is emitted via `<h:outputText>` or even EL in template text, Jakarta Faces will look up the converter by class, invoke its `Converter#getAsString()` method, and render the result. In case you want to explicitly use a specific or a different converter, then you have to replace any EL in template text by `<h:outputText>` and explicitly register the converter on it. Generally, it is those kinds of number- or datetime-related properties that need to be formatted in a locale-specific pattern.

```
<h:outputText value="#{product.price}">
    <f:convertNumber type="currency" locale="en_US" />
</h:outputText>
```

The last purpose of `<h:outputText>` is being able to reference a piece of inline text in `<f:ajax render>`. By default, `<h:outputText>` doesn't generate any HTML code. But if it has at least an attribute specified that must end up in the generated HTML output, such as `id` or `styleClass`, then it will generate an HTML `<span>` element. This is referenceable via JavaScript and thus useful for Ajax-updating specific parts of text. Of course, you could also opt for Ajax-updating some common container component, but this is far less efficient than Ajax-updating only specific parts that really need to be updated.

The `<h:outputFormat>` is an extension of `<h:outputText>` that parses the value using `java.text.MessageFormat` API[4] beforehand. This is particularly useful in combination with localized resource bundles. An example can be found in the section "Parameterized Resource Bundle Values" in Chapter 14.

The `<h:outputLabel>` basically generates the HTML `<label>` element, which is an essential part of HTML forms. This was already described in the section "Label and Message Components" in Chapter 4. It is important to note that the `<h:outputLabel>` and `<h:outputText>` are, in HTML perspective, absolutely not interchangeable. In a relatively recent burst of low-quality programming tutorial sites on the Internet that basically show code snippets without any technical explanation for the sake of advertisement incomes, the `<h:outputLabel>` is often incorrectly being used to output a piece of text in a Hello World Jakarta Faces page. Such tutorial sites can better be ignored entirely.

---

[4] https://docs.oracle.com/en/java/javase/15/docs/api/java.base/java/text/
MessageFormat.html

The <h:outputLink> generates an HTML <a> element. It's somewhat a leftover of Jakarta Faces 1.x and isn't terribly useful since the introduction of the much more useful <h:link> in Jakarta Faces 2.0. When you don't need to reference a Jakarta Faces view with a link, for which you'd use <h:link> instead, then you could as well just use a plain HTML <a> element instead of <h:outputLink>. The following tags generate exactly the same HTML:

```
<h:outputLink value="http://google.com">Google</h:outputLink>
<a href="http://google.com">Google</a>
```

The plain HTML equivalent is terser.

Navigation-Based Output Components

These components are <h:link> and <h:button>, both extending from the UIOutcomeTarget superclass. They have an outcome attribute that accepts a logical path to a Jakarta Faces view. The path will actually be validated if it's a valid Jakarta Faces view; otherwise, the link or button will be rendered as disabled. In other words, they don't accept a path to a non-Jakarta Faces resource, let alone an external URL. For this, you'd need <h:outputLink> or plain HTML <a> instead.

The <h:link> will generate an HTML <a> element with the URL of the target Jakarta Faces view specified as an href attribute. The <h:button> will generate an HTML <input type="button"> element with an onclick attribute that assigns, with the help of JavaScript, the URL of the target Jakarta Faces view to window.location.href property. This is indeed somewhat awkward, but that's just a limitation of HTML. Neither <input type="button"> nor <button> supports an href-like attribute.

Given the following folder structure of a Maven WAR project in Eclipse:

```
▼ 🗁 src
    ▼ 🗁 main
        ▸ 🗁 java
        ▸ 🗁 resources
        ▼ 🗁 webapp
            ▼ 🗁 folder1
                📄 page1.xhtml
                📄 page2.xhtml
            ▼ 🗁 folder2
                📄 page1.xhtml
                📄 page2.xhtml
            ▸ 🗁 WEB-INF
                📄 page1.xhtml
                📄 page2.xhtml
```

The following <h:link> and <a> pairs enclosed in /folder1/page1.xhtml will all generate exactly the same links in the HTML output.

```
<h:link outcome="page2" value="link1" />
<a href="#{request.contextPath}/folder1/page2.xhtml">link1</a>

<h:link outcome="/folder2/page1" value="link2" />
<a href="#{request.contextPath}/folder2/page1.xhtml">link2</a>

<h:link outcome="/folder2/page2" value="link3" />
<a href="#{request.contextPath}/folder2/page2.xhtml">link3</a>

<h:link outcome="/page1" value="link4" />
<a href="#{request.contextPath}/page1.xhtml">link4</a>

<h:link outcome="/page2" value="link5" />
<a href="#{request.contextPath}/page2.xhtml">link5</a>
```

Note thus that <h:link> already automatically prepends any context path of the web application project and appends the currently active URL pattern of the FacesServlet mapping. Also note that without the leading slash, the outcome is interpreted relative to the current folder, and with a leading slash, the outcome is interpreted relative to the context path.

Panel-Based Output Components

These components are the <h:panelGroup> and <h:panelGrid>, both extending from the UIPanel superclass. The <h:panelGroup> has multiple responsibilities. It can generate an HTML <span>, or <div>, or even <td>, depending on the layout attribute and whether it's enclosed in a <h:panelGrid>.

By default, the <h:panelGroup> generates just an HTML <span> element, exactly like <h:outputText>. The main difference is that the <h:panelGroup> doesn't have a value attribute. Instead, the content is represented by its children. It also doesn't support disabling HTML escaping or attaching a converter. That's up to any <h:outputText> child. In this context, it's not terribly useful. The <h:panelGroup> is only more useful than <h:outputText> when you need to be able to reference using <f:ajax render> an inline element that in turn groups a bunch of closely related inline elements. Something like the following that represents the "user profile," which should be Ajax updatable from within some sort of user profile edit form further down the page.

```
<p>
    Welcome,
    <h:panelGroup id="userProfile">
        <img src="#{user.imageUrl}" />
        #{user.name}
    </h:panelGroup>
</p>
...
<h:form>
    ...
    <f:ajax ... render=":userProfile" />
    ...
</h:form>
```

When setting the layout attribute of <h:panelGroup> to block, then it will generate an HTML <div> element. In standard HTML, "inline elements"[5] don't start at a new line by default and don't allow block element children. And "block-level elements"[6] always start at a new line by default and allow inline as well as block-level elements as children.

---

[5] https://developer.mozilla.org/en-US/docs/Web/HTML/Inline_elements
[6] https://developer.mozilla.org/en-US/docs/Web/HTML/Block-level_elements

Hence, the supported values of the layout attribute of <h:panelGroup> are "inline" and "block". Historically, the layout attribute was only added in Jakarta Faces 1.2 after complaints from Jakarta Faces developers about a missing Jakarta Faces component to represent an HTML <div> element. This could then be used to wrap larger block-level sections that need to be Ajax updatable; otherwise, a plain HTML <div> is also sufficient.

```
<h:panelGroup layout="block" id="userProfile">
    <p>
        Welcome,
        <img src="#{user.imageUrl}" />
        #{user.name}
    </p>
</h:panelGroup>
```

Note that it's illegal in HTML to have a block-level element nested in an inline element. The <p> is a block-level element, and hence, the layout="block" is absolutely mandatory in the preceding construct. If you don't specify this attribute and thus effectively let Jakarta Faces render an HTML <span> element, then the web browser behavior is unspecified. The average web browser will render the block-level element children outside the inline element and even possibly error out when this construct is traversed by JavaScript, because it wouldn't necessarily find the expected block-level children within an inline element.

Also keep in mind that in the preceding construct, the <p> tags and the "Welcome" text are also updated during any Jakarta Faces Ajax update action on the <h:panelGroup>. This is essentially a waste of hardware resources, on both the server side and the client side, as those are static and never subject to changes. When Ajax-updating things, you should preferably ensure that <f:ajax render> only references components that absolutely need to be Ajax-updated and thus not an unnecessarily large section that also covers static parts.

When the <h:panelGroup> is being nested in a <h:panelGrid> component, which generates an HTML <table> element, then the layout attribute of <h:panelGroup> is ignored, and the component will basically act as a container of components that should ultimately end up in the very same cell of the table. That is, the renderer of <h:panelGrid> considers every direct child component as an individual table cell.

Given the following two-column `<h:panelGrid>`, which should generate a two-column HTML table, what would you guess the actual generated HTML output would look like?

```
<h:panelGrid columns="2">
    one
    <h:outputText value="two" />
    three
    four
    <h:panelGroup>five</h:panelGroup>
    six
    seven
    <h:panelGroup>
        eight
        nine
    </h:panelGroup>
</h:panelGrid>
```

Each section of template text between two Jakarta Faces components is internally considered a single Jakarta Faces component. In Mojarra, it's represented by the internal `UIInstructions` component. After the view build time, the actual component tree hierarchy is thus roughly represented as follows:

```
<h:panelGrid columns="2">
    <ui:instructions>one</ui:instructions>
    <h:outputText value="two" />
    <ui:instructions>
        three
        four
    </ui:instructions>
    <h:panelGroup>five</h:panelGroup>
    <ui:instructions>
        six
        seven
    </ui:instructions>
```

```
    <h:panelGroup>
        eight
        nine
    </h:panelGroup>
</h:panelGrid>
```

Note again that there's no such component as <ui:instructions> in Facelets. The preceding markup is purely for visualization of the actual component tree hierarchy so that your brain can better process it. This <h:panelGrid> has thus effectively six direct children that will each end up in their own table cell. With two columns, this will thus effectively generate three rows. Here's the actual generated HTML output (reformatted for readability).

```
<table>
    <tbody>
        <tr>
            <td>one</td>
            <td>two</td>
        </tr>
        <tr>
            <td>three four</td>
            <td>five</td>
        </tr>
        <tr>
            <td>six seven</td>
            <td>eight nine</td>
        </tr>
    </tbody>
</table>
```

Rendering in Chrome browser:

one   two
three four five
six seven eight nine

You see, the `<h:panelGroup>` makes sure that "five" and "eight nine" don't end up in the very same table cell as "six seven." Also note that it's unnecessary to wrap any Jakarta Faces component in a `<h:panelGroup>` if it should represent a single cell already. That's why the `<h:outputText>` behind "two" didn't need to be wrapped in a `<h:panelGroup>`. You can, of course, do so for better readability of the source code, but this is technically unnecessary. The following code with explicit `<h:panelGroup>` declarations generates exactly the same HTML output, but it is undoubtedly better parsable by a human.

```
<h:panelGrid columns="2">
    <h:panelGroup>
        one
    </h:panelGroup>
    <h:panelGroup>
        two
    </h:panelGroup>

    <h:panelGroup>
        three
        four
    </h:panelGroup>
    <h:panelGroup>
        five
    </h:panelGroup>

    <h:panelGroup>
        six
        seven
    </h:panelGroup>
    <h:panelGroup>
        eight
        nine
    </h:panelGroup>
</h:panelGrid>
```

If you happen to have a dynamic amount of cells based on a view-scoped iterable model, then you can nest a Jakarta Tags `<c:forEach>` in `<h:panelGrid>` to have it generate them as a data grid with a fixed amount of columns.

```
<h:panelGrid columns="3">
    <c:forEach items="#{viewProducts.products}" var="product">
        <h:panelGroup>
            <h3>#{product.name}</h3>
            <p>#{product.description}</p>
        </h:panelGroup>
    </c:forEach>
</h:panelGrid>
```

Note thus that `<ui:repeat>` is unsuitable here as compared to `<c:forEach>`, as explained in the section "Jakarta Tags" in Chapter 3. It will technically work just fine, but the renderer of `<h:panelGrid>` will interpret it as a single table cell.

Also note that it's very important for this iterable model to be view scoped, particularly if you have Jakarta Faces form components inside `<h:panelGrid>`. The technical reason is that during processing the postback request, Jakarta Faces expects the iterated item behind the submitted iteration index to be exactly the same item as it was when the page was presented to the end user. In other words, when Jakarta Faces is about to process a form submit, and an item has been added or removed or even reordered in the meanwhile, causing its iteration index to be possibly changed, then the submitted values and/or the invoked action would possibly be performed against the wrong item currently at the initially known index. This is dangerous for the integrity of the model. If you don't have any Jakarta Faces form components inside `<h:panelGrid>`, or if the model isn't subject to changes during the view scope, e.g., because it's only created or updated during application startup, then the backing bean behind `#{viewProducts}` can safely be request scoped.

Data Iteration Component

There's only one, `<h:dataTable>`, which extends from the `UIData` superclass and generates an HTML `<table>` based on an iterable data model whereby each item is represented as a single row. The other data iteration component available in Jakarta Faces, the Facelets `<ui:repeat>`, doesn't extend from the `UIData` superclass and doesn't emit any HTML output and therefore doesn't technically count as an "output component." Also, in the standard Jakarta Faces component set, no such component generates an HTML `<ul>`, `<ol>`, or `<dl>`, but this can relatively easily be created as a custom component extending from `UIData` (see also the section "Creating New Component and Renderer" in Chapter 11).

215

The value attribute of UIData supports java.lang.Iterable. In other words, you can supply any Java collection as a model value. As index-based access is most used in UIData, most efficient is the java.util.ArrayList as it offers O(1) access by index. The renderer of the <h:dataTable> component supports only <h:column> as a direct child component. Anything else is ignored. As its name hints, <h:column> represents a single column. Each iteration round over the value of <h:dataTable> will basically re-render all columns against the currently iterated item. As with <c:forEach> and <ui:repeat>, the currently iterated item is exposed in EL scope by the var attribute. The following is a basic example that iterates over a List<String>.

```
<h:dataTable id="strings" value="#{bean.strings}" var="string">
    <h:column>#{string}</h:column>
</h:dataTable>
```

Backing bean class com.example.project.view.Bean:

```
@Named @RequestScoped
public class Bean {

    private List<String> strings;

    @PostConstruct
    public void init() {
        strings = Arrays.asList("one", "two", "three");
    }

    public List<String> getStrings() {
        return strings;
    }
}
```

Generated HTML output:

```
<table>
    <tbody>
        <tr><td>one</td></tr>
        <tr><td>two</td></tr>
        <tr><td>three</td></tr>
    </tbody>
</table>
```

Rendering in Chrome browser:

one

two

three

It is important to note that the variable name as specified by the var attribute shouldn't clash with existing managed bean names or even with implicit EL objects. Implicit EL objects have higher precedence in EL resolving. One example of an implicit EL object is #{header}, which refers to ExternalContext#getRequestHeaderMap().[7] So when you happen to have #{bean.headers} and you'd like to present it in an iterating component, then you can't use var="header" and you'd better think of a different name, such as var="head".

The following is a more elaborate example that shows a list of products. A similar table was shown earlier in the section "Custom Converters" in Chapter 5.

```
<h:dataTable id="products" value="#{products.list}" var="product">
    <h:column>
        <f:facet name="header">ID</f:facet>
        #{product.id}
    </h:column>
    <h:column>
        <f:facet name="header">Name</f:facet>
        #{product.name}
    </h:column>
    <h:column>
        <f:facet name="header">Description</f:facet>
        #{product.description}
    </h:column>
</h:dataTable>
```

---

[7]https://jakarta.ee/specifications/platform/10/apidocs/jakarta/faces/context/ExternalContext.html#getRequestHeaderMap

Backing bean class com.example.project.view.Products:

```
@Named @RequestScoped
public class Products {

    private List<Product> list;

    @Inject
    private ProductService productService;

    @PostConstruct
    public void init() {
        list = productService.list();
    }

    public List<Product> getList() {
        return list;
    }
}
```

Product entity: com.example.project.model.Product:

```
@Entity
public class Product {

    @Id @GeneratedValue(strategy=IDENTITY)
    private Long id;

    @Column(nullable = false)
    private @NotNull String name;

    @Column(nullable = false)
    private @NotNull String description;

    // Add/generate getters+setters.
}
```

Product service: com.example.project.service.ProductService:

```
@Stateless
public class ProductService {

    @PersistenceContext
    private EntityManager entityManager;

    @TransactionAttribute(SUPPORTS)
    public List<Product> list() {
        return entityManager
            .createQuery("FROM Product ORDER BY id DESC", Product.class)
            .getResultList();
    }
}
```

Generated HTML output:

```
<table>
    <thead>
        <tr>
            <th scope="col">ID</th>
            <th scope="col">Name</th>
            <th scope="col">Description</th>
        </tr>
    </thead>
    <tbody>
        <tr>
            <td>3</td>
            <td>Three</td>
            <td>The third product</td>
        </tr>
        <tr>
            <td>2</td>
            <td>Two</td>
            <td>The second product</td>
        </tr>
```

```
    <tr>
        <td>1</td>
        <td>One</td>
        <td>The first product</td>
    </tr>
  </tbody>
</table>
```

Rendering in Chrome browser:

```
3 Three The third product
2 Two   The second product
1 One   The first product
```

It is important to note that the iterable model behind the `value` attribute of `<h:dataTable>` must refer a bean property that is already prepared beforehand in a one-time life cycle event, such as `@PostConstruct` or `<f:viewAction>`. This doesn't apply specifically to `UIData` components but to basically every Jakarta Faces component. That is, the getter method may be invoked multiple times during the Jakarta Faces life cycle, especially when referenced in the `value` attribute of an iteration component or in the `rendered` attribute of any Jakarta Faces component.

The technical reason is that any EL value expression is, behind the scenes, created as a `jakarta.el.ValueExpression` instance which internally basically just holds the literal EL string as in `"#{products.list}"` and every single `ValueExpression#getValue()` call on it would simply reevaluate the expression against the provided EL context. This is normally a very cheap operation, done in nanoseconds, but it may slow down drastically when the getter method in turn performs a relatively expensive database query which may take tens or hundreds or even thousands of milliseconds.

Iteration components may invoke the getter method during every phase of the Jakarta Faces life cycle when the iteration component happens to have Jakarta Faces form components nested. When you prepare the iterable model by obtaining a list from the database in the getter method, then this would cause the database to be queried on every single getter method call, which is plainly inefficient. Moreover, the same problems with regard to resolving the iterated item of interest based on the submitted iteration index may occur as described in the last paragraph of the previous section about `<h:panelGrid>` with `<c:forEach>`.

Another thing to note is `<f:facet name="header">`. This generates basically a `<thead>` element with the content in a `<th>` element. The `<h:dataTable>` also supports `<f:facet name="footer">` which will then generate a `<tfoot>` element with the content in a `<td>` element. You can usually find all supported `<f:facet>` names in the tag documentation, as well as in the `<h:dataTable>` tag documentation.[8]

Basically, you can put anything inside `<h:column>` to represent the cell content. Even form components or a nested `<h:dataTable>` or `<ui:repeat>`. The following is a small example that shows a fictive `Set<Tag>` tags property of `Product` entity in a nested `<ui:repeat>`.

```
<h:dataTable id="products" value="#{products.list}" var="product">
    ...
    <h:column>
        <ui:repeat value="#{product.tags}" var="tag">
            #{tag.name}<br/>
        </ui:repeat>
    </h:column>
</h:dataTable>
```

Editable <h:dataTable>

As to form components nested inside `<h:column>`, you can substitute EL in template text with input components as follows:

```
<h:form id="list">
    <h:dataTable id="products" value="#{products.list}" var="product">
        <h:column>
            <f:facet name="header">ID</f:facet>
            #{product.id}
        </h:column>
        <h:column>
            <f:facet name="header">Name</f:facet>
            <h:inputText id="name" value="#{product.name}" />
            <h:message for="name" />
        </h:column>
```

---

[8]https://jakarta.ee/specifications/faces/4.0/vdldoc/facelets/h/dataTable.html

```
        <h:column>
            <f:facet name="header">Description</f:facet>
            <h:inputTextarea id="description"
                value="#{product.description}">
            </h:inputTextarea>
            <h:message for="description" />
        </h:column>
    </h:dataTable>
    <h:commandButton id="save" value="Save" action="#{products.save}">
        <f:ajax execute="@form" render="@form" />
    </h:commandButton>
</h:form>
```

whereby the save() method of the backing bean class basically looks as follows, after having changed the backing bean class to be a @ViewScoped one instead of a @RequestScoped one:

```
public void save() {
    productService.update(products);
}
```

And the update() method of the service class in turn looks as follows:

```
@TransactionAttribute(REQUIRED)
public void update(Iterable<Product> products) {
    products.forEach(entityManager::merge);
}
```

Note that you don't need to worry at all about collecting the submitted values. Jakarta Faces has already done that task for you. Also note that you don't need to worry about uniqueness of the component IDs within <h:dataTable>, as that component already implements the NamingContainer interface and prepends its own client ID and the iteration index to the client ID of the child components, as you can see in the following generated HTML output:

```
<table id="list:products">
    <thead>
        <tr>
            <th scope="col">ID</th>
```

```
            <th scope="col">Name</th>
            <th scope="col">Description</th>
        </tr>
    </thead>
    <tbody>
        <tr>
            <td>3</td>
            <td>
                <input id="list:products:0:name" type="text"
                    name="list:products:0:name" value="Three">
                </input>
            </td>
            <td>
                <textarea id="list:products:0:description"
                    name="list:products:0:description"
                >The third product</textarea>
            </td>
        </tr>
        <tr>
            <td>2</td>
            <td>
                <input id="list:products:1:name" type="text"
                    name="list:products:1:name" value="Two">
                </input>
            </td>
            <td>
                <textarea id="list:products:1:description"
                    name="list:products:1:description"
                >The second product</textarea>
            </td>
        </tr>
        <tr>
            <td>1</td>
```

```
            <td>
                <input id="list:products:2:name" type="text"
                    name="list:products:2:name" value="One">
                </input>
            </td>
            <td>
                <textarea id="list:products:2:description"
                    name="list:products:2:description"
                >The first product</textarea>
            </td>
        </tr>
    </tbody>
</table>
```

It must be said that having an editable table like this is not terribly efficient, certainly not when the table contains a lot of columns and rows. Jakarta Faces can handle it pretty well; only the average web browser will have a hard time handling it, certainly when the number of rows exceeds a few thousand. And then I'm not speaking about the end user potentially going crazy from scrolling through the whole page all the time and basically having no clear overview. There are several solutions to this: first and foremost is pagination; second is filtering; third is row-based inline editing and updating; and fourth is external editing in a dialog or detail page.

All the mentioned table-specific performance and usability solutions are not offered by the standard `<h:dataTable>` and therefore require quite an amount of custom code. It's strongly recommended that you look for an existing Jakarta Faces component library supporting these features in order to make your Jakarta Faces life easier without the need to reinvent the wheel. Currently, the most widely used one is PrimeFaces with its `<p:dataTable>`.[9] This can even be further simplified with `<op:dataTable>` of OptimusFaces,[10] which is in turn based on `<p:dataTable>`. Editing the selected item in a detail page is doable with standard Jakarta Faces, and it's demonstrated in the "Custom Converters" section in Chapter 5.

---

[9] https://www.primefaces.org/showcase/ui/data/datatable/basic.xhtml
[10] https://github.com/omnifaces/optimusfaces

It should be said that in the specific case of a List<String> as model value, using input components in columns isn't as easily done as demonstrated with the List<Product> example. In other words, the following example won't work at all:

```
<h:form>
    <h:dataTable value="#{bean.strings}" var="string">
        <h:column>
            <h:inputText value="#{string}" />
        </h:column>
    </h:dataTable>
    <h:commandButton value="Save" action="#{bean.save}">
        <f:ajax execute="@form" />
    </h:commandButton>
</h:form>
```

The technical problem is that java.lang.String is immutable and doesn't have a public setter method for its internal value. True, it indeed actually also doesn't have a getter method, but EL already defaults to Object#toString() which in case of String just returns the very string itself. This can be solved by explicitly referencing the specific item of the model value using an index as follows:

```
<h:form>
    <h:dataTable binding="#{table}" value="#{bean.strings}" var="string">
        <h:column>
            <h:inputText value="#{bean.strings[table.rowIndex]}" />
        </h:column>
    </h:dataTable>
    <h:commandButton value="Save" action="#{bean.save}">
        <f:ajax execute="@form" />
    </h:commandButton>
</h:form>
```

Note the binding attribute. Basically, during the view build time, this sets the current UIComponent instance as an EL variable identified by the given name. In this particular snippet, it will thus make the #{table} variable to reference the concrete HtmlDataTable instance behind the <h:dataTable> tag. The #{table} variable is during the view build time referenceable only after the tag location in the view and during the view render time referenceable anywhere in the view. In this way, you can access the UIComponent properties as if it were a bean. The #{table.rowIndex} basically thus refers to the UIData#getRowIndex() method,[11] which returns the current iteration index. And, finally, this is used to reference the item of interest in the list. During the update model values phase (fourth phase), Jakarta Faces will simply replace the item at the specified index.

Also for the binding attribute, it's very important that the variable name shouldn't clash with existing managed bean names or implicit EL objects and for sure not with other components in the same view. You can alternatively let the binding attribute reference a backing bean property as follows:

```
<h:dataTable binding="#{bean.table}" ...>
```

with

```
private UIData table; // +getter +setter
```

But this is fairly useless if it isn't used anywhere else in the backing bean. Moreover, this is dangerous when the managed bean scope is wider than request (see also the section "View Build Time" in Chapter 3). It is better not to bind component instances to a backing bean at all; it might indicate a poor practice. The only reasonable real-world use case for this is binding composite component children to a backing component (see also the section "Composite Components" in Chapter 7).

In case you're using <ui:repeat> or <c:forEach> instead of <h:dataTable> on something like a List<String>, then you can obtain the iteration index in a much simpler way, via the varStatus attribute.

```
<h:form>
    <ui:repeat value="#{bean.strings}" var="string" varStatus="loop">
        <h:inputText value="#{bean.strings[loop.index]}" /><br/>
    </ui:repeat>
    <h:commandButton value="Save" action="#{bean.save}">
        <f:ajax execute="@form" />
    </h:commandButton>
</h:form>
```

---

[11] https://jakarta.ee/specifications/platform/10/apidocs/jakarta/faces/component/
UIData.html#getRowIndex

Add/Remove Rows in <h:dataTable>

Coming back to the <h:dataTable> with List<Product>, there may be cases in which you'd like to be able to add or remove items while staying in the same view, usually in some sort of an admin page. In order to add a new Product, we need to prepare a new instance in the managed bean, fill it in a separate form, persist it, and then refresh the table.

```
<h:form id="list">
    <h:dataTable id="products" value="#{products.list}" ...>
        ...
    </h:dataTable>
</h:form>
<h:form id="add">
    <h:outputLabel for="name" value="Name" />
    <h:inputText id="name" value="#{products.product.name}" />
    <h:message for="name" />
    <h:outputLabel for="description" value="Description" />
    <h:inputTextarea id="description"
        value="#{products.product.description}">
    </h:inputTextarea>
    <h:message for="description" />
    <h:commandButton id="add" value="Add" action="#{products.add}">
        <f:ajax execute="@form" render="@form :list:products" />
    </h:commandButton>
</h:form>
```

whereby the relevant backing bean code looks as follows:

```
private List<Product> list; // +getter
private Product product = new Product(); // +getter

@PostConstruct
public void init() {
    list = productService.list();
}
```

```
public void add() {
    productService.create(product);
    list.add(0, product);
    product = new Product();
}
```

with this create() method in service class:

```
@TransactionAttribute(REQUIRED);
public Long create(Product product) {
    entityManager.persist(product);
    return product.getId();
}
```

Removing could be done in several ways. In any case, you may need an additional column to hold the submit buttons or radio buttons or check boxes. The easiest way is a column with a command button that deletes the currently iterated item and then refreshes the table.

```
<h:form id="list">
    <h:dataTable id="products" value="#{products.list}" var="product">
        ...
        <h:column>
            <h:commandButton id="delete" value="Delete"
                action="#{products.delete(product)}">
                <f:ajax render="@namingcontainer" />
            </h:commandButton>
        </h:column>
    </h:dataTable>
</h:form>
```

with this delete(Product) method in a @ViewScoped backing bean class:

```
public void delete(Product product) {
    productService.delete(product);
    list.remove(product);
}
```

and this delete() method in service class:

```
@TransactionAttribute(REQUIRED)
public void delete(Product product) {
    if (entityManager.contains(product)) {
        entityManager.remove(product);
    }
    else {
        Product managedProduct = getById(product.getId());

        if (managedProduct != null) {
            entityManager.remove(managedProduct);
        }
    }
}
```

Note the render attribute of <f:ajax>. It specifies @namingcontainer, which basically references the closest parent NamingContainer component. From the standard Jakarta Faces HTML component set, only <h:form> and <h:dataTable> are instances of NamingContainer. In this specific construct, @namingcontainer thus references the <h:dataTable>. You could also have used <f:ajax render=":list:products"> instead; it's only slightly verbose. The <f:ajax render="products"> wouldn't work because it will try to find it within the context of the currently iterated row, which is basically within all <h:column> components.

Select Rows in <h:dataTable>

Having a radio button column in a <h:dataTable> is natively possible since Jakarta Faces 2.3, thanks to the new group attribute of the <h:selectOneRadio> (see also the section "Selection Components" in Chapter 4).

```
<h:form id="list">
    <h:dataTable id="products" value="#{products.list}" var="product">
        <h:column>
            <h:selectOneRadio id="selected" group="selected"
                value="#{products.selected}">
                <f:selectItem itemValue="#{product}" />
```

```
            </h:selectOneRadio>
        </h:column>
        ...
    </h:dataTable>
    <h:commandButton id="deleteSelected" value="Delete selected product"
        action="#{products.deleteSelected}">
        <f:ajax execute="@form" render="products" />
    </h:commandButton>
</h:form>
```

With this deleteSelected() method in a @ViewScoped backing bean class:

```
private Product selected; // +getter +setter

public void deleteSelected() {
    productService.delete(selected);
    list.remove(selected);
}
```

Note that you need a ProductConverter or BaseEntityConverter here as well.
Those are elaborated in the section "Custom Converters" in Chapter 5.

The check box selection is a little more convoluted. You'd intuitively grab
<h:selectManyCheckbox>, but this doesn't support the group attribute as
<h:selectOneRadio> does. You'd need to fall back to <h:selectBooleanCheckbox> with
a Map<Product, Boolean> whereby the map key represents the currently iterated product
and the map value represents the check box value.

```
<h:form id="list">
    <h:dataTable id="products" value="#{products.list}" var="product">
        <h:column>
            <h:selectBooleanCheckbox id="selection"
                value="#{products.selection[product]}">
            </h:selectBooleanCheckbox>
        </h:column>
        ...
    </h:dataTable>
```

```
<h:commandButton id="deleteSelected" value="Delete selected products"
    action="#{products.deleteSelected}">
    <f:ajax execute="@form" render="products" />
</h:commandButton>
</h:form>
```

The modified deleteSelected() method in the @ViewScoped backing bean looks as follows:

```
private Map<Product, Boolean> selection = new HashMap<>(); // +getter

public void deleteSelected() {
    List<Product> selected = selection.entrySet().stream()
        .filter(Entry::getValue)
        .map(Entry::getKey)
        .collect(Collectors.toList());
    productService.delete(selected);
    selected.forEach(list::remove);
    selection.clear();
}
```

The overloaded ProductService#delete(Iterable) method looks as follows:

```
@TransactionAttribute(REQUIRED)
public void delete(Iterable<Product> products) {
    products.forEach(this::delete);
}
```

Dynamic Columns in <h:dataTable>

In a <h:dataTable>, with the help of Jakarta Tags <c:forEach>, it is also possible to dynamically create multiple <h:column> instances based on a Java model that is at least view scoped. A request-scoped model can also, but this doesn't guarantee that it is during a postback request exactly the same as it was during the preceding request, and therefore there is a risk of the dynamic <h:column> composition being off.

The value of the `<c:forEach>` should reference a collection of entity property names or map keys. You can then use the brace notation in EL as in #{entity[propertyName]} or #{map[key]} to reference the actual value. This works for both UIOutput and UIInput components. The following example illustrates how you could achieve this for a List<Product>.

Backing bean:

```
@Named @RequestScoped
public class Products {
    private List<Product> list;
    private List<String> properties;

    @Inject
    private ProductService productService;

    @PostConstruct
    public void init() {
        list = productService.list();
        properties = Arrays.asList("id", "name", "description");
    }

    // Add/generate getters (setters not needed here).
}
```

Facelets file:

```
<h:dataTable value="#{products.list}" var="product">
    <c:forEach items="#{products.properties}" var="property">
        <h:column>#{product[property]}</h:column>
    </c:forEach>
</h:dataTable>
```

You could even generalize this further for other entities of a common superclass, such as BaseEntity, whereby you obtain the relevant property names from the entity service.

Resource Components

Jakarta Faces offers three resource components, the `<h:graphicImage>`, `<h:outputScript>`, and `<h:outputStylesheet>`, for image resources, JavaScript resources, and CSS resources, respectively. They can reference physical resource files as well as dynamic resource files. The physical resource files themselves must be placed in the `/resources` subfolder of the main web folder. The dynamic resource files can be handled with a custom `ResourceHandler` that intercepts on a specific library name and/or resource name. Given the following folder structure in a Maven WAR project in Eclipse:

```
▼ ⬒ src
    ▼ ⬒ main
        ▸ ⬒ java
        ▸ ⬒ resources
        ▼ ⬒ webapp
            ▼ ⬒ resources
                ▼ ⬒ images
                    ▣ some.svg
                ▼ ⬒ scripts
                    ▤ some.js
                ▼ ⬒ styles
                    ▤ some.css
            ▸ ⬒ WEB-INF
```

the resources are referenceable as follows:

```
<h:graphicImage name="images/some.svg" />
<h:outputScript name="scripts/some.js" />
<h:outputStylesheet name="styles/some.css" />
```

The generated HTML output looks as follows, provided that `/project` is the context path of the web application:

```
<img src="/project/jakarta.faces.resource/images/some.svg.xhtml" />
<script type="text/javascript"
src="/project/jakarta.faces.resource/scripts/some.js.xhtml"></script>
<link type="text/css" rel="stylesheet"
    href="/project/jakarta.faces.resource/styles/some.css.xhtml" />
```

You'll see that it's prefixed with `/jakarta.faces.resource` path and suffixed with the currently active URL pattern of the `FacesServlet`. The `/jakarta.faces.resource` is represented by the constant `ResourceHandler#RESOURCE_IDENTIFIER`.[12] That the resource URL matches the URL pattern of the `FacesServlet` ensures that it will actually invoke the `FacesServlet` which in turn knows how to handle the resource. It will first invoke `ResourceHandler#isResourceRequest()`, which by default determines if the URL prefix starts with the known `RESOURCE_IDENTIFIER` constant and if so then immediately delegates to `ResourceHandler#handleResourceRequest()` instead of going through the entire Jakarta Faces life cycle.

Also note that these web resources are not placed in the `src/main/resources` folder but in the `src/main/webapp/resources` folder. The `src/main/resources` folder is only for non-class resources that must end up in the classpath, such as resource bundle files and configuration properties files. These classpath resources are obtainable by `ClassLoader#getResource()`.[13] The `src/main/webapp/resources` doesn't end up in the classpath; instead, it ends up in the web content. These web resources are obtainable by `ExternalContext#getResource()`,[14] which delegates under the hood to `ServletContext#getResource()`.[15]

The `name` attribute thus basically represents the path to the resource relative to the `src/main/webapp/resources` folder. These components also support a `library` attribute. The `library` attribute must represent the unique resource library name of a Jakarta Faces library. For standard Jakarta Faces, the resource library name is "`jakarta.faces`"; for PrimeFaces,[16] the resource library name is "`primefaces`"; for OmniFaces,[17] the resource library name is "`omnifaces`"; for BootsFaces,[18] the resource library name is "`bsf`"; and so on. Normally, these library-specific resources are already automatically included by the Jakarta Faces library in question, usually declaratively via the

---

[12] https://jakarta.ee/specifications/platform/10/apidocs/jakarta/faces/application/ResourceHandler.html#RESOURCE_IDENTIFIER

[13] https://docs.oracle.com/en/java/javase/17/docs/api/java.base/java/lang/ClassLoader.html#getResource(java.lang.String)

[14] https://jakarta.ee/specifications/platform/10/apidocs/jakarta/faces/context/ExternalContext.html#getResource-java.lang.String

[15] https://jakarta.ee/specifications/platform/10/apidocs/jakarta/servlet/ServletContext.html#getResource-java.lang.String

[16] https://primefaces.org

[17] https://omnifaces.org

[18] https://bootsfaces.net

@ResourceDependency annotation on the UIComponent or Renderer class and sometimes programmatically via UIViewRoot#addComponentResource(). This is elaborated in the section "Resource Dependencies" in Chapter 11. Those resources can, if necessary, be referenced using a resource component whereby you thus explicitly specify the library attribute.

The following example explicitly includes the standard Jakarta Faces faces.js file:

```
<h:head>
    ...
    <h:outputScript library="jakarta.faces" name="faces.js" />
</h:head>
```

This is usually unnecessary as the Jakarta Faces components depending on this script, such as <h:commandLink>, <f:ajax>, and <f:websocket>, already automatically include it. Here's another example that explicitly includes the jquery.js file from the PrimeFaces library—this works of course only if you actually have PrimeFaces installed.

```
<h:head>
    ...
    <h:outputScript library="primefaces" name="jquery/jquery.js" />
</h:head>
```

This approach can be useful when you'd like to reuse the PrimeFaces-provided jQuery library on a page that doesn't necessarily contain any PrimeFaces component, for example, when you have some web project–specific scripts that in turn depend on jQuery. By default, all PrimeFaces components automatically include this jQuery library, but that thus won't happen if the page doesn't contain any PrimeFaces component. The Jakarta Faces resource management will already make sure that both automatically included and explicitly included JavaScript and CSS resources don't get duplicated in the generated HTML output. In other words, the preceding line that explicitly includes jQuery can safely be used on a page that does actually contain a PrimeFaces component.

Note that there are currently a relatively large number of poor-quality Jakarta Faces tutorials on the Internet that don't correctly use the library attribute. Instead, those tutorials incorrectly demonstrate the library attribute to represent the subfolder within the src/main/webapp/resources folder, something like the following:

```
<h:graphicImage library="images" name="some.svg" />
<h:outputScript library="scripts" name="some.js" />
<h:outputStylesheet library="styles" name="some.css" />
```

This is outright wrong. It doesn't offer the custom resource handler any possibility to distinguish library-specific resources from each other. In the previous example, you'd basically need to check three different resource libraries even though all those resources belong to the very same library–the web project itself.

Talking about custom resource handlers, imagine that you want to compel the web browser to forcibly reload the image, JavaScript, and/or CSS resource when it has changed in the server side. This can be achieved by adding a query string parameter to the resource URL whose value represents the version of the resource. This is also called "cache busting." In Jakarta Faces, this can be achieved with the following example of a custom ResourceHandler that decorates the Resource to return its last modified timestamp as a query string parameter.

```
public class VersionResourceHandler extends ResourceHandlerWrapper {

    public VersionResourceHandler(ResourceHandler wrapped) {
        super(wrapped);
    }

    @Override
    public Resource createResource(String name, String library) {
        Resource resource = super.createResource(name, library);

        if (resource == null || library != null) {
            return resource;
        }

        return new ResourceWrapper(resource) {

            @Override
            public String getRequestPath() {
                String url = super.getRequestPath();
                return url
                    + (url.contains("?") ? "&" : "?")
                    + "v=" + getLastModified();
            }
```

```java
        private long getLastModified() {
            try {
                return getWrapped().getURL()
                    .openConnection().getLastModified();
            }
            catch (IOException ignore) {
                return 0;
            }
        }
    };
  }
}
```

In order to activate it, register it in the `faces-config.xml` as follows:

```xml
<application>
    <resource-handler>
        com.example.project.resourcehandler.VersionResourceHandler
    </resource-handler>
</application>
```

Note that the `createResource()` method returns the created resource unmodified when it's `null`, or when the `library` is not `null`. The resource itself is `null` when the name is unknown. The `library` is `null` when it's unspecified and thus specific to the web project. You could of course also apply this logic to all resources of other libraries, but they usually already have their own internal implementation of this kind of a resource handler.

Coming back to the resource components, you can place the `<h:graphicImage>` only inside the body, which can be both the plain HTML `<body>` or the Jakarta Faces `<h:body>`. Obviously, in a plain HTML document, you can have an `<img>` element only inside the document body. You can place the `<h:outputScript>` and `<h:outputStylesheet>` basically anywhere in the Jakarta Faces page. The `<h:outputScript>` will by default generate the HTML `<script>` element at exactly the declared location, regardless of being in the head or the body of the document. The `<h:outputStylesheet>`, however, will by default be moved to the end of `<h:head>` when declared inside `<h:body>`. That is because in HTML, it's illegal to have a `<link rel="stylesheet">` outside the `<head>`. The `<h:outputScript>` can also be automatically moved to the end of the document head when declared inside the <h:body> with the target attribute set to head. When the target attribute of the <h:outputScript> is set to body, then it will be automatically moved to the end of the document body. The <h:outputStylesheet> doesn't support it. In other words, the following test Facelet:

```
<h:head>
    <title>Resource component relocation demo.</title>
    <h:outputStylesheet name="style1.css" />
    <h:outputScript name="script1.js" />
    <h:outputScript name="script2.js" target="head" />
    <h:outputScript name="script3.js" target="body" />
</h:head>
<h:body>
    <p>Paragraph 1</p>
    <h:outputStylesheet name="style2.css" />
    <h:outputScript name="script4.js" />
    <h:outputScript name="script5.js" target="head" />
    <h:outputScript name="script6.js" target="body" />
    <p>Paragraph 2</p>
</h:body>
```

will basically generate the following HTML output (URLs simplified for brevity):

```
<head>
    <title>Resource component relocation demo.</title>
    <script type="text/javascript" src="script1.js"></script>
    <link type="text/css" rel="stylesheet" href="style1.css" />
    <script type="text/javascript" src="script2.js"></script>
    <link type="text/css" rel="stylesheet" href="style2.css" />
    <script type="text/javascript" src="script5.js"></script>
</head>
<body>
    <p>Paragraph 1</p>
    <script type="text/javascript" src="script4.js"></script>
    <p>Paragraph 2</p>
```

```
<script type="text/javascript" src="script3.js"></script>
<script type="text/javascript" src="script6.js"></script>
</body>
```

In other words, the resource rendering order in the document head is

1. `<h:outputScript>` from `<h:head>` without `target`

2. `<h:outputStylesheet>` from `<h:head>`

3. `<h:outputScript>` from `<h:head>` with `target="head"`

4. `<h:outputStylesheet>` from `<h:body>`

5. `<h:outputScript>` from `<h:body>` with `target="head"`

Note that `<h:outputStylesheet>` implicitly infers `target="head"` and is therefore rendered *after* `<h:outputScript>` without any target. All JavaScript and CSS resources that are automatically included via the `@ResourceDependency` annotation of components will end up between the resources declared in `<h:head>` and those declared in `<h:body>`. So if you happen to use a Jakarta Faces library that automatically includes a bunch of CSS resources, and you'd like to override some of them, then you'd best put such `<h:outputStylesheet>` in the `<h:body>` instead of in the `<h:head>` so that you can guarantee that it's loaded *after* the library's CSS resources.

Beware though, some Jakarta Faces libraries will automatically override the default renderer of `<h:head>` that may mess up the default resource ordering. In such a case, you'd best consult the documentation of the Jakarta Faces library in question for new ordering rules, or to restore the default renderer of `<h:head>` via the web project's `faces-config.xml`.

```
<render-kit>
    <renderer>
        <component-family>jakarta.faces.Output</component-family>
        <renderer-type>jakarta.faces.Head</renderer-type>
        <renderer-class>
            com.sun.faces.renderkit.html_basic.HeadRenderer
        </renderer-class>
    </renderer>
</render-kit>
```

In case you're using MyFaces instead of Mojarra as Jakarta Faces implementation, then use `org.apache.myfaces.renderkit.html.HtmlHeadRenderer` instead as the renderer class.

In case you intend to develop such a Jakarta Faces library that automatically includes specific resources, then keep in mind to use `@ResourceDependency` or `UIViewRoot#addComponentResource()` instead of replacing the default renderer of `<h:head>` for the purpose. As annotations don't allow specifying dynamic values, any dynamic resources can best be added during the `PostAddToView` event of `<h:head>`. This can be achieved application-wide with a `SystemEventListener` as follows assuming that your library's resource library name is "foo":

```
public class DynamicResourceListener implements SystemEventListener {

    private static final String LIBRARY = "foo";

    @Override
    public boolean isListenerForSource(Object source) {
        UIOutput output = (UIOutput) source;
        return "jakarta.faces.Head".equals(output.getRendererType());
    }

    @Override
    public void processEvent(SystemEvent event) {
        FacesContext context = event.getFacesContext();
        String scriptName = "foo.js"; // Can be dynamic.
        addResource(context, scriptName);
        String stylesheetName = "foo.css"; // Can be dynamic.
        addResource(context, stylesheetName);
    }

    private void addResource(FacesContext context, String name) {
        UIComponent resource = new UIOutput();
        resource.getAttributes().put("library", LIBRARY);
        resource.getAttributes().put("name", name);
        resource.setRendererType(context.getApplication()
            .getResourceHandler().getRendererTypeForResourceName(name));
```

```
        context.getViewRoot()
            .addComponentResource(context, resource, "head");
    }
}
```

which is registered in `faces-config.xml` as follows:

```
<system-event-listener>
    <system-event-listener-class>
        com.example.project.listener.DynamicResourceListener
    </system-event-listener-class>
    <system-event-class>
        jakarta.faces.event.PostAddToViewEvent
    </system-event-class>
    <source-class>
        jakarta.faces.component.UIOutput
    </source-class>
</system-event-listener>
```

Note that `<source-class>` could better have been a `jakarta.faces.component.html.HtmlHead`, but this doesn't necessarily work across all Jakarta Faces implementations. In, for example, Mojarra, `<h:head>` implicitly creates an instance of `UIOutput` instead of `HtmlHead`.

Once installed, this `DynamicResourceListener` will result in the following HTML output for exactly the last shown test Facelet with `style1.css`, `script1.js`, `script2.js`, etc. (also here, URLs are simplified for brevity).

```
<head>
    <title>Resource component relocation demo.</title>
    <script type="text/javascript" src="script1.js"></script>
    <script type="text/javascript" src="foo.js"></script>
    <link type="text/css" rel="stylesheet" href="foo.css" />
    <link type="text/css" rel="stylesheet" href="style1.css" />
    <script type="text/javascript" src="script2.js"></script>
    <link type="text/css" rel="stylesheet" href="style2.css" />
    <script type="text/javascript" src="script5.js"></script>
</head>
```

```
<body>
    <p>Paragraph 1</p>
    <script type="text/javascript" src="script4.js"></script>
    <p>Paragraph 2</p>
    <script type="text/javascript" src="script3.js"></script>
    <script type="text/javascript" src="script6.js"></script>
</body>
```

The resource rendering order in the document head is thus

1. `<h:outputScript>` from `<h:head>` without `target`

2. Dynamic script added to `head` during `PostAddToView`

3. Dynamic stylesheet added to `head` during `PostAddToView`

4. `<h:outputStylesheet>` from `<h:head>`

5. `<h:outputScript>` from `<h:head>` with `target="head"`

6. `<h:outputStylesheet>` from `<h:body>`

7. `<h:outputScript>` from `<h:body>` with `target="head"`

You see, the ordering is quite predictable. It shouldn't have been necessary to override the renderer of `<h:head>`. Moreover, overriding the renderer of `<h:head>` from a Jakarta Faces library risks the possibility that it becomes incompatible with any other Jakarta Faces library that coincidentally also overrides the renderer of `<h:head>`. You'd really want to avoid that.

Another advantage of using resource components is that Jakarta Faces can this way automatically push all resources associated with the page to the client so that the client will be able to retrieve them sooner than the time needed to parse the HTML document and locate all `<link>`, `<script>`, and `<img>` elements. This is new since Jakarta Faces 2.3. This only requires that the Jakarta Faces 2.3 web application is deployed to a Servlet 4.0–compatible container (Payara 5, GlassFish 5, Tomcat 9, WildFly 12, etc.), and that HTTPS is being used instead of HTTP, and that the client supports HTTP/2 protocol.[19] This does not require additional configuration from the Jakarta Faces side on.

---

[19] `https://caniuse.com/#feat=http2`

Pass-Through Elements

Jakarta Faces also supports implicitly interpreting any arbitrary HTML element as a full-fledged Jakarta Faces component. This feature was introduced in Jakarta Faces 2.2 and is formally known as "pass-through elements." This is particularly useful when you want to use HTML5 elements such as `<main>`, `<article>`, `<section>`, `<aside>`, `<nav>`, `<header>`, and `<footer>` and you want to be able to reference them in `<f:ajax render>`. Previously, before Jakarta Faces 2.2, those elements didn't have a Jakarta Faces component equivalent and you're therefore forced to wrap them in `<h:panelGroup layout="block">` that only makes the generated HTML output less semantic. The pass-through element trigger is available by the `jakarta.faces` namespace. All you need to do is to specify at least one attribute on this namespace. The default namespace prefix is just "`faces`".

```
<!DOCTYPE html>
<html lang="en"
    xmlns:faces="jakarta.faces"
    xmlns:h="jakarta.faces.html"
>
    <h:head>
        <title>Title</title>
    </h:head>
    <h:body>
        <header>
            ...
            <nav faces:id="menu">
                ...
            </nav>
        </header>
        <main faces:id="main">
            ...
        </main>
        <footer>
            ...
        </footer>
    </h:body>
</html>
```

Under the hood, in the Jakarta Faces component tree, those HTML5 elements are turned into a `UIPanel` component and are treated in the Jakarta Faces component tree exactly like `<h:panelGroup>`. This way you can cleanly keep using semantic HTML5 markup while still being able to reference them via `<f:ajax render>`. In other words, the following construct won't work:

```
<main id="main">
    ...
    <h:form id="form">
        ...
        <h:commandButton id="submit" ...>
            <f:ajax render=":main" />
        </h:commandButton>
    </h:form>
</main>
```

It fails because `UIViewRoot#findComponent()` doesn't return anything when passing "`main`" as search keyword. Jakarta Faces can't find any component with the given ID. The `<main>` element is here basically interpreted as template text. But the following construct will work:

```
<main faces:id="main">
    ...
    <h:form id="form">
        ...
        <h:commandButton id="submit" ...>
            <f:ajax render=":main" />
        </h:commandButton>
    </h:form>
</main>
```

`UIViewRoot#findComponent()` on "`main`" will then return a `UIPanel` instance representing the `<main>` element. Jakarta Faces will then be able to render it into the Ajax response. The pass-through element feature also works on other HTML elements; only they don't necessarily turn into a `UIPanel` instance. Instead, they will be turned into a Jakarta Faces component whose generated HTML output matches the very HTML element (see Table 6-1). The following construct is, under the hood, identical to the previous one:

```
<main faces:id="main">
    ...
    <form faces:id="form">
        ...
        <input type="submit" faces:id="submit" ...>
            <f:ajax render=":main" />
        </input>
    </form>
</main>
```

Table 6-1. *Passthrough Elements Recognized by Jakarta Faces*

Passthrough HTML element	Implied Jakarta Faces component
<a faces:action="…">	<h:commandLink>
<a faces:actionListener="…">	<h:commandLink>
<a faces:value="…">	<h:outputLink>
<a faces:outcome="…">	<h:link>
<body faces:id="…">	<h:body>
<button faces:id="…">	<h:commandButton type="button">
<button faces:outcome="…">	<h:button>
<form faces:id="…">	<h:form>
<head faces:id="…">	<h:head>
<img faces:id="…">	<h:graphicImage>
<input faces:id="…" type="button">	<h:commandButton type="button">
<input faces:id="…" type="checkbox">	<h:selectBooleanCheckbox>
<input faces:id="…" type="file">	<h:inputFile>
<input faces:id="…" type="hidden">	<h:inputHidden>
<input faces:id="…" type="password">	<h:inputSecret>

(continued)

Table 6-1. (*continued*)

Passthrough HTML element	Implied Jakarta Faces component
<input faces:id="…" type="reset">	<h:commandButton type="reset">
<input faces:id="…" type="submit">	<h:commandButton type="submit">
<input faces:id="…" type="*">	<h:inputText>
<label faces:id="…">	<h:outputLabel>
<link faces:id="…">	<h:outputStylesheet>
<script faces:id="…">	<h:outputScript>
<select faces:id="…">	<h:selectOneListbox>
<select faces:id="…" multiple="*">	<h:selectManyListbox>
<* faces:id="…">	<h:panelGroup>

Any attribute specified on such a pass-through element is implicitly mapped to the corresponding attribute of the Jakarta Faces component. In the following example, the Jakarta Faces component and pass-through element pairs are equivalent.

```
<h:graphicImage library="common" name="some.svg" />
<img faces:library="common" name="some.svg" />

<h:inputText value="#{bean.name}" />
<input type="text" faces:value="#{bean.name}" />

<h:inputText type="email" value="#{bean.email}" />
<input type="email" faces:value="#{bean.email}" />

<h:link outcome="contact" value="Contact" />
<a faces:outcome="contact">Contact</a>
```

Note that you don't necessarily need to register every single attribute of a pass-through element on the "faces" namespace. Only one is sufficient to trigger the pass-through element feature, preferably the first one. This keeps the code concise.

CHAPTER 7

Facelets Templating

When Jakarta Faces came out for first time in 2004, only Jakarta Pages (formerly known as Jakarta Pages) was available as view technology. It was immediately clear that it was an ill-suited view technology for web development with Jakarta Faces. The problem with Jakarta Pages is that it writes to the HTTP response as soon as it encounters template text, while Jakarta Faces would like to first create a component tree based on the view declaration in order to be able to perform the life cycle processing on it. For example, the following Jakarta Faces 1.0/1.1 page using Jakarta Pages view technology:

```
<h:commandLink action="...">
    <strong>strong link text</strong>
</h:commandLink>
```

would produce the following HTML output, with template text emitted by Jakarta Pages *before* the generated HTML output of Jakarta Faces components:

```
<strong>strong link text</strong>
<a href="..." onclick="..."></a>
```

The "correct approach" would be to wrap template text in `<f:verbatim>` tags:

```
<h:commandLink action="...">
    <f:verbatim><strong>strong link text</strong><f:verbatim>
</h:commandLink>
```

which would correctly produce the following HTML output:

```
<a href="..." onclick="...">
  <strong>strong link text</strong>
</a>
```

© Bauke Scholtz and Arjan Tijms 2022
B. Scholtz and A. Tijms, *The Definitive Guide to Jakarta Faces in Jakarta EE 10*,
https://doi.org/10.1007/978-1-4842-7310-4_7

This has obviously received a lot of criticism, and the general recommendation became that people should not be mixing Jakarta Faces with HTML. Another problem with Jakarta Faces 1.0/1.1 was that there was no component to represent an HTML <div>. That was around the time "Web 2.0" had just started, when people also started to discommend the use of HTML tables to lay out a web page. The prevailing view was that only divs should be used, which made people dislike Jakarta Faces 1.0/1.1 even more.

The peculiar Jakarta Pages behavior of causing a disorganized HTML output was internally worked around in Jakarta Faces 1.2, which was released only 2 years later in 2006, and the missing component to represent an HTML <div> was solved by giving the existing <h:panelGroup> component a new layout="block" attribute so that it renders a <div> instead of a <span>. So people can already, since Jakarta Faces 1.2, safely mix plain HTML with Jakarta Faces components in a Jakarta Pages page and continue using divs in both plain HTML and Jakarta Faces ways. However, the old recommendation to avoid plain HTML while authoring Jakarta Faces 1.0/1.1 pages turned into a persistent myth that is even today still alive among some people.

Another problem with Jakarta Pages is that existing Jakarta Pages–specific tags, such as Jakarta Tags (formerly known as Jakarta Tags), and existing Jakarta Pages–specific expression language in the form of ${...} didn't integrate at all into the Jakarta Faces life cycle and therefore mixing existing Jakarta Pages–specific taglibs and expressions with Jakarta Faces components in a Jakarta Pages page would result in confusing and unintuitive behavior. People couldn't use the Jakarta Tags <c:forEach> to render a list of Jakarta Faces components as those components wouldn't see the variable declared by <c:forEach var>. There was no dedicated Jakarta Faces component to loop over a list other than <h:dataTable>, and ultimately people are stuck with HTML tables while creating lists in the Jakarta Faces page.

Finally, Jakarta Pages also offers very limited templating capabilities with actually only one "templating" tag, the <jsp:include>; therefore, templating with Jakarta Pages would require a fairly complicated approach of creating a bunch of custom tags for every definition of a reusable template section.[1] This contradicts the philosophy of Jakarta Faces, to have reusable components to minimize code duplication. With Jakarta Pages, you would end up duplicating Jakarta Faces components themselves. Existing templating frameworks such as Tiles and Thymeleaf are either Jakarta Pages centric or don't support Jakarta Faces at all and thus cannot be used.

---

[1] https://stackoverflow.com/q/1296235/157882

There was clearly a strong need for a new Jakarta Faces–oriented view technology that should supplant Jakarta Pages and solve all of its problems with the Jakarta Faces life cycle. And then Facelets was introduced in 2006. It could be installed separately for Jakarta Faces 1.1 and 1.2, and it shipped built-in with Jakarta Faces 2.0. It became the default view technology for Jakarta Faces, and Jakarta Pages was immediately deprecated as view technology for Jakarta Faces. New tags introduced in Jakarta Faces 2.0, such as `<f:ajax>`, `<h:head>`, `<h:body>`, `<h:outputScript>`, and `<h:outputStylesheet>`, are only available for Facelets and not for Jakarta Pages. Jakarta Faces 2.0 also introduced a new interface to more easily plug a custom view declaration language (VDL) as alternative to Jakarta Pages and even Facelets, the `ViewDeclarationLanguage` API. This way, one could create, for example, a pure Javabased VDL for Jakarta Faces.[2]

XHTML

The Facelets VDL specifies that the views are defined in XML-based files that are compiled using a SAX parser and kept around in memory. This memory cache is, since Jakarta Faces 2.1, configurable using a custom `FaceletCacheFactory`. When the Jakarta Faces project stage is set to `Development`, the SAX-compiled representations of Facelets files are by default not cached. This allows easier development against an already running server by just editing the Facelets files from inside an IDE (integrated development environment) that supports hot-publishing the local changes to the target runtime.

The Facelets files themselves usually use the `.xhtml` extension, and therefore, starters often call them "XHTML" instead of "Facelets." This is okay when talking in the context of Jakarta Faces, but the term "XHTML" has another side in the web development world. At its core, XHTML is a markup language for HTML pages that need to be compiled using an XML-based tool. In other words, developers basically create XML files with HTML markup mixed with web framework–specific XML tags, after which the web framework will parse them into an XML tree, generate some web framework–specific representation of the XML tree (which is in Jakarta Faces the `UIViewRoot`), and ultimately generate the desired HTML output based on the framework's internal representation of the XML tree.

---

[2]`https://arjan-tijms.omnifaces.org/2011/09/authoring-jsf-pages-in-pure-java.html`

But around the time of Facelets' introduction in 2006, XHTML was being overhyped by another group of web developers who were basically disappointed by seeing the W3 validator to invalidate their HTML4 documents–generally because of the desire to explicitly close all tags for consistency, including those which should actually not be closed as per HTML4 specification, such as `<link>`, `<meta>`, `<br>`, and `<hr>`, and sometimes because of the desire to specify custom tag attributes in order to have some JavaScript plug-ins to interact more cleanly with the HTML document, which is also disallowed by the HTML4 specification.

Even though basically every single web browser in the world leniently accepted that, including the jurassic IE6, those developers didn't want to see their carefully crafted HTML4 documents being invalidated by the W3 validator and changed their HTML doctype declaration to use the XHTML DTD, an extension to HTML that requires every tag to be closed and allows custom attributes to be specified on existing tags. However, this is essentially abuse of XHTML as they didn't at all actually use any XML tool to compile the document and generate the desired HTML output. It was merely to keep the W3 validator happy.

Coincidentally, also around that time, HTML5 was just started in draft. Essentially, developers could just strip out any DTD from the HTML doctype declaration in order to get an HTML document that allows XML-based syntax wherein all tags are always closed and custom elements and attributes are allowed and, importantly, validated correctly in the W3 validator. In other words, `<!DOCTYPE html>` has been sufficient for those developers, even in IE6. Unfortunately, it took ages before HTML5 was officially finished, so developers kept abusing the XHTML doctype before they could switch back to the HTML doctype. When talking about Facelets to those group of developers, don't call it "XHTML" but just "Facelets"; otherwise, it will cause confusion.

Template Compositions

Facelets provides tags for easily creating template compositions based on a single master template file. This should reduce code duplication for site-wide sections that are repeated across all web pages, such as header, navigation menu, and footer. The master template file should represent a full-blown web page layout with all site-wide sections, and it should use `<ui:insert>` tags to represent places where the page-specific sections can be inserted. The following is a basic example of such a master template file, `/WEB-INF/templates/layout.xhtml`:

```
<!DOCTYPE html>
<html lang="en"
    xmlns:h="jakarta.faces.html"
    xmlns:ui="jakarta.faces.facelets"
>
    <h:head>
        <title>#{title}</title>
    </h:head>
    <h:body>
        <header>
            <ui:include src="/WEB-INF/includes/layout/header.xhtml" />
        </header>
        <main>
            <ui:insert name="content" />
        </main>
        <footer>
            <ui:include src="/WEB-INF/includes/layout/footer.xhtml" />
        </footer>
    </h:body>
</html>
```

Note that the master template file and the include files are explicitly placed in the /WEB-INF folder. This is done in order to prevent direct access by users who are guessing the path in URL. Also note that the page title is declared as a simple EL (Expression Language) expression #{title} instead of as a <ui:insert>. Namely, it is not allowed to have any markup in the <title> element.

The xmlns attribute basically defines, via a URI (uniform resource identifier), which tags can be used in the declared XML namespace. The default root XML namespace URI is the W3 XHTML standard http://www.w3.org/1999/xhtml that thus defines "any XHTML and HTML5+ tag," such as <html>, <title>, <header>, <main>, and <footer> in the preceding example. The Facelets compiler is aware of this standard XML namespace and will pass through all elements as "general UI instructions." It is not necessary to explicitly declare the root XML namespace in a Facelets file. Only tooling like IDEs may require them for proper code completion, but Jakarta Faces itself does not require the root XML namespace being present in the Facelet.

The "h" XML namespace specifies the HTML taglib URI and the "ui" XML namespace specifies the Facelets taglib URI, which are both present in the Jakarta Faces implementation JAR file and registered to Facelets during the web application's startup. The Facelets compiler can this way find the associated tag handlers, components, and composite components, which in turn do the hard work of building the view, decoding the HTTP request, and encoding the HTTP response. Those URIs are thus not per definition live Internet addresses. You can even specify your own via a *.taglib.xml file. This will be expanded later in the section "Tag Files."

The following is what the include file /WEB-INF/includes/layout/header.xhtml looks like:

```
<ui:composition
    xmlns:h="jakarta.faces.html"
    xmlns:ui="jakarta.faces.facelets"
>
    <a href="#{request.contextPath}/">
        <h:graphicImage name="images/layout/logo.svg" />
    </a>
    <nav>
        <ul>
            <li><h:link outcome="/about" value="About" /></li>
            <li><h:link outcome="/help" value="Help" /></li>
            <li><h:link outcome="/contact" value="Contact" /></li>
        </ul>
    </nav>
</ui:composition>
```

Note the link around the logo. It points to #{request.contextPath}/. This basically prints the domain-relative URL to the application's root. #{request} is an implicit EL object referring the current HttpServletRequest instance. contextPath refers to one of its properties, implied by the getContextPath() method.

The following is what the include file /WEB-INF/includes/layout/footer.xhtml looks like:

```
<ui:composition
    xmlns:h="jakarta.faces.html"
    xmlns:ui="jakarta.faces.facelets"
>
```

```
    <nav>
        <ul>
            <li><h:link outcome="/terms-of-service"
                        value="Terms of Service" /></li>
            <li><h:link outcome="/privacy-policy"
                        value="Privacy Policy" /></li>
            <li><h:link outcome="/cookie-policy"
                        value="Cookie Policy" /></li>
        </ul>
    </nav>
    <small>© Example Company</small>
</ui:composition>
```

Finally, here's how the template client can look, for example, /home.xhtml:

```
<ui:composition template="/WEB-INF/templates/layout.xhtml"
    xmlns:h="jakarta.faces.html"
    xmlns:ui="jakarta.faces.facelets"
>
    <ui:param name="title" value="Welcome!" />

    <ui:define name="content">
        <h1>Welcome to Example Company!</h1>
        <p>Lorem ipsum dolor sit amet.</p>
    </ui:define>
</ui:composition>
```

Note the template attribute of the <ui:composition>. This must represent the server-side path to the master template, preferably as an absolute path, thus starting with "/".

In a template client, the <ui:param> lets you define a simple parameter specific to the master template. Basically, you can use any parameter name, as long as it is supported by the master template and it doesn't clash with an existing managed bean name. In this specific case, the value for the EL variable #{title} is specified as "Welcome!". This will ultimately end up inside the <title> element of the master template.

And the `<ui:define>` lets you define a block of markup specific for the master template. It will ultimately end up in the place where the `<ui:insert>` with exactly the same name is declared in the master template. Figure 7-1 gives a clear overview of how this all fits together.

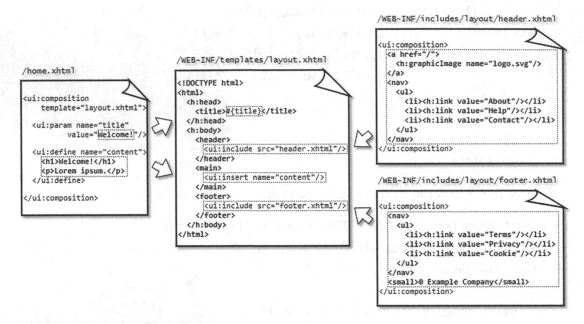

Figure 7-1. *The relationship between the master template* `layout.xhtml`, *include files* `header.xhtml`, *and* `footer.xhtml`, *and the template client* `home.xhtml`. *Note that template file paths and some tag attributes are omitted for brevity. Refer to the previously shown code snippets for the actual coding*

Finally, opening `/home.xhtml` should produce the final HTML output that you can inspect by right-clicking *View page source* in the average web browser.

Single Page Application

A recent trend is the so-called Single Page Application (SPA). This concept is on its own not so new; in fact, it is older than Jakarta Faces itself, but it was heavily popularized during "Web 2.0" with JavaScript-based frameworks such as Angular. Basically, an SPA lets the web application behave like a desktop-oriented application by dynamically changing the main content with an Ajax request when navigating to a different page instead of loading the entire page via a GET request. Gmail is one such known example of an SPA.

Such an SPA is also achievable with Jakarta Faces by simply using `<ui:include>` whose src attribute is dynamically updated by Ajax. The following is an example utilizing the same master template as shown in the previous section, /spa.xhtml:

```
<ui:composition template="/WEB-INF/templates/layout.xhtml"
    xmlns:faces="jakarta.faces"
    xmlns:f="jakarta.faces.core"
    xmlns:h="jakarta.faces.html"
    xmlns:ui="jakarta.faces.facelets"
>
    <ui:param name="title" value="Single Page Application" />

    <ui:define name="content">
        <aside>
            <nav>
                <h:form>
                    <f:ajax render=":content">
                        <ul>
                            <li><h:commandLink value="page1"
                                action="#{spa.set('page1')}" /></li>
                            <li><h:commandLink value="page2"
                                action="#{spa.set('page2')}" /></li>
                            <li><h:commandLink value="page3"
                                action="#{spa.set('page3')}" /></li>
                        </ul>
                    </f:ajax>
                </h:form>
            </nav>
        </aside>
        <article faces:id="content" data-page="#{spa.page}">
            <ui:include src="/WEB-INF/includes/spa/#{spa.page}.xhtml" />
        </article>
    </ui:define>
</ui:composition>
```

Do note that the `<article>` element is declared as a so-called pass-through element by explicitly specifying a Jakarta Faces identifier via `faces:id="..."`. Under the hood, when declaring an HTML element that has no Jakarta Faces component equivalent, such as `<header>`, `<footer>`, `<main>`, `<article>`, and `<section>`, as a pass-through element, this way, it is turned into a `UIPanel` component and is treated in the Jakarta Faces component tree exactly like `<h:panelGroup>`. This way, you can cleanly keep using semantic HTML5 markup while still being able to reference it as if it were a Jakarta Faces component and thus be able to Ajax-update it. See also the section "Pass-Through Elements" in Chapter 6.

As you might have deciphered in the previous `/spa.xhtml` example, there's a side navigation menu that sets the current page in the managed bean identified by `#{spa}` and Ajax-updates the component identified by `id="content"` that in turn contains a dynamic include. The previous example excepts the following include files to be present in the `/WEB-INF/includes/spa` folder: `page1.xhtml`, `page2.xhtml`, and `page3.xhtml`. Each of them is a simple include file that looks as follows:

```
<ui:composition
    xmlns:h="jakarta.faces.html"
    xmlns:ui="jakarta.faces.facelets"
>
    <h1>First page</h1>
    <p>Lorem ipsum dolor sit amet.</p>
</ui:composition>
```

The backing bean associated with the `#{spa}` managed bean is fairly simple; it looks as follows:

```
@Named @ViewScoped
public class Spa implements Serializable {

    private String page;

    @PostConstruct
    public void init() {
        page = "page1";
    }
```

```
    public void set(String page) {
        this.page = page;
    }

    public String getPage() {
        return page;
    }
}
```

The default page is defined in @PostConstruct. Otherwise, the user might face an error page with the message "Invalid path : /WEB-INF/includes/spa/.xhtml".

Note that the backing bean is declared @ViewScoped. This is important in order to remember across postbacks which page is currently being opened. If it were @RequestScoped, and the user navigates to, for example, page2 and submits a form therein, which creates a new HTTP request, then the @RequestScoped managed bean would be recreated again, with page1 as default value of the page property and thus not anymore the initially selected value of page2. This has the consequence that the <ui:include> won't anymore reference page2.xhtml when Jakarta Faces is about to decode any input components in order to process the form submit during the postback request, and therefore Jakarta Faces would fail to find the input components declared in page2.xhtml. A @ViewScoped bean lives as long as the user postbacks to the very same view, in this case, /spa.xhtml, and therefore correctly remembers the currently selected page.

When playing around with this SPA example, you might have noticed one disadvantage: the pages are not bookmarkable. This is caused by the fact that the pages are not opened by an idempotent GET request. You can solve that by utilizing the HTML5 history.pushState API.[3] Basically, on completion of the Ajax request, you should push the intended URL to the browser history, which will be reflected in the browser's address bar. And you should modify the Spa backing bean to check if any specific page has been opened and then prepare the page variable accordingly.

The following is a kickoff example that just appends the ?page=xxx query string parameter. First, adjust the <f:ajax> of the spa.xhtml to specify the onevent attribute as follows:

```
<f:ajax ... onevent="pageChangeListener">
```

---

[3] https://developer.mozilla.org/en-US/docs/Web/API/History_API

And create the following JavaScript function:

```javascript
function pageChangeListener(event) {
    if (event.status == "success") {
        var page = document.getElementById("content").dataset.page;
        var url = location.pathname + "?page=" + page;
        history.pushState(null, document.title, url);
    }
}
```

And, finally, adjust the Spa backing bean as follows:

```java
@Inject @ManagedProperty("#{param.page}")
Private String page;
public void init() {
    if (page == null) {
        page = "page1";
    }
}
```

Also, note that you might want to validate the provided page parameter. Path probing by hackers is innocent, by the way, as Jakarta Faces already doesn't allow traversing into the parent path as in /spa.xhtml?page=../../templates/layout.

Template Decorations

In case you would like to have a reusable include file that is capable of inserting template definitions as if you would be using <ui:include> to reference an include file with one or more <ui:insert> sections, then you can use <ui:decorate>. The following is one such example, the /WEB-INF/decorations/contact.xhtml:

```xml
<ui:composition
    xmlns:ui="jakarta.faces.facelets"
>
    <section class="contact">
        <header><ui:insert /></header>
        <nav>
```

```
        <ul>
            <li>∅ <a href="tel:+31612345678"
                title="Phone">+31 (0)6 1234 5678</a></li>
            <li>✉ <a href="mailto:info@example.com"
                title="Email">info@example.com</a></li>
        </ul>
    </nav>
  </section>
</ui:composition>
```

Here is how it can be used; you can put the <ui:decorate> anywhere in your template client, as a <ui:include>:

```
<ui:decorate template="/WEB-INF/decorations/contact.xhtml">
    <h2>Questions? Contact us!</h2>
</ui:decorate>
```

Note that the contact.xhtml has only one <ui:insert> and that it has no name. This will insert the entire <ui:decorate> tag body at the declared place of <ui:insert>. You can, of course, specify a name, but then you would need to explicitly specify <ui:define> with a name for that. That would be only useful if you have more than one insert section.

You can, if necessary, use <ui:param> to pass parameters. This works the same way as with <ui:composition template>. The following example parameterizes the email username /WEB-INF/decorations/contact.xhtml with a default value of "info."

```
...
<li>✉ <a href="mailto: #{empty mailto ? 'info' : mailto}@example.com"
    title="Email">#{empty mailto ? 'info' : mailto}@example.com</a></li>
...
```

This can then be used as follows:

```
<ui:decorate template="/WEB-INF/decorations/contact.xhtml">
    <ui:param name="mailto" value="press" />
    <h3>Contact us</h3>
    <p>
```

```
        For press inquiries you can contact us by the below
        phone number and email address.
    </p>
</ui:decorate>
```

Tag Files

As with <ui:composition template> and <ui:decorate>, you can also use <ui:param> in <ui:include>.

```
<ui:include src="/WEB-INF/includes/field.xhtml">
    <ui:param name="id" value="firstName" />
    <ui:param name="label" value="First Name" />
    <ui:param name="value" value="#{profile.user.firstName}" />
</ui:include>
```

wherein the /WEB-INF/includes/field.xhtml looks something like the following:

```
<ui:composition
    xmlns:faces="jakarta.faces"
    xmlns:h="jakarta.faces.html"
    xmlns:ui="jakarta.faces.facelets"
    xmlns:c="jakarta.tags.core"
>
    <div class="field" faces:rendered="#{rendered ne false}">
        <h:outputLabel id="#{id}_l" for="#{id}" value="#{label}" />
        <c:choose>
            <c:when test="#{type eq 'password'}">
                <h:inputSecret id="#{id}" label="#{label}"
                    value="#{value}">
                </h:inputSecret>
            </c:when>
            <c:when test="#{type eq 'textarea'}">
                <h:inputTextarea id="#{id}" label="#{label}"
                    value="#{value}">
                </h:inputTextarea>
            </c:when>
```

```
        <!-- More types can be added as c:when here -->
        <c:otherwise>
            <h:inputText id="#{id}" label="#{label}"
                value="#{value}" type="#{type}">
            </h:inputText>
        </c:otherwise>
    </c:choose>
    <h:messages id="#{id}_m" for="#{id}" styleClass="messages" />
    </div>
</ui:composition>
```

However, watch out that you don't go overboard with the amount of `<ui:param>` tags in a `<ui:include>`. In such a case, you would prefer to have something more concise, like the following, instead:

```
<t:field id="firstName" label="First Name"
    value="#{profile.user.firstName}">
</t:field>
```

Having `<ui:include>` with three or more `<ui:param>` tags is a strong sign that the include file can better be registered as a tag file so that it can be used with less boilerplate code in the Facelet.

First, move the include file into a different subfolder, `/WEB-INF/tags/field.xhtml`. This is not a technical requirement. It will work just fine wherever you put it, but we just want to organize the files clearly. Master template files go in `/WEB-INF/templates`, include files go in `/WEB-INF/includes`, decorate files go in `/WEB-INF/decorations`, and tag files go in `/WEB-INF/tags`.

Then, create the following `/WEB-INF/example.taglib.xml`:

```
<?xml version="1.0" encoding="UTF-8"?>
<facelet-taglib
    xmlns="https://jakarta.ee/xml/ns/jakartaee"
    xmlns:xsi="https://www.w3.org/2001/XMLSchema-instance"
    xsi:schemaLocation="https://jakarta.ee/xml/ns/jakartaee
        https://jakarta.ee/xml/ns/jakartaee/web-facelettaglibrary_4_0.xsd"
    version="4.0"
>
```

```
<namespace>example.tags</namespace>
<short-name>t</short-name>
<tag>
    <description>Renders label + input + message field.</description>
    <tag-name>field</tag-name>
    <source>tags/field.xhtml</source>
    <attribute>
        <description>The type of the input component.</description>
        <name>type</name>
        <required>false</required>
        <type>java.lang.String</type>
    </attribute>
    <attribute>
        <description>The ID of the input component.</description>
        <name>id</name>
        <required>true</required>
        <type>java.lang.String</type>
    </attribute>
    <attribute>
        <description>The label of the input component.</description>
        <name>label</name>
        <required>true</required>
        <type>java.lang.String</type>
    </attribute>
    <attribute>
        <description>The value of the input component.</description>
        <name>value</name>
        <required>false</required>
        <type>java.lang.Object</type>
    </attribute>
    <attribute>
        <description>Whether the field is rendered.</description>
        <name>rendered</name>
        <required>false</required>
        <type>boolean</type>
```

```
      </attribute>
   </tag>
</facelet-taglib>
```

That's admittedly quite some boilerplate code. It is good to know that the `<attribute>` elements aren't mandatory for the technical functioning of the tag file. You could even omit them altogether. But then the IDE won't be able to load them into autosuggest boxes while attempting to autocomplete the custom tag. This is not really developer-friendly. So you'd better keep them in. The `<required>` property of the tag attribute, by the way, only results in a runtime error when the Jakarta Faces project stage is set to `Development`. In other Jakarta Faces project stages, it's ignored. And the average IDE will immediately prompt those required attributes during autocompleting the tag.

The file name, `example.taglib.xml`, is free to your choice. In order for Jakarta Faces to automatically pick up a taglib file during the application's startup, there are only two requirements: it must have a `.taglib.xml` extension, and it must be placed in `/WEB-INF` folder (or in case of a JAR file that ends up in `/WEB-INF/lib`, then it must be placed in `/META-INF` folder of that JAR file). Unfortunately, placing the file in `/WEB-INF` doesn't always work quite well in some servers, such as GlassFish/Payara. In that case, you'd have to explicitly register it via the following context parameter in `web.xml` whose value represents the full path to the `*.taglib.xml` file from the web root on.

```
<context-param>
    <param-name>jakarta.faces.FACELETS_LIBRARIES</param-name>
    <param-value>/WEB-INF/example.taglib.xml</param-value>
</context-param>
```

In order to use any tag defined in the `*.taglib.xml`, you first have to declare exactly the `<namespace>` URI of the taglib in the XML namespace of your Facelet, along with an arbitrary XML namespace prefix. For better maintainability of the code, it's recommended to consistently pick the taglib's preferred XML namespace prefix as specified in the `<short-name>` of the `*.taglib.xml`, which is "t" in case of our `example.taglib.xml`.

```
<ui:composition template="/WEB-INF/templates/layout.xhtml"
    xmlns:h="jakarta.faces.html"
    xmlns:ui="jakarta.faces.facelets"
    xmlns:t="example.tags"
>
```

```
    <ui:param name="title" value="Log In" />
    <ui:define name="content">
        <h:form>
            <fieldset>
                <header>
                    <h1>Log In</h1>
                </header>
                <t:field type="email" id="email" label="Email"
                    value="#{login.email}">
                </t:field>
                <t:field type="password" id="password" label="Password"
                    value="#{login.password}">
                </t:field>
                <footer>
                    <t:button id="submit" label="Log In"
                        action="#{login.submit()}">
                    </t:button>
                </footer>
            </fieldset>
        </h:form>
    </ui:define>
</ui:composition>
```

Do note that the type="email" of the email field thus ends up in <c:otherwise>
of the tag file implementation wherein it gets passed through the type="#{type}"
attribute of <h:inputText>. This allows you to easily use HTML5 input fields, such as
type="email", type="number", and type="tel".

You might also have noticed another custom tag, <t:button>. Here's how it is
implemented in /WEB-INF/tags/button.xhtml.

```
<ui:composition
    xmlns:faces="jakarta.faces"
    xmlns:f="jakarta.faces.core"
    xmlns:h="jakarta.faces.html"
    xmlns:ui="jakarta.faces.facelets"
>
```

```
  <div class="button" faces:rendered="#{rendered ne false}">
    <h:commandButton id="#{id}" value="#{label}">
        <f:actionListener binding="#{action}" />
        <f:ajax execute="@form" render="@form" />
    </h:commandButton>
    <h:messages id="#{id}_m" globalOnly="true" redisplay="false" />
  </div>
</ui:composition>
```

It's registered in example.taglib.xml nearly the same way as <t:field>, with one exception for the action attribute. Technically, you need to specify a <method-signature> instead of a (property) <type>:

```
<attribute>
    <description>
        Action method of the button.
        NOTE: must include method parenthesis.
    </description>
    <name>action</name>
    <required>true</required>
    <method-signature>void action()</method-signature>
</attribute>
```

You might have noticed that the actual tag implementation uses <f:actionListener binding="#{action}"> instead of action="#{action}". This is actually a necessary trick in order to get it to properly invoke the method. That is, the <method-signature> was initially intended for UI components, not for tag files. It's ignored in tag files. This may be worked on for Faces.next. For now, you can get away with the <f:actionListener binding> trick. This has only one additional requirement: you need to explicitly include the method parenthesis in the tag file client as in <t:button action="#{login.submit()}">. When you omit the method parenthesis as in <t:button action="#{login.submit}">, then the submit will fail with *jakarta. el.PropertyNotFoundException: The class 'com.example.project.view.Login' does not have the property 'submit'.*

In case you would like to customize tag files from the tag file client side on, for example, by adding more specific input attributes, or nesting core tags, or by prepending or appending content to the label or message, then you can use <ui:define> and

`<ui:insert>` the same way you're used to doing with master template files and decorate files. The following example demonstrates how you can enhance the `/WEB-INF/tags/ field.xhtml` on this with a bunch of new `<ui:insert>` tags:

```
<ui:composition
    xmlns:faces="jakarta.faces"
    xmlns:h="jakarta.faces.html"
    xmlns:ui="jakarta.faces.facelets"
    xmlns:c="jakarta.tags.core"
>
    <div class="field" faces:rendered="#{rendered ne false}">
        <ui:insert name="beforeLabel" />
        <ui:insert name="label">
            <h:outputLabel id="#{id}_l" for="#{id}" value="#{label}">
                <span><ui:insert name="insideLabel" /></span>
            </h:outputLabel>
        </ui:insert>
        <ui:insert name="beforeInput" />
        <ui:insert name="input">
            <c:choose>
                <c:when test="#{type eq 'password'}">
                    <h:inputSecret id="#{id}" label="#{label}"
                        value="#{value}">
                        <ui:insert />
                    </h:inputSecret>
                </c:when>
                <c:when test="#{type eq 'textarea'}">
                    <h:inputTextarea id="#{id}" label="#{label}"
                        value="#{value}">
                        <ui:insert />
                    </h:inputTextarea>
                </c:when>
```

```
                <!-- More types can be added as c:when here -->
                <c:otherwise>
                    <h:inputText id="#{id}" label="#{label}"
                        value="#{value}" type="#{type}">
                        <ui:insert />
                    </h:inputText>
                </c:otherwise>
            </c:choose>
        </ui:insert>
        <ui:insert name="beforeMessages" />
        <ui:insert name="messages">
            <h:messages id="#{id}_m" for="#{id}" styleClass="messages" />
        </ui:insert>
    </div>
</ui:composition>
```

Now, that's a lot of flexibility! In the tag file client, you can use `<ui:define name="beforeLabel">` to define some content that should appear before the label of the field. And you can use `<ui:define name="label">` to override the label altogether. And you can use `<ui:define name="insideLabel">` to append some (HTML) content inside the label and so forth. The following example demonstrates how `insideLabel` can be used to append a "Forgot password?" link to the label of the password field:

```
<t:field ...>
    <ui:define name="insideLabel">
        <h:link outcome="/reset-password" value="Forgot password?" />
    </ui:define>
</t:field>
```

Note that `<ui:insert name="insideLabel">` is wrapped in an HTML `<span>`. This allows you to more easily select "anything" that ends up in there via CSS so that you can, for example, let it float to the right using just the following CSS:

```
.field label > span {
    float: right;
}
```

Anything else in the tag file client that is not nested in a `<ui:define>` will end up inside the nameless `<ui:insert>` tag nested in the chosen input component. This allows you to easily nest any `<f:xxx>` core tag specifically for the input component:

```
<t:field ...>
    <f:attribute name="onkeypress" value="return event.key != 'Enter'" />
    <f:validateRegex pattern="[0-9]{4}" />
    <f:ajax render="otherField" />
</t:field>
```

This specific example prevents the form from submitting when the *Enter* key is pressed by returning `false` when the `KeyBoardEvent.key` equals "`Enter`", and registers a regex validator to accept only a value of four digits by matching against a regular expression pattern of "`[0-9]{4}`", and instructs Jakarta Faces to update the component identified by "`otherField`" by Ajax when the value change event has occurred.

Coming back to the tag file implementation in `/WEB-INF/tags/field.xhtml`, you might have noticed that Jakarta Tags `<c:when>` is being used there instead of the `rendered` attribute of the Jakarta Faces components. This has advantages as Jakarta Tags has a different life cycle than Jakarta Faces components. Jakarta Tags is executed when the Jakarta Faces component tree is about to be built, during the view build time. Jakarta Faces components are executed when HTML output is about to be generated, during the view render time. Moreover, if you were using Jakarta Faces' own `rendered` attribute, then you would face "duplicate component ID" errors because of multiple components with the same ID physically ending up in the Jakarta Faces component tree.

Might it happen that you are considering the use of plain Java code to dynamically create the component tree based on at least a view-scoped model, then you should absolutely reconsider using Jakarta Tags instead. As Jakarta Tags itself is also XML based and you can thus just put together everything in an XHTML file, you will end up with much better readable and maintainable code for a "dynamic" component.

Composite Components

Sometimes, you would like to have a group of related input components to represent a single model value. A classic example is having three `<h:selectOneMenu>` dropdowns representing day, month, and year that are ultimately bound to a single `java.time.LocalDate` property in the backing bean. This is not trivial to implement with just an include file or a tag file. You would need some additional Java-based logic that makes sure that, for example, the day drop-down doesn't show the value 29, 30, or 31 depending on the currently selected month and that it converts the submitted values to a fullfledged `LocalDate` instance, and vice versa. But you can't and shouldn't put any Java code in any Facelet.

You'll perhaps think of just creating a dedicated backing bean for this case. But this is not sufficient either. It doesn't allow you to cleanly hook on the component's life cycle through the Jakarta Faces phases: collecting the individual submitted values from multiple components, converting them into a single `LocalDate` instance, if necessary throwing a converter exception during the validations phase, and letting the Jakarta Faces life cycle automatically skip the remaining phases. A backing bean's setter method or action method is far from the right place for that logic. It would be invoked too late anyway. And it would feel strange to be able to reference and potentially manipulate the very same backing bean via an EL expression on an arbitrary place in the Facelet.

This is exactly where composite components come into the picture: composing a bunch of existing Jakarta Faces components into virtually a single component tied to a single model value and ultimately using it exactly the same way as you would be using a plain `<h:inputText>`. Imagine a `<t:inputLocalTime>` composite component composed of two `<h:selectOneMenu>` components tied to a single `java.time.LocalTime` model value. Instead of a backing bean, you can use a full-fledged `UIComponent` instance as a so-called backing component.

First, create a dedicated subfolder in `main/webapp/resources` folder (and thus not `main/java/resources!`), for example, `main/webapp/resources/components`. There you can put Facelets files representing composite components. The path representing the subfolder, as in `/components`, is then to be used in the XML namespace URI after the `jakarta.faces.composite` as shown next.

```
xmlns:t="jakarta.faces.composite/components"
```

Note that the XML namespace prefix of "t" clashes with one which we already defined before for tag files. This is of course not the intent. You may choose a different XML namespace for composite components. It's, however, also possible to let them share the same custom XML namespace URI `example.tags`. This can be achieved by adding a `<composite-library-name>` to the `*.taglib.xml` which in turn must represent the name of the dedicated subfolder.

```
<composite-library-name>components</composite-library-name>
```

This way, all composite components are also available by the same XML namespace as tag files.

```
<... xmlns:t="example.tags">
...
<t:inputLocalTime ... />
```

The file name of the Facelets file representing the composite component will become the tag name. So in order to have a `<t:inputLocalTime>`, we need an `inputLocalTime.xhtml` file in the `main/webapp/resources/components` folder. The following is a kickoff example of what it can look like:

```
<ui:component
    xmlns:f="jakarta.faces.core"
    xmlns:h="jakarta.faces.html"
    xmlns:ui="jakarta.faces.facelets"
    xmlns:cc="jakarta.faces.composite"
>
    <cc:interface componentType="inputLocalTime">
        <cc:attribute name="value" type="java.time.LocalTime"
            shortDescription="Selected time. Defaults to 00:00.">
        </cc:attribute>
        <cc:attribute name="required" type="boolean"
            shortDescription="Required state. Defaults to false.">
        </cc:attribute>
    </cc:interface>
    <cc:implementation>
        <span id="#{cc.clientId}" class="inputLocalTime">
            <h:selectOneMenu id="hour" binding="#{cc.hour}"
                required="#{cc.attrs.required}">
                <f:selectItem itemValue="#{null}" />
                <f:selectItems value="#{cc.hours}" />
            </h:selectOneMenu>
            :
            <h:selectOneMenu id="minute" binding="#{cc.minute}"
                required="#{cc.attrs.required}">
                <f:selectItem itemValue="#{null}" />
```

```
                <f:selectItems value="#{cc.minutes}" />
            </h:selectOneMenu>
        </span>
    </cc:implementation>
</ui:component>
```

There are several things to notice here, which makes a composite component different from a tag file. First, the composite component's body is always divided into two sections: an interface and an implementation.

The interface declares a `componentType` attribute which should reference the value of either the `@FacesComponent` annotation on a `UIComponent` subclass or the `<component-type>` entry of a `<component>` as declared in either `faces-config.xml` or `*.taglib.xml`. When the `componentType` attribute is absent, then it defaults to `UINamingContainer`. The interface also declares the supported component attributes as `<cc:attribute>` entries. To keep it simple, we restrict to only two in the example interface: `value` and `required`. There are also implicitly inherited attributes from the `UIComponent` superclass, which we don't need to explicitly define as `<cc:attribute>` entries: `id`, `binding`, and `rendered`. That makes it a total of five attributes which you can use in the implementation.

The implementation defines the actual markup of the composite component. In the example implementation, you can find two `<h:selectOneMenu>` drop-downs wrapped in a `<span>` element. There you can also find several occurrences of the special EL variable `#{cc}` that refers to the current `UIComponent` instance behind the composite component, which is thus an instance of the type as declared in the `componentType` attribute, or, if absent, an instance of `UINamingContainer`. The `#{cc.attrs}` is a shortcut to the component attribute map as available by `UIComponent#getAttributes()`. The `#{cc.attrs.required}` as used in the `required` attributes thus refers to `<cc:attribute name="required">` which you in turn can define in the client side as `<t:inputLocalTime required="true">`.

The `#{cc.clientId}` in the `<span>` element just prints the composite component's client ID as the `id` attribute of the `<span>` element. This is actually a trick in order to be able to reference the "whole" composite component using a client ID search expression from the template client on. Imagine the following case:

```
<h:inputText ...>
    <f:ajax render="time" />
</h:inputText>
<t:inputLocalTime id="time" ... />
```

This case wouldn't have worked without the #{cc.clientId} being rendered as
an ID of any plain HTML element that wraps the entire body of <cc:implementation>,
usually a <span> or <div>. The technical problem is while the composite component
itself is findable in the Jakarta Faces component tree by the component ID search
expression, the HTML representation of the composite component is by default not
available by document.getElementById(clientId) in JavaScript. In other words, Jakarta
Faces Ajax wouldn't be able to update it. Explicitly adding a plain HTML element with
the composite component's client ID thus solves that.

Finally, there are a bunch of #{cc} expressions that don't reference the #{cc.attrs}
directly. Both <h:selectOneMenu> components are via the binding attribute directly
bound as properties of the so-called backing component, the concrete UIComponent
instance behind the composite component. And both <f:selectItems> option lists
obtain their values directly from the backing component as well. Here's how the
backing component class is implemented, the com.example.project.composite.
InputLocalTime:

```
@FacesComponent("inputLocalTime")
public class InputLocalTime extends UIInput implements NamingContainer {

    private static final List<String> HOURS =
        IntStream.rangeClosed(0, 23).boxed()
            .map(InputLocalTime::pad).collect(Collectors.toList());

    private static final List<String> MINUTES =
        IntStream.rangeClosed(0, 59).boxed()
            .map(InputLocalTime::pad).collect(Collectors.toList());

    private UIInput hour;
    private UIInput minute;

    @Override
    public String getFamily() {
        return UINamingContainer.COMPONENT_FAMILY;
    }

    @Override
    public void encodeBegin(FacesContext context) throws IOException {
        LocalTime localTime = (LocalTime) getValue();
```

```java
        if (localTime != null) {
            hour.setValue(pad(localTime.getHour()));
            minute.setValue(pad(localTime.getMinute()));
        }

        super.encodeBegin(context);
    }

    @Override
    public Object getSubmittedValue() {
        String submittedHour = (String) hour.getSubmittedValue();
        String submittedMinute = (String) minute.getSubmittedValue();

        if (submittedHour == null || submittedMinute == null) {
            return null;
        }
        else if (submittedHour.isEmpty() || submittedMinute.isEmpty()) {
            return "";
        }
        else {
            return submittedHour + ":" + submittedMinute;
        }
    }

    @Override
    protected Object getConvertedValue
        (FacesContext context, Object submittedValue)
    {
        String submittedTime = (String) submittedValue;

        if (submittedTime == null || submittedTime.isEmpty()) {
            return null;
        }

        try {
            return LocalTime.parse(submittedTime,
                DateTimeFormatter.ISO_LOCAL_TIME);
        }
```

273

```
        catch (DateTimeParseException e) {
            throw new ConverterException(e);
        }
    }

    private static String pad(Integer value) {
        return String.format("%02d", value);
    }

    public UIInput getHour() { return hour; }
    public void setHour(UIInput hour) { this.hour = hour; }
    public UIInput getMinute() { return minute; }
    public void setMinute(UIInput minute) { this.minute = minute; }
    public List<String> getHours() { return HOURS; }
    public List<String> getMinutes() { return MINUTES; }
}
```

Now, that was a bit of code. Not only will you see that the getters and setters are collapsed for brevity, but you'll also see that our composite extends UIInput and implements NamingContainer. Extending from UIInput gives us the benefit that we don't need to repeat most of the default encoding and decoding behavior of UIInput in our backing component, so we only need to override a few methods. Implementing NamingContainer is a technical requirement of <cc:interface>. This enables you to use multiple instances of the composite component in the same context without facing "duplicate component ID" errors. This requirement is also reflected by the overridden getFamily() method.

The actual UIInput components composing the composite component are declared as properties of the backing component. In this case, they are both <h:selectOneMenu> drop-downs that are, via the binding attribute, tied to those properties. This enables us to easily set their values during encoding (read: processing the HTTP response) and to obtain the submitted values during decoding (read: processing the HTTP request). You can find the logic for that in the overridden encodeBegin() and getSubmittedValue() methods, respectively.

In the encodeBegin() method, you thus have the opportunity to prepare the displayed values based on the model value, if any. The getValue() method is inherited from the UIInput superclass and is tied to the value attribute of the composite component. You can break down the model value and set the desired values in the individual UIInput components of the composite component. The pad() helper method just pads the digit with a leading zero so that, for example, the "1" gets displayed as "01". This helper method is also used during static initialization of the lists of available hours and minutes specifically for <f:selectItems>.

In the getSubmittedValue() method, you should compose the submitted values of the individual UIInput components together to a single String. In the specific case of <t:inputLocalTime>, we compose a String following the ISO local time pattern HH:mm. In turn, the UIInput superclass passes this value through the getConvertedValue() wherein we thus have the opportunity to convert the composed String to the concrete model value, which is in our case the LocalTime. Ultimately, the UIInput superclass will make sure that this gets set in the backing bean during the update model values phase. Now you can use it as follows:

```
<ui:composition template="/WEB-INF/templates/layout.xhtml"
    xmlns:f="jakarta.faces.core"
    xmlns:h="jakarta.faces.html"
    xmlns:ui="jakarta.faces.facelets"
    xmlns:cc="jakarta.faces.composite/components"
>
    <ui:define name="content">
        <h:form>
            <h:outputLabel for="time:hour" value="Time" />
            <t:inputLocalTime id="time" value="#{bean.time}" />
            <h:commandButton value="Submit" action="#{bean.submit}">
                <f:ajax execute="@form" />
            </h:commandButton>
        </h:form>
    </ui:define>
</ui:composition>
```

where the backing bean represented by #{bean} looks as follows:

```
@Named @RequestScoped
public class Bean {

    private LocalTime time;
```

```
    public void submit() {
        System.out.println("Submitted local time: " + time);
    }

    public LocalTime getTime() {
        return time;
    }

    public void setTime(LocalTime time) {
        this.time = time;
    }
}
```

Might it happen that you need to nest `<f:ajax>` inside the composite component in order to run some Ajax during the change event of any of the individual drop-downs, then you can achieve that by adding `<cc:clientBehavior>` targeting both drop-downs as follows:

```
<cc:interface ...>
    ...
    <cc:clientBehavior name="change" default="true"
        targets="hour minute" event="change">
    </cc:clientBehavior>
</cc:interface>
```

The name attribute of `<cc:clientBehavior>` represents the event name that you should declare in template client in order to trigger it.

```
<t:inputLocalTime id="time" ...>
    <f:ajax event="change" ... />
</t:inputLocalTime>
```

The `default` attribute of `<cc:clientBehavior>` being set to `"true"` indicates that this is the default event, which means that you could just omit it, as you could do with `event="change"` for existing input text and drop-down components, and with `event="click"` for existing check box and radio button components, and with `event="action"` for existing command components.

```
<t:inputLocalTime id="time" ...>
    <f:ajax ... />
</t:inputLocalTime>
```

The `targets` attribute of `<cc:clientBehavior>` must define a space-separated collection of IDs of target `UIInput` components enclosed in the implementation of the composite component on which you would like to trigger the Ajax event, and the `event` attribute of `<cc:clientBehavior>` must define the desired event name to be actually triggered on the target `UIInput` components. In other words, this does, under the hood, effectively the same as if the following is implemented in the composite component:

```
<h:selectOneMenu id="hour" ...>
    <f:ajax event="change" ... />
</h:selectOneMenu>
<h:selectOneMenu id="minute" ...>
    <f:ajax event="change" ... />
</h:selectOneMenu>
```

In this specific example, the value of the `event` attribute coincidentally has just the same value as the value of the `name` attribute. This is perhaps confusing at first, but it allows you to easily define a custom event name. For example, the following is the code to use when you want to trigger an event solely on the change of the `hour` drop-down:

```
<cc:interface ...>
    ...
    <cc:clientBehavior name="hourChange"
        targets="hour" event="change">
    </cc:clientBehavior>
</cc:interface>
```

With this, the following Ajax listener will thus be fired only when the `hour` drop-down is changed and not when the `minute` drop-down is changed.

```
<t:inputLocalTime id="time" ...>
    <f:ajax event="hourChange" listener="#{bean.hourChanged}" />
</t:inputLocalTime>
```

All in all, it must be said that composite components have been overhyped after they were first introduced in Jakarta Faces 2.0. People started using them to "composite" whole templates, includes, decorations, and even multiple tags, without using any backing component. That is, the zero-configuration nature as compared to tag files is very attractive. Everything is declared in the composite component file itself via `<cc:interface>`. And they can be directly used in the template client just by following a convention without the need to configure it in some XML file.

The caveat is that composite components are, due to their internal design, relatively expensive during building and restoring the view as compared to plain include files, decorate files, and tag files, especially when deeply nested. The best practice is therefore to use them only and only if you actually need a backing component via `<cc:interface componentType>`. For any other case, just use an include, a decorate, or a tag file instead. In the previous section, you may already have learned that tag files can be quite powerful with the help of Jakarta Tags.

Recursive Composite Component

You can safely nest composite components in each other. However, when you nest the very same composite component recursively in itself, then it would fail with a stack overflow error when EL attempts to resolve the concrete composite component instance behind #{cc}.[4]

Imagine that you've got a recursive tree model that represents some sort of a discussion thread, such as email messages and all their replies, or blog comments and all their replies, whereby each reply can in turn have another set of replies. This can be represented as a single Jakarta Persistence entity as follows:

```
@Entity
public class Message {

    @Id @GeneratedValue(strategy=IDENTITY)
    private Long id;

    @Lob @Column(nullable = false)
    private @NotNull String text;
```

---

[4]https://balusc.omnifaces.org/2016/02/recursive-tree-of-composite-components.html

```
@ManyToOne
private Message replyTo;

@OneToMany(mappedBy = "replyTo")
private List<Message> replies = Collections.emptyList();

// Add/generate remaining getters and setters.
}
```

Note that the replyTo property represents the parent message which the current message is a reply to and that the replies property represents all replies to the current message. The tree structure can then be queried as follows in a MessageService:

```
public List<Message> tree() {
    return entityManager.createQuery(
        "SELECT DISTINCT m FROM Message m"
            + " LEFT JOIN FETCH m.replies r"
            + " ORDER BY m.id ASC", Message.class)
        .getResultList().stream()
        .filter(m -> m.getReplyTo() == null)
        .collect(toList());
}
```

Note that the filtering of the result list afterward is at first glance inefficient, but in reality, every single message is retrieved only once and simply referenced in the replies property.

Now, you'd intuitively implement the <t:message> composite component as something like the following:

```
<cc:interface>
    <cc:attribute name="value" type="com.example.Message" />
</cc:interface>
<cc:implementation>
    #{cc.attrs.value.text}
    <c:if test="#{not empty cc.attrs.value.replies}">
        <ul>
            <c:forEach items="#{cc.attrs.value.replies}" var="reply">
```

```
            <li>
                <t:message value="#{reply}" />
            </li>
        </c:forEach>
    </ul>
</c:if>
</cc:implementation>
```

which is in turn used as follows:

```
<c:forEach items="#{messages.tree}" var="message">
    <t:message value="#{message}" />
</c:forEach>
```

You'll perhaps only wonder why `<c:forEach>` is being used instead of `<ui:repeat>` inside the implementation of the composite component. The explanation is relatively simple: `<ui:repeat>` is ignored during view build time. In other words, when using `<ui:repeat>` there, then the `<t:message>` would include itself in an infinite loop. If you need to remember the why and how, head back to the section "Jakarta Tags" in Chapter 3.

But even with the previous implementation, you would still run into an infinite loop. You know that the #{cc} references the current instance of the composite component. Under the hood, when #{reply} is passed to the nested composite, then in reality, a reference to #{cc.attrs.value.replies[index]} is being passed. This is, on its own, no problem. But when the nested composite in turn evaluates the #{cc} part from this alias, then it would reference itself instead of the parent composite. Hence, the infinite loop.

Theoretically, you could solve this by replacing #{cc} with #{cc.parent} which returns UIComponent#getParent().

```
<c:forEach items="#{cc.attrs.value.replies}" varStatus="loop">
    ...
    <t:message value="#{cc.parent.attrs.value.replies[loop.index]}" />
    ...
</c:forEach>
```

However, it still doesn't work. Under the hood, inside the nested composite, when the EL evaluator comes to #{cc.parent} and attempts to evaluate "attrs.value" on it, then the parent composite component would return yet another EL expression in the form of #{cc.attrs.value} which ultimately gets evaluated. However, the #{cc} part still gets interpreted as "current composite component," which is inside the nested composite component and thus the nested composite itself.

We could only solve it to let the parent composite component not return yet another EL expression but instead the already-evaluated value. This can be achieved by overriding UIComponent#setValueExpression() in the backing component where you check whether the ValueExpression representing #{cc.attrs.value} is about to be set on the component and then immediately evaluate it and store the result as a local variable of the composite component. This shouldn't cause harm as it's supposed to be a read-only attribute.

```java
@FacesComponent("messageComposite")
public class MessageComposite extends UINamingContainer {

    private Message message;

    @Override
    public void setValueExpression
        (String attributeName, ValueExpression expression)
    {
        if ("value".equals(attributeName)) {
            ELContext elContext = getFacesContext().getELContext();
            message = (Message) expression.getValue(elContext);
        }
        else {
            super.setValueExpression(attributeName, expression);
        }
    }

    public Message getMessage() {
        return message;
    }
}
```

With this backing component in place, and replacing "attrs.value" by "message" in the implementation, then it finally works.

```
<cc:interface componentType="messageComposite">
    <cc:attribute name="value" type="com.example.Message" />
</cc:interface>
<cc:implementation>
    #{cc.message.text}
    <c:if test="#{not empty cc.message.replies}">
        <ul>
            <c:forEach items="#{cc.message.replies}" varStatus="loop">
                <li>
                    <t:message
                        value="#{cc.parent.message.replies[loop.index]}">
                    </t:message>
                </li>
            </c:forEach>
        </ul>
    </c:if>
</cc:implementation>
```

Implicit EL Objects

In Facelets files, there are a bunch of implicit EL objects available. They are mainly shortcuts to important artifacts, scopes, maps, and components available in the current faces context. Table 7-1 provides an overview of them.

Table 7-1. *Implicit EL Objects Available in EL Context of Jakarta Faces*

Implicit EL object	Resolves to	Returns	Since
#{facesContext}	FacesContext#getCurrentInstance( )	FacesContext	2.0
#{externalContext}	FacesContext#getExternalContext( )	ExternalContext	2.3
#{view}	FacesContext#getViewRoot( )	UIViewRoot	2.0
#{component}	UIComponent#getCurrentComponent( )	UIComponent	2.0
#{cc}	UIComponent#getCurrentComposite Component( )	UIComponent	2.0
#{request}	ExternalContext#getRequest( )	HttpServletRequest	1.0
#{session}	ExternalContext#getSession( )	HttpSession	1.0
#{application}	ExternalContext#getContext( )	ServletContext	1.0
#{flash}	ExternalContext#getFlash( )	Flash	2.0
#{requestScope}	ExternalContext#getRequestMap( )	Map<String, Object>	1.0
#{viewScope}	UIViewRoot#getViewMap( )	Map<String, Object>	2.0
#{flowScope}	FlowHandler#getCurrentFlowScope( )	Map<Object, Object>	2.2
#{sessionScope}	ExternalContext#getSessionMap( )	Map<String, Object>	1.0
#{applicationScope}	ExternalContext#getApplicationMap( )	Map<String, Object>	1.0
#{initParam}	ExternalContext#getInitParameterMap( )	Map<String, String>	1.0
#{param}	ExternalContext#getRequestParameter Map( )	Map<String, String>	1.0
#{paramValues}	ExternalContext#getRequestParameter ValuesMap( )	Map<String, String[ ]>	1.0
#{header}	ExternalContext#getRequestHeaderMap( )	Map<String, String>	1.0
#{headerValues}	ExternalContext#getRequestHeader ValuesMap( )	Map<String, String[ ]>	1.0
#{cookie}	ExternalContext#getRequestCookieMap( )	Map<String, Cookie>	1.0
#{resource}	ResourceHandler#createResource( )	Resource	2.0

For all implicit EL objects, if the class in turn specifies a getter method somewhere, such as `HttpServletRequest#getContextPath()`, then you can of course access it in EL the usual way as in `#{request.contextPath}`.

For scoped maps, any property will be interpreted as the map key. If the property happens to contain period characters, then you can use the brace notation as in `#{map['key.with.periods']}` in order to access the map value. Note that `#{flash}` essentially extends from `Map<String, Object>`, so it could be treated as such. It should also be said that `#{flowScope}` indeed deviates from other scoped maps by accepting `Object` instead of `String` as a map key. This is most likely a historical mistake. The canonical approach to access scoped maps is to use a `String`-based key.

`#{cookie}` is mapped by the cookie name, and the value actually returns a `jakarta.servlet.http.Cookie` instance that in turn has a `getValue()` property. So in order to access the `JSESSIONID` cookie, you basically need `#{cookie.JSESSIONID.value}`. Of course, you can in this specific example of the session ID also just use `#{session.id}` instead.

`#{resource}` actually has its own EL resolver that interprets any property as a resource identifier in "`library:name`" format and then passes it to `ResourceHandler#createResource()` and finally returns the URL of the resource via `Resource#getRequestPath()`. This is very useful in CSS resources in order to reference a Jakarta Faces image resource as a CSS background image. The following example will actually render the URL of `src/main/webapp/resources/images/background.svg`.

```
body {
    background-image: url("#{resource['images/background.svg']}");
    background-size: cover;
}
```

Note that resolving EL expressions in CSS resources only works when the CSS resource itself is included via `<h:outputStylesheet>` instead of `<link>`. Also noted should be that Jakarta Faces remembers by default only on the very first request of the CSS resource whether it contains EL expressions or not. If it didn't, then Jakarta Faces won't recheck it on a later request, even not in the development stage. So if you notice that your first EL expression in an existing CSS resource doesn't seem to work, then you'd better restart the web application. This feature of EL resolving in CSS resources is actually pretty useful.

This feature of EL resolving in CSS resources isn't available in JS resources. For them, you'd instead need to print a JS object in the global scope and let your JS resources intercept it if necessary. For example:

```
<h:outputScript>var config = #{configuration.script};</h:outputScript>
<h:outputScript name="scripts/some.js" />
```

whereby the #{configuration.script} just returns a JSON object as string from your managed bean. Or you could let EL print it as a data attribute of an HTML element, such as the context path in the following example:

```
<html lang="en" data-baseuri="#{request.contextPath}/">
    ...
</html>
```

which is in turn accessible in JS as follows:

```
var baseuri = document.documentElement.dataset.baseuri;
```

or if you're a jQuery fan:

```
var baseuri = $("html").data("baseuri");
```

That said, when creating managed beans on the Java side, or when declaring custom EL variables on the Facelets side, such as <h:dataTable var="foo">, <ui:repeat var="foo">, or <c:set var="foo">, then you need to make absolutely sure that you don't explicitly or implicitly choose a managed bean name or EL variable name that clashes with one of the previously listed implicit EL objects. This is because implicit EL objects have higher precedence in EL resolving than user-defined names. So, for example, the following construct wouldn't work as you might expect:

```
<ui:repeat value="#{bean.parameters}" var="param">
    #{param}<br />
</ui:repeat>
```

It would by default print literally "{}" for each iteration round, which is basically the default Map#toString() format of an empty Map. When you reopen the same page with a query string like ?foo=bar, then it would print literally "{foo=bar}" for each iteration round. You'd better rename the var="param" to something else, such as var="parameter".

CHAPTER 8

Backing Beans

The "backing bean" is a Jakarta Faces–specific concept. It represents the sole JavaBean class that is ultimately used as a "managed bean" responsible for providing data, actions, and/or components in a Jakarta Faces page.

Model, View, or Controller?

Jakarta Faces is an MVC (model-view-controller) framework. MVC is a widely used architectural design pattern for software applications that has its roots in desktop application development.[1]

In a Jakarta Faces framework's point of view, the model is represented by the backing bean; the view is represented by the component tree, which in turn is usually defined in a Facelets file; and the controller is represented by the `FacesServlet` that is already provided by Jakarta Faces. From a Jakarta EE application server's point of view, however, the model is represented by the service layer that in turn is usually using Jakarta Persistence entities, the view is represented by all your Jakarta Faces–based code, and the controller is the `FacesServlet`. In a Jakarta Faces developer's point of view, the model is represented by the service layer, the view is represented by the Facelets file, and the controller is represented by the backing bean.

The backing bean class can thus be either the model, view, or controller, depending on your point of view, while the service layer is always the model, and the Facelets file is always the view, and the `FacesServlet` is always the controller. Note that in this context, the "Jakarta Faces developer" is you, who develops a web application using the Jakarta Faces framework for a Jakarta EE application server.

---

[1] `https://en.wikipedia.org/wiki/Model-view-controller`

Figure 8-1 illustrates the position of the backing bean in Jakarta Faces' MVC paradigm. It's a Venn diagram where the intersection of the controller and the view is represented by the Jakarta Faces component tree which could be bound to a backing bean via the component's `binding` attribute. The intersection of the view and the model is represented by property getters and setters of EL value expressions which could be bound to a backing bean, usually via the component's `value` attribute. The intersection of the controller and the model is represented by action method invocations of EL method expressions which could be bound to a backing bean via the component's `action` attribute. Finally, the intersection of all intersections is represented by the backing bean itself.

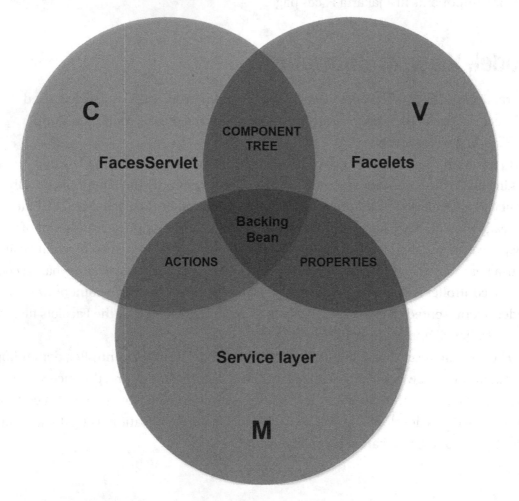

Figure 8-1. *The position of the backing bean in Jakarta Faces' MVC paradigm*

In this MVC paradigm, the backing bean has thus a rather unique position. Note that the backing bean doesn't necessarily need to be represented by a single class. It can even be represented by multiple classes, each with its own managed bean scope, like as that the view can be represented by multiple Facelets files and the model can be represented by multiple Jakarta Enterprise Beans and Jakarta Persistence classes.

Coming back to the Jakarta Faces developer's point of view, we can even get a step further with considering whether the backing bean is a model or a controller, depending on how you code the backing bean class. The following is one way:

```
@Named @RequestScoped @Stateful
public class ProductBacking {

    private String productName;
    private String productDescription;

    @Inject
    private ActiveUser activeUser;

    @PersistenceContext
    private EntityManager entityManager;

    public void save() {
        Product product = new Product();
        product.setName(productName);
        product.setDescription(productDescription);
        product.setCreatedBy(activeUser.get());
        entityManager.persist(product);
        FacesContext.getCurrentInstance().addMessage(null,
            new FacesMessage("Product created!"));
    }

    // Add/generate getters and setters for product name and description.
}
```

In this rather naive way, the entity's properties are essentially duplicated in the backing bean class, and the business logic is tightly coupled in the backing bean class. In other words, the backing bean class has incorrectly taken over the responsibilities of the real model. One would misinterpret such backing bean class as being the sole model. When we eliminate this duplication and unreusability, we find another way:

```
@Named @RequestScoped
public class ProductBacking {

    private Product product = new Product();

    @Inject
    private ProductService productService;

    public void save() {
        productService.create(product);
        FacesContext.getCurrentInstance().addMessage(null,
            new FacesMessage("Product created!"));
    }

    public Product getProduct() {
        return product;
    }
}
```

whereby the ProductService looks as follows:

```
@Stateless
public class ProductService {

    @PersistenceContext
    private EntityManager entityManager;

    @Inject
    private ActiveUser activeUser;

    public Long create(Product product) {
        product.setCreatedBy(activeUser.get());
        entityManager.persist(product);
        return product.getId();
    }
}
```

This is actually the correct way of authoring backing beans. When comparing it to the first way, you could argue that the backing bean has, in the Jakarta Faces developer's point of view, become a controller for the real model. The backing bean being a controller is not wrong from the Jakarta Faces developer's point of view, but this is not actually correct from the Jakarta Faces framework's point of view where the `FacesServlet` is the real controller. The `FacesServlet` treats the backing bean as a model, because the `FacesServlet` doesn't have direct access to the real model, the service layer. You as the Jakarta Faces developer can, of course, in your context treat the backing bean as a controller, because you can easily ignore all duties of the `FacesServlet` as you don't need to worry about its job while writing Jakarta Faces code. All you need to worry about while writing Jakarta Faces code is the view, the model, and the backing bean. The rest is done transparently by Jakarta Faces.

Managed Beans

The conceptual difference between a "backing bean" and a "managed bean" can be represented by the following lines of code that is executed under the hood of the bean management facility:

```
BackingBeanClass managedBeanInstance = new BackingBeanClass();
someContext.put("managedBeanName", managedBeanInstance, someScope);
```

In other words, the backing bean is the concrete class created by you, the Jakarta Faces developer, and registered into some bean management facility, such as CDI. The bean management facility will automatically manage the bean's life cycle by performing construction, dependency injection, and destruction when necessary, without you having to do it manually. If you've ever developed with plain vanilla Servlets and Jakarta Pages, then this basically removes the need to manually instantiate beans and put them as an attribute of the `ServletContext`, `HttpSession`, or `ServletRequest`.[2] To register a backing bean class as a CDI managed bean for Jakarta Faces views, simply put the `@jakarta.inject.Named` annotation[3] on the class signature.

---

[2] https://stackoverflow.com/q/3106452/157882
[3] https://jakarta.ee/specifications/platform/10/apidocs/jakarta/inject/Named.html

```
@Named
public class BackingBeanClass {
    // ...
}
```

It will then immediately be available in EL context by #{backingBeanClass} and in all other managed beans via @Inject. The EL context is directly available in Facelets files. By default, the managed bean name is derived from the backing bean's class name by lowercasing the first character. This can optionally be overridden by specifying the value of the @Named annotation.

```
@Named("managedBeanName")
public class BackingBeanClass {
    // ...
}
```

This is now in EL context available by #{managedBeanName}. Nothing has changed for the @Inject approach. Once a backing bean becomes a managed bean, it will be automatically instantiated and initialized whenever it's accessed for the first time in the context associated with the bean's scope. It will be automatically destroyed when the life cycle associated with the bean's scope has ended. More about managed bean scopes in the next section.

Historically, Jakarta Faces provided a native way to register backing bean classes as managed beans: first, in version 1.x via <managed-bean> entries in faces-config.xml and since version 2.0 via @jakarta.faces.bean.ManagedBean annotation, which is, since version 2.3, officially deprecated in favor of CDI @Named and, since version 4.0, completely removed.

CDI is natively available in Jakarta EE application servers and relatively easy to install in bare-bones servlet containers. For example, JBoss Weld, one of the CDI implementations, can already be installed in Tomcat by simply adding the single dependency org.jboss.weld.servlet:weld-servlet-shaded to the project[4] without any further effort.

---

[4] https://balusc.omnifaces.org/2013/10/how-to-install-cdi-in-tomcat.html

Scopes

The managed bean scope basically represents the lifetime of the managed bean. As hinted in the previous section, in plain vanilla Jakarta Servlet perspective, the scopes are represented by the object being put as an attribute of the `ServletContext`, `HttpSession`, or `ServletRequest`. Those objects will then become "application scoped," "session scoped," and "request scoped," respectively. This is still how it works with CDI and all; it only adds an extra abstract layer over it so that you don't anymore need to manually create and put the objects in a certain scope.

In standard Jakarta Faces, the following CDI based managed bean scopes are available for backing beans, ordered from the longest living to the shortest living:

1. `@jakarta.enterprise.context.ApplicationScoped`

2. `@jakarta.enterprise.context.SessionScoped`

3. `@jakarta.faces.lifecycle.ClientWindowScoped`

4. `@jakarta.enterprise.context.ConversationScoped`

5. `@jakarta.faces.flow.FlowScoped`

6. `@jakarta.faces.view.ViewScoped`

7. `@jakarta.enterprise.context.RequestScoped`

8. `@jakarta.enterprise.context.Dependent`

@ApplicationScoped

An application-scoped managed bean instance is tied to the lifetime of the web application itself. It's under the hood represented as an attribute of the `ServletContext` that is created on the web application's deployment and destroyed on the web application's undeployment. Note that this is not equal to the server's startup and shutdown. Web applications can be deployed and undeployed on a running server.

In other words, there's only one instance of an application-scoped managed bean throughout the web application's lifetime that is shared across all requests and sessions. You could argue that it behaves like a singleton. However, it doesn't actually follow the singleton design pattern. It follows the "just create one" design pattern.[5] A real singleton

---

[5] `http://butunclebob.com/ArticleS.UncleBob.SingletonVsJustCreateOne`

doesn't have any public constructor but only a static method that returns a statically initialized lazy loaded instance. A real JavaBean, on the other hand, requires the presence of a default constructor.

By default, an application-scoped bean managed instance is created for the first time when the web application's code accesses it for the first time during the web application's lifetime. It's thus not, per definition, immediately created when the ServletContext instance is created. It is, however, guaranteed to be destroyed when the ServletContext instance is destroyed.

Application-scoped managed beans are useful for application-wide data that needs to be initialized only once in the application's lifetime, or needs to provide nonstatic getters that delegate to static variables, or needs to provide functions for usage in EL. The following example makes sure that application settings stored in the database are loaded only once and provided as a Map by #{settings} during the rest of the application's lifetime.

```
@ApplicationScoped
public class ApplicationSettingsProducer {

    private Map<String, String> settings;

    @Inject
    private ApplicationSettingsService applicationSettingsService;

    @PostConstruct
    public void init() {
        settings = applicationSettingsService.getAll();
    }

    @Produces @Named
    public Map<String, String> getSettings() {
        return settings;
    }
}
```

Note that the @Named annotation is placed on the getter, which implies a managed bean name matching the property name: #{settings}. Also note that the getter in turn needs the @Produces annotation in order to be recognized as a managed bean producer. The following is another example that offers text formatting functions:

```
@Named @ApplicationScoped
public class Format {

    public String date(LocalDate localDate) {
        if (localDate != null) {
            return localDate.format(DateTimeFormatter.ISO_LOCAL_DATE);
        }
        else {
            return "n/a";
        }
    }

    public String currency(BigDecimal amount) {
        if (amount != null) {
            return NumberFormat.getCurrencyInstance(Locale.US)
                .format(amount);
        }
        else {
            return "n/a";
        }
    }
}
```

This could be useful in, for example, a data table to keep the Facelets code terse.

```
<h:dataTable value="#{cart.products}" var="product">
    <h:column>#{format.date(product.lastModified)}</h:column>
    <h:column>#{format.currency(product.discount)}</h:column>
</h:dataTable>
```

It's also useful in case you need a formatted value in an attribute that doesn't allow a nested <h:outputText><f:convertXxx>.

```
<h:commandLink ... title="Last visited #{format.date(user.lastVisited)}">
```

@SessionScoped

A session-scoped managed bean instance is tied to the lifetime of the established HTTP session. It's under the hood represented as an attribute of the `HttpSession` that is created for every unique client on demand of the web application's code. When the web application's code directly or indirectly pokes the `HttpSession` for the first time via `HttpServletRequest#getSession()`, then the servlet container will create a new `HttpSession` instance, generate a long and unique string as session ID, and store it in server's memory, usually as an entry of some internal `Map`. The servlet container will also set a session cookie on the HTTP response with "JSESSIONID" as the cookie name and the session ID as the cookie value. A "session cookie" is identified by the absence of the "maximum age" attribute.

As per the HTTP cookie specification, the client (the web browser) is required to send this cookie back in the header of the subsequent requests as long as the cookie is valid. In any decent web browser, you can inspect the request and response headers in the "Network" section of the web developer's toolset that is accessible by pressing F12 in the web browser. The servlet container will check every incoming HTTP request for the presence of the cookie with the name "JSESSIONID" and use its value (the session ID) to get the associated `HttpSession` instance from server's memory.

On the server side, the `HttpSession` instance stays alive until it has not been accessed for more than the timeout value as specified in the `<session-timeout>` setting of `web.xml`, which defaults to 30 minutes on most, if not all, servlet containers. So when the client doesn't visit the web application for longer than the time specified, then the servlet container will destroy the `HttpSession` instance. Every subsequent HTTP request, even with the cookie specified, will not have access to the associated `HttpSession` instance anymore; the servlet container will create a new `HttpSession` instance and overwrite the cookie value with the new session ID.

On the client side, by default, all session cookies stay alive for as long as the browser instance is running. So when the client shuts down the browser instance, then all session cookies are destroyed on the client side. In a new browser instance, the session cookies from a previous browser session are not available anymore, so the browser won't send any JSESSIONID cookie. The server will then interpret it as a brand-new session. The `HttpSession` instance associated with the previous browser session will silently expire on the server side.

By default, a session-scoped managed bean instance is created for the first time when the web application's code accesses it for the first time during the HTTP session's lifetime. It's thus not, per definition, immediately created when the HttpSession instance is created. It is, however, guaranteed to be destroyed when the HttpSession instance is destroyed. Session-scoped managed beans are effectively shared across all browser tabs and windows within the same browser session.

Session-scoped managed beans are useful for keeping track of client-specific data, such as the entity representing the currently logged-in user, the selected language, and other user-related preferences. The following example calculates the current locale and provides a getter/setter for it so that it can be obtained in the view and modified by a UIInput component.

```
@Named @SessionScoped
public class ActiveLocale implements Serializable {

    private Locale current;

    @PostConstruct
    public void init() {
        FacesContext context = FacesContext.getCurrentInstance();
        current = context.getApplication()
            .getViewHandler().calculateLocale(context);
    }

    // Getter+setter.
}
```

A more elaborate example can be found in the section "Changing the Active Locale" in Chapter 14. Do note that session-scoped managed beans must implement Serializable because the HttpSession instance itself, where those beans are being stored, is subject to being written to disk in case of a server restart, or even to being transferred over the network to a different server in case of a server cluster configuration with a distributable session.

Another classic example is a "shopping cart."

```
@Named @SessionScoped
public class Cart implements Serializable {

    private List<Product> products = new ArrayList<>();
```

```
public void addProduct(Product product) {
    products.add(product);
}

// ...
}
```

@ClientWindowScoped

A client-window-scoped managed bean is basically tied to the lifetime of the established `jakarta.faces.lifecycle.ClientWindow` instance, already introduced in Jakarta Faces 2.2 along with @FlowScoped. Only the @ClientWindowScoped annotation is new since Jakarta Faces 4.0.

The `ClientWindow` instance is in turn identified by a predefined HTTP request parameter with the name of "jfwid" ("Jakarta Faces Window ID") whose value represents the client window ID. The client window ID in turn basically references an isolated mapping in the current HTTP session where the client-window-scoped managed beans are stored. It needs to be activated first by adding the following context parameter to the `web.xml`.

```
<context-param>
    <param-name>jakarta.faces.CLIENT_WINDOW_MODE</param-name>
    <param-value>url</param-value>
</context-param>
```

The only other supported value is "none", which is also the default value. The absence of this context parameter will cause any usage of a @ClientWindowScoped bean to throw a `jakarta.enterprise.context.ContextNotActiveException`.

When having a @ClientWindowScoped bean referenced in a Jakarta Faces page, and it is opened for the first time and thus the bean is constructed for the first time, then a new value for the "jfwid" request parameter will be generated. This parameter will be visible in the URL when using a `UIOutcomeTarget` component to navigate through other pages. Jakarta Faces will, with the help of the `ViewHandler`, automatically append the "jfwid" request parameter to the outcome URLs.

The associated @ClientWindowScoped bean instance will remain active for the rest of the session as long as the same value of the "jfwid" request parameter is reused during subsequent postbacks and navigations, regardless of the browser tab or window it took place in. Only opening a brand new browser tab/window on the same URL without the "jfwid" request parameter will start a new ClientWindow and therefore also create a brand new @ClientWindowScoped bean.

When the end user manipulates the value of the "jfwid" request parameter to a custom value, then this will also start a new ClientWindow with its own new instance of the @ClientWindowScoped bean. There is, however, a maximum limit to the amount of allowable ClientWindow instances per HTTP session, which defaults to ten per session in case of Mojarra. This is configurable with the following context parameter in web.xml.

```
<context-param>
    <param-name>jakarta.faces.NUMBER_OF_CLIENT_WINDOWS</param-name>
    <param-value>25</param-value>
</context-param>
```

The ClientWindow will only end and destroy all associated beans when this limit is hit and thus the least recently used one will be evicted.

@ConversationScoped

A conversation-scoped managed bean is tied to the lifetime of the injected jakarta. enterprise.context.Conversation instance that offers begin() and end() methods which must be explicitly invoked by the web application's code in order to indicate the start and end of the conversation scope. The conversation scope is represented by a predefined HTTP request parameter with a default name of "cid" ("Conversation ID") whose value represents the conversation ID. The conversation ID in turn references an isolated mapping in the current HTTP session where the conversation-scoped managed bean instances will be stored.

As long as the conversation scope has not started, the conversation-scoped managed bean will behave like a request-scoped managed bean. When the application code explicitly invokes Conversation#begin(), then the conversation scope will start, and a custom jakarta.faces.application.ViewHandler provided by the CDI implementation will make sure that all its getXxxURL() methods such as getActionURL() and getBookmarkableURL() return a URL (uniform resource locator) with the conversation ID parameter included. In case of Weld, that's the

ConversationAwareViewHandler.[6] All Jakarta Faces `UIForm` and `UIOutcomeTarget`
components derive their action and target URLs from those methods of the
`ViewHandler`. The generated HTML output of those components will thus ultimately
include the conversation ID in the target URL.

On an incoming HTTP request, when the conversation ID parameter is present
in the request, and it is still valid, the CDI implementation will obtain the associated
conversation scope from the HTTP session and make sure that all conversation-scoped
managed beans are obtained from exactly this conversation scope identified by the
conversation ID. This works on both GET and POST requests. Any form submit or any
link/navigation to a URL with the conversation ID included will provide access to the very
same conversation scope, as long as it's still valid. The conversation scope ends when the
application code explicitly invokes `Conversation#end()`. When the end user reuses the
"cid" request parameter later or manipulates its value to one which isn't started in its
own browser session, or when the underlying `HttpSession` instance is destroyed, then
CDI will throw a `jakarta.enterprise.context.NonexistentConversationException`.

Conversation-scoped managed beans are particularly useful in order to be able
to return to a particular stateful page within the same browser session after being
redirected elsewhere. A classic example is a third-party web service that is included in an
HTML `<iframe>` or opened in a new browser tab or even targeted in the `action` attribute
of a plain HTML `<form>` and can, via a specific request parameter, be configured to
redirect back to your web application after completing the service. When you include
the conversation ID in the redirect URL, then you will in the redirected page be able to
resume with exactly the same conversation-scoped managed bean instance as it was
before the redirect. This allows you the opportunity to finalize and unlock any pending
transactions and, of course, end the conversation.

Given a checkout button that looks as follows:

```
<h:form>
    ...
    <ui:fragment rendered="#{empty payment.url}">
        ...
        <h:commandButton value="Checkout" action="#{payment.checkout}">
            <f:ajax render="@form" />
```

---

[6]https://github.com/weld/core/blob/4.0.0.Final/modules/jsf/src/main/java/org/jboss/
weld/module/jsf/ConversationAwareViewHandler.java

```
        </h:commandButton>
    </ui:fragment>
    <ui:fragment rendered="#{not empty payment.url}">
        <iframe src="#{payment.url}"></iframe>
    </ui:fragment>
</h:form>
```

here's what the associated conversation-scoped bean behind #{payment} looks like:

```
@Named @ConversationScoped
public class Payment implements Serializable {
    private Order order;
    private String url;

    @Inject
    private Cart cart;

    @Inject
    private OrderService orderService;

    @Inject
    private Conversation conversation;

    public void checkout() {
        order = orderService.lockProductsAndPrepareOrder(cart);
        conversation.begin();
        url = "https://third.party.com/pay?returnurl="
            + URLEncoder.encode("https://my.site.com/paid?cid="
            + conversation.getId(), "UTF-8");
    }

    public void confirm() {
        orderService.saveOrderAndCreateInvoice(order);
        conversation.end();
    }

    @PreDestroy
    public void destroy() {
        orderService.unlockProductsIfNecessary(order);
    }
```

```
public String getUrl() {
    return url;
}
```
}

Basically, the checkout button is only rendered when there's no payment URL set. Once the button is pressed, all products of the shopping cart are locked, and the order is prepared. Also, depending on the third-party payment service, the URL referring it must be prepared whereby you include the return URL as some query parameter in the URL of the payment service. The return URL should in turn include the "cid" request parameter representing the conversation ID. In the redirected page which will actually be loaded in the <iframe>, you can just mark the conversation complete with <f:viewAction>.

```
<f:metadata>
    <f:viewAction action="#{payment.confirm}" />
</f:metadata>
```

Of course, the average third-party payment service should have a more elaborate Java or even JavaScript API instead of <iframe>; also, it should be possible to provide different return pages for each payment outcome such as payment failed and payment aborted. The preceding example is just to give the general idea.

@FlowScoped

A flow-scoped managed bean is tied to the lifetime of a Jakarta Faces flow. It basically extends the client-window-scope with its predefined HTTP request parameter "jfwid"; only the scope is further narrowed down to a specific set of Jakarta Faces views in an isolated subfolder. Once the end user clicks a Jakarta Faces link or button component that navigates to a specific entry page of a Jakarta Faces flow, then the flow scope will automatically start. The flow scope cannot be started when you open the entry page without navigating to it via a Jakarta Faces link or button component.

Additionally, particularly when using a UIOutcomeTarget component instead of a UICommand component to navigate, then the query string may be accompanied with another predefined HTTP request parameters "jffi" ("Jakarta Faces Flow Identifier") and "jftfdi" ("Jakarta Faces To Flow Document Identifier"). Those are actually only mandatory for starting a Jakarta Faces flow using a GET request. Technically, for the rest of the flow, the "jfwid" parameter alone is sufficient. As long as the "jfwid" parameter is present and is still valid, then the Jakarta Faces flow is idempotent and can be resumed using a GET request. When you open a new browser tab and navigate into the Jakarta Faces flow, then actually a new flow scope will be started, independent of the flow scope in another tab. Once a postback request within the Jakarta Faces flow navigates to a page outside the flow, then the flow scope will automatically end. When the end user reuses the "jfwid" request parameter later, or manipulates its value to one which isn't started in its own browser session, or enters the flow directly, or when the underlying HttpSession instance is destroyed, then CDI will throw a jakarta.enterprise.context.ContextNotActiveException.

The major difference between the flow scope and the client window and conversation scopes is thus that the pages within a Jakarta Faces flow cannot be entered directly. They will automatically start when the end user navigates to the entry page of the flow, and they will automatically end when a postback navigates outside the flow. Flow-scoped managed beans are useful in order to isolate a conversation to a specific set of Jakarta Faces pages. A classic real-world example is a booking application that is spread over multiple forms in physically different pages.

There are various ways to define a Jakarta Faces flow. One way is by convention, another way is by declarative configuration in the /[flowId]/[flowId]-flow.xml file, and yet another way is by programmatic configuration using jakarta.faces.flow.FlowBuilder API.[7] In this book, we'll restrict ourselves to convention over configuration. First, create the following folder structure:

```
▾ ⌂ src
  ▾ ⌂ main
    ▸ ⌂ java
    ▸ ⌂ resources
    ▾ ⌂ webapp
      ▾ ⌂ booking
          booking.xhtml
          booking-flow.xml
          confirm.xhtml
          payment.xhtml
          persons.xhtml
      ▸ ⌂ WEB-INF
        home.xhtml
```

[7]https://jakarta.ee/specifications/platform/10/apidocs/jakarta/faces/flow/builder/FlowBuilder.html

The first convention is that the flow entry page must have exactly the same name as the subfolder it is sitting in. In this case, that's "booking". This is considered the Flow ID. The second convention is that there must be a *-flow.xml file in the subfolder whose name is prefixed with the Flow ID, that is, booking-flow.xml. This XML configuration file can be kept empty for now. It's only useful when you want to fine-grain the Jakarta Faces flow configuration, for example, by specifying a different entry page. Without this file, the flow scope won't be activated. One disadvantage of having at least one activated flow somewhere in the web application, however, is that the Jakarta Faces client Window ID parameter "jfwid" will be appended to every single navigation URL, even when it doesn't target a Jakarta Faces flow. This URL pollution may for some developers be the main reason to not use the flow scope at all.

The navigation component in order to enter a Jakarta Faces flow must be placed in a Jakarta Faces page outside the flow subfolder. The navigation outcome must reference the name of the flow subfolder, which is the Flow ID. Here's an example in /home.xhtml.

```
<h:button value="Start booking" outcome="booking" />
```

Of course, this can be substituted with <h:link>. It's recommended to use GET instead of POST for this so that the booking page's URL properly reflects in the browser's address bar. Then, in all pages within the subfolder, you can reference a flow-scoped managed bean which will be shared across all these pages. You can navigate back and forth between these pages as well while retaining the flow-scoped managed bean instance. It's recommended that you use Ajax with redirect for this. The Ajax submits will improve the user experience. The redirects will make sure that the individual pages are still bookmarkable.

Here's an example of how these pages look like. The /booking/booking.xhtml page has an input field requesting the start date as first step:

```
<h:form>
    <h:inputText value="#{booking.startDate}" />
    ...
    <h:commandButton value="Next" action="persons?faces-redirect=true">
        <f:ajax execute="@form" render="@form" />
    </h:commandButton>
</h:form>
```

The /booking/persons.xhtml page has several input fields requesting the person's details:

```
<h:form>
    <ui:repeat value="#{booking.persons}" var="person">
        <h:inputText value="#{person.name}" />
        ...
    </ui:repeat>
    ...
    <h:commandButton value="Back" action="booking?faces-redirect=true">
        <f:ajax execute="@form" render="@form" />
    </h:commandButton>
    <h:commandButton value="Next" action="confirm?faces-redirect=true">
        <f:ajax execute="@form" render="@form" />
    </h:commandButton>
</h:form>
```

The /booking/confirm.xhtml page shows a summary of the so far entered details:

```
<h:form>
    <h:outputText value="#{booking.startDate}" />
    ...
    <h:commandButton value="Back" action="persons?faces-redirect=true">
        <f:ajax execute="@form" render="@form" />
    </h:commandButton>
    <h:commandButton value="Next" action="payment?faces-redirect=true">
        <f:ajax execute="@form" render="@form" />
    </h:commandButton>
</h:form>
```

The /booking/payment.xhtml page shows a payment method drop-down and performs the payment:

```
<h:form>
    <h:selectOneMenu value="#{booking.paymentMethod}">
        ...
    </h:selectOneMenu>
    ...
```

```
    <h:commandButton value="Back" action="confirm?faces-redirect=true">
        <f:ajax execute="@form" render="@form" />
    </h:commandButton>
    <h:commandButton value="Submit" actionListener="#{booking.submit()}"
        action="/home?faces-redirect=true">
        <f:ajax execute="@form" render="@form" />
    </h:commandButton>
</h:form>
```

And, finally, the flow-scoped bean behind #{booking} can look like this:

```
@Named @FlowScoped("booking")
public class Booking implements Serializable {

    private LocalDate startDate;
    private List<Person> persons;
    private PaymentMethod paymentMethod;

    // ...

    public void submit() {
        // ...
    }
}
```

You see, the majority of navigation task is done by the `action` attribute of the command components. The `faces-redirect=true` is a special request parameter that is internally recognized by Jakarta Faces as an instruction to perform a redirect after postback. Of course, this request parameter is stripped of the target URL before performing the actual redirect. Once the postback leaves the flow, then the flow-scoped managed bean is destroyed, and the previously presented page URLs are not reusable anymore.

@ViewScoped

A view-scoped managed bean is tied to the lifetime of the Jakarta Faces view state. The Jakarta Faces view state is elaborated in the section "View State" in Chapter 3. In a nutshell, a view-scoped managed bean lives as long as the end user is performing postback requests on the very same Jakarta Faces view and the invoked action methods keep returning null or void. Once the action method returns non-null, even if it's an empty string or represents the same view, then the view scope will end. View-scoped managed beans are not shared across browser tabs within the same browser session. Each one gets its own unique instance. Effectively, they are indirectly identified by the jakarta.faces.ViewState hidden input field in the generated HTML representation of a Jakarta Faces form.

However, view-scoped managed beans are actually not stored in the Jakarta Faces view state, not even when client-side state saving is enabled. They are actually stored in the HTTP session, regardless of the Jakarta Faces state saving method. They are not immediately destroyed when the end user unloads the web page either by performing a GET request via a link or bookmark or editing the URL in browser's address bar, or by closing the browser tab. They will stick around in the HTTP session and only get destroyed when the HTTP session expires.

Because an end user can in theory spawn an unlimited amount of browser tabs within the same session, and thus also as many view states and view-scoped managed beans, there's a configurable maximum limit on the amount of view states and view-scoped managed beans which will be stored in the HTTP session. Once this limit is reached, the least recently used view state and view-scoped managed bean will be expired and destroyed. When the end user actually goes back to the tab that originally referenced the now expired view state and performs a postback request on it, then Jakarta Faces will throw a ViewExpiredException. The limit on the amount of view states is dependent on the Jakarta Faces implementation used. In Mojarra, this limit is configurable by the com.sun.faces.numberOfLogicalViews context parameter in web.xml whose default value is 15.[8]

```
<context-param>
    <param-name>com.sun.faces.numberOfLogicalViews</param-name>
    <param-value>25</param-value>
</context-param>
```

If your web application, however, invites being opened in many more browser tabs, such as a discussion forum or a Q&A site, then you'd better switch to client-side state saving. This way, the Jakarta Faces view states are no longer stored in the HTTP session and will therefore also never expire. However, the associated view-scoped managed

---

[8] https://stackoverflow.com/q/4105439/157882

beans are still stored in the HTTP session and expirable. When the end user actually goes back to the tab that originally referenced the now expired view-scoped managed bean and performs a postback request on it, then Jakarta Faces will not throw a `ViewExpiredException` but instead will create a new one from scratch, hereby losing all the state changes to the original managed bean instance. The limit on the amount of view-scoped managed beans is also dependent on the Jakarta Faces implementation used. In Mojarra, this limit is configurable by the `com.sun.faces.numberOfActiveViewMaps` context parameter in `web.xml` whose default value is 25.

```
<context-param>
    <param-name>com.sun.faces.numberOfActiveViewMaps</param-name>
    <param-value>15</param-value>
</context-param>
```

This configuration actually decreases the default value to be equal to default maximum amount of Jakarta Faces view states in session. This is fine when you're using serverside state saving and all your Jakarta Faces views effectively reference only one view-scoped managed bean instance. However, in a decently developed and refactored Jakarta Faces web application, the average Jakarta Faces page usually references multiple view-scoped managed beans. If you have, for example, a maximum amount of three different view-scoped managed beans per Jakarta Faces view, then you'd best set the limit to three times the value of `com.sun.faces.numberOfLogicalViews`. You only need to take into account the possible memory consumption. It will quickly go overboard when the view-scoped managed beans in turn hold relatively a lot of data.

View-scoped managed beans are very useful for retaining state across Ajax-based postbacks on the same Jakarta Faces view, particularly if those postbacks result in changes in the value of the `rendered` attribute of any `UIComponent`, or the `disabled` or `readonly` attribute of any `UIInput` component, or the disabled attribute of any `UICommand` component within the same Jakarta Faces view. That is, on a subsequent postback, Jakarta Faces will, as part of a safeguard against a tampered request, recheck them before actually processing the component. If the managed bean holding the state was request scoped instead of view scoped, then those changes in the conditions would get lost in a subsequent postback, and the postback wouldn't get processed as intuitively expected. In other words, view-scoped managed beans are particularly useful in dynamic forms.

One example is a drop-down that conditionally renders a free text field when the "other" option is chosen.

```
<f:metadata>
    <f:importConstants type="com.example.project.model.Title" />
</f:metadata>
...
<h:form>
    <h:selectOneMenu value="#{bean.customer.title}">
        <f:selectItems value="#{Title}" />
        <f:ajax render="other" />
    </h:selectOneMenu>
    <h:panelGroup id="other">
        <h:inputText rendered="#{bean.customer.title eq 'OTHER'}"
            value="#{bean.customer.titleOther}" required="true" />
    </h:panelGroup>
    ...
    <h:commandButton value="Save" action="#{bean.save}" />
</h:form>
```

This construct won't work when the managed bean is request scoped and is thus recreated on every request. When the drop-down changes, then it creates a new instance of the request-scoped bean, sets the title there, and renders the free text field, and finally the request-scoped bean instance gets destroyed. When the form submits, then it creates a new instance of the request-scoped bean, thus without the customer title, and when Jakarta Faces checks the `rendered` attribute during the apply request values phase (second phase) of the free text field and notices that it's `false`, then it ultimately won't process the free text field at all. This construct will only work when the managed bean is view scoped, because the customer title set during the drop-down change is still available during the apply request values phase (second phase) of the form submit.

There is, however, a work-around. You could let the rendered attribute check the HTTP request parameter instead of the model value. As explained in Chapter 4, the HTTP request parameter name is specified by the component's client ID. You could bind the drop-down component to the view and use its client ID to obtain the HTTP request parameter value.

```
<h:selectOneMenu binding="#{title}" value="#{bean.customer.title}">
    <f:selectItems value="#{Title}" />
    <f:ajax render="other" />
</h:selectOneMenu>
<h:panelGroup id="other">
    <h:inputText rendered="#{param[title.clientId] eq 'OTHER'}"
        value="#{bean.customer.titleOther}" required="true" />
</h:panelGroup>
```

This way, when Jakarta Faces checks the rendered attribute during the apply request values phase (second phase) of the form submit, then it will notice that it's true and continue processing the free text field, even when the managed bean is request scoped and thus #{bean.customer.title} is still null at that point. Note that the binding attribute doesn't reference a managed bean property. This is unnecessary as it wouldn't be used over there.

This example of Jakarta Faces behavior on the rendered attribute is also fully applicable on the readonly attribute of any UIInput component and the disabled attribute of any UIInput and UICommand component.

There may also be cases wherein a request-scoped managed bean will work just fine but imposes a risk of a corrupted state as compared to a view-scoped managed bean, certainly when relying on data coming from a shared database which could be mutated by other users. This affects primarily use cases whereby UIInput or UICommand components are nested in an iterating component such as <h:dataTable>, <ui:repeat>, and <c:forEach> that iterates over a model coming from the database. This was explained previously in Chapter 6, but for the sake of refreshment, we will explain it once more. Imagine a table of products with a delete button in a column.

```
<f:form id="list">
    <h:dataTable id="products" value="#{products.list}" var="product">
        ...
        <h:column>
            <h:commandButton id="delete" value="Delete"
```

```
                action="#{products.delete(product)}">
                    <f:ajax render="@namingcontainer" />
            </h:commandButton>
        </h:column>
    </h:dataTable>
</h:form>
```

with this backing bean:

```
@Named @ViewScoped
public class Products implements Serializable {

    private List<Product> list;

    @Inject
    private ProductService productService;

    @PostConstruct
    public void init() {
        list = productService.list();
    }

    public void delete(Product product) {
        productService.delete(product);
        list.remove(product);
    }

    public List<Product> getList() {
        return list;
    }
}
```

The submitted button is under the hood identified by the iteration index. When Jakarta Faces is about to process the form submit, and a product has been added or removed or even reordered in the meanwhile, causing the iteration index to be changed, then the invoked action would possibly be performed against the wrong item currently at the initially known index. This is dangerous for the integrity of the model. In such a case, the value of the iteration component must refer a view-scoped model.

Also here, there is a work-around. Instead of relying on the iteration index, you can also rely on the unique identifier of the iterated object which must be passed as an HTTP request parameter instead of as an EL method argument.

```
<f:form id="list">
    <h:dataTable id="products" value="#{products.list}" var="product">
        ...
        <h:column>
            <h:commandButton id="delete" value="Delete"
                action="#{products.delete}">
                <f:param name="id" value="#{product.id}" />
                <f:ajax render="@namingcontainer" />
            </h:commandButton>
        </h:column>
    </h:dataTable>
</h:form>
```

whereby the backing bean is adjusted as follows:

```
@Named @RequestScoped
public class Products {

    private List<Product> list;

    @Inject @ManagedProperty("#{param.id}")
    private Long id;

    @Inject
    private ProductService productService;

    @PostConstruct
    public void init() {
        list = productService.list();
    }

    public void delete() {
        productService.delete(id);
        list.removeIf(product -> product.getId().equals(id));
    }
```

```
    public List<Product> getList() {
        return list;
    }
}
```

No, the `action="#{products.delete(product.id)}"` instead of using `<f:param>` won't work. The technical reason is that `<f:param>` is executed immediately during the render response phase of the form, long before the end user presses the delete button. Thus, at the moment the end user presses the delete button, it's guaranteed to have the correct value. The EL method argument, on the contrary, is only evaluated during the postback request after the end user has pressed the delete button. When the model has changed in the meanwhile, then it would thus evaluate to the wrong ID when the iteration index of the particular product has changed.

As explained in the beginning of this section, the standard Jakarta Faces view-scoped bean management facility has thus two major disadvantages: first, the instances don't immediately expire when the end user unloads the web page and stick around in the HTTP session; second, even with client-side state saving enabled, they are stored in the HTTP session. Those problems are currently not yet solved in the standard Jakarta Faces API.

For now, the Jakarta Faces utility library OmniFaces offers an enhanced `@ViewScoped` annotation that solves those two disadvantages.[9] View-scoped managed beans annotated with `@org.omnifaces.cdi.ViewScoped` will actually get destroyed when the end user unloads the page. This is under the hood done with the help of `Navigator.sendBeacon` API[10] in JavaScript and a specialized `ViewHandler` implementation provided by OmniFaces that listens on those unload requests. There have been production applications making heavy use of view-scoped managed beans whereby the memory usage has reduced for up to 80% after switching from standard Jakarta Faces `@ViewScoped` to OmniFaces `@ViewScoped`. This makes the destroy-on-unload feature a major candidate to be added to the future version of the standard Jakarta Faces API.

In order to save the physical view-scoped managed bean in the Jakarta Faces view state when client-side state saving is enabled, the `saveInViewState` attribute of the OmniFaces `@ViewScoped` annotation must be set to `true`. You only need to keep in mind that those beans will never expire, not even when the page gets unloaded, or

---

[9] https://showcase.omnifaces.org/cdi/ViewScoped
[10] https://developer.mozilla.org/en-US/docs/Web/API/Navigator/sendBeacon

when the HTTP session expires. In fact, the entire bean has physically become part of the generated HTML output, in the `jakarta.faces.ViewState` hidden input field. There have been community requests to make Jakarta Faces state management more flexible, such as toggling between client- and server-side state saving on a per-view (per `UIViewRoot`) or even per-form (per `UIForm`) basis and being able to store view-scoped managed beans in the actual view state instead of in the HTTP session. This may also be reconsidered in a future version of the standard Jakarta Faces API.

@RequestScoped

A request-scoped managed bean is among others tied to the lifetime of the HTTP request, which is for Jakarta Faces the most important case. Other cases include the lifetimes of a call to an asynchronous method invocation on a session bean (a method annotated by `@Asynchronous`), a timer timeout method, or when a message-driven bean (MDB) processes a message, all in Jakarta Enterprise Beans (previously known as Jakarta Enterprise Beans). Note that an Ajax request also counts as a single HTTP request.

When the client sends an HTTP request to the server, then the servlet container will create `HttpServletRequest` and `HttpServletResponse` instances representing the HTTP request and response and pass them through the authentication modules, servlet filters, and servlets. They will be destroyed immediately after all authentication modules, servlet filters, and servlets are finished processing the request and response. In other words, every HTTP request creates a new instance of a request-scoped managed bean that is available only during that request and not in other requests.

Request-scoped managed beans are useful for simple and static forms which don't have any dynamic Ajax-based updates, for which you would rather use a view-scoped managed bean. Think of a login form or a contact form.

```
@Named @RequestScoped
public class Login {

    private String username;
    private String password;

    // ...
}
```

Sure, those forms can be tied to a view-scoped managed bean as well without problems, but that's a waste of memory space. Note that you should absolutely not make the Jakarta Persistence entity itself a managed bean. In other words, the following approach is factually wrong:

```
@Named @RequestScoped // or @Model
@Entity
public class Product {
    // ...
}
```

Not only does this violate the Law of Demeter,[11] but it also risks that Jakarta Persistence won't be able to persist it, because CDI actually wraps the managed bean in a proxy class and Jakarta Persistence would then not be able to obtain the entity information from it when you're about to pass an injected instance to the entity manager. Hibernate would in such case throw "Unknown entity: com.example.Entity$Proxy$_$$_WeldClientProxy", which thus actually represents the CDI proxy class.

You might at this point wonder how exactly CDI actually works. First, it will, during the web application's startup, collect all classes that are annotated with a CDI-compatible scope annotation. Then, it will generate proxy classes for all of them. Ultimately, instances of those proxy classes are being injected. Given an example bean class com.example.Bean, the generated CDI proxy class may look as follows:

```
public class Bean$Proxy$_$$_CDI extends Bean implements Serializable {

    public String getSomeProperty() {
        Bean actualInstance = CDI.resolveItSomehow();
        return actualInstance.getSomeProperty();
    }

    public void setSomeProperty(String someProperty) {
        Bean actualInstance = CDI.resolveItSomehow();
        actualInstance.setSomeProperty(someProperty);
    }
}
```

---

[11] https://en.wikipedia.org/wiki/Law_of_Demeter

You see, it extends the bean class, makes it serializable, and uses an "impossible to clash" class name and lets all methods delegate to the actual instance obtained from the CDI context. You'll probably also immediately understand why the CDI bean management facility requires the bean classes to be public and have a public default constructor. You'll also see that when such a proxy class is created and injected, the underlying actual instance is not necessarily created. It's only automatically created when the fictive `CDI.resolveItSomehow()` method is invoked. Under the hood, it will obtain the context from a thread local variable, exactly how `FacesContext#getCurrentInstance()` works.

By the way, Jakarta Enterprise Beans also works with serializable proxies this way. That's why it could seemingly magically perform all the heavy lifting of starting or joining a transaction and using pooled instances. This is all thus actually done in the proxied methods, before and after calling the actual instance method.

Note that CDI has also a `@jakarta.enterprise.inject.Model` stereotype annotation that basically bundles both `@Named` and `@RequestScoped` into a single annotation. This is in no way different from a request-scoped managed bean. Unfortunately, it does not represent a non-proxy instance; otherwise, it would be nice to put it on an `@Entity`. The `@Model` annotation exists just for convenience.

@Dependent

A dependent-scoped managed bean is tied to the lifetime of the scope wherein it's being created for the first time. So if you inject it into an `@ApplicationScoped`, then it will become application scoped too. And if you inject it into a `@ViewScoped`, then it will become view scoped too. And so on. This is the default CDI scope.

This has, however, a caveat. When you forget to declare any CDI scope annotation on your `@Named` backing bean, and you reference it directly in EL, as in `#{dependentScopedBean}`, instead of referencing it via another managed bean, as in `#{requestScopedBean.dependentScopedBean}`, then every EL evaluation will basically create a brand-new instance that exists only within that EL context. In other words, imagine a Jakarta Faces form with two input fields and a submit button, each bound to a dependent-scoped managed bean, then you will effectively end up with three separate instances. One wherein the first input field is set, one wherein the second input field is set, and one wherein the action method is invoked. So if you ever observe odd behavior of `null` submitted values in the action method even though the required validation has passed, then the first thing to check is whether the CDI managed bean scope is present and correct.

The major technical difference with other scopes is that dependent-scoped managed beans are not proxied. In other words, what's being injected is the actual instance. Here's an example of how it could be used to prepare a new (and unproxied!) Jakarta Persistence entity via @Inject:

```
@Dependent
public class Entities {

    @Produces
    public Product getProduct() {
        return new Product();
    }
}

@Named @RequestScoped
public class Products {

    @Inject
    private Product product;

    @Inject
    Private ProductService productService;

    public void add() {
        productService.create(product);
    }

    public Product getProduct() {
        return product;
    }
}
```

Note that you still can't use `<h:inputText value="#{product.name}">` because it would get its own instance. You still need to use #{products.product.name}. For exactly this reason, the producer method isn't @Named. Also note that in case of a view-scoped managed bean, you'd need to force Jakarta Faces to restart the view scope by returning a nonnull outcome from action method; otherwise, the injected Product instance would be reused for the next view.

In the end, this example is not terribly useful because the behavior is not necessarily intuitive. You'd better use `private Product product = new Product();` instead without the `@Inject`.

Which Scope to Choose?

Which scope to choose depends solely on the data (instance variables, a.k.a. the state) the bean holds and represents. You should strive to put the state in the shortest possible acceptable scope. Start with a `@RequestScoped` bean. Once you notice that some state needs to be retained after a postback on the same view, split that state exactly into a new `@ViewScoped` bean which you, in turn, `@Inject` in the `@RequestScoped` bean. Once you notice that some state needs to be retained on another request within the same session, split that state exactly into a new `@SessionScoped` bean which you in turn `@Inject` in the `@RequestScoped` bean. And so on.

Abusing an `@ApplicationScoped` bean for session-, conversation-, flow-, view-, or request-scoped data would make it to be shared among all users, so anyone else can see each other's data, which is just plain wrong. Abusing a `@SessionScoped` bean for conversation-, flow-, view-, or request-scoped data would make it to be shared among all browser tabs in the same session, so the end user may experience inconsistencies when interacting with every view after switching between tabs, which is bad for user experience. Abusing a `@RequestScoped` bean for view-, flow-, or conversation-scoped data would make view-, flow-, or conversation-scoped data be reinitialized to default on every single (Ajax) postback, causing possibly nonworking forms. Abusing a `@ViewScoped`, `@FlowScoped`, or `@ConversationScoped` bean for request-, session-, or application-scoped data and abusing a `@SessionScoped` bean for application-scoped data doesn't affect the end user, but it unnecessarily occupies server memory and is plain inefficient.

Note that the scope should rather not be chosen based on performance implications, unless you really have a low memory footprint and want to go completely stateless. You'd then need to exclusively use stateless forms with `@RequestScoped` beans and fiddle with request parameters to maintain any client's state. In other words, you would possibly need to reinvent whatever already is being done by the `jakarta.faces.ViewState` hidden input field.

Where Is @FlashScoped?

At last, Jakarta Faces also supports the flash scope. It is backed by a short living cookie that is associated with a data entry in the session scope. Before the redirect, a cookie will be set on the HTTP response with a value that represents the unique key of the data entry in the session scope. After the redirect, the presence of the flash scope cookie will be checked, and the data entry associated with the cookie value as key will be removed from the session scope and will be put in the request scope of the redirected request. Finally, the cookie will be removed from the HTTP response. This way, the redirected request has access to request-scoped data that has been prepared in the initial request.

This is actually not available as a managed bean scope by standard Jakarta Faces API. In other words, there is no such thing as @FlashScoped. The flash scope is only available as a map via ExternalContext#getFlash() in managed beans and #{flash} in EL. Historically, the flash scope was primarily introduced in order to be able to show a faces message set in the action method in the redirected page. Imagine the use case of saving an edited product in a detail page and redirecting back to the master page.

```
public String save() {
    FacesContext context = FacesContext.getCurrentInstance();

    try {
        productService.update(product);
        context.addMessage(null, new FacesMessage("Product saved!"));
        return "/products?faces-redrect=true";
    }
    catch (Exception e) {
        context.addMessage(null, new FacesMessage(
            "Cannot save product. Error: " + e.getMessage()));
        return null;
    }
}
```

The faces message "Product saved!" wouldn't show up in the <h:messages globalOnly> of the redirected page because faces messages are inherently request scoped (actually, "faces context scoped"). Historically, during the Jakarta Faces 1.x era, this problem was solved with a phase listener that copies after the render response phase all undisplayed faces messages into the HTTP session and re-adds after the restore view phase any of them back into the faces context. Since the introduction of the flash scope in Jakarta Faces 2.0, this problem could be solved in an easier way by simply invoking `Flash#setKeepMessages()`[12].

```
productService.update(product);
context.addMessage(null, new FacesMessage("Product saved!"));
context.getExternalContext().getFlash().setKeepMessages(true);
return "/products?faces-redirect=true";
```

This way, the faces messages are before redirect automatically stored in the flash scope and restored after redirect.

The flash scope is not only useful for faces messages. It's also useful for passing entire objects while redirecting from one view to another view, without needing to pass some object identifier as a request parameter. The following is an example that prepares an entity for the next step without needing to save it in the database first:

```
@Named @RequestScoped // or @ViewScoped
public class Home {

    private Product product = new Product();

    public String prepareProduct() {
        FacesContext context = FacesContext.getCurrentInstance();
        context.getExternalContext().getFlash().put("product", product);
        return "/next?faces-redirect=true";
    }

    public Product getProduct() {
        return product;
    }
}
```

whereby the bean of the next step looks as follows:

```
@Named @ViewScoped
public class Next implements Serializable {

    @Inject @ManagedProperty("#{flash.product}")
    private Product product;
```

---

[12] https://jakarta.ee/specifications/platform/10/apidocs/jakarta/faces/context/Flash.html#setKeepMessages-boolean

```
public void save() {
    // ...
}

public Product getProduct() {
    return product;
}
```
}

And the /next.xhtml redirects back to /home.xhtml when the entity is absent in the flash scope.

```
<f:metadata>
    <f:viewAction action="/home" if="#{empty flash.product}" />
</f:metadata>
```

Note that this redirect will thus take place when you open /next.xhtml directly, or when you refresh the page in the web browser. In case you'd like to avoid that, then you can instruct the flash scope to keep the entry value in the flash scope by prefixing the entry key with the predefined key "keep" on the #{flash} map.

```
@Named @RequestScoped
public class Next {

    @Inject @ManagedProperty("#{flash.keep.product}")
    private Product product;
    // ...
}
```

This way, the lifetime of the flash scope will expand until the end user closes the browser window, or when the application navigates to a different view, or when the underlying HTTP session expires. This way, you can even make the managed bean request scoped instead of view scoped and not lose the entity while submitting a form in the /next.xhtml page or even refreshing the page. This is a relatively powerful feature of the flash scope.

Managed Bean Initialization and Destruction

Managed bean instances can be initialized based on injected dependencies in a @ PostConstruct annotated method. Managed bean instances can hook on destroy event in a @PreDestroy annotated method.

```
@Named
public class Bean {

    @PostConstruct
    public void init() {
        // ...
    }

    @PreDestroy
    public void destroy() {
        // ...
    }
}
```

The method names are not predefined. The exact method names init() and destroy() are basically taken over from the existing HttpServlet API. You can of course choose your own method names, such as onload() and cleanup(). It's useful to know that those annotations are inheritable. In other words, you could put those initialization and destruction methods in an abstract base class.

In the postconstruct method, you have the opportunity to perform initialization based on injected dependencies. Those injected dependencies are not available in the constructor yet. The bean management facility can only inject the dependencies after having constructed the managed bean instance. It will then immediately invoke the @PostConstruct annotated method. In the pre-destroy method, you have the opportunity to perform any necessary cleanup, such as closing resources, deleting files, and saving state.

Injecting Jakarta Faces Vended Types

Managed beans can obviously be injected in each other via CDI's @Inject as demonstrated several times so far in this book. Next to injecting your own types, a variety of Jakarta Faces vended types can be injected via CDI as well. These types largely correspond to the implicit EL objects we saw in Table 7-1 in the "Implicit EL Objects" section in Chapter 7. This is no coincidence. Internally, implicit objects in Jakarta Faces are implemented by so-called Bean<T> instances from CDI. These CDI Bean<T> instances are effectively the factory objects that know how to generate beans, with what type and optional qualifier and/or with what name.

When the name of an implicit object is used in expression language, the CDI EL resolver does a lookup for that object by name, which results in a call to a certain Bean<T> instance. When we're injecting, the type into which we inject, together with any explicit or implicit qualifiers, forms an alternative key that's being used for this lookup. Both types of keys will result in the exact same CDI Bean<T> instance being used.

Table 8-1 shows the Jakarta Faces vended types that are injectable via CDI.

Table 8-1. *Injectable Jakarta Faces Vended Types, All Since 2.3*

Injectable Jakarta Faces type	Resolves to
jakarta.faces.context.FacesContext	FacesContext#getCurrentInstance()
jakarta.faces.context.ExternalContext	FacesContext#getExternalContext()
jakarta.faces.component.UIViewRoot	FacesContext#getViewRoot()
jakarta.faces.context.Flash	ExternalContext#getFlash()
@RequestMap Map<String, Object>	ExternalContext#getRequestMap()
@ViewMap Map<String, Object>	UIViewRoot#getViewMap()
@FlowMap Map<Object, Object>	FlowHandler#getCurrentFlowScope()
@SessionMap Map<String, Object>	ExternalContext#getSessionMap()
@ApplicationMap Map<String, Object>	ExternalContext#getApplicationMap()
@InitParameterMap Map<String, String>	ExternalContext#getInitParameterMap()
@RequestParameterMap Map<String, String>	ExternalContext#getRequestParameterMap()
@RequestParameterValuesMap Map<String, String[ ]>	ExternalContext#getRequestParameterValuesMap()
@HeaderMap Map<String, String>	ExternalContext#getRequestHeaderMap()
@HeaderValuesMap Map<String, String[ ]>	ExternalContext#getRequestHeaderValuesMap()
@RequestCookieMap Map<String, Cookie>	ExternalContext#getRequestCookieMap()
jakarta.faces.application.ResourceHandler	Application#getResourceHandler()

It should be noted that compared to the implicit EL objects mentioned in Table 7-1, a few are missing for CDI-injectable Jakarta Faces vended types mentioned in Table 8-1, namely:

- `#{component}`
- `#{cc}`
- `#{request}`
- `#{session}`
- `#{application}`

Both `#{component}` and `#{cc}` resolve to `UIComponent` that is not injectable, since this would require a special proxy or custom scope that's narrow enough to resolve the "current" instance of those at the time the injected type is accessed. Since such scope is not available in Jakarta Faces yet, these had been excluded from CDI injection.

The `#{request}`, `#{session}`, and `#{application}`, respectively, representing `HttpServletRequest`, `HttpSession`, and `ServletContext` in a Servlet container have been omitted since these types are not owned by Jakarta Faces and therefore Jakarta Faces should not provide CDI injection capabilities for those. The fact that Jakarta Faces does provide implicit EL objects for those is mostly historical. The only specification that should provide injection for those types is the Servlet API, which owns those types directly.

As can be seen from Table 8-1, for objects for which there is only one instance and that instance is vended (owned) by Jakarta Faces, no qualifier is needed. When it concerns more general types, such as the various maps, a qualifier is needed. All these qualifier annotations are available from the `jakarta.faces.annotation` package.[13]

A caveat is that all of the preceding types are request scoped, but the time during which they are valid is actually smaller, namely, from shortly after the moment the `service()` method of the `FacesServlet` is called until shortly before the moment that method is exited. Care should be taken not to inject and access these types outside that time. It's expected that a future revision of the Jakarta Faces spec will address this problem.

---

[13] https://jakarta.ee/specifications/platform/10/apidocs/jakarta/faces/annotation/package-summary.html

324

The following shows an example of injecting two of the Jakarta Faces vended types:

```
@Named @RequestScoped
public class Bean {

    @Inject
    private Flash flash;

    @Inject @RequestParameterMap
    private Map<String, String> requestParameterMap;

    public void someMethod() {
        if (requestParameterMap.containsKey("something")) {
            flash.put("aKey", "aValue");
        }
    }
}
```

Eager Initialization

Managed beans are by default lazily initialized whenever they are for the first time referenced in an EL expression or as an injected dependency. Managed beans can be eagerly initialized on the start of any scope by an observer method that observes the initialization of the scope of interest. One example was previously given in the "@ViewScoped" section. The general pattern of the eager initialization method is as follows:

```
public void startup(@Observes @Initialized(XxxScoped.class) S scope) {
    // ...
}
```

where XxxScoped.class can be any CDI-compatible scope and the S represents the owner of the scope. For the following scopes that are thus:

- ApplicationScoped.class – jakarta.servlet.ServletContext

- SessionScoped.class – jakarta.servlet.http.HttpSession

- ConversationScoped.class – jakarta.servlet.ServletRequest

- FlowScoped.class – jakarta.faces.flow.Flow

- ViewScoped.class – jakarta.faces.component.UIViewRoot

- RequestScoped.class – jakarta.servlet.ServletRequest

Note that the containing bean must be of at least the same scope in order to have
@Observes @Initialized take effect. Eager initialization has for an application-scoped
managed bean the advantage that you can configure it as a "startup" bean without
needing to reference it in some other bean in order to get it initialized.

```
@ApplicationScoped
public class Startup {
    public void contextInitialized
        (@Observes @Initialized(ApplicationScoped.class)
            ServletContext context)
    {
        // ...
    }
}
```

Eager initialization has for a request-scoped bean the advantage that you can, if
necessary, invoke an asynchronous DB query long before the FacesServlet is invoked.

```
@Named @RequestScoped
public class EagerProducts {

    private Future<List<Product>> list;

    @Inject
    private ProductService productService;

    public void requestInitialized
        (@Observes @Initialized(RequestScoped.class)
            HttpServletRequest request)
    {
        if ("/products.xhtml".equals(request.getServletPath())) {
            list = productService.asyncList();
        }
    }
```

```
    public List<Product> getList() {
        try {
            return list.get();
        }
        catch (InterruptedException e) {
            Thread.currentThread().interrupt();
            throw new FacesException(e);
        }
        catch (ExecutionException e) {
            throw new FacesException(e);
        }
    }
}
```

where the ProductService looks like this:

```
@Stateless
public class ProductService {

    @TransactionAttribute(SUPPORTS)
    public List<Product> list() {
        return entityManager
            .createQuery("FROM Product ORDER BY id DESC", Product.class)
            .getResultList();
    }

    @Asynchronous
    public Future<List<Product>> asyncList() {
        return new AsyncResult<>(list());
    }
}
```

Note particularly that the requestInitialized() method needs to determine the actual path before invoking the business service method. This is because the @Observes @Initialized(RequestScoped.class) is basically invoked on every single request. In this specific example, the business service method will thus only be hit when the request hits the /products.xhtml page. That page can in turn just reference the product list as usual.

```
<h:dataTable value="#{eagerProducts.list}" var="product">
    ...
</h:dataTable>
```

When opening this page, then the request scoped bean will thus be initialized directly upon start of the request, long before the `FacesServlet` is invoked, and asynchronously fetch the `List<Products>` from the database. Depending on the server hardware used, the available server resources, and all synchronous code running between the creation of the bean and entering the Jakarta Faces render response phase, this approach may give you a time space of 10–500ms (or perhaps even more when there's some inefficient code in the pipeline) to fetch data from DB in a different thread parallel with the HTTP request and thus a speed improvement equivalent to the time the DB needs to fetch the data.

Layers

While implementing backing beans, it's very important to understand the importance of the separation of the Jakarta Faces backing bean from the Jakarta Persistence entity and the Jakarta Enterprise Beans service. In other words, when developing backing beans, you should make sure that your backing beans are as slick as possible and that they delegate as much as possible model properties to entities and business logic to services. You should realize that entities and services should be fully reusable on a completely different front end than Jakarta Faces, such as Jakarta RESTful Web Services or even plain vanilla Jakarta Pages/Servlets.

This thus also means that you should make sure that you don't directly or indirectly include a Jakarta Faces–specific dependency in an entity or a service. For example, the following approach is factually wrong:

```
@Entity
public class Product {

    private String name;
    private String description;

    public static Product of(ProductBacking backingBean) {
        Product product = new Product();
        product.setName(backingBean.getName());
```

```
        product.setDescription(backingBean.getDescription());
        return product;
    }

    // ...
}
```

Here, the Jakarta Persistence entity is tightly coupled to a Jakarta Faces backing bean. Not only are the entity properties reused in the backing bean, but also the entity has a dependency on the backing bean. It wouldn't be possible to extract the entity into a stand-alone JAR module that is reusable across different web applications.

And the following approach is also factually wrong:

```
@Stateless
public class ProductService {

    @Inject
    private EntityManager entityManager;

    public void create(Product product) {
        entityManager.persist(product);
        FacesContext.getCurrentInstance().addMessage(null,
            new FacesMessage("Product created!"));
    }
}
```

Here, the Jakarta Enterprise Beans method pokes the faces context and sets a message there. This would fail with a `NullPointerException` when the method is being invoked from, for example, a web service or a servlet because there's no instance of the faces context available anywhere over there. This UI messaging task is clearly not the responsibility of the back-end code but of the front-end code. In other words, adding a faces message should only and only happen in a Jakarta Faces artifact, such as a backing bean.

The correct approach is as follows, as demonstrated previously in the section "Model, View, or Controller?":

```
@Named @RequestScoped
public class ProductBacking {

    private Product product = new Product();
```

```
@Inject
private ProductService productService;

public void save() {
    productService.create(product);
    FacesContext.getCurrentInstance().addMessage(null,
        new FacesMessage("Product created!"));
}

public Product getProduct() {
    return product;
}
}
```

Naming Conventions

There is no strict convention specified by Jakarta Faces itself. I've seen the following conventions across various projects:

- Foo

- FooBean

- FooBacking

- FooBackingBean

- FooManager

- FooManagedBean

- FooController

whereby Foo can in turn represent one of the following:

- Jakarta Faces view ID,

  for example, EditProduct for /edit/product.xhtml

- Jakarta Faces view name,

  for example, Products for /view/products.xhtml

- Jakarta Persistence entity name,

  for example, Product for @Entity class Product

- Jakarta Faces form ID,

    for example, `EditProduct` for `<h:form id="editProduct">`

First and foremost, names ending with `Bean` like `FooBean`, `FooBackingBean`, and `FooManagedBean` must be avoided to all extent. The "bean" suffix is superfluous and too ambiguous as practically any stateful class in Java can be marked as a JavaBean. You don't immediately use "`ProductBean`" for your entity or "`ProductServiceBean`" or even "`ProductServiceEnterpriseBean`" for your service, right? True, #{bean} or #{myBean} or even #{yourBean} to indicate a managed bean is very often used across generic code examples in blogs, forums, Q&A sites, and even this book. But this is merely done for clarity and simplicity of the code snippets.

That leaves us with `Foo`, `FooBacking`, `FooManager`, and `FooController`. All are equally acceptable. Personally, I tend to use `FooBacking` for request-, view-, flow-, and conversation-scoped beans and `FooManager` for session- and application-scoped beans. As to the naming convention of `Foo` part, that generally depends on whether the backing bean is tightly tied to a particular Jakarta Faces view or a Jakarta Faces form, or generally reusable across multiple Jakarta Faces views or forms referring a particular entity.

In any case, this is a pretty subjective item that can hardly be answered objectively with "the One and Correct" answer. It really doesn't matter that much to me or anyone else what you make of it, as long as you're consistent with it throughout the entire project.

CHAPTER 9

Exception Handling

Sometimes, things can unexpectedly go wrong. In Java, that usually manifests as an `Exception` being thrown. In Jakarta EE, it's basically no different. The issue is how and when to properly handle them. By default, any uncaught exception during an HTTP request will end up in a default error page provided by the application server. Figure 9-1 shows what WildFly's default HTTP 500 error page looks like.

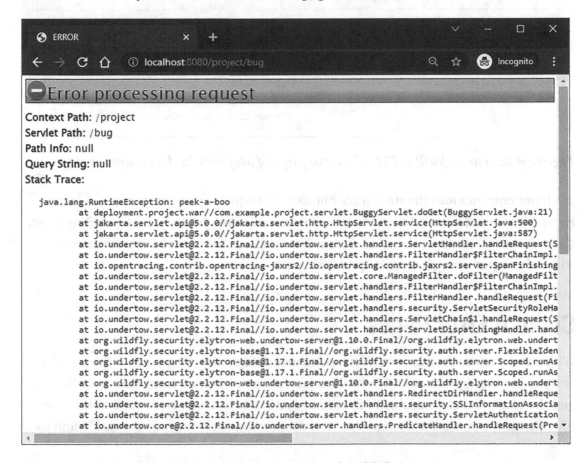

Figure 9-1. *The default HTTP 500 error page of WildFly*

© Bauke Scholtz and Arjan Tijms 2022
B. Scholtz and A. Tijms, *The Definitive Guide to Jakarta Faces in Jakarta EE 10*,
https://doi.org/10.1007/978-1-4842-7310-4_9

The Jakarta Faces implementation being used may even provide its own default error page. Both Mojarra and MyFaces provide an internal default implementation based on the `jakarta.faces.context.ExceptionHandler` API,[1] which is only shown when the Jakarta Faces project stage is set to `Development`. Figure 9-2 shows how that page looks for Mojarra.

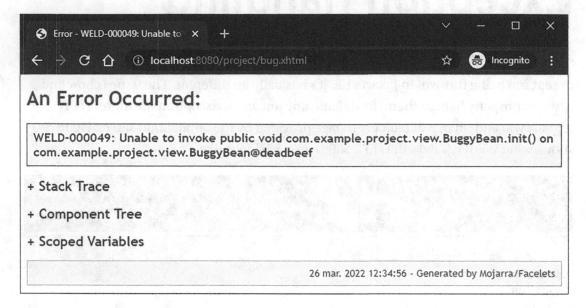

Figure 9-2. *The default HTTP 500 error page of Mojarra in development stage*

It not only includes the stack trace but also the textual representation of the Jakarta Faces component tree and any scoped variables, which might be helpful in nailing down the root cause, although, in reality, the stack trace alone and reexecuting the use case with a debugger is much more helpful than that.

Custom Error Pages

While useful to the average web developer, those default error pages are, quite frankly, scary to the average end user. The look and feel is completely off from the rest of the site, and the text is like abracadabra to the average end user. Such an error page doesn't even provide escape points for the end user. The disgruntled end user cannot quickly find its

---

[1] https://jakarta.ee/specifications/platform/10/apidocs/jakarta/faces/context/ExceptionHandler.html

way to the home or contact page. Fortunately for the end user, you can override those default error pages by including an error page in the web application and registering its location in an <error-page> entry in web.xml.

```
<error-page>
    <error-code>500</error-code>
    <location>/WEB-INF/errorpages/500.xhtml</location>
</error-page>
```

The custom error page is purposefully being placed in a /WEB-INF folder so that end users can't access or bookmark them directly. By default, the servlet container will set error page–related attributes in the request scope whose keys are defined as jakarta. servlet.RequestDispatcher.ERROR_XXX constants.[2] This way, you can, if necessary, include them in the custom error page. The following is an example:

```
<dl>
    <dt>Request URI</dt>
    <dd>#{requestScope['jakarta.servlet.error.request_uri']}</dd>
    <dt>Exception type</dt>
    <dd>#{requestScope['jakarta.servlet.error.exception']['class']}</dd>
    <dt>Exception message</dt>
    <dd>#{requestScope['jakarta.servlet.error.exception'].message}</dd>
    <dt>Stack trace</dt>
    <dd><pre>#{
        facesContext.externalContext.response.writer.flush()
    }#{
        requestScope['jakarta.servlet.error.exception'].printStackTrace
            (facesContext.externalContext.response.writer)
    }</pre></dd>
</dl>
```

Note the trick to print the stack trace. It's important that the response writer is flushed before printing the stack trace and that there's no whitespace in template text outside the EL (Expression Language) expressions within the <pre> element; otherwise, it would be appended to the stack trace.

---

[2] https://jakarta.ee/specifications/platform/10/apidocs/jakarta/servlet/RequestDispatcher.html#ERROR_EXCEPTION

Coming back to the scariness of such an error page, you'd better hide away all the error detail behind a condition that evaluates only true when the Jakarta Faces project stage equals Development. First, set an application-scoped shortcut variable in some master template:

```
<c:set var="DEV" scope="application"
    value="#{facesContext.application.projectStage eq 'Development'}">
</c:set>
```

Now you can conditionally display any technical information in the error page when the Jakarta Faces project stage equals Development.

```
<c:if test="#{DEV}">
    <h3>Error detail for developer</h3>
    <dl>
        ...
    </dl>
</c:if>
```

In any case, it's very important that the error page is entirely stateless. In other words, a decent error page may not contain any Jakarta Faces forms, not even a logout form. Not only will you avoid the risk that the form submit fails because the initial exception was actually caused by a corrupted Jakarta Faces state, but those forms will actually submit to the wrong URL (uniform resource locator), namely, the one of the error page itself. As the error page is hidden in the /WEB-INF folder, the form submit would only result in a 404 error. Instead of moving the error page outside the /WEB-INF folder, you could work around the logout case by using a plain HTML form which submits to a plain Servlet. The SecurityContext is also just injectable over there, as are session-scoped managed beans, if any.

Ajax Exception Handling

By default, when an exception occurs during a Jakarta Faces Ajax request, then the end user would not get any form of feedback whether or not the action was successfully performed. In Mojarra, only when the Jakarta Faces project stage is set to Development, then the end user would see a bare JavaScript alert with only the exception type and message (see Figure 9-3).

Figure 9-3. *The JavaScript alert when an exception is thrown during an Ajax request in Mojarra in Development stage*

This isn't terribly useful. And in the `Production` stage, the end user wouldn't even get any feedback. The web application would fail silently, leaving the end user behind as if nothing had happened, which is just confusing and bad for user experience. It would make more sense if exceptions during Jakarta Faces Ajax requests are handled the same way as exceptions during synchronous requests, which reuse exactly the same error page as the one declared as `<error-page>` in `web.xml`. In other words, the end user should be able to see the error page in full glory. This can be achieved by creating a custom `ExceptionHandler` implementation that basically instructs Jakarta Faces to create a new `UIViewRoot` based on the error page and then build and render it. It's only quite a bit of code. At its simplest, it can look as follows:

```
public class AjaxExceptionHandler extends ExceptionHandlerWrapper {

    public AjaxExceptionHandler(ExceptionHandler wrapped) {
        super(wrapped);
    }

    @Override
    public void handle() {
        handleAjaxException(FacesContext.getCurrentInstance());
        getWrapped().handle();
    }
```

```
    protected void handleAjaxException(FacesContext context) {
        Iterator<ExceptionQueuedEvent> unhandledExceptionQueuedEvents =
            getUnhandledExceptionQueuedEvents().iterator();

        if (context == null
            || context.getExternalContext().isResponseCommitted()
            || !context.getPartialViewContext().isAjaxRequest()
            || !unhandledExceptionQueuedEvents.hasNext()
        ) {
            return;
        }

        Throwable exception = unhandledExceptionQueuedEvents
            .next().getContext().getException();

        while (exception.getCause() != null
            && (exception instanceof FacesException
                || exception instanceof ELException)
        ) {
            exception = exception.getCause();
        }

        ExternalContext external = context.getExternalContext();
        String uri = external.getRequestContextPath()
            + external.getRequestServletPath();
        Map<String, Object> requestScope = external.getRequestMap();
        requestScope.put(RequestDispatcher.ERROR_REQUEST_URI, uri);
        requestScope.put(RequestDispatcher.ERROR_EXCEPTION, exception);

        String viewId = "/WEB-INF/errorpages/500.xhtml";
        Application application = context.getApplication();
        ViewHandler viewHandler = application.getViewHandler();
        UIViewRoot viewRoot = viewHandler.createView(context, viewId);
        context.setViewRoot(viewRoot);

        try {
            external.responseReset();
            ViewDeclarationLanguage viewDeclarationLanguage =
                viewHandler.getViewDeclarationLanguage(context, viewId);
```

```
            viewDeclarationLanguage.buildView(context, viewRoot);
            context.getPartialViewContext().setRenderAll(true);
            viewDeclarationLanguage.renderView(context, viewRoot);
            context.responseComplete();
        }
        catch (IOException e) {
            throw new FacesException(e);
        }
        finally {
            requestScope.remove(RequestDispatcher.ERROR_EXCEPTION);
        }

        unhandledExceptionQueuedEvents.remove();

        while (unhandledExceptionQueuedEvents.hasNext()) {
            unhandledExceptionQueuedEvents.next();
            unhandledExceptionQueuedEvents.remove();
        }
    }

    public static class Factory extends ExceptionHandlerFactory {

        public Factory(ExceptionHandlerFactory wrapped) {
            super(wrapped);
        }

        @Override
        public ExceptionHandler getExceptionHandler() {
            return new AjaxExceptionHandler
                (getWrapped().getExceptionHandler());
        }
    }
}
```

The handleAjaxException() will first check if there is a faces context, if the response isn't yet committed, if the request is an Ajax request, and if there's any unhandled exception event in the queue. If none of those conditions matches, it will return and let Jakarta Faces continue as usual.

The HTTP response is considered committed when the response or a part thereof has physically already been sent to the client. This is a point of no return. You can't take the already-sent bytes back. This may happen when the exception occurs halfway during the render response phase. The first half of the HTTP response may already have been sent to the client. Also the default exception handler of Jakarta Faces and the server can't deal with it. Effectively, the client gets a half-baked HTML page. Best what you could do to avoid this situation is to make sure that you aren't performing business logic in getter methods of backing beans, which on its own is always a bad idea, and that backing beans are initialized as soon as possible. That could be achieved by executing exception-sensitive business logic in <f:viewAction> instead of @PostConstruct. Another option is to increase the HTTP response buffer size to match the size of the generated HTML response of the largest exception-sensitive page. Assuming that it's 100KB, the following web.xml context parameter can be used.

```
<context-param>
    <param-name>jakarta.faces.FACELETS_BUFFER_SIZE</param-name>
    <param-value>102400</param-value> <!-- 100 kB. -->
</context-param>
```

The next step in handleAjaxException() is extracting the root cause of interest from the unhandled exception events queue. Any exception that occurs during the processing of the Jakarta Faces life cycle will be wrapped in a jakarta.faces.FacesException. Any exception that occurs during the evaluation of an EL expression will be wrapped in a jakarta.el.ELException. Those are not of interest, and therefore, we need to unwrap them to find the underlying root cause.

Next, the #{requestScope['jakarta.servlet.error.request_uri']} and #{requestScope['jakarta.servlet.error.exception']} variables will be set so that the error page can access them. Also the UIViewRoot instance representing the error page will be created with the help of the ViewHandler and set in the faces context. You could, if necessary, conditionally prepare the view ID of the error page based on the actual root cause of the exception. For example:

```
String viewId;

if (exception instanceof ViewExpiredException) {
    viewId = "/WEB-INF/errorpages/expired.xhtml";
}
```

```
else {
    viewId = "/WEB-INF/errorpages/500.xhtml";
}
```

Coming back to the handleAjaxException(), in the try block, the HTTP response buffer will be cleared, the UIViewRoot will be populated with components, the Ajax context will be instructed to render the entire view, the UIViewRoot will be rendered, the faces context will be instructed that the response is already manually taken care of so that it won't perform any navigation, and, finally, the exception will be removed from the request scope. The removal of the exception from the request scope in the finally block is not mandatory, but there exist servlet containers that consider this as a trigger to append an internal error page to the response, such as Tomcat. We'd like to avoid this behavior to keep our custom error page clean.

Finally, the queue of unhandled exception events will be drained. This is also not mandatory, but it is done on purpose so that it matches the default behavior of web.xml-configured error pages and also to prevent any next ExceptionHandler in the chain from handling any remaining exception events.

In order to get it to run, you actually need to create a factory as well. As many other application-wide customizations in Jakarta Faces, custom exception handlers can only be registered through a factory. It might look verbose, but that's just part of the design. In this specific case, it allows you to return a different exception handler implementation depending on some global configuration setting. You can find the Factory as a nested class in the bottom of the previously shown AjaxExceptionHandler class. It extends from jakarta.faces.context.ExceptionHandlerFactory[3] and can be registered in faces-config.xml as follows:

```
<factory>
    <exception-handler-factory>
        com.example.project.exceptionhandler.AjaxExceptionHandler$Factory
    </exception-handler-factory>
</factory>
```

By the way, it must be said that such an exception handler is also suitable on non-Ajax requests. You just have to remove the PartialViewContext#isAjaxRequest() check. You only need to keep in mind to manually set the HTTP response status code to

---

[3] https://jakarta.ee/specifications/platform/10/apidocs/jakarta/faces/context/ExceptionHandlerFactory.html

500 depending on whether or not it's an Ajax request. Do this after the `ExternalContext` `#responseReset()` line.

```
if (!context.getPartialViewContext().isAjaxRequest()) {
    external.setResponseStatus
        (HttpServletResponse.SC_INTERNAL_SERVER_ERROR);
}
```

When you do so on an Ajax request, then the Jakarta Faces Ajax script won't process the Ajax response as you'd expect. Instead of displaying the error page, it will trigger the onerror handler.

ViewExpiredException Handling

If you've worked with Jakarta Faces before, then the chance is high that you've seen or heard about a `ViewExpiredException`. It will be thrown when the Jakarta Faces view state associated with the postback cannot be found in the HTTP session anymore. In other words, when the `jakarta.faces.STATE_SAVING_METHOD` context parameter is set to its default value of "`server`" and the end user submits a Jakarta Faces form whose view state cannot be found anymore on the server side. Note that when the context parameter is set to "`client`", then you still need a "`faces/ClientSideSecretKey`" environment entry in order to avoid expired views when the server restarts. This all was elaborated in the section "View State" in Chapter 3. Also, in the section "@ViewScoped" in Chapter 8, you can find how to configure the amount of views and managed beans Jakarta Faces will save in the HTTP session.

There are several circumstances where a `ViewExpiredException` may unexpectedly occur. All of them are related to page navigation and the browser cache while the end user has recently logged out from the web application. Normally, the HTTP session is during logout invalidated as a security measure, and the end user is redirected to some landing page. When the previously visited web page is cacheable, and the end user presses the browser's back button after logout, then the end user may successfully get to see the previously visited web page from the browser cache. If it contains any Jakarta Faces form, then its `jakarta.faces.ViewState` hidden input field will actually refer a view state that does not exist in the current session anymore. When the end user submits such form, then Jakarta Faces will inevitably throw a `ViewExpiredException`.

Although this is an excellent security measure, the end user may get confused as the previously visited web page actually got successfully loaded in end user's experience. This confusion is not good for user experience. You'd therefore best make sure that stateful Jakarta Faces pages are not cacheable so that the web browser is forced to actually hit the web server when the end user presses the back button and thus load a fresh new page with a view state that is actually valid in the current HTTP session. This can be achieved with a servlet filter that sets specific response headers to instruct the client not to cache the HTTP response. The following is an example of such a servlet filter:

```
@WebFilter(servletNames="facesServlet")
public class NoCacheFilter implements Filter {

    @Override
    public void doFilter
        (ServletRequest req, ServletResponse res, FilterChain chain)
            throws IOException, ServletException
    {
        HttpServletRequest request = (HttpServletRequest) req;
        HttpServletResponse response = (HttpServletResponse) res;
        String resourcePath = request.getContextPath()
            + ResourceHandler.RESOURCE_IDENTIFIER;

        if (!request.getRequestURI().startsWith(resourcePath)) {
            response.setHeader
                ("Cache-Control", "no-store, must-revalidate");
        }

        chain.doFilter(request, response);
    }
}
```

Basically, it hooks on all requests that are going to hit the FacesServlet, provided that it's configured on a servlet name of "facesServlet" in web.xml as follows:

```
<servlet>
    <servlet-name>facesServlet</servlet-name>
    <servlet-class>jakarta.faces.webapp.FacesServlet</servlet-class>
</servlet>
```

Alternatively, if you have divided your web application into a public area with only stateless Jakarta Faces pages and a restricted area with only stateful Jakarta Faces pages, then you could also map this filter on a more specific URL pattern that matches only the stateful section, such as /admin/*.

```
@WebFilter("/admin/*")
```

This filter checks first if the HTTP request doesn't represent a Jakarta Faces resource request before setting the cache control header. Those requests are identified by the /jakarta.faces.resource path after the context path, which is available by the ResourceHandler#RESOURCE_IDENTIFIER constant. This is automatically used when you use a Jakarta Faces resource component, such as <h:graphicImage>, <h:outputScript>, or <h:outputstyleSheet>. See also the section "Resource Components" in Chapter 6. You don't want to disable the browser cache on them as that would otherwise impact the page loading performance.

The Cache-Control header being set is actually only recognized by HTTP 1.1–capable clients. HTTP 1.1 was introduced in 1997. In case you would like to cover HTTP 1.0 clients as well, which these days are generally only ancient proxies or poor users who can't get something better than Internet Explorer 6.0, then you'd best add two more response headers along the Cache-Control.

```
response.setHeader("Pragma", "no-cache"); // HTTP 1.0.
response.setDateHeader("Expires", 0); // Proxies.
```

Now, with this filter in place, the end user won't anymore get to see any Jakarta Faces page from the browser cache and thus can no longer get a ViewExpiredException on them. However, there are still cases where a ViewExpiredException is unavoidable. One such case is an end user who has several Jakarta Faces pages open in different browser tabs and logs out in one of them and then performs an action in another tab without refreshing the page beforehand. For such a case, you'd really need a "Sorry, your session has expired" error page. This can easily be configured as another error page in web.xml as follows:

```
<error-page>
    <exception-type>
        jakarta.faces.application.ViewExpiredException
    </exception-type>
    <location>/WEB-INF/errorpages/expired.xhtml</location>
</error-page>
```

Do not let the `<location>` point to a public page, such as a login page. Error pages must stay in /WEB-INF folder in order to avoid it being directly accessible, bookmarkable, or even crawlable. In case you really need the end user to end up in an existing public page, then better use a meta refresh header in the error page that in turn redirects the end user further to the desired public page. This way, you can ensure that the URL in browser's address bar gets reflected to the correct one and thus not be the one of the previous page, where the error occurred.

```
<!DOCTYPE html>
<html lang="en">
    <head>
        <title>Session expired</title>
        <meta http-equiv="refresh"
            content="0;url=#{request.contextPath}/login.xhtml" />
    </head>
    <body>
        <h1>Sorry, your session has expired</h1>
        <h3>You will be redirected to login page</h3>
        <p>
            <a href="#{request.contextPath}/login.xhtml">
                Click here if the redirect didn't work,
                or when you're impatient.
            </a>
        </p>
    </body>
</html>
```

Note that the "0" in the meta refresh content represents the amount of seconds before redirect. Thus, "0" means "redirect immediately." You can use, for example, "3" to let the browser wait 3 seconds before the redirect.

Keep in mind to also configure this exact error page `<location>` in any custom exception handler such as the `AjaxExceptionHandler` demonstrated in the previous section. You also need to make sure that your "general" error page is mapped on an error code of 500 instead of an exception type of, for example, `java.lang.Exception` or `java.lang.Throwable`. This was already demonstrated in the first section of this chapter.

```
<error-page>
    <error-code>500</error-code>
    <location>/WEB-INF/errorpages/500.xhtml</location>
</error-page>
```

Otherwise, all exceptions wrapped in `ServletException` would still end up in the general error page. Jakarta Faces will wrap any exception in a `ServletException` when it's thrown during a synchronous (non-Ajax) postback instead of an asynchronous (Ajax) postback. The `web.xml` error page mechanism will only extract the root cause from the `ServletException` for a second pass through error pages by exception type when no matching error page by exception type is found.

A completely different alternative to avoid `ViewExpiredException` is to use stateless Jakarta Faces views. This way, nothing of the Jakarta Faces view state will be saved, and the Jakarta Faces views will never expire but will just be rebuilt from scratch on every request. You can turn on stateless views by setting the `transient` attribute of `<f:view>` to `true`. This is elaborated in the section "Stateless Forms" in Chapter 4.

IOException Handling

Some methods of the underlying `HttpServletRequest` and `HttpServletResponse` objects may throw an `IOException`. Usually, that only happens when the network connection unexpectedly breaks: for example, when the end user abruptly stops the HTTP request by pressing the Esc button in the web browser, or the end user abruptly navigates to a different web page while the current page is still loading, or even when the end user's computer catches fire or the network cable gets chewed by a mouse. Those circumstances are really unavoidable. For you, as web application developer, it's best to let any `IOException` bubble up all the way into the servlet container. In other words, there's absolutely no need to catch it as follows:

```
public void someAjaxListener() {
    try {
        FacesContext.getCurrentInstance()
            .getExternalContext().redirect(url);
    }
```

```
    catch (IOException e) {
        throw new UncheckedIOException(e);
    }
}
```

Instead, just let it go.

```
public void someAjaxListener() throws IOException {
    FacesContext.getCurrentInstance()
        .getExternalContext().redirect(url);
}
```

EJBException Handling

Sometimes, invoking service methods may also cause an exception. Generally, those
are on purpose, such as "entity not found," "unique constraint violation," "invalid user
credentials," and "entity is in meanwhile modified by another user." By default, any
non-application-specific RuntimeException, which is thrown from a Jakarta Enterprise
Beans service method, such as NullPointerException and even Jakarta Persistence's
PersistenceException, is wrapped in an EJBException. This makes it clumsy to nail
down the actual root cause in the Jakarta Faces action method.

```
public void addProduct() {
    FacesMessage message;

    try {
        Long id = productService.create(product);
        message = new FacesMessage(FacesMessage.SEVERITY_INFO,
            "Product successfully saved", "ID is " + id);
    }
    catch (EJBException e) {
        if (e.getCause() instanceof ConstraintViolationException) {
            message = new FacesMessage(FacesMessage.SEVERITY_ERROR,
                "Duplicate product!", e.getMessage());
            context.validationFailed();
        }
```

```
    else {
        throw e;
    }
}

context.addMessage(null, message);
}
```

This is not the best practice. Not only would you need to determine the root cause of the EJBException by inspecting Exception#getCause(), but the web.xml error page mechanism would also not be able to show a specific error page for, for example, a ConstraintViolationException because it's wrapped in an EJBException. In order to get the service method to throw it unwrapped, you need to create a custom exception superclass first which you then annotate with @jakarta.ejb.ApplicationException.[4]

```
@ApplicationException(rollback=true)
public abstract class BusinessException extends RuntimeException {

    public BusinessException() {
        super();
    }

    public BusinessException(Exception cause) {
        super(cause);
    }

}
```

Note the rollback=true attribute on the annotation. This is very important in case you'd like the Jakarta Enterprise Beans container to roll back any active transaction from where this exception is being thrown. The following are some examples of subclasses of this custom business exception:

```
public abstract class QueryException extends BusinessException {}
public class EntityNotFoundException extends QueryException {}
public class DuplicateEntityException extends QueryException {}
public abstract class CredentialsException extends BusinessException {}
```

---

[4]https://jakarta.ee/specifications/platform/10/apidocs/jakarta/ejb/
ApplicationException.html

```
public class InvalidUsernameException extends CredentialsException {}
public class InvalidPasswordException extends CredentialsException {}
```

Note that you don't necessarily need to repeat the @ApplicationException over all subclasses as it's already @Inherited. The following are some concrete use cases on which those exceptions could be thrown:

```
public User getById(Long id) {
    try {
        return entityManager
            .createQuery("FROM User u WHERE u.id = :id", User.class)
            .setParameter("id", id)
            .getSingleResult();
    }
    catch (NoResultException e) {
        throw new EntityNotFoundException(e);
    }
}

public Optional<User> findByEmail(String email) {
    try {
        return Optional.of(entityManager
            .createQuery("FROM User u"
                + " WHERE u.email = :email", User.class)
            .setParameter("email", email)
            .getSingleResult());
    }
    catch (NoResultException e) {
        return Optional.empty();
    }
}

public User getByEmailAndPassword(String email, String password) {
    User user = findByEmail(email)
        .orElseThrow(InvalidUsernameException::new);
    Credentials credentials = user.getCredentials();
    byte[] passwordHash = digest(password, credentials.getSalt());
```

```
    if (!Arrays.equals(passwordHash, credentials.getPasswordHash())) {
        throw new InvalidPasswordException();
    }

    return user;
}
public Long create(User user) {
    if (findByEmail(user.getEmail()).isPresent()) {
        throw new DuplicateEntityException();
    }

    entityManager.persist(user);
    return user.getId();
}
```

In the backing bean action methods, you could then handle them accordingly.

```
public void signup() {
    FacesMessage message;

    try {
        userService.create(user);
        message = new FacesMessage("You are successfully signed up!");
    }
    catch (DuplicateEntityException e) {
        message = new FacesMessage(FacesMessage.SEVERITY_ERROR,
            "Sorry, username already taken!", e.getMessage());
        context.validationFailed();
    }

    context.addMessage(null, message);
}
```

In order to further reduce the boilerplate code, you could even let all business exceptions go and have a custom exception handler to handle them.

```
public class BusinessExceptionHandler extends ExceptionHandlerWrapper {

    public BusinessExceptionHandler(ExceptionHandler wrapped) {
        super(wrapped);
    }
```

```
@Override
public void handle() {
    handleBusinessException(FacesContext.getCurrentInstance());
    getWrapped().handle();
}

protected void handleBusinessException(FacesContext context) {
    Iterator<ExceptionQueuedEvent> unhandledExceptionQueuedEvents =
        getUnhandledExceptionQueuedEvents().iterator();

    if (context == null
        || !unhandledExceptionQueuedEvents.hasNext()
    ) {
        return;
    }

    Throwable exception = unhandledExceptionQueuedEvents
        .next().getContext().getException();

    while (exception.getCause() != null
        && (exception instanceof FacesException
            || exception instanceof ELException)
    ) {
        exception = exception.getCause();
    }

    if (!(exception instanceof BusinessException)) {
        return;
    }

    context.addMessage(null, new FacesMessage(
        FacesMessage.SEVERITY_FATAL,
        exception.toString(),
        exception.getMessage()));
    context.validationFailed();
    context.getPartialViewContext()
        .getRenderIds().add("globalMessages");

    unhandledExceptionQueuedEvents.remove();
```

```
    while (unhandledExceptionQueuedEvents.hasNext()) {
        unhandledExceptionQueuedEvents.next();
        unhandledExceptionQueuedEvents.remove();
    }
}

public static class Factory extends ExceptionHandlerFactory {

    public Factory(ExceptionHandlerFactory wrapped) {
        super(wrapped);
    }

    @Override
    public ExceptionHandler getExceptionHandler() {
        return new BusinessExceptionHandler
            (getWrapped().getExceptionHandler());
    }
}
}
```

Yes, it's indeed similar to the AjaxExceptionHandler as shown in the earlier section "Ajax Exception Handler." However, the first difference is that it doesn't skip handling the exception when the response is already committed or when it's not an Ajax request. The second difference is the logic between extracting the root cause of the exception and draining the remaining unhandled exception events. This BusinessExceptionHandler will instead check if the root cause is an instance of BusinessException, and if so, it will add a faces message and instruct Jakarta Faces to explicitly Ajax-update the component identified by "globalMessages", which should refer to a global messages component in your master template something like the following:

```
<h:messages id="globalMessages" globalOnly="true" />
```

Ultimately, all business exception–related faces messages will end up there. You might have noticed that the faces context is explicitly marked as "validation failed" via the FacesContext#validationFailed() call. This is generally useful in case any code in the Facelet template is relying on it. If you would like to run it together with the AjaxExceptionHandler for nonbusiness exceptions, then you need to register it in the faces-config.xml *after* the AjaxExceptionHandler. Anything that is declared later in the `faces-config.xml` will effectively wrap the previously declared one. This also applies to custom exception handler factories. When the `BusinessExceptionHandler` confirms that the exception is not an instance of `BusinessException`, then it will leave the unhandled exception in the queue and return from the method and finally delegate to the `handle()` method of the wrapped `ExceptionHandler`, which shall be the `AjaxExceptionHandler`.

```
<factory>
    <exception-handler-factory>
        com.example.project.AjaxExceptionHandler$Factory
    </exception-handler-factory>
    <exception-handler-factory>
        com.example.project.BusinessExceptionHandler$Factory
    </exception-handler-factory>
</factory>
```

With the `BusinessExceptionHandler` in place, you could further reduce the backing bean action method as follows:

```
public void signup() {
    userService.create(user);
    context.addMessage(null,
        new FacesMessage("You are successfully signed up!");
}
```

CHAPTER 10

WebSocket Push

WebSocket support is represented by the `<f:websocket>` tag, the `PushContext` interface, and the `@Push` annotation, introduced in Jakarta Faces 2.3. It is built on top of the JSR-356 WebSocket specification, introduced in Jakarta EE 7. JSR-356 is even natively supported in Tomcat since 7.0.27 and in Jetty since 9.1.0.

In Mojarra, the `<f:websocket>` has an additional Jakarta EE dependency: JSON-P (JSR-353). In case you're targeting Tomcat or Jetty instead of a Jakarta EE application server, you might need to install it separately. JSON-P is internally used to convert Java objects to a JSON string so that it can, without much hassle, be transferred to the client side and be provided as an argument of JavaScript listener function attached to `<f:websocket>`.

Configuration

The JSR-356 WebSocket specification does not officially support programmatic initialization of the socket end point during runtime. So we cannot initialize it by simply declaring `<f:websocket>` in the view and wait until a Jakarta Faces page referencing it is being opened for the first time. We really need to explicitly initialize it during deployment time. Jakarta Faces could do that by default, but having an unused WebSocket end point open forever is not really resource efficient if it's never going to be used by the web application. So we cannot avoid having a context parameter in order to instruct Jakarta Faces to explicitly initialize it during deployment time.

```
<context-param>
    <param-name>jakarta.faces.ENABLE_WEBSOCKET_ENDPOINT</param-name>
    <param-value>true</param-value>
</context-param>
```

© Bauke Scholtz and Arjan Tijms 2022
B. Scholtz and A. Tijms, *The Definitive Guide to Jakarta Faces in Jakarta EE 10*,
https://doi.org/10.1007/978-1-4842-7310-4_10

If you prefer programmatic initialization over declarative initialization, then you can always use ServletContext#setInitParameter() in a ServletContainerInitializer of your web fragment library as follows:

```
public class YourInitializer implements ServletContainerInitializer {

    @Override
    public void onStartup(Set<Class<?>> types, ServletContext context) {
        context.setInitParameter(
            PushContext.ENABLE_WEBSOCKET_ENDPOINT_PARAM_NAME, "true");
    }
}
```

Note that it is not possible to perform this task in a ServletContextListener as Jakarta Faces will actually check for the context parameter in its own ServletContainerInitializer implementation which thus always runs before any ServletContextListener.

Once the WebSocket end point is enabled and successfully initialized during deployment, then it will listen for WebSocket handshake requests on the URL (uniform resource locator) pattern /jakarta.faces.push/*. The first path element will represent the WebSocket channel name.

Coming back to "officially," some WebSocket implementations do, however, support programmatic initialization, such as the one provided by Undertow, which is in turn used in WildFly. Unfortunately, the spec doesn't say so, and there may be WebSocket implementations that simply do not support programmatic initialization, such as Tyrus as used in Payara.[1]

The WebSocket container will, by default, listen for handshake requests on the same port as the application server is listening for HTTP requests. You can optionally change the port with another web.xml context parameter:

```
<context-param>
    <param-name>jakarta.faces.WEBSOCKET_ENDPOINT_PORT</param-name>
    <param-value>8000</param-value>
</context-param>
```

---

[1] https://github.com/eclipse-ee4j/websocket-api/issues/211

or programmatically in a `ServletContainerInitializer`:

```
context.setInitParameter(
    PushContext.WEBSOCKET_ENDPOINT_PORT_PARAM_NAME, "8000");
```

Usage

In your Jakarta Faces page, just declare the `<f:websocket>` tag along with the required `channel` attribute representing the channel name and the optional `onmessage` attribute representing a reference to a JavaScript function.

```
<f:websocket channel="test" onmessage="logMessage" />

<script>
    function logMessage(message, channel, event) {
        console.log(message);
    }
</script>
```

The JavaScript function will be invoked with three arguments:

1. `message`: The push message as JSON object.

2. `channel`: The WebSocket channel name. This may be useful in case you intend to have a global listener or want to manually control the close of the WebSocket.

3. `event`: The original `MessageEvent` object. This may be useful in case you intend to inspect it in the JavaScript function.

On the WAR side, you can inject the `PushContext` via the `@Push` annotation in any web artifact that supports CDI injection. This can be a simple CDI managed bean, but it can also be a `@WebServlet`, `@WebFilter`, or `@WebListener`.

```
import jakarta.inject.Named;
import jakarta.enterprise.context.RequestScoped;
import jakarta.inject.Inject;
import jakarta.faces.push.Push;
import jakarta.faces.push.PushContext;
```

```
@Named @RequestScoped
public class Bean {

    @Inject @Push
    private PushContext test;

    public void submit() {
        test.send("Hello World!");
    }
}
```

The PushContext variable name *test* must match the channel name declared in the Jakarta Faces page. In case you cannot match the variable name with the channel name, then you can always specify the channel name in the optional `channel` attribute of the `@Push` annotation.

```
@Inject @Push(channel="test")
private PushContext foo;
```

Once the `submit()` method of the bean shown before is invoked by some Jakarta Faces command component, even in a different Jakarta Faces page, then the push message "Hello World!" will be sent to **all** opened sockets on the very same channel name, application-wide.

Scopes and Users

As you may have realized, `<f:websocket>` is thus, by default, application scoped. You can control the scope by the optional `scope` attribute. Allowed values are `application`, `session`, and `view`.

When set to `session`, then the message will be sent to all opened sockets on the very same channel in the current session only.

```
<f:websocket channel="progress" scope="session" />
```

This is particularly useful for progress messages coming from long-running session-scoped background tasks initiated by the user itself. This way, the user can just continue browsing the site without the need to wait for the result on the very same page.

Alternatively, you can also set the optional user attribute to a serializable value representing the unique user identifier, which can be, for example, a String representing the user login name or a Long representing the user ID. When this attribute is set, then the scope of the socket will automatically default to session, and it cannot be set to application.

```
<f:websocket channel="chat" user="#{loggedInUser.id}" />
```

This offers the opportunity to send a message to a specific user as follows:

```
private String message;
private User recipient;

@Inject @Push
private PushContext chat;

public void sendMessage() {
    Long recipientId = recipient.getId();
    chat.send(message, recipientId);
}
```

You can even send it to multiple users by providing a Set argument.

```
private String message;
private Set<User> recipients;

@Inject @Push
private PushContext chat;

public void sendMessage() {
    Set<Long> recipientIds = recipients.stream()
        .map(User::getId)
        .collect(Collectors.toSet());
    chat.send(message, recipientIds);
}
```

In other words, you can easily implement a chat box this way. Incidentally, real-time user-targeted notifications at, for example, Stack Overflow work this way.

When the scope is set to view, then the message will be sent to the opened socket on the specified channel in the current view only. This won't affect any sockets on the same channel in all other views throughout the application.

```
<f:websocket channel="push" scope="view" />
```

This is also supported in combination with the user attribute.

```
<f:websocket channel="chat" user="#{user.id}" scope="view" />
```

This construct of having a view-scoped socket targeted to a specific user is somewhat unusual though and should only be used if the logged-in user represented by user attribute can have a shorter lifetime than the HTTP session. This is, however, in turn considered a poor security practice. The best security practice is, namely, that the HTTP session is invalidated during login as well as during logout. Invalidating the HTTP session during login prevents session fixation attacks, and invalidating the session during logout prevents dirty user-specific data lingering around in HTTP session.

Channel Design Hints

You can declare multiple push channels on different scopes with or without user target throughout the application. However, be aware that the same channel name can easily be reused across multiple views, even if it is view scoped. It's more efficient if you use as few different channel names as possible and tie the channel name to a specific push socket scope/user combination, not to a specific Jakarta Faces view. In case you intend to have multiple view-scoped channels for different purposes, then it is best to use only one view-scoped channel and have a global JavaScript listener that can distinguish its task based on the delivered message, for example, by sending the message in a server as follows:

```
Map<String, Object> message = new HashMap<>();
message.put("functionName", "someFunction");
message.put("functionData", functionData); // Can be Map or Bean.
someChannel.send(message);
```

which is then processed in the onmessage JavaScript listener function as follows:

```
function someSocketListener(message) {
```

```
    window[message.functionName](message.functionData);
}

function someFunction(data) {
    // ...
}

function otherFunction(data) {
    // ...
}

// ...
```

One-Time Push

You can use the connected attribute to prevent the socket from automatically connecting during page load.

```
<f:websocket ... connected="false" />
```

This is particularly useful when you want to perform a one-time push of the result after invoking a view-scoped Ajax action method which might take a bit more time to complete, and you'd like the user to immediately continue using the very same page without being annoyed about a "slow web site" experience. This approach only requires a bit of additional work with the faces.push JavaScript API (application programming interface). It has three functions, but only two are of interest to us: faces.push.open(...) and faces.push.close(...). The third one, faces.push.init(...), basically initializes the socket, and it should not be your concern to invoke it; that's up to the renderer of the <f:websocket> tag.

In order to explicitly open the unopened socket right before invoking the Ajax action method, you need to invoke the faces.push.open(...) function with the socket client ID as argument. In order to explicitly close the opened socket right after the push message has arrived, you need to invoke the faces.push.close(...) function with the socket client ID as argument. The following example demonstrates the one-time push approach in its entirety:

```
<script>
    function startLongRunningProcess() {
```

```
        faces.push.open("push");
        document.getElementById("status").innerHTML =
            "Long running process has started ...";
    }

    function endLongRunningProcess(result) {
        faces.push.close("push");
        document.getElementById("status").innerHTML = result;
    }
</script>

<h:form>
    <h:commandButton value="submit"
        onclick="startLongRunningProcess()"
        action="#{longRunningProcess.submit}">
        <f:ajax />
    </h:commandButton>
</h:form>

<div id="status" />

<f:websocket id="push" channel="push" scope="view"
    connected="false" onmessage="endLongRunningProcess">
</f:websocket>
```

It must be said that it's a poor practice to put JavaScript code right in the HTML source as shown before. It's, of course, for demonstration purposes only. For better maintenance, performance, and tooling support, you should, in real-world code, put JavaScript code in a JS file and include it via `<h:outputScript>`. And then I'm not talking about the lack of jQuery magic for demonstration purposes.

In the example, opening the socket is performed during the `onclick` of the command button. The `onmessage` listener function in turn closes the socket. Of course, you can also keep the socket open all the time without fiddling with JavaScript, but it may be a waste of resources if the socket isn't used for purposes other than presenting the result of a view-scoped Ajax action method. Here is how the associated backing bean can look like.

```
@Named @RequestScoped
```

```java
public class LongRunningProcess {

    @Inject
    private LongRunningProcessService service;

    @Inject @Push
    private PushContext push;

    public void submit() {
        service.asyncSubmit(result -> push.send(result));
    }
}
```

And here is what the service class looks like.

```java
@Stateless
public class LongRunningProcessService {

    @Asynchronous
    public void asyncSubmit(Consumer<String> callback) {
        String result = someLongRunningProcess();
        callback.accept(result);
    }
}
```

Note the Jakarta Enterprise Beans @Asynchronous annotation. This is very important in this construct. It will ensure that the enterprise bean method is executed in a separate thread. This allows the backing bean method to return immediately without waiting for the enterprise bean method to complete.

Stateful UI Updates

As you may have noticed, the onmessage JavaScript listener function is generally only useful for small stateless tasks, such as displaying a feedback message or adding a new item to some stateless list using JavaScript. It isn't terribly useful when you want to update a stateful UI (user interface) represented by another Jakarta Faces component. Think of replacing a trivial loading image with a whole Jakarta Faces table.

For that, you'd better nest a <f:ajax> listening on a specific push message. Via its render attribute, you have the opportunity to automatically update an arbitrary Jakarta Faces component as response to an incoming push message. The following is an example that initially shows a loading image and then the table when it's ready to load:

```
<h:form>
    <f:websocket channel="push" scope="view">
        <f:ajax event="loaded" render=":results" />
    </f:websocket>
</h:form>
<h:panelGroup id="results" layout="block">
    <h:graphicImage name="images/loading.gif"
        rendered="#{empty longRunningSearch.results}">
    </h:graphicImage>
    <h:dataTable value="#{longRunningSearch.results}" var="result"
        rendered="#{not empty longRunningSearch.results}">
        <h:column>#{result.id}</h:column>
        <h:column>#{result.name}</h:column>
        <h:column>#{result.value}</h:column>
    </h:dataTable>
</h:panelGroup>
```

Note that <f:websocket> is placed in <h:form>. This is mandatory when it has <f:ajax> nested. Normally, this is not required. Here is how the backing bean can look like.

```
@Named @ViewScoped
public class LongRunningSearch implements Serializable {

    private List<Result> results;

    @Inject
    private LongRunningSearchService service;

    @Inject @Push
    private PushContext push;

    @PostConstruct
```

```
public void init() {
    service.asyncLoadResults(results -> {
        this.results = results;
        push.send("loaded");
    });
}

public List<Result> getResults() {
    return results;
}
}
```

Note that the push message "loaded" matches exactly the <f:ajax event> value. You can use any value you want, and you can nest as many <f:ajax> tags as you need. It's important that the managed bean is @ViewScoped as the Ajax call is basically performed in a different request within the same view. Finally, the service class looks as follows:

```
@Stateless
public class LongRunningSearchService {

    @Asynchronous
    public void asyncLoadResults(Consumer<List<Result>> callback) {
        List<Result> results = someLongRunningProcess();
        callback.accept(results);
    }
}
```

The someLongRunningProcess() method represents your implementation of some long-running process (e.g., calling a third-party web service API).

Site-Wide Push Notifications

For this, you can use an application-scoped socket. Such a socket is particularly useful for application-wide feedback messages triggered by the web application itself on a particular event which may be of interest to all application users. Think of site-wide statistics, real-time lists, stock updates, etc. The following example shows the case of a real-time top ten list:

```
<h:dataTable id="top10" value="#{bean.top10}" var="item">
    <h:column>#{item.ranking}</h:column>
    <h:column>#{item.name}</h:column>
    <h:column>#{item.score}</h:column>
</h:dataTable>
<h:form>
    <f:websocket channel="top10Observer">
        <f:ajax event="updated" render=":top10" />
    </f:websocket>
</h:form>
```

Here is what the service class looks like, with a little help from CDI events.

```
@Stateless
public class ItemService {

    @Inject
    private EntityManager entityManager;

    @Inject
    private BeanManager beanManager;

    public void update(Item item) {
        List<Item> previousTop10 = getTop10();
        entityManager.merge(item);
        List<Item> currentTop10 = getTop10();

        if (!currentTop10.equals(previousTop10)) {
            beanManager.fireEvent(new Top10UpdatedEvent());
        }
    }

    @TransactionAttribute(NOT_SUPPORTED)
    pulic List<Item> getTop10() {
        return entityManager
            .createNamedQuery("Item.top10", Item.class)
```

```
        .getResultList();
    }
}
```

Note that the `Top10UpdatedEvent` is, in this specific example, basically just an empty class like `public class Top10UpdatedEvent {}`. Also note that we're not injecting the `PushContext` in the service class. This is otherwise considered tight coupling of layers. All Jakarta Faces–related code belongs in the front end, not in the back end. This way, the back-end service classes are better reusable across all kinds of front-end frameworks other than Jakarta Faces, such as Jakarta RESTful Web Services or even plain vanilla Jakarta Pages/Servlet. In other words, you should ensure that none of your back-end classes directly or indirectly use any front end–specific classes such as those from `jakarta.faces.*`, `jakarta.ws.*`, and `jakarta.servlet.*` packages.

Any event fired with the `BeanManager#fireEvent()` method can be observed using CDI `@Observes` annotation. This works across all layers. In other words, even when it's fired in the back end, you can observe it in the front end. The only requirement is that the backing bean must be `@ApplicationScoped`. That is, there's not necessarily any means of an HTTP request, HTTP session, or Jakarta Faces view anywhere at that moment.

```
@Named @ApplicationScoped
public class Bean {

    private List<Item> top10;

    @Inject
    private ItemService service;

    @Inject @Push
    private PushContext top10Observer;

    @PostConstruct
    public void load() {
        top10 = service.getTop10();
    }

    public void onTop10Updated(@Observes Top10UpdatedEvent event) {
        load();
```

```
        top10Observer.send("updated");
    }

    public List<Item> getTop10() {
        return top10;
    }
}
```

Keeping Track of Active Sockets

In order to keep track of active sockets, you can in an application-scoped bean observe
@WebsocketEvent.Opened and @WebsocketEvent.Closed events. The following example
assumes that you have <f:websocket channel="chat" user="..."> and that you
intend to collect "active chat users":

```
@ApplicationScoped
public class WebsocketEventObserver {

    private Map<Serializable, AtomicInteger> users;

    @PostConstruct
    public void init() {
        users = new ConcurrentHashMap<>();
    }

    public void onopen(@Observes @Opened WebsocketEvent event) {
        if ("chat".equals(event.getChannel())) {
            getCounter(event.getUser()).incrementAndGet();
        }
    }

    public void onclose(@Observes @Closed WebsocketEvent event) {
        if ("chat".equals(event.getChannel())) {
            getCounter(event.getUser()).decrementAndGet();
        }
    }

    private AtomicInteger getCounter(Serializable user) {
```

```
        return users.computeIfAbsent(user, k -> new AtomicInteger());
    }

    public Set<Serializable> getActiveUsers() {
        return users.entrySet().stream()
            .filter(entry -> entry.getValue().intValue() > 0)
            .map(entry -> entry.getKey())
            .collect(Collectors.toSet());
    }
}
```

You can use the preceding getActiveUsers() method to obtain a set of "active chat users." Do note that a single user can open the same web page multiple times within the same session (e.g., multiple browser tabs), and that's exactly why a counter is used instead of simply adding and removing users from a Set.

Client Side Event Handling

The <f:websocket> tag will by default keep the connection open forever, as long as the document is open, as long as there's no connected="false" being set, and as long as faces.push.close(clientId) is not being invoked. When the first connection attempt fails, then it will immediately close the socket. You can optionally use the onclose attribute to reference a JavaScript function that acts as a close listener.

```
<f:websocket ... onclose="closeListener" />

<script>
    function closeListener(code, channel, event) {
        if (code == -1) {
            // WebSocket API not supported by client. E.g. IE9.
        }
        else if (code == 1000) {
            // Normal close as result of expired view or session.
        }
        else if (code == 1008) {
            // Normal close as result of unknown channel ID.
        }
```

369

```
        else {
            // Abnormal close as result of a client or server error.
            // You might want to show a message and/or refresh the page.
        }
    }
</script>
```

The JavaScript function will be invoked with three arguments:

1. code: The close reason code as integer. If this is -1, then the
   WebSocket JavaScript API is simply not supported[2] by the client. If
   this is 1000, then a normal closure has occurred as consequence
   of an expired view or session in the server side. If this is 1008, then
   a normal closure has occurred because the provided channel ID is
   unknown. This will usually only happen when it is spoofed by the
   client, or when the server has restarted with a new deployment
   with a changed channel ID while the client hasn't yet refreshed
   the page.

2. channel: The WebSocket channel name. This may be useful in
   case you intend to have a global listener.

3. event: The original CloseEvent object. This may be useful in case
   you intend to inspect it in the JavaScript function.

As you might have noticed in the aforementioned onclose listener function example, you could thus just check if the close code of a <f:websocket> equals 1000 in order to perform some client-side action via JavaScript (e.g., displaying a warning message and/ or redirecting to some "Session expired" page).

```
<f:websocket channel="push" scope="session" onclose="closeListener" />

<script>
    function closeListener(code) {
        if (code == 1000) {
            window.location = faces.contextPath + "/expired.xhtml";
```

---

[2]https://caniuse.com/#feat=websockets

```
        }
    }
</script>
```

This works for both view- and session-scoped sockets. Application-scoped sockets, however, remain open forever as long as the document is still open on client side, even when the underlying view or session has expired.

When the first connection attempt succeeds, but the socket later gets disconnected for some reason (e.g., because the server is restarting), then it will by default trigger an error event and keep trying to reconnect at incremental intervals. In the case of Mojarra, it will keep retrying up to 25 times, with an interval that is incremented 500ms each time, and in case all reconnect attempts have failed, it will eventually completely close the socket and invoke the onclose listener. You can optionally use the onerror attribute to reference a JavaScript function that listens for those error events.

```
<f:websocket ... onerror="errorListener" />

<script>
    function errorListener(code, channel, event) {
        if (code == 1001) {
            // Server is reachable, but has returned an unexpected
            // response code. E.g. 503 when it's shutting down.
        }
        else if (code == 1006) {
            // Server is not anymore reachable, this can happen if it
            // is completely down, or if client's network is down.
        }
        else {
            // Any other reason which is usually not -1, 1000 or 1008,
            // as the onclose will be invoked instead.
        }

        // In any case, the websocket will attempt to reconnect. This
        // onerror function will be invoked again. Once the websocket
        // gives up reconnecting, the onclose will finally be invoked.
    }
</script>
```

Breaking Down Mojarra's f:websocket Implementation

The `<f:websocket>` API specifies the following classes and methods:

- `jakarta.faces.push.Push`: A CDI qualifier to for @Inject. With the help of this qualifier, the socket channel name can be specified.

- `jakarta.faces.push.PushContext`: An interface with three `send()` methods: `send(Object message)`, `send(Object message, S user)`, and `send(Object message, Collection<S> users)`. All those methods accept the push message as `Object` and will for JavaScript convert it to a JSON string. All those methods return a `Set<Future<Void>>`. If it returns an empty set, then there was no open socket associated with given channel and user. For each `Future<Void>`, if it doesn't throw `ExecutionException` on `Future#get()` method call, then the message was successfully delivered.

- `jakarta.faces.component.UIWebsocket`: A component that implements `ClientBehaviorHolder` in order to support nested `<f:ajax>`. Historically, the prototype socket tag extended from `TagHandler` instead of `UIComponent`. It was later decided to let the tag support `<f:ajax>` as that would make complex and stateful UI updates much easier. However, it isn't possible to let a `TagHandler` implement `ClientBehaviorHolder` and benefit all of built-in Ajax magic, hence the final conversion to `UIComponent`.

- `ViewHandler#getWebsocketURL()` method that takes a channel name and returns the absolute WebSocket URL in the form of `ws://host:port/context/jakarta.faces.push/channel` with help of `ExternalContext#encodeWebsocketURL()`.

- `ExternalContext#encodeWebsocketURL()` method that basically takes a relative WebSocket URI in the form of `/context/jakarta.faces.push/channel` and returns the absolute WebSocket URL.

The actual implementation is fairly extensive. It's directly based on OmniFaces `<o:socket>`[3] with, here and there, a few adjustments such as using a component's client ID instead of a channel name in JavaScript API functions.

- `com.sun.faces.renderkit.html_basic.WebsocketRenderer`: A faces renderer class that registers during encoding the socket channel, scope, and user in `WebsocketChannelManager` and retrieves the WebSocket URL from it. Then it auto-includes the `faces.js` script containing the necessary `faces.push.*` functions and renders the `faces.push.init(...)` inline script function call with among others the WebSocket URL as an argument. This function should in turn in JavaScript create a `new WebSocket(url)`. The `WebsocketRenderer` will also subscribe the `WebsocketFacesListener` to the current view.

- `com.sun.faces.push.WebsocketChannelManager`: A session-scoped CDI managed bean that keeps track of all so far registered `<f:websocket>` channels, scopes, and users and ensures that each socket gets its own unique channel identifier. It will register every channel identifier in `WebsocketSessionManager` and those of user-targeted sockets in `WebsocketUserManager`.

- `com.sun.faces.push.WebsocketFacesListener`: A system event listener that listens on `PreRenderViewEvent` and renders, if necessary, the `faces.push.open(...)` or `faces.push.close(...)` inline script function calls depending on whether the `connected` attribute represents a dynamic EL expression which got changed during an Ajax request.

- `com.sun.faces.push.WebsocketEndpoint`: A class that implements JSR-356 `jakarta.websocket.Endpoint` and listens on the URI template `/jakarta.faces.push/{channel}`. When a `new WebSocket(url)` is created and opened on client-side JavaScript, then a new `jakarta.websocket.Session` is created on server-side Java, and the `WebsocketEndpoint` will add this `Session` to `WebsocketSessionManager`. Equivalently, when a socket is closed, then the `WebsocketEndpoint` will remove it from `WebsocketSessionManager`.

---

[3] `https://showcase.omnifaces.org/push/socket`

- `com.sun.faces.push.WebsocketSessionManager`: An application-scoped CDI managed bean that collects all so far opened socket sessions and validates that their unique WebSocket URL has been registered by `WebsocketChannelManager`.

- `com.sun.faces.push.WebsocketUserManager`: An application-scoped CDI managed bean that collects the channel identifiers of all so far opened user-targeted sockets.

- `com.sun.faces.push.WebsocketPushContext`: The concrete implementation of the `PushContext` interface. It will send the push message via `WebsocketSessionManager` and, if necessary, obtain the user-targeted channels via `WebsocketUserManager`.

- `com.sun.faces.push.WebsocketPushContextProducer`: The CDI producer that creates the `WebsocketPushContext` instance based on channel name as obtained from `@Push` qualifier, the `WebsocketSessionManager`, and `WebsocketUserManager`.

CHAPTER 11

Custom Components

In Chapter 7, you should have learned that Facelets `<ui:composition>`, `<ui:include>`, and `<ui:decorate>` are useful when you want to split main page layout fragments into reusable templates, such as header, menu, main content, and footer. And that Facelet tag files such as `<t:field>` are useful when you want to have a reusable group of components in order to minimize code duplication. And that composite components such as `<t:inputLocalTime>` are useful when you want to create a custom component with a single responsibility based on existing components and, if necessary, a bunch of HTML.

However, there may be cases in which no single component exists for the purpose you had in mind, even not when composed of existing components and/or a bunch of HTML. Or perhaps the component does exist, but its renderer is not doing things you had in mind. At this point, you would need to create a custom component or a custom renderer.

Jakarta Faces has since the beginning offered a high degree of abstraction around the `UIComponent` API (application programming interface). You can customize components by creating a brand-new custom `UIComponent`, or by extending an existing component from the standard HTML component set, or by plugging a custom `Renderer` for an existing component.

Component Type, Family, and Renderer Type

Each `UIComponent` instance has "component type," "component family," and "renderer type" associated with it. The component type basically represents the unique component identifier associated with the component tag. It can be registered into Jakarta Faces via

375

© Bauke Scholtz and Arjan Tijms 2022
B. Scholtz and A. Tijms, *The Definitive Guide to Jakarta Faces in Jakarta EE 10*,
https://doi.org/10.1007/978-1-4842-7310-4_11

either the @FacesComponent annotation or the <component> entry in faces-config.xml. The following example demonstrates the usage of the @FacesComponent annotation on a minimal component class:

```
@FacesComponent(SomeComponent.COMPONENT_TYPE)
public class SomeComponent extends UIComponentBase {

    public static final String COMPONENT_TYPE = "project.SomeComponent";
    public static final String COMPONENT_FAMILY = "project.SomeFamily";

    public SomeComponent() {
        setRendererType(SomeRenderer.RENDERER_TYPE);
    }

    @Override
    public String getFamily() {
        return COMPONENT_FAMILY;
    }
}
```

And the following example demonstrates the usage with the <component> entry in faces-config.xml:

```
<component>
    <component-type>project.SomeComponent</component-type>
    <component-class>
        com.example.project.component.SomeComponent
    </component-class>
</component>
```

Note that when you register a Jakarta EE artifact via *both* the annotation and the XML ways using the same identifier, then the XML declaration will always get precedence over the annotation declaration. The same holds true for all Jakarta Faces annotations.

The public constants COMPONENT_TYPE and COMPONENT_FAMILY in the component class are not mandatory, but they follow the same convention as the standard Jakarta Faces component set and therefore give more consistency while developing with Jakarta Faces. The public constant COMPONENT_TYPE namely allows the developer to programmatically create the component as below without the need to hard-code the component type.

```
UIComponent component = FacesContext.getCurrentInstance()
    .getApplication().createComponent(SomeComponent.COMPONENT_TYPE);
```

Note that programmatically creating UIComponent instances this way is generally not the normal practice in an average Jakarta Faces web application. Instead, you normally define the components in the view and leave the job of creating UIComponent instances up to Jakarta Faces or any pluggable component library.

In the case of Facelets view technology, the component tag as in <x:someComponent> can be registered into Jakarta Faces via either @FacesComponent(createTag=true) or a <tag> entry in a *.taglib.xml file along with the component type as follows:

```
<tag>
    <tag-name>someComponent</tag-name>
    <component>
        <component-type>project.SomeComponent</component-type>
    </component>
</tag>
```

As said, the standard Jakarta Faces component set has the COMPONENT_TYPE constant also defined in the concrete UIComponent classes behind the component tags. Those UIComponent classes are all located in the jakarta.faces.component.html package. The UIComponent class name can be derived from the component tag name by prefixing it with "Html". So, for example, the standard Jakarta Faces component tag <h:outputText> is actually backed by the HtmlOutputText component class. Jakarta Faces can, via either the @FacesComponent annotation or the <component> entry in faces-config.xml, figure out which component class exactly is associated with the component type, so Jakarta Faces knows that, for the <h:outputText> tag, it should create a concrete HtmlOutputText instance.

Once Jakarta Faces has the concrete UIComponent instance at hand, it can figure out the component family as well as the renderer type by invoking the methods UIComponent#getFamily() and UIComponent#getRendererType(), respectively. This information is mandatory in order to create a concrete Renderer instance for the given UIComponent instance, as you can see in the following snippet:

```
Renderer renderer = FacesContext.getCurrentInstance().getRenderKit()
    .getRenderer(component.getFamily(), component.getRendererType());
```

The component family is basically a "hard-coded" constant which can be shared across multiple component types. It's "hard-coded" in such a way that there's no setter for it. This is needed in order to get the concrete Renderer instances as they are not registered by component type but rather by component family. This allows the developer of the pluggable render kit to register the renderer type just once by the component family instead of multiple times for each known standard component type and unknown custom component type. Normally, the component family and renderer type are registered into the Jakarta Faces application via either the @FacesRenderer annotation or the <renderer> entry in faces-config.xml. The following example demonstrates the usage with the annotation on a minimal renderer class.

```
@FacesRenderer(
    componentFamily=SomeComponent.COMPONENT_FAMILY,
    rendererType=SomeRenderer.RENDERER_TYPE)
public class SomeRenderer extends Renderer {
    public static final String RENDERER_TYPE = "project.SomeRenderer";
}
```

And the following example demonstrates the usage with the entry in faces-config.xml:

```
<render-kit>
    <renderer>
        <component-family>project.SomeFamily</component-family>
        <renderer-type>project.SomeRenderer</renderer-type>
        <renderer-class>
            com.example.project.renderer.SomeRenderer
        </renderer-class>
    </renderer>
</render-kit>
```

The renderer type is by default defined in the constructor of the concrete component class, as can be seen in the code snippet of the SomeComponent class as shown previously. In case it's needed, the component subclass developer or even yourself as component end user can always override the default renderer instance of a component with the desired renderer instance. This can be done in various ways, all via XML. The first way is via the <tag> entry associated with the component tag in the *.taglib.xml file.

```
<tag>
    <tag-name>someComponent</tag-name>
    <component>
        <component-type>project.SomeComponent</component-type>
        <renderer-type>custom.OtherRenderer</renderer-type>
    </component>
</tag>
```

This affects application-wide and targets only the specific component tag. The second way is via a new `<renderer>` entry in `faces-config.xml` that targets exactly the desired component family and its default renderer type.

```
<render-kit>
    <renderer>
        <component-family>project.SomeFamily</component-family>
        <renderer-type>project.SomeRenderer</renderer-type>
        <renderer-class>
            com.example.custom.renderers.OtherRenderer
        </renderer-class>
    </renderer>
</render-kit>
```

This affects application-wide and targets *every* component tag associated with the given component family currently associated with the given renderer type. The third way is via the `rendererType` attribute of the component tag.

```
<x:someComponent ... rendererType="custom.OtherRenderer" />
```

This affects only the declared component tag and not others. Table 11-1 provides an overview of all component types, families, and renderer types of the standard Jakarta Faces component set.

Table 11-1. *Component Class, Component Type, Component Family, and Renderer Type of Standard Jakarta Faces HTML Component Set*

Component tag	Component class	Component type	Component family	Renderer type
<h:body>	HtmlBody	jakarta.faces.OutputBody	jakarta.faces.Output	jakarta.faces.Body
<h:button>	HtmlOutcomeTargetButton	jakarta.faces.HtmlOutcomeTargetButton	jakarta.faces.OutcomeTarget	jakarta.faces.Button
<h:column>	HtmlColumn	jakarta.faces.HtmlColumn	jakarta.faces.Column	null
<h:commandButton>	HtmlCommandButton	jakarta.faces.HtmlCommandButton	jakarta.faces.Command	jakarta.faces.Button
<h:commandLink>	HtmlCommandLink	jakarta.faces.HtmlCommandLink	jakarta.faces.Command	jakarta.faces.Link
<h:commandScript>	HtmlCommandScript	jakarta.faces.HtmlCommandScript	jakarta.faces.Command	jakarta.faces.Script
<h:dataTable>	HtmlDataTable	jakarta.faces.HtmlDataTable	jakarta.faces.Data	jakarta.faces.Table
<h:doctype>	HtmlDoctype	jakarta.faces.OutputDoctype	jakarta.faces.Output	jakarta.faces.Doctype
<h:form>	HtmlForm	jakarta.faces.HtmlForm	jakarta.faces.Form	jakarta.faces.Form
<h:graphicImage>	HtmlGraphicImage	jakarta.faces.HtmlGraphicImage	jakarta.faces.Graphic	jakarta.faces.Image
<h:head>	HtmlHead	jakarta.faces.OutputHead	jakarta.faces.Output	jakarta.faces.Head
<h:inputFile>	HtmlInputFile	jakarta.faces.HtmlInputFile	jakarta.faces.Input	jakarta.faces.File

Table 11-1. *(continued)*

Component tag	Component class	Component type	Component family	Renderer type
<h:inputHidden>	HtmlInputHidden	jakarta.faces.HtmlInputHidden	jakarta.faces.Input	jakarta.faces.Hidden
<h:inputSecret>	HtmlInputSecret	jakarta.faces.HtmlInputSecret	jakarta.faces.Input	jakarta.faces.Secret
<h:inputText>	HtmlInputText	jakarta.faces.HtmlInputText	jakarta.faces.Input	jakarta.faces.Text
<h:inputTextarea>	HtmlInputTextarea	jakarta.faces.HtmlInputTextarea	jakarta.faces.Input	jakarta.faces.Textarea
<h:link>	HtmlOutcomeTargetLink	jakarta.faces.HtmlOutcomeTargetLink	jakarta.faces.OutcomeTarget	jakarta.faces.Link
<h:message>	HtmlMessage	jakarta.faces.HtmlMessage	jakarta.faces.Message	jakarta.faces.Message
<h:messages>	HtmlMessages	jakarta.faces.HtmlMessages	jakarta.faces.Messages	jakarta.faces.Messages
<h:outputFormat>	HtmlOutputFormat	jakarta.faces.HtmlOutputFormat	jakarta.faces.Output	jakarta.faces.Format
<h:outputLabel>	HtmlOutputLabel	jakarta.faces.HtmlOutputLabel	jakarta.faces.Output	jakarta.faces.Label
<h:outputText>	HtmlOutputText	jakarta.faces.HtmlOutputText	jakarta.faces.Output	jakarta.faces.Text
<h:outputScript>	UIOutput	jakarta.faces.Output	jakarta.faces.Output	jakarta.faces.Script

(continued)

Table 11-1. (*continued*)

Component tag	Component class	Component type	Component family	Renderer type
<h:outputStylesheet>	UIOutput	jakarta.faces.Output	jakarta.faces.Output	jakarta.faces. resource.Stylesheet
<h:panelGrid>	HtmlPanelGrid	jakarta.faces.HtmlPanelGrid	jakarta.faces.Panel	jakarta.faces.Grid
<h:panelGroup>	HtmlPanelGroup	jakarta.faces.HtmlPanelGroup	jakarta.faces.Panel	jakarta.faces.Group
<h:selectBoolean Checkbox>	HtmlSelectBoolean Checkbox	jakarta.faces.HtmlSelect BooleanCheckbox	jakarta.faces. SelectBoolean	jakarta.faces. Checkbox
<h:selectManyCheckbox>	HtmlSelectMany Checkbox	jakarta.faces. HtmlSelectManyCheckbox	jakarta.faces. SelectMany	jakarta.faces. Checkbox
<h:selectManyListbox>	HtmlSelectManyListbox	jakarta.faces. HtmlSelectManyListbox	jakarta.faces. SelectMany	jakarta.faces. Listbox
<h:selectManyMenu>	HtmlSelectManyMenu	jakarta.faces. HtmlSelectManyMenu	jakarta.faces. SelectMany	jakarta.faces.Menu
<h:selectOneListbox>	HtmlSelectOneListbox	jakarta.faces. HtmlSelectOneListbox	jakarta.faces. SelectOne	jakarta.faces. Listbox
<h:selectOneMenu>	HtmlSelectOneMenu	jakarta.faces.HtmlSelect OneMenu	jakarta.faces. SelectOne	jakarta.faces.Menu
<h:selectOneRadio>	HtmlSelectOneRadio	jakarta.faces.HtmlSelect OneRadio	jakarta.faces. SelectOne	jakarta.faces.Radio

If you carefully inspect the table, then you'll see a certain pattern in the component family and renderer type, particularly with input, select, and command components. You'll notice that a renderer type can be shared across multiple components, even of a different family.

You'll also notice that there's one HTML component without a renderer type, the `<h:column>`. This is a special component which cannot be used stand-alone but can only be used when nested in a specific parent component. From the standard Jakarta Faces component set, that's so far only the `<h:dataTable>`. Its renderer basically iterates over all children and performs an `instanceof` check for `UIColumn` and then acts on them accordingly.

Creating New Component and Renderer

If you have paid close attention to Table 3-1 in Chapter 3, then you might have noticed that Jakarta Faces doesn't provide any component to render a dynamic `<ul>` or `<ol>` or even `<dl>` element based on a provided array or collection value. It only supports that for the `<table>` element. True, the same could be achieved with Facelets `<ui:repeat>` and a bit of custom HTML code, but we'll take this as an opportunity to create a new custom component that renders a `<ul>` or `<ol>`.

The first step is to check which `UIComponent` subclass is suitable for the task we have in mind so that we can reduce the custom code logic to a minimum. In the `jakarta.faces.component` package, you can find a bunch of `UIXxx` component subclasses. If you want to create a new form component, then extend from `UIForm`. If you want to create a new input component, then extend from `UIInput`. If you want to create a new output component, then extend from `UIOutput`. If you want to create a new data iterator component, then extend from `UIData`. There is rarely any need to extend from `UIComponent` directly. We'd like to be able to iterate over a collection in order to generate `<li>` elements inside the `<ul>`, so we'll pick `UIData`. It has a lot of iteration and state saving logic already implemented. The following is the custom component class `com.example.project.component.DataList`:

```
@FacesComponent(createTag=true)
public class DataList extends UIData {
```

```
    public DataList() {
        setRendererType(DataListRenderer.RENDERER_TYPE);
    }

}
```

Is that really all? Yes, the UIData superclass already has everything we need, and all the HTML producing code just goes into the DataListRenderer, which will be shown shortly. You'll notice that the @FacesComponent annotation declares a createTag=true attribute. This basically instructs Jakarta Faces that it should automatically create a component tag, the predefined XML namespace jakarta.faces.component. In other words, the preceding tag is available in the Facelets file as follows:

```
< ... xmlns:my="jakarta.faces.component">
    ...
    <my:dataList ...>
        ...
    </my:dataList>
```

The XML namespace prefix "my" is of course your choice. Generally, you'd like to pick some sort of abbreviation of your company name here. You can also override the predefined XML namespace with the namespace attribute.

```
@FacesComponent(createTag=true, namespace="example.components")
```

This will then be available as follows:

```
< ... xmlns:ex="example.components">
    ...
    <ex:dataList ...>
        ...
    </ex:dataList>
```

This namespace is unfortunately not unifiable with the <namespace> of a custom *.taglib.xml file. If you use the same namespace for both, then Jakarta Faces will prefer the *.taglib.xml one over the @FacesComponent one and hence be unable to find the custom component tag. In practically anything Jakarta EE related, any XML-based registration of a thing has higher precedence than a Java annotation-based registration of the very same thing.

You'd basically need to explicitly register the custom component over there in the `*.taglib.xml` file as well. Here's how the `/WEB-INF/example.taglib.xml` as created in the section "Tag Files" in Chapter 7 could be extended with the registration of the custom component, which is essentially the same as what the `@FacesComponent` is doing for you.

```xml
<?xml version="1.0" encoding="UTF-8"?>
<facelet-taglib
    xmlns="https://jakarta.ee/xml/ns/jakartaee"
    xmlns:xsi="http://www.w3.org/2001/XMLSchema-instance"
    xsi:schemaLocation="https://jakarta.ee/xml/ns/jakartaee
        https://jakarta.ee/xml/ns/jakartaee/web-facelettaglibrary_4_0.xsd"
    version="4.0"
>
    <namespace>example.tags</namespace>
    <short-name>t</short-name>
    <!-- Other tags here -->
    <tag>
        <description>Renders a HTML list.</description>
        <tag-name>dataList</tag-name>
        <component>
            <component-type>dataList</component-type>
        </component>
    </tag>
</facelet-taglib>
```

This way, the custom component is available in the same namespace as the other tags.

```
< ... xmlns:t="example.tags">
    ...
    <t:dataList ...>
        ...
    </t:dataList>
```

Now, you can essentially remove all attributes of the `@FacesComponent` so that it becomes just `@FacesComponent`. Yes, as you have seen in the `example.taglib.xml`, the component type defaults to the class name with the first character lowercased. You can always override it by explicitly specifying it as the value of the `@FacesComponent` annotation. Generally, you'd like to prefix it with the name of the company. It's a good practice to define it as a public constant so that others could, if necessary, look it up in the Javadoc and/or use it for `Application#createComponent()`.

```java
@FacesComponent(DataList.COMPONENT_TYPE)
public class DataList extends UIData {

    public static final String COMPONENT_TYPE = "example.DataList";

    public DataList() {
        setRendererType(DataListRenderer.RENDERER_TYPE);
    }
}
```

Now adjust the component type in the `example.taglib.xml` accordingly.

```xml
<component>
    <component-type>example.DataList</component-type>
</component>
```

The `*.taglib.xml` also gives you room to register the attributes via `<attribute>` entries, although that may end up in some verbose code. You should already have seen that in the section "Tag Files" in Chapter 7. Unfortunately, the current Faces version doesn't offer an annotation to declaratively declare an "official" component attribute. There's no such thing as `@FacesAttribute private Iterable value`. Yet. This might come in a Faces.next. The non-official way, without any `<attribute>`, also works just fine. You can declare any attribute you want on the component tag in the view.

```xml
<t:dataList foo="bar" bar="foo" />
```

That's just the freedom of XML. Whether the actual component or renderer implementation actually does something with it is another story. You could even declare a custom attribute on an existing component and just plug an extended Renderer in order to process that attribute. More later in the section "Extending Existing Renderer." Talking about renderers, our `<t:dataList>` still needs its renderer. Here's what the `com.example.project.renderer.DataListRenderer` looks like.

```java
@FacesRenderer(
    componentFamily=UIData.COMPONENT_FAMILY,
    rendererType=DataListRenderer.RENDERER_TYPE)
```

```java
public class DataListRenderer extends Renderer {

    public static final String RENDERER_TYPE = "example.List";

    @Override
    public void encodeBegin
        (FacesContext context, UIComponent component)
            throws IOException
    {
        ResponseWriter writer = context.getResponseWriter();
        UIData data = (UIData) component;

        if (data.getRowCount() > 0) {
            writer.startElement("ul", component);
        }
    }

    @Override
    public boolean getRendersChildren() {
        return true;
    }

    @Override
    public void encodeChildren
        (FacesContext context, UIComponent component)
            throws IOException
    {
        ResponseWriter writer = context.getResponseWriter();
        UIData data = (UIData) component;

        for (int i = 0; i < data.getRowCount(); i++) {
            data.setRowIndex(i);
            writer.startElement("li", component);
            if (component.getChildCount() > 0) {
                for (UIComponent child : component.getChildren()) {
                    child.encodeAll(context);
                }
            }

            writer.endElement("li");
        }
```

```
        data.setRowIndex(-1);
    }

    @Override
    public void encodeEnd
        (FacesContext context, UIComponent component)
            throws IOException
    {
        ResponseWriter writer = context.getResponseWriter();
        UIData data = (UIData) component;

        if (data.getRowCount() > 0) {
            writer.endElement("ul");
        }
    }
}
```

In hindsight, it's relatively simple. We're delegating as much as possible of the hard work to the Jakarta Faces–provided UIData superclass. In the encodeBegin(), you start the <ul> element when the data model is not empty. This is to be checked by examining the result of UIData#getRowCount(). Its Javadoc[1] basically says:

> *Return the number of rows in the underlying data model. If the number of available rows is unknown, return -1.*

The term "rows" is indeed strongly related to tables. This is also what this superclass is originally designed for: <h:dataTable>. The term "items" would have been more general than "rows," but it is what it is.

Then, in the encodeChildren() method, we set the current row index via the UIData#setRowIndex() method, start the <li> element, encode all children as-is via UIComponent#encodeAll() on each of them, and finally end the <li> element. Once the loop is done, we explicitly make it clear to the UIData superclass by invoking UIData#setRowIndex() with a value of -1. Its Javadoc[2] says:

---

[1] https://jakarta.ee/specifications/platform/10/apidocs/jakarta/faces/component/ UIData.html#getRowCount

[2] https://jakarta.ee/specifications/platform/10/apidocs/jakarta/faces/component/ UIData.html#setRowIndex-int

If the new `rowIndex` *value is* `-1`*: If the* `var` *property is not* `null`*, remove the corresponding request scope attribute (if any). Reset the state information for all descendant components.*

It thus clears out any state related to the iteration. This is very important; otherwise, it might cause side effects further down in the component tree or even cause a corrupted view state when it by itself needs to traverse the data model. Finally, in the `encodeEnd()` method, it will end the `<ul>` element based on same conditions as in `encodeBegin()`.

The `UIData#setRowIndex()` call in the `encodeChildren()` method will under the hood extract the data model from the `value` attribute and wrap it in a suitable implementation of the `jakarta.faces.model.DataModel` abstract class.[3] So far, as per the Javadoc of `UIData#getValue()`,[4] the following types of the object behind the `value` attribute are supported, in this scanning order:

1. `java.util.List` (since 1.0).

2. Arrays (since 1.0).

3. `java.sql.ResultSet` (since 1.0).

4. `java.util.Collection` (since 2.2).

5. `java.lang.Iterable` (since 2.3).

6. `java.util.Map` (since 2.3).

7. Types for which a suitable `DataModel` has been registered via `@FacesDataModel` (since 2.3).

8. All other types will be adapted using the `ScalarDataModel` class, which will treat the object as a single row of data (since 1.0).

You would indeed not expect to see anyone passing around a plain `java.sql.ResultSet` in a modern Jakarta EE application, but this all is for backward compatibility. Remember, Jakarta Faces was introduced in 2004. Backward compatibility was one of its strongest keys in surviving up to today. It's certainly a candidate to be removed, but not now.

---

[3] https://jakarta.ee/specifications/platform/10/apidocs/jakarta/faces/model/DataModel.html

[4] https://jakarta.ee/specifications/platform/10/apidocs/jakarta/faces/component/UIData.html#getValue

And there's indeed an overlap between some types; List and Collection could easily be covered by Iterable as they both implement this interface. But this has a performance reason. For a List, the items are accessed directly by index by the ListDataModel; for a Collection, the items are extracted first via Collection#toArray() and then accessed by index by the CollectionDataModel; and for an Iterable, the items are simply iterated and collected into a new List first by the IterableDataModel. It may make a difference.

You'll also see that Faces 2.3 has not only added two new data models but even introduced a new annotation to register a custom one. Previously, you'd need to manually wrap the custom collection in the custom data model every time before passing to a UIData component. The DataModel abstract class has the disadvantage of not being Serializable itself which more or less forces you to make a @ViewScoped bean holding such a data model to have a lazy loading getter on a transient data model property as follows:

```
private YourCollection yourCollection;
private transient YourDataModel dataModel;

public DataModel getDataModel() {
    if (dataModel == null) {
        dataModel = new YourDataModel(yourCollection);
    }

    return dataModel;
}
```

Ideally, the UIData should by itself recognize YourCollection type and automatically wrap it in a YourDataModel. The @FacesDataModel annotation does exactly that.

```
@FacesDataModel(forClass=YourCollection.class)
public class YourDataModel<E> extends DataModel<E> {}
```

Coming back to the custom renderer, there's one method left unexplained: the getRendersChildren(). It's been overridden to explicitly return true. You'll probably ask yourself, why was it initially false? Why not just let it be the default behavior of encodeChildren() and rely on any overridden encodeChildren() method whether it wants to invoke encodeAll() on the children? This was actually a historic oversight in the specification. Originally, the encodeAll() method didn't exist. It was only added in Faces 1.2, and it basically made the getRendersChildren() obsolete. But for backward compatibility, this complexity was introduced.

In a nutshell, always let getRendersChildren() return true if you have overridden the encodeChildren() method. Otherwise, the children won't be encoded at all.

Last but not least, you'll probably also wonder why we don't "simply" override the encodeBegin(), encodeChildren(), (and getRendersChildren()), and encodeEnd() of the DataList component but instead create a "whole" renderer implementation. The main reason is: simplicity and extensibility. Those methods are on UIComponent specified to do more than only rendering. They also check if the UIComponent#isRendered() returns true. The encodeBegin() also fires PreRenderComponentEvent and pushes the current component into the EL (Expression Language) scope as #{component}. The encodeEnd() pops #{component} out of the EL scope. And they also check if there's a renderer attached and, if so, delegate to it. That's all specified in their Javadoc. You'd need to manually take care of them yourself when you override those methods. That's unnecessarily repeated work. And when someone in the future wants to adjust the rendering of the component, then they won't be able to simply plug a custom renderer if your component doesn't check for it.

Extending Existing Component

Imagine that there's an existing component whose behavior you'd like to adjust, usually by adding one or more new custom attributes. If those attributes are purely output only, then you could just make use of the pass-through attributes feature that was introduced in Faces 2.2. Previously, any custom attribute that wasn't officially supported by the component was simply ignored during view render time. For example, when you'd like to add the directory attribute to the existing <h:inputFile> component,[5] then simply adding the attribute as follows won't work.

```
<h:inputFile id="photo" value="#{editProfile.photo}" directory="true" />
```

With the pass-through attributes feature, you could explicitly instruct Jakarta Faces to render the custom attribute anyway. This can be done in two ways. The first way is registering it via the jakarta.faces.passthrough XML namespace.

---

[5] https://jakarta.ee/specifications/faces/4.0/vdldoc/facelets/h/inputFile.html

```
< ... xmlns:h="jakarta.faces.html"
    xmlns:a="jakarta.faces.passthrough">
    ...
    <h:form enctype="multipart/form-data">
        <h:inputFile ... multiple="true" a:directory="true" />
    </h:form>
```

Another way is declaring it via the `<f:passThroughAttribute>` tag.

```
< ... xmlns:f="jakarta.faces.core"
    xmlns:h="jakarta.faces.html">
    ...
    <h:form enctype="multipart/form-data">
        <h:inputFile ... multiple="true">
            <f:passThroughAttribute name="directory" value="true" />
        </h:inputFile>
    </h:form>
```

Do note that you need to explicitly set `multiple="true"` as well; otherwise, you wouldn't be able to send a directory containing more than one file. On the browsers supporting the `directory` attribute, the file browse dialog will allow folder selection. However, this won't work in browsers not supporting this nonstandard attribute;[6] on the WebKit-based ones, you need to set `webkitdirectory` attribute instead. So you ultimately end up like this when you merely want to support directory selection with a broad as possible browser support.

```
< ... xmlns:f="jakarta.faces.core"
    xmlns:h="jakarta.faces.html">
    ...
    <h:form enctype="multipart/form-data">
        <h:inputFile ... multiple="true">
            <f:passThroughAttribute name="directory" value="true" />
            <f:passThroughAttribute name="webkitdirectory" value="true" />
        </h:inputFile>
    </h:form>
```

---

[6]https://caniuse.com/#feat=input-file-directory

One way to reduce this boilerplate is to extend the `<h:inputFile>` component to add a new `directory` attribute that automatically sets all these three attributes accordingly. The first step is looking at which `UIComponent` class exactly is represented by `<h:inputFile>`. As you can see in Table 11-1, that's `jakarta.faces.component.html.HtmlInputFile`. Let's start by extending it and adding the new `directory` attribute.

```
@FacesComponent(createTag=true)
public class InputFile extends HtmlInputFile {

    @Override
    public void encodeBegin(FacesContext context) throws IOException {
        boolean directory = isDirectory();

        if (directory) {
            setMultiple(true);
            getPassThroughAttributes().put("directory", true);
            getPassThroughAttributes().put("webkitdirectory", true);
        }

        super.encodeBegin(context);
    }

    public boolean isDirectory() {
        return (boolean) getStateHelper().eval("directory", true);
    }

    public void setDirectory(boolean directory) {
        getStateHelper().put("directory", directory);
    }
}
```

Note that there's no property for the `directory` attribute. Any public component attribute must be represented by a getter/setter pair that delegates further to `UIComponent#getStateHelper()`. Basically, you must delegate all view-scoped component attributes to the `StateHelper`. This will in turn take care that the right deltas end up in the Jakarta Faces view state. This is of course optional, but not doing so will make the component instance not programmatically manipulatable. Any changes performed during a previous HTTP request would get lost during the subsequent HTTP postback request for the very simple reason that the UIComponent instance is recreated from scratch.

Also note that the directory and webkitdirectory attributes are simply added as pass-through attributes in the encodeBegin() method before delegating to the superclass method where the actual rendering job takes place. This removes the need to create a whole custom renderer for the particular purpose of rendering new attributes. Let's test it now.

```
< ... xmlns:f="jakarta.faces.core"
    xmlns:h="jakarta.faces.html"
    xmlns:my="jakarta.faces.component">
    ...
    <h:form enctype="multipart/form-data">
        <my:inputFile id="files" value="#{bean.files}" directory="true">
            <f:ajax listener="#{bean.upload}" render="files_m" />
        </my:inputFile>
        <h:message id="files_m" for="files" />
    </h:form>
```

For the sake of completeness, here's what the backing bean looks like.

```
@Named @RequestScoped
public class Bean {

    private List<Part> files;

    public void upload() {
        for (Part file : files) {
            String fileName = file.getSubmittedFileName();
            String fileType = file.getContentType();
            long fileSize = file.getSize();
            System.out.println("File name: " + fileName);
            System.out.println("File type: " + fileType);
            System.out.println("File size: " + fileSize);
        }
    }
```

```
    // Add/generate getter and setter.
}
```

Now we have basically created the `UIComponent` equivalent of `<h:inputFile>` with a pass-through `directory` attribute.

In Jakarta Faces 4.0, the `<h:inputFile>` got a new `accept` attribute. It can be used as follows:

```
< ... xmlns:f="jakarta.faces.core"
    xmlns:h="jakarta.faces.html"
    xmlns:my="jakarta.faces.component">
    ...
    <h:form enctype="multipart/form-data">
        <my:inputFile id="photo" value="#{bean.photo}" accept="image/*">
            <f:ajax listener="#{bean.upload}" render="photo_m" />
        </my:inputFile>
        <h:message id="photo_m" for="photo" />
    </h:form>
```

On the browsers supporting this attribute, the file browse dialog will only show the files matching the comma-separated IANA (Internet Assigned Numbers Authority) media types[7] specified in the `accept` attribute. However, this won't work in browsers not supporting this attribute,[8] nor will it validate anything on the server side. Even if the browser supports it, any malicious-minded end user can easily manipulate the retrieved HTML document and remove the `accept` attribute and hence be able to upload a different file type.

In order to be able to validate in the server side whether the media type of the uploaded file actually matches the specified `accept` attribute, you can override the `UIInput#validateValue()` method of the `InputFile` class as below. This runs during the process validations phase (third phase).

```
@Override
protected void validateValue(FacesContext context, Object newValue) {
    String accept = getAccept();
```

---

[7] https://www.iana.org/assignments/media-types/media-types.xhtml
[8] https://caniuse.com/#feat=input-file-accept

```
    if (accept != null && newValue instanceof Part) {
        Part part = (Part) newValue;
        String contentType = context.getExternalContext()
            .getMimeType(part.getSubmittedFileName());
        String acceptPattern = accept.trim()
            .replace("*", ".*").replaceAll("\\s*,\\s*", "|");

        if (contentType == null || !contentType.matches(acceptPattern)) {
            String message = "Unacceptable file type";
            context.addMessage(getClientId(context), new FacesMessage(
                FacesMessage.SEVERITY_ERROR, message, null));
            setValid(false);
        }
    }

    if (isValid()) {
        super.validateValue(context, newValue);
    }
}
```

As you see, it will basically check if the `accept` attribute is specified and if there's a submitted file, and if so, then convert the `accept` attribute to a regular expression pattern and match the content type of the submitted file against it. The `accept` attribute represents a comma-separated string of IANA media types wherein the asterisk is used as a wildcard and the comma is used as a disjunction operator. An example `accept` value of `"image/*,application/pdf"` is this way converted to a regular expression of `"image/.*|application/pdf"`. If it doesn't match, then it will add a faces message associated with the component to the faces context and mark the component as invalid by calling `UIInput#setValid()` with `false`. In the end, if the component is valid, it will continue the validation call to the superclass.

Further, there's another thing to mention: the content type is not obtained from `Part#getContentType()` but from `ExternalContext#getMimeType()` based on the submitted file name. This is just to cover the corner case that the client doesn't send a content type along or even sends one that is not understood by the server. `ExternalContext#getMimeType()` basically obtains the list of known content types from `<mime-mapping>` entries in `web.xml`. The server itself has some default values, and you can override or extend them in the web application's own `web.xml`.

Now the file's content type attribute is filtered on the client side and validated on the server side. All good and well, but this of course only validates the file's content type based on the file name and not the file's actual content. Imagine that one creates a ZIP file and simply renames the file extension to become an image file, or even an executable file with malware. It would still pass through the file type validation on both the client and server side. Frankly, this responsibility is not up to the component itself, but to you, the Jakarta Faces developer. The correct solution would be to create a custom validator and attach it to the component. Here's what such an image file validator can look like, with a little help from the Java 2D API that is capable of parsing image files. If it throws an exception or returns null, then it's very definitely not an image file.

```java
@FacesValidator("project.ImageFileValidator")
public class ImageFileValidator implements Validator<Part> {

    @Override
    public void validate
        (FacesContext context, UIComponent component, Part value)
            throws ValidatorException
    {
        if (value == null) {
            return; // Let @NotNull or required="true" handle.
        }

        try {
            ImageIO.read(value.getInputStream()).toString();
        }
        catch (Exception e) {
            String message = "Not an image file";
            throw new ValidatorException(new FacesMessage(message), e);
        }
    }
}
```

In order to get it to run, declare it as validator attribute of the component tag.

```
<my:inputFile ... validator="project.ImageFileValidator" />
```

It works beautifully. Now, when validation passes as well, the backing bean action method is invoked wherein you can save the uploaded file to the desired location. This could be implemented as follows:

```
public void upload() {
    Path folder = Paths.get("/path/to/uploads");
    String fileName = Paths.get(photo.getSubmittedFileName())
        .getFileName().toString();
    int indexOfLastDot = fileName.lastIndexOf('.');
    String name = fileName.substring(0, indexOfLastDot);
    String extension = fileName.substring(indexOfLastDot);
    FacesMessage message = new FacesMessage();

    try (InputStream contents = photo.getInputStream()) {
        Path file = Files.createTempFile(folder, name + "-", extension);
        Files.copy(contents, file, StandardCopyOption.REPLACE_EXISTING);
        message.setSummary("Uploaded file successfully saved.");
    }
    catch (IOException e) {
        message.setSummary("Could not save uploaded file, try again.");
        message.setSeverity(FacesMessage.SEVERITY_ERROR);
        e.printStackTrace();
    }

    FacesContext.getCurrentInstance().addMessage(null, message);
}
```

You might wonder why it seems to save the uploaded file as a temporary file. This is actually not true. We're just utilizing the `Files#createTempFile()` facility in order to guarantee the uniqueness of the file name of the saved file. It will automatically include a unique random string between the file name and the file extension. Otherwise, when multiple people upload different files with coincidentally the same name, they may overwrite each other and we'd lose information.

Extending Existing Renderer

Imagine that there's an existing renderer that has logic bugs or shortcomings and you'd like to quickly patch it by extending it instead of rewriting from scratch. Unfortunately, it sounds far easier than it actually is. That is, standard renderer implementations are not part of the standard Jakarta Faces API, contrary to standard HTML component implementations that are available in the `jakarta.faces.component.html` package. The actual standard HTML renderer implementations are provided by the Jakarta Faces implementation itself. Mojarra has them in the `com.sun.faces.renderkit.html_basic` package, and MyFaces has them in the `org.apache.myfaces.renderkit.html` package.

Another problem with those standard HTML renderers is relatively poor abstraction of the code. Basically, all those standard HTML renderers don't have abstracted-out pieces of code that solely emit HTML markup in such a way that it's fully separated from the logic. In other words, when you need to fix some logic, you'd almost always also have to rewrite or copy/paste all of the code responsible for emitting HTML.

A common real-world example is the desire to let `<h:message>` or `<h:messages>` render the faces message unescaped so that you can embed some HTML code in a faces message, more than often to provide a link to the desired target page (e.g., "Unknown user, perhaps you want to `<a href="login">Log in</a>`?"). The standard `<h:message>` component doesn't support such facility, and the HTML escaping is controlled by its renderer that in turn is thus Jakarta Faces implementation dependent. This Jakarta Faces built-in HTML escaping is found over all place and is a very important guard against possible XSS attack holes when you're about to embed user-controlled data in the web page. There are a handful of components that have an explicit attribute to turn off this HTML escaping, such as `<h:outputText>` with its `escape` attribute, `<f:selectItem>` with its `itemEscaped` attribute, and `<f:selectItems>` with its `itemLabelEscaped` attribute. Such an attribute is, however, absent in `<h:message>` and `<h:messages>`. See also Jakarta Faces API spec issue 634.[9] Perhaps it will be added in Faces.next, but for now, you can't go around using a third-party component library or extending the existing standard HTML renderer.

---

[9] https://github.com/eclipse-ee4j/faces-api/issues/634

We'll take that as an example to extend an existing standard HTML renderer for
<h:message>. The first step is looking at which renderer exactly is currently used by the
<h:message> component. In Table 11-1, you will see that this component is backed by
the HtmlMessage class. The currently used renderer implementation can be figured out
programmatically as follows:

```
String componentFamily = HtmlMessage.COMPONENT_FAMILY;
String rendererType = new HtmlMessage().getRendererType();
Renderer renderer = FacesContext.getCurrentInstance().getRenderKit()
    .getRenderer(componentFamily, rendererType);
System.out.println(renderer.getClass());
```

In case you're using Mojarra as Jakarta Faces implementation, it'll print as follows:

```
class com.sun.faces.renderkit.html_basic.MessageRenderer
```

That's thus exactly the renderer class we'd like to extend. Mojarra is open source, and
its source code is currently available at https://github.com/eclipse-ee4j/mojarra.
Once you've gotten the MessageRenderer source code at hand, the next step is to figure
out where exactly the summary and detail of the FacesMessage is being rendered and
how exactly we can override it with a minimum of code. We can see in the source code
that it takes place in the encodeEnd() method which, in the current Mojarra 4.0 version,
is already 160 lines of code. It's using ResponseWriter#writeText()[10] to render the
summary and detail. We'd like to replace this by ResponseWriter#write() so that it
doesn't perform any escaping.

We can of course extend the class, copy/paste all the 160 lines of the encodeEnd()
method, and adjust the writeText() calls for the summary as well as detail variables as
follows:

```
Object escape = component.getAttributes().get("escape");

if (escape == null || Boolean.parseBoolean(escape.toString())) {
    writer.writeText(summary, component, null);
}
```

---

[10] https://jakarta.ee/specifications/platform/10/apidocs/jakarta/faces/context/
ResponseWriter.html#writeText-java.lang.Object-jakarta.faces.component.
UIComponent-java.lang.String

```
else {
    writer.write(summary);
}
```

However, this is not terribly elegant. What if we were to capture all writeText() calls during the encodeEnd() method and transparently delegate to write()? That would look much better. You can achieve this by wrapping the ResponseWriter, setting it on the faces context, and passing it through the superclass. Almost any public Jakarta Faces API artifact has an equivalent XxxWrapper class as well in the API. You can find them all in the "All known implementing classes" section of the jakarta.faces.FacesWrapper Javadoc.[11] All those wrapper classes make Jakarta Faces very easily customizable and extensible. All of them have a constructor taking the to-be-wrapped class, and you basically just need to pick one or more of the methods you'd like to decorate.

All in all, here's how we could extend the MessageRenderer to delegate all writeText() calls during the encodeEnd() method to write().

```
public class EscapableMessageRenderer extends MessageRenderer {
    @Override
    public void encodeEnd
        (FacesContext context, UIComponent component)
            throws IOException
    {
        ResponseWriter writer = context.getResponseWriter();
        try {
            context.setResponseWriter(new ResponseWriterWrapper(writer) {
                @Override
                public void writeText
                    (Object text, UIComponent component, String property)
                        throws IOException
                {
                    String string = text.toString();
                    Object escape = component.getAttributes()
                        .get("escape");
```

---

[11] https://jakarta.ee/specifications/platform/10/apidocs/jakarta/faces/FacesWrapper.html

```
                    if (escape == null
                        || Boolean.parseBoolean(escape.toString()))
                    {
                        super.writeText(string, component, property);
                    }
                    else {
                        super.write(string);
                    }
                }
            });
            super.encodeEnd(context, component);
        }
        finally {
            context.setResponseWriter(writer);
        }
    }
}
```

Do note that it's very important to restore the original response writer in the `finally` of the `try` block wherein the wrapped response writer is being used. In order to get it to run, register it as follows in `faces-config.xml` on the component family and renderer type as associated with the `<h:message>` component:

```xml
<render-kit>
    <renderer>
        <component-family>jakarta.faces.Message</component-family>
        <renderer-type>jakarta.faces.Message</renderer-type>
        <renderer-class>
            com.example.project.renderer.EscapableMessageRenderer
        </renderer-class>
    </renderer>
</render-kit>
```

No, you cannot use the `@FacesRenderer` annotation for this. This won't work when extending an existing renderer. The original renderers are by themselves already registered on the very same component family and renderer type, somewhere in an XML file. And you know, an XML-based configuration always gets higher precedence over an annotation-based configuration when both are discovered.

Now you can just set the escape attribute of the existing <h:message> component to false in order to get the extended renderer to do its job.

```
<h:message ... escape="false" />
```

Beware that you don't embed user-controlled input in any faces message that gets displayed in there, or you'll open up a potential XSS attack hole.

Custom Tag Handlers

In Chapter 3, you learned about the difference between the view build time and the view render time, and that tag handlers such as Jakarta Tags run while building the Jakarta Faces component tree while Jakarta Faces components run while processing the HTTP request and response through the Jakarta Faces life cycle. Not only Jakarta Faces components can be customized, but tag handlers can also be customized. This is particularly useful when you want to control the building of the Jakarta Faces component tree instead of processing the HTTP request and response.

The <f:viewParam> is useful on master-detail pages. From the master page, you can link to the detail page with the entity ID as the parameter. In the detail page, you can load the entity by ID via <f:viewParam>. It goes as follows:

```
<f:metadata>
    <f:viewParam name="id" value="#{editItem.item}"
        converter="project.ItemConverter" converterMessage="Unknown item"
        required="true" requiredMessage="Bad request">
    </f:viewParam>
</f:metadata>
```

When conversion or validation fails, a faces message will be added to the faces context of the current page. However, more often you'd just like to directly redirect the user back to the master page. This is relatively trivial to implement with <f:event> on PostValidateEvent. No, <f:viewAction> won't work as that wouldn't be invoked in first place when there's a conversion or validation error.

```
<f:metadata>
    ...
    <f:event type="postValidate" listener="#{editItem.onload()}" />
</f:metadata>
```

wherein the onload() method looks as follows:

```java
public void onload() throws IOException {
    FacesContext context = FacesContext.getCurrentInstance();

    if (context.isValidationFailed()) {
        ExternalContext ec = context.getExternalContext();
        ec.redirect(ec.getRequestContextPath() + "/items.xhtml");
    }
}
```

Okay, that works, but this will end up in boilerplate code when you have more of such pages. Ideally, you'd like to be able to declaratively register an event listener on <f:viewParam> itself in a self-documenting way like the following so that you can keep the backing bean code free of manual request-response processing clutter.

```xml
<f:metadata>
    <f:viewParam ...>
        <t:viewParamValidationFailed redirect="/items.xhtml" />
    </f:viewParam>
</f:metadata>
```

This can be achieved with a tag handler that basically registers a new system event listener on the UIViewParameter component represented by the <f:viewParam> tag. The tag handler class must extend from jakarta.faces.view.facelets.TagHandler.

```java
public class ViewParamValidationFailed extends TagHandler
    implements ComponentSystemEventListener
{
    private String redirect;

    public ViewParamValidationFailed(TagConfig config) {
        super(config);
        redirect = getRequiredAttribute("redirect").getValue();
    }

    @Override
    public void apply(FaceletContext context, UIComponent parent)
        throws IOException
```

```
{
    if (parent instanceof UIViewParameter
        && !context.getFacesContext().isPostback())
    {
        parent.subscribeToEvent(PostValidateEvent.class, this);
    }
}

@Override
public void processEvent(ComponentSystemEvent event)
    throws AbortProcessingException
{
    UIComponent parent = event.getComponent();
    parent.unsubscribeFromEvent(PostValidateEvent.class, this);
    FacesContext context = event.getFacesContext();

    if (context.isValidationFailed()) {
        try {
            ExternalContext ec = context.getExternalContext();
            ec.redirect(ec.getRequestContextPath() + redirect);
        }
        catch (IOException e) {
            throw new AbortProcessingException(e);
        }
    }
}
}
```

Indeed, this also implements jakarta.faces.event.ComponentSystemEventListener. This is not strictly required for a tag handler; it's just done for code convenience in this specific example. The overridden apply() method is for TagHandler, and the overridden processEvent() method is for ComponentSystemEventListener. In the apply() method, we have the opportunity to programmatically manipulate the parent component before it's being added to the component tree.

We can programmatically achieve the same behavior as <f:event> by calling UICo mponent#subscribeToEvent(), passing the component system event type and listener instance of interest. The listener instance of interest happens to be just the current tag handler instance. When the component system event of interest has been published by the application, then the processEvent() method of the listener instance will be invoked.

The first thing we do in processEvent() is to unsubscribe the listener instance. This is done on purpose because component system event listeners are considered stateful and therefore are inherently saved in the Jakarta Faces view state. An easy way to observe this is to reconfigure Jakarta Faces to save the view state on the client side by explicitly setting the jakarta.faces.STATE_SAVING_METHOD context parameter to client in web.xml and inspecting the size of the jakarta.faces.ViewState hidden input field in the generated HTML output of any Jakarta Faces form. Every time when you add a <f:event>, or don't unsubscribe ComponentSystemEventListener after it has done its job, then the size of the Jakarta Faces view state grows with the serialized form of the listener instance. In this specific use case of a listener that should only run during a nonpostback request, that's just unnecessary, hence the explicit unsubscribe.

Now, in order to get it to run, register it in /WEB-INF/example.taglib.xml as follows:

```
<tag>
    <tag-name>viewParamValidationFailed</tag-name>
    <handler-class>
        com.example.project.taghandler.ViewParamValidationFailed
    </handler-class>
</tag>
```

Packaging in a Distributable JAR

In case you have developed a bunch of reusable components, renderers, tag handlers, tag files, composite components, and whatnot, and you'd like to package it in a JAR file for inclusion in /WEB-INF/lib of a web application, then you need to create a so-called web fragment project. Basically, all Jakarta Faces–oriented components and utility libraries such as OmniFaces, PrimeFaces, OptimusFaces, BootsFaces, ButterFaces, and DeltaSpike are built like this. In Maven perspective, it's merely a JAR project. The key is to put files that you normally put in the src/main/webapp folder of a Maven WAR project in the src/main/resources/META-INF/resources/[libraryName] folder of the Maven JAR project. There is one main exception, all deployment descriptor files that you normally put in `src/main/webapp/WEB-INF` such as `web.xml`, `faces-config.xml`, `*.taglib.xml`, and `beans.xml` go directly in the `src/main/resources/META-INF` folder. Another exception is that the `web.xml` file is to be replaced by `web-fragment.xml`.

The `[libraryName]` subfolder in the resources folder represents the "library name" that is generally the URL-friendly form of the project name, for example, "omnifaces", "primefaces", "optimusfaces", "bsf", "butterfaces", etc. Exactly this library name is then usable in the `library` attribute of resource components such as `<h:outputScript>`, `<h:outputStylesheet>`, and `<h:graphicImage>`. The following is what such a Maven JAR project looks like in Eclipse when organized to conform to the "web fragment" rules. Note particularly the structure of the `src/main/resources` folder. Of course, any Java classes can go inside the `src/main/java` folder in the usual way.

whereby the common.taglib.xml looks like the following, with the composite library name set to a path relative to src/main/resources/META-INF/resources and the tag file source set to a path relative to the location of the *.taglib.xml file itself.

```
<?xml version="1.0" encoding="UTF-8"?>
<facelet-taglib
    xmlns="https://jakarta.ee/xml/ns/jakartaee"
    xmlns:xsi="http://www.w3.org/2001/XMLSchema-instance"
    xsi:schemaLocation="https://jakarta.ee/xml/ns/jakartaee
        https://jakarta.ee/xml/ns/jakartaee/web-facelettaglibrary_4_0.xsd"
    version="4.0"
>
    <namespace>com.example/common</namespace>
    <short-name>common</short-name>
    <composite-library-name>common/components</composite-library-name>
    <tag>
        <tag-name>someTag</tag-name>
        <source>resources/common/tags/someTag.xhtml</source>
    </tag>
</facelet-taglib>
```

and whereby the web-fragment.xml looks as follows, nearly identical to web.xml, only with a different root element, <web-fragment> instead of <web-app>.

```
<?xml version="1.0" encoding="UTF-8"?>
<web-fragment
    xmlns="https://jakarta.ee/xml/ns/jakartaee"
    xmlns:xsi="http://www.w3.org/2001/XMLSchema-instance"
    xsi:schemaLocation="https://jakarta.ee/xml/ns/jakartaee
        https://jakarta.ee/xml/ns/jakartaee/web-fragment_6_0.xsd"
    version="6.0"
>
    <name>common</name>
</web-fragment>
```

Once such a web fragment project is built as a JAR file and included in /WEB-INF/lib of the main web application project, then the resources of the JAR are available in the Facelets files of the main web application project via the library name "common" as follows:

```
<ui:composition template="/common/templates/some.xhtml"
    xmlns:h="jakarta.faces.html"
    xmlns:ui="jakarta.faces.facelets"
    xmlns:common="com.example/common"
>
    <ui:define name="content">
        <common:someComposite />
        <h:graphicImage library="common" name="js/some.svg" />
        <ui:include src="/common/includes/some.xhtml" />
        <h:outputScript library="common" name="scripts/some.js" />
        <h:outputStylesheet library="common" name="styles/some.css" />
        <common:someTag />
    </ui:define>
</ui:composition>
```

Resource Dependencies

There may be cases whereby your custom component or renderer depends on a specific JavaScript or Stylesheet resource, for which you would like to avoid the end user having to manually include it via <h:outputScript> or <h:outputStylesheet>. In such cases, you may find the @jakarta.faces.application.ResourceDependency annotation[12] useful. Imagine that you would like to automatically include common:scripts/some.js and common:styles/some.css along with a particular custom component; then you can do so as follows:

```
@ResourceDependency(library="common", name="some.css", target="head")
@ResourceDependency(library="common", name="some.js", target="head")
public class SomeCustomComponent extends UIComponent {
    // ...
}
```

---

[12] https://jakarta.ee/specifications/platform/10/apidocs/jakarta/faces/application/ResourceDependency.html

You can of course also include Jakarta Faces own `jakarta.faces:faces.js` when necessary, that is, when your custom component happens to rely on, for example, the `faces.ajax.request()` or other functions provided by the standard Jakarta Faces JavaScript API. The `jakarta.faces:faces.js` can be included as follows, with the script library and name available as constants of `ResourceHandler`.

```
@ResourceDependency(
    library=ResourceHandler.FACES_SCRIPT_LIBRARY_NAME,
    name=ResourceHandler.FACES_SCRIPT_RESOURCE_NAME,
    target="head")
public class SomeCustomComponent extends UIComponent {
    // ...
}
```

CHAPTER 12

Search Expressions

As stated in the sections "Ajax Life Cycle" in Chapter 3 and "Ajaxifying Components" in Chapter 4, the execute and render attributes of `<f:ajax>` tag take a space-separated collection of so-called component search expressions.

The search expressions have always been part of Jakarta Faces since the beginning as this was used in the for attribute of `<h:outputLabel>`, `<h:message>`, and `<h:messages>` components, but they have only become essential knowledge for the Jakarta Faces developer since the introduction of `<f:ajax>` in Jakarta Faces 2.0. Namely, labels and messages are in almost any case already within the very same naming container parent as the target input component, so simply specifying the ID of the target input component in the for attribute already suffices, but this is not necessarily true for the execute and render attributes of `<f:ajax>` as the target component may sit in a different naming container context or even in a physically different Facelets file.

To overcome these difficulties, Jakarta Faces 2.0 introduced a few more abstract search expressions: "@this", "@form", "@all", and "@none". Something like "@form" is particularly easy to use, as it just means target whatever the current form is. If that current form is defined two parent templates up from the page where it's referenced, then this really makes referencing it much easier.

Although they made things much easier, these keywords were quite limited. Not only are there just four of them, but they're also not extensible and the default Jakarta Faces component set only uses them internally in the `<f:ajax>` tag. Using them in other components, even in Jakarta Faces' own `<h:outputLabel>`, `<h:message>`, and `<h:messages>` components, as well as using them programmatically, was left out. Therefore, in Jakarta Faces 2.3, a "Component Search Expression Framework" was introduced that greatly expands upon those four keywords. It was largely based on a proven API (application programming interface) of PrimeFaces.[1]

---

[1] https://www.primefaces.org/search-expression-framework/

© Bauke Scholtz and Arjan Tijms 2022
B. Scholtz and A. Tijms, *The Definitive Guide to Jakarta Faces in Jakarta EE 10*,
https://doi.org/10.1007/978-1-4842-7310-4_12

Relative Local IDs

This is the simplest form of a component search expression. The most common use cases are found in the for attribute of <h:outputLabel>, <h:message>, and <h:messages> components. It simply references the sole ID of the target UIInput component.

```
<h:outputLabel for="email" value="Email address" />
<h:inputText id="email" value="#{login.email}" required="true" />
<h:message for="email" />
```

This only prerequires that the target component is also sitting within the very same naming container parent. A naming container parent is a component that implements the NamingContainer interface.[2] In standard Jakarta Faces, only <h:form>, <h:dataTable>, <ui:repeat>, and <f:subview> are an instance of NamingContainer. All composite components are also an instance of NamingContainer, but tag files are not.

In case you need to reference a specific UIInput component within a naming container from <h:outputLabel> on, then you need to append the so-called naming container separator character to the ID of the naming container component and then the ID of the target UIInput component. The default naming container separator character is a colon ":". The currently configured separator character is programmatically available by UINamingContainer#getSeparatorCharacter().[3]

```
char separatorCharacter = UINamingContainer
    .getSeparatorCharacter(FacesContext.getCurrentInstance);
```

This is configurable via the jakarta.faces.SEPARATOR_CHAR context parameter in web.xml.

```
<context-param>
    <param-name>jakarta.faces.SEPARATOR_CHAR</param-name>
    <param-value>-</param-value>
</context-param>
```

---

[2] https://jakarta.ee/specifications/platform/10/apidocs/jakarta/faces/component/NamingContainer.html

[3] https://jakarta.ee/specifications/platform/10/apidocs/jakarta/faces/component/UINamingContainer.html#getSeparatorChar-jakarta.faces.context.FacesContext

> **Caution**   Changing this to something else like a hyphen "-" or even an
> underscore "_" is **not** recommended.[4]

In the long term, such a change is confusing and brittle as those characters are also allowed in the ID attribute itself. Jakarta Faces does not validate the component ID against the currently configured naming container separator character, and thus, it may easily slip through and cause trouble while referencing such a component in a search expression. It's therefore the best to rely on the default of ":".

Coming back to referencing a specific `UIInput` component within a naming container from `<h:outputLabel>` on, in the example composite component `<t:inputLocalTime>` as demonstrated in the section "Composite Components" in Chapter 7, the hour drop-down component has an ID of "hour". Thus, for `<h:outputLabel>`, when using the default naming container separator character, the relative local ID of the hour drop-down inside the composite component is "time:hour".

```
<h:outputLabel id="l_time" for="time:hour" value="Time" />
<t:inputLocalTime id="time" value="#{schedule.time}" required="true" />
<h:message id="m_time" for="time" />
```

Note that this is not necessary for `<h:message>` as faces messages are under the hood already added to the faces context with the client ID of the composite component itself.

Using relative local IDs also works within the context of `<h:column>` of `<h:dataTable>`. It's then interpreted in the context of the currently iterated row, even when the target component is sitting in another column. The following example demonstrates that

```
<h:dataTable id="users" value="#{admin.users}" var="user">
    ...
    <h:column>
        <f:facet name="header">Country</f:facet>
        <h:selectOneMenu id="country" value="#{user.address.country}">
            <f:selectItems value="#{data.countries}" />
            <f:ajax render="city" />
        </h:selectOneMenu>
```

---

[4]https://stackoverflow.com/q/10726653/157882

```
    </h:column>
    <h:column>
        <f:facet name="header">City</f:facet>
        <h:selectOneMenu id="city" value="#{user.address.city}">
            <f:selectItems value="#{user.address.country.cities}" />
        </h:selectOneMenu>
    </h:column>
    ...
</h:dataTable>
```

Under the hood, relative local IDs are resolved using the algorithm as described in the UIComponent#findComponent() API.[5] This means that you can also resolve them programmatically. You only need to ensure that the findComponent() method is invoked on the correct base component, and thus not on, for example, the UIViewRoot.

Absolute Hierarchical IDs

In case the target component is not within the same naming container parent as the current component, then you need an absolute hierarchical ID instead of a local relative ID. The key difference is that an absolute hierarchical ID starts with the naming container separator character. It will then search for the target component from the UIViewRoot on. Such construct is often used in the render attribute of <f:ajax> when it needs to reference a component that is not located inside the same form.

```
<h:form id="search">
    ...
    <h:commandButton id="submit" ...>
        <f:ajax execute="@form" render=":results" />
    </h:commandButton>
</h:form>
<h:panelGroup id="results" layout="block">
    ...
</h:panelGroup>
```

---

[5] https://jakarta.ee/specifications/platform/10/apidocs/jakarta/faces/component/
UIComponent.html#findComponent-java.lang.String

A less common use case where an absolute hierarchical ID is needed is when you need to reference a component that is in turn nested in another naming container. For example, when you want to update a `<h:message>` associated with a composite component during a `<cc:clientBehavior>` event inside the composite component.

```
<h:form id="form">
    <h:outputLabel id="l_time" for="time:hour" value="Time" />
    <t:inputLocalTime id="time" value="#{schedule.time}" required="true">
        <f:ajax render=":form:m_time" />
    <h:message id="m_time" for="time" />
</h:form>
```

You could argue that this is a bug or an oversight in the Jakarta Faces specification. This is very true and should be worked on for a next version of Jakarta Faces. Another yet less common use case is when you need to update a specific iteration round of an iteration component, such as `<h:dataTable>` and `<ui:repeat>`.

```
<h:form id="form">
    <h:dataTable id="table" value="#{bean.items}" var="item">
        <h:column>
            <h:panelGroup id="column1" layout="block">
                ...
            </h:panelGroup>
        </h:column>
        <h:column>
            <h:panelGroup id="column2" layout="block">
                ...
            </h:panelGroup>
        </h:column>
    </h:dataTable>
    <h:commandButton value="Update second row">
        <f:ajax render=":form:table:1:column1
                        :form:table:1:column2">
        </f:ajax>
    </h:commandButton>
</h:form>
```

Note that the iteration index is zero based as with normal Java collections and arrays. Also note that you basically need to wrap the cell's content in another component in order to properly reference the cell's content and that you need to explicitly specify every column in order to update the entire row, as demonstrated before. Updating the entire column is also possible, but less convenient because you basically need to specify the search expression for every single row. Fortunately, the render attribute can take an EL (Expression Language) expression, and the EL stream API can be used to concatenate a bunch of strings in the :form:table:[i]:column format depending on the amount of items in the table.

```
<h:commandButton value="Update second column">
    <f:ajax render="#{bean.items.stream()
        .map(i -> ' :form:list:' += bean.items.indexOf(i) += ':column2')
        .reduce((l, r) -> (l += r)).get()}">
    </f:ajax>
</h:commandButton>
```

Admittedly, this is not the most elegant approach. You'd better delegate to a custom function in an application-scoped bean. It could look something like the following:

```
<h:commandButton value="Update second column">
    <f:ajax
        render="#{ajax.columnIds(bean.items, ':form:table::column2')}"
    </f:ajax>
</h:commandButton>
```

whereby the #{ajax} application-scoped bean looks something like the following:

```
@Named @ApplicationScoped
public class Ajax {
    public String columnIds(List<?> list, String idTemplate) {
        return IntStream.range(0, list.size()).boxed()
            .map(i -> idTemplate.replace("::", ":" + i + ":"))
            .collect(Collectors.joining(" "));
    }
}
```

That's already something better, but still boilerplate-ish. If necessary, you can also programmatically add Ajax render IDs from a backing bean on. You can use the PartialViewContext#getRenderIds()[6] for this. Namely, the returned collection is mutable and only consulted during the render response phase (sixth phase). You also need to specify an absolute hierarchical ID here, but with only one important difference: it cannot start with the naming container separator character. In other words, ":form:table:0:column2" isn't going to work; you need to specify "form:table:0:column2" instead. It's always resolved relative to UIViewRoot.

```
FacesContext context = FacesContext.getCurrentInstance();
PartialViewContext ajaxContext = context.getPartialViewContext();
ajaxContext.getRenderIds().add("form:table:0:column2");
```

As a tip, in case you're having a hard time figuring out the absolute hierarchical ID and/or memorizing which components exactly are naming containers, then you can always look in the generated HTML output. Open the Jakarta Faces page in your favorite web browser, do a *View Page Source*, locate the HTML element representation of the Jakarta Faces component of interest, take the value of its ID attribute, and finally prefix it with the naming container separator character.

Also, in case you encounter an autogenerated ID prefixed with j_id, then you absolutely need to give the associated Jakarta Faces component a fixed ID; otherwise, its value would be off when the component's position in the component tree is subject to be changed because of, for example, a conditionally included component somewhere before the position of the component of interest. (See also the section "Text-Based Input Components" in Chapter 4.)

Like relative local IDs, absolute hierarchical IDs can be programmatically resolved using the algorithm as described in the UIComponent#findComponent() API.[7] The following example demonstrates how to get hold of the UIData component representing <h:form id="form"><h:dataTable id="table">.

```
UIViewRoot root = FacesContext.getCurrentInstance().getViewRoot();
UIData table = (UIData) root.findComponent("form:table");
```

---

[6] https://jakarta.ee/specifications/platform/10/apidocs/jakarta/faces/context/
PartialViewContext.html#getRenderIds

[7] https://jakarta.ee/specifications/platform/10/apidocs/jakarta/faces/component/
UIComponent.html#findComponent-java.lang.String

Standard Search Keywords

Jakarta Faces provides a set of more abstract search expressions, known as "search keywords." They all start with the "@" character. They can be used to substitute a fixed component ID in the search expression. Table 12-1 provides an overview of them.

Table 12-1. *Standard Search Keywords Provided by Jakarta Faces*

Keyword	Resolves to	Since
@this	UIComponent#getCurrentComponent()	2.0
@form	UIComponent#getNamingContainer() until an UIForm is encountered	2.0
@all	Everything	2.0
@none	Nothing	2.0
@parent	UIComponent#getParent( )	2.3
@child(index)	UIComponent#getChildren( ) at given index	2.3
@next	UIComponent#getParent( ) and then UIComponent#getChildren( ) at next index	2.3
@previous	UIComponent#getParent( ) and then UIComponent#getChildren( ) at previous index	2.3
@namingcontainer	UIComponent#getNamingContainer( )	2.3
@composite	UIComponent#getCompositeComponentParent( )	2.3
@id(id)	UIComponent#findComponent() with given ID.	2.3
@root	FacesContext#getViewRoot()	2.3

In a standard Jakarta Faces component set, all search keywords, including custom ones, can be used in the following component attributes:

- `<f:ajax execute>`: Specifies components which must be processed during the apply request values, process validations, update model values, and invoke application phases (second, third, fourth, and fifth phases) of the Ajax postback request. Defaults to `@this`

- `<f:ajax render>`: Specifies components which must be processed during the render response phase (sixth phase) of the Ajax postback request. Defaults to `@none`

- `<h:outputLabel for>`: Specifies the target component of the generated HTML `<label>` element. Defaults to `@none`

- `<h:message for>`: Specifies the target component for which the first faces message must be rendered. Defaults to `@none`

- `<h:messages for>`: Specifies the target component for which all faces messages must be rendered. Defaults to `@none`

Note that using search keywords in the `for` attribute of `<h:outputLabel>`, `<h:message>`, and `<h:messages>` has only been possible since Jakarta Faces 2.3. In older versions, only relative and absolute IDs were supported.

The most commonly used search keyword is undoubtedly `@form`. You have basically no other choice when using `<f:ajax>` in a `UICommand` component which is supposed to process the entire form.

```
<h:form>
    ...
    <h:commandButton value="Submit" ...>
        <f:ajax execute="@form" />
    </h:commandButton>
</h:form>
```

Also new since Jakarta Faces 2.3 is that search keywords can be chained with regular component IDs. The following is an example that expands on the example given before in the section "Absolute Hierarchical IDs":

```
<h:form>
    <h:outputLabel id="l_time" for="time:hour" value="Time" />
    <t:inputLocalTime id="time" value="#{schedule.time}" required="true">
        <f:ajax render="@form:m_time" />
    <h:message id="m_time" for="time" />
</h:form>
```

And the following is an example that updates the entire table when a row is deleted:

```
<h:form>
    <h:dataTable value="#{products.list}" var="product">
        ...
        <h:column>
            <h:commandButton id="delete" value="Delete"
                action="#{products.delete(product)}">
                <f:ajax render="@namingcontainer" />
            </h:commandButton>
        </h:column>
    </h:dataTable>
</h:form>
```

Note particularly that it thus references the closest component implementing the NamingContainer interface, which, in this context, is <h:dataTable> and thus not <h:form>.

As to programmatic resolution, search expressions with keywords cannot be programmatically resolved using UIComponent#findComponent(). For that, you need SearchExpressionHandler#resolveComponent() or resolveComponents()[8] instead. SearchExpressionHandler is in turn available by Application#getSearchExpressionHandler(). You also need to create SearchExpressionContext[9] beforehand which wraps the component to start searching from.

```
FacesContext context = FacesContext.getCurrentInstance();
UIComponent base = context.getViewRoot(); // Can be any component.
String expression = "@namingcontainer";
SearchExpressionContext searchContext = SearchExpressionContext
    .createSearchExpressionContext(context, base);
SearchExpressionHandler searchHandler = context.getApplication()
```

---

[8]https://jakarta.ee/specifications/platform/10/apidocs/jakarta/faces/component/search/SearchExpressionHandler.html#resolveComponent-jakarta.faces.component.search.SearchExpressionContext-java.lang.String-jakarta.faces.component.ContextCallback

[9]https://jakarta.ee/specifications/platform/10/apidocs/jakarta/faces/component/search/SearchExpressionContext.html.

```
      .getSearchExpressionHandler();
handler.resolveComponent(searchContext, expression, (ctx, found) -> {
    System.out.println(found);
});
```

Frankly, it's quite verbose, but it's Jakarta Faces API's own. Fortunately, utility libraries such as OmniFaces exist.

Custom Search Keywords

The Component Search Expression Framework introduced in Jakarta Faces 2.3 also comes with an API that allows us to create custom search keywords. Imagine that you have a form with multiple <h:message> components and that you'd like to re-render them all when submitting the form. Then you'd be tempted also to use @form in the render attribute of <f:ajax>.

```
<h:form>
    <h:outputLabel for="input1" ... />
    <h:inputText id="input1" ... />
    <h:message for="input1" />

    <h:outputLabel for="input2" ... />
    <h:inputText id="input2" ... />
    <h:message for="input2" />

    <h:outputLabel for="input3" ... />
    <h:inputText id="input3" ... />
    <h:message for="input3" />

    <h:commandButton value="Submit" ...>
        <f:ajax execute="@form" render="@form" />
    </h:commandButton>
</h:form>
```

But this is not terribly efficient. In fact, it also unnecessarily re-renders all label and input components and any other static content inside the very same form which doesn't at all change during the Ajax postback request. This is a waste of resources. Ideally, we should have a search keyword like "@messages" that basically references all message components within the same form.

```
<h:form>
    <h:outputLabel for="input1" ... />
    <h:inputText id="input1" ... />
    <h:message id="m_input1" for="input1" />

    <h:outputLabel for="input2" ... />
    <h:inputText id="input2" ... />
    <h:message id="m_input2" for="input2" />

    <h:outputLabel for="input3" ... />
    <h:inputText id="input3" ... />
    <h:message id="m_input3" for="input3" />

    <h:commandButton value="Submit" ...>
        <f:ajax execute="@form" render="@messages" />
    </h:commandButton>
</h:form>
```

Note that each <h:message> component has an explicit ID set, because without an explicit ID, they will by default render nothing to the HTML output, and then the Jakarta Faces Ajax API JavaScript wouldn't be able to find them in order to update its content based on the Ajax response.

In order to get Jakarta Faces to recognize the new search keyword @messages, first extend the jakarta.faces.component.search.SearchKeywordResolver[10] as follows:

```
public class MessagesKeywordResolver extends SearchKeywordResolver {

    @Override
    public boolean isResolverForKeyword
        (SearchExpressionContext context, String keyword)
    {
        return "messages".equals(keyword);
    }

    @Override
    public void resolve
        (SearchKeywordContext context, UIComponent base, String keyword)
    {
```

---

[10] https://jakarta.ee/specifications/platform/10/apidocs/jakarta/faces/component/search/SearchKeywordResolver.html

```
    UIComponent form = base.getNamingContainer();

    while (!(form instanceof UIForm) && form != null) {
        form = form.getNamingContainer();
    }

    if (form != null) {
        Set<String> messageClientIds = new HashSet<>();
        VisitContext visitContext = VisitContext.createVisitContext
            (context.getSearchExpressionContext().getFacesContext());
        form.visitTree(visitContext, (visit, child) -> {
            if (child instanceof UIMessage) {
                messageClientIds.add(child.getClientId());
            }
            return VisitResult.ACCEPT;
        });

        if (!messageClientIds.isEmpty()) {
            context.invokeContextCallback(new UIMessage() {
                @Override
                public String getClientId(FacesContext context) {
                    return String.join(" ", messageClientIds);
                }
            });
        }
    }

    context.setKeywordResolved(true);
    }
}
```

It should be noted that this approach is already slightly hacky. Namely, the intent of the SearchKeywordResolver is to resolve a keyword to exactly one component whose client ID will then be used to substitute the keyword. This component will then be passed to SearchKeywordContext#invokeContextCallback(). In the aforementioned approach, we instead collect the client IDs of all UIMessage components found within the parent UIForm and then supply a fake UIMessage component to invokeContextCallback() who will in turn call the getClientId() of the fake UIMessage component that actually returns the desired collection of client IDs.

It should also be noted that UIComponent#visitTree()[11] is being used instead of recursing over UIComponent#getChildren() in order to collect the client IDs of any UIMessage component. Namely, when plain iterating over children, you may sooner or later come across an iterator component such as <h:dataTable> or <ui:repeat>, and if it happens to have only one UIMessage component nested, then you'll effectively end up with only one client ID, namely, the one without the iteration index. UIComponent#visitTree() doesn't do that; any iterator component in the path will actually iterate over its model value and effectively give back multiple UIMessage components, each with the correct client ID with the iteration index included.

In the end, SearchKeywordContext#setKeywordResolved() must be called with true in order to inform the search context that the keyword has successfully been resolved, even if it actually resolved to nothing. It doesn't actually do any harm if you forgot this, but if you don't mark the search keyword resolved this way, then the search context will continue consulting all other search keyword resolvers, which might end up being less efficient.

Finally, in order to get the new MessagesKeywordResolver to run, register it in faces-config.xml as follows:

```
<application>
    <search-keyword-resolver>
        com.example.project.MessagesKeywordResolver
    </search-keyword-resolver>
</application>
```

or programmatically in a @WebListener as follows:

```
@WebListener
public class ApplicationConfig implements ServletContextListener {

    @Override
    public void contextInitialized(ServletContextEvent event) {
        FacesContext.getCurrentInstance().getApplication()
            .addSearchKeywordResolver(new MessagesKeywordResolver());
    }
}
```

---

[11] https://jakarta.ee/specifications/platform/10/apidocs/jakarta/faces/component/ UIComponent.html#visitTree-jakarta.faces.component.visit.VisitContext-jakarta. faces.component.visit.VisitCallback

Note that the FacesContext must be available at this point and hence a ServletContainerInitializer won't necessarily work, and that the FacesServlet may not have serviced a request yet and hence registration in some managed bean won't necessarily work.

CHAPTER 13

Security

Security for web applications is a broad field and includes a number of topics such as protecting access to resources, shielding against injection attacks of various kinds, and preventing users from being tricked into doing malicious actions on behalf of an attacker.

Jakarta Faces supports these topics in various ways, either by providing native solutions or by integrating with the Jakarta EE platform's facilities. For access to resources, which includes both authentication (the caller proving its identity) and authorization (the system determining to which resources the caller has access), Jakarta Faces (JavaServer Faces) integrates with the Jakarta EE Security machinery, which in turn is defined by, among others, the Servlet spec and the Jakarta EE Security spec.

Jakarta EE Security (JSR 375) is supported by both the Web and Full profile in Jakarta EE 8. Additionally, the reference implementation Soteria works on Jakarta EE 7 servers, and because it's built on JASPIC (Jakarta EE authentication SPI) (JSR 196), it also works on Servlet containers that support JASPIC (such as Tomcat since 8.5 and Jetty since 7.0).

Jakarta EE Security Overview and History

In Jakarta EE, security is not specified in a single specification but is in fact spread over multiple specifications that integrate with each other in various ways. While this allows for different aspects of security to be evolved at their own pace, and practically speaking even allows some to be replaced by non-spec implementations, it does muddy the waters of what spec is responsible for what.

In this introductory section, we'll start off with providing a somewhat broad overview of what some of the pieces are and how they fit together. We'll focus on the web aspects of security. Security is also present in things like Jakarta Enterprise Beans (Enterprise JavaBeans) and JCA (Java Connector Architecture) connectors, but these are outside the scope of this book.

427

© Bauke Scholtz and Arjan Tijms 2022
B. Scholtz and A. Tijms, *The Definitive Guide to Jakarta Faces in Jakarta EE 10*,
https://doi.org/10.1007/978-1-4842-7310-4_13

Historically, security in Jakarta EE is mostly based on the security model introduced by the Jakarta Servlet specification, that is, a model where the core elements are an "authentication mechanism" (FORM, BASIC, etc.), a set of security constraints in web.xml where a specific pattern (the URL pattern) is combined with a collection of roles (including the empty collection), and a few ways to programmatically test the caller's details, such as HttpServletRequest.isUserInRole.

While effective, many details were left out in the early days. The Servlet spec did ask for implementations (Servlet containers) to be extendable with respect to the authentication mechanisms but did not specify how exactly this should be done. Likewise, the Servlet spec implicitly requires an "identity store" (File, Database, LDAP, etc.) that holds the caller details such as credentials, name, and roles but left all details about how to configure these to the Servlet container.

The Servlet spec did not define any way to access the security constraints defined in web.xml in a programmatic way, or to programmatically influence their execution (e.g., to make certain constraints time based). Furthermore, the very early versions of the Servlet spec did not specify the constraint resolution in the strictest way, which allowed for some small differences in interpretation between various Servlet containers.

The first additional spec to address these concerns was JACC (JSR 115), which, simply stated, deals with authorization concerns. JACC specifies how the web.xml security constraints should be represented in code, namely, as a collection of *Permission* instances. JACC also specifies how these can be accessed (queried) by code and finally allows for custom authorization modules that can replace or augment the logic that the container executes to determine its access decision. A perhaps somewhat difficult thing to understand about JACC is that it's not so much something that can be implemented on its own and then added to a Servlet container (as we can do with Jakarta Faces), but it standardizes and more concisely specifies what all Servlet containers internally are already doing.

The second additional spec to address the abovementioned concerns was JASPIC (JSR 196), which deals with authentication concerns. JASPIC specifies at what moments the Servlet container should call the authentication mechanism and defines an explicit interface type for these authentication mechanisms, so custom authentication mechanisms can use this interface instead of the Servlet container's proprietary one and thus be portable. JASPIC says a few things about the identity store, but too little to be really usable in practice. Like JACC, JASPIC isn't something that can be implemented independently, but it standardizes something that all Servlet containers are already doing.

Both JACC and JASPIC define low-level SPIs (server provider interfaces) that are mainly intended to be implemented and used by vendors to provide extension products. They are quite bare and fairly abstract. As such, they are not (rich) APIs (application programming interfaces) that are targeted at application developers. Here is where the Jakarta EE Security API (JSR 375) comes in. Jakarta EE Security offers a higher-level and easier-to-register (just implement the interface) and easier-to-use (CDI based) version of the JASPIC authentication module. The Jakarta EE Security API also fully defines the identity store artifact, but perhaps most importantly, it provides a number of concrete implementations of all of these, among which is a FORM-based authentication mechanism optimized for use with Jakarta Faces and several identity stores such as a JDBC (Java Database Connectivity) store and an LDAP (Lightweight Directory Access Protocol) store.

The RI (reference implementation) of the Jakarta EE Security API is called Soteria. This implementation is of course provided by the Jakarta EE RI GlassFish. Soteria, like Mojarra and MyFaces, has been designed to run independently on basically every Servlet container provided that it adheres to the JASPIC specs (which both Tomcat and Jetty do as mentioned in the chapter's introduction). Its dependencies (at the time of writing, for Soteria 2.0) are CDI 3.0 and Expression Language 4.0. These two dependencies are provided by all Jakarta EE implementations. Servlet containers typically provide EL (Expression Language) support, while CDI can be added separately, for instance, using the RI Weld. For a few *optional* features, Soteria takes advantage of Servlet containers that adhere to the JACC spec.

Protect Access to Resources

In Jakarta Faces, the main resources to protect are views, which are accessed via URL patterns. It's therefore these URL patterns we need to define security constraints. These constraints are primarily defined in web.xml. In fact, as of Jakarta EE 10, web.xml is pretty much the only viable place to define security constraints for Jakarta Faces views.

Jakarta EE has three kinds of security constraints:

- Excluded

- Unchecked

- By role

Excluded

"**Excluded**," a.k.a. "deny all," means that no external caller will be granted access to the resources covered by this constraint. One might ask what the purpose of such a constraint is. If the resources can never be accessed, why are those resources there in the first place?

The answer is twofold. For one, a single application may be configured for different purposes. An excluded security constraint is an easy way then to quickly disable a number of resources that are not applicable to a certain configuration of the application. A more important use case is to be able to make a distinction between external use and internal use of a resource. The key insight here is that security constraints are only applied to external requests for that resource, that is, to a caller requesting `https://example.com/resources/template.xhtml`, but **not** to internal requests such as includes, forwards, and any of the methods to load a resource from the classpath or file system.

This is specifically important for Jakarta Faces because of a somewhat unfortunate design choice regarding composite components. Composite components are components that are implemented via a Facelet instead of a Java class. By convention, they have to be placed in a directory inside a directory named `/resources` that resides in the web root, for instance, `/resources/bar/foo.xhtml`. This will make a composite component "`foo`" available in the namespace `jakarta.faces.composite/bar`.

Components are of course not views, and the caller should not be able to request those directly. Unfortunately, `/resources` is not in any way a special directory to Jakarta EE. Jakarta Faces assigns a special meaning to it by convention, but to the Servlet container, it's a directory like any other. This specifically means there's no protection applied to it and any caller can directly request resources from it. In other words, this directory is "unchecked," a.k.a. "world readable." Even with an `*.xhtml` mapping, this not only allows the user to guess which components we have but lets the user attempt to execute those as well. Clearly, this is not what we want. There are two solutions for this:

- Configure another directory to be the Jakarta Faces resources directory.

- Add the mentioned security constraint to `web.xml`.

Via the `jakarta.faces.WEBAPP_RESOURCES_DIRECTORY` context parameter, another directory can be configured to be the Jakarta Faces resources directory instead of `/resources`. For example:

```
<context-param>
    <param-name>jakarta.faces.WEBAPP_RESOURCES_DIRECTORY</param-name>
    <param-value>WEB-INF/resources</param-value>
</context-param>
```

Note that the path is relative to the web root and must not begin with a "/".

While this is a good default for our own applications, it still doesn't totally protect us. Namely, third-party JARs can still provide their resources via /`resources` and aren't affected by that context parameter. For that reason, the aforementioned "Excluded" constraint is needed. It looks as follows:

```
<security-constraint>
    <web-resource-collection>
        <web-resource-name>The /resources folder</web-resource-name>
        <url-pattern>/resources/*</url-pattern>
    </web-resource-collection>
</security-constraint>
```

As can be seen, defining an *excluded* constraint boils down to defining the URL pattern that we wish to constrain, without defining any specific constraints.

Unchecked

"**Unchecked**," a.k.a. "permit all," "public," and "world readable," means that all callers, independent of whether or not they are authenticated, have access to the resources covered by the "constraint." Internally, an explicit constraint may exist for this, but in `web.xml`, this "constraint" is defined simply by not defining any constraint at all for a URL pattern. In other words, every URL that's not covered explicitly by any other pattern is "unchecked."

By Role

"**By role**" means a so-called role is associated with a URL pattern, and the authenticated caller must have that role in order to access the resource. A role itself is frequently seen as a concept with strict semantics, but it's essentially little more than just an opaque string that needs to match from the set of such strings associated with an authenticated caller and the set of strings associated with a URL pattern. The content of that string is completely up to the application, meaning it could be a "type of caller," like "admin", "user", etc., but also something fine-grained as "may_add_item", or even tokens such as "AYUDE-OPWR-BM1OP".

The following gives an example:

```
<security-constraint>
    <web-resource-collection>
        <web-resource-name>User pages</web-resource-name>
        <url-pattern>/user/*</url-pattern>
    </web-resource-collection>
    <auth-constraint>
        <role-name>VIEW_USER_PAGES</role-name>
    </auth-constraint>
</security-constraint>
<security-constraint>
    <web-resource-collection>
        <web-resource-name>Admin pages</web-resource-name>
        <url-pattern>/admin/*</url-pattern>
    </web-resource-collection>
    <auth-constraint>
        <role-name>VIEW_ADMIN_PAGES</role-name>
    </auth-constraint>
</security-constraint>
<security-role>
    <role-name>VIEW_USER_PAGES</role-name>
</security-role>
<security-role>
    <role-name>VIEW_ADMIN_PAGES</role-name>
</security-role>
```

In the preceding fragment, we define two security constraints—one for the /user/* pattern, for which the caller needs to have the role "VIEW_USER_PAGES", and one for the /admin/* pattern, for which the caller needs the role "VIEW_ADMIN_PAGES". With the aforementioned constraints in place, a caller accessing, say, /user/account.xhtml has to be authenticated and has to have the mentioned role.

An auth-constraint can contain multiple roles, for which OR semantics are applied. This means the authenticated caller only needs to have one of the roles in that constraint in order to be granted access. Constraints can additionally be restricted to a specific HTTP method (such as GET or POST). This does come with a caveat, since by default all methods that are not specified will be unchecked (public). This can be countered by using the top-level `<deny-uncovered-http-methods/>` tag. The following gives an example of this:

```
<deny-uncovered-http-methods />
<security-constraint>
    <web-resource-collection>
        <web-resource-name>User pages</web-resource-name>
        <url-pattern>/user/*</url-pattern>
        <http-method>GET</http-method>
        <http-method>POST</http-method>
    </web-resource-collection>
    <auth-constraint>
        <role-name>VIEW_USER_PAGES</role-name>
    </auth-constraint>
</security-constraint>
```

Setting the Authentication Mechanism

After the security constraints have been defined, we need to set how the caller will authenticate. The artifact that handles the interaction with the caller (i.e., asks the caller for credentials in a certain way) is called an "authentication mechanism." Jakarta EE provides a number of these out of the box. The Servlet spec provides four, namely, FORM, BASIC, DIGEST, and CERT, while Jakarta EE Security provides FORM and BASIC as well (with the difference that these correspond to CDI beans), but also a variant of FORM called "Custom FORM."

FORM and Custom FORM are both suitable for interactive web applications, such as the ones we would build primarily with Jakarta Faces. Contrary to, say, BASIC, the FORM authentication mechanisms call back into the application and let it render the form that asks the caller for credentials, hence the name of these mechanisms.

The difference between the two is mainly in how the mechanism requires the application to continue the so-called authentication dialog after it has rendered the form. In FORM, this is done by letting the caller post the filled-out form to the virtual URL j_security_check, while in Custom FORM, this is done programmatically via a call to the injected SecurityContext. This small difference makes all the difference for Jakarta Faces though. In Jakarta Faces, a form view by default submits to the same URL it was requested from, so posting back to a single mechanism mandated URL is not at all natural. In addition to that, in Jakarta Faces, we often need to have server-side code running after a postback; just think about converters and validators and the ability to emit a faces message. We can't really do any of this if we have to post back to the virtual nonfaces j_security_check URL, but it's quite doable when we can continue the authentication dialog programmatically from the backing bean's action method.

We'll first show you how to configure a web application to use the Custom FORM authentication mechanism. Later on, we'll explain how to actually use Jakarta Faces to fulfill the requirements this mechanism imposes on the application.

All of the authentication mechanisms provided by Jakarta EE Security are installed and configured via its own AuthenticationMechanismDefinition annotation. This annotation tells the container which type of authentication mechanism to install and with which configuration. The annotation can be placed on pretty much every class on the classpath. Logically, it fits in quite well with the @FacesConfig annotation. The following shows an example:

```
@CustomFormAuthenticationMechanismDefinition(
    loginToContinue = @LoginToContinue(
        loginPage = "/login.xhtml",
        errorPage = ""
    )
)
@FacesConfig @ApplicationScoped
public class ApplicationConfig {
    // ...
}
```

A perhaps somewhat unfortunate requirement here is that the `errorPage` attribute has to be specified and set to the empty string. This is needed since the `@LoginToContinue` element has a default value for an actual error page. In Jakarta Faces, we rarely use an explicit error page to display errors but instead redisplay the original page with the error messages rendered on it via faces messages.

Do note that the current version of Jakarta EE Security only allows one authentication mechanism to be active at the same time. Technically what happens when the container encounters the `@CustomFormAuthenticationMechanismDefinition` annotation is that it adds an enabled CDI bean to the system of type `HttpAuthenticationMechanism`. This is important to know, since its being a regular CDI bean means we can inject it, decorate it, intercept it, and basically do everything with it that we can normally do with CDI beans.

The `loginToContinue` attribute is used to configure the view that the container forwards to whenever the caller tries to access a protected view. This is called "container initiated authentication"; the container starts the authentication dialog as opposed to the application.

Note that the default is to *forward* to the login page, meaning that if the caller tries to access `https://example.com/foo.xhtml`, and `/foo.xhtml` is protected, the caller will still see `/foo.xhtml` in the address bar and not `/login.xhtml`. However, the postback is to `/login.xhtml`, so after entering credentials, the caller would get to see this in the address bar. Alternatively, we can configure the `loginToContinue` attribute to use a redirect instead.

```
@CustomFormAuthenticationMechanismDefinition(
    loginToContinue = @LoginToContinue(
        loginPage = "/login.xhtml",
        useForwardToLogin = false,
        errorPage = ""
    )
)
@FacesConfig @ApplicationScoped
public class ApplicationConfig {
    // ...
}
```

Setting the Identity Store

After having declared the security constraints and setting the mechanism that we'd like to use to authenticate, there's one final piece of the puzzle remaining: setting the artifact that contains the caller's data, such as credentials, name, and roles. In Jakarta EE Security, this artifact is called an identity store.

Jakarta EE provides two of these out of the box: one to connect to a database and one to connect to LDAP (Lightweight Directory Access Protocol). The Jakarta EE Security RI (Soteria) additionally ships with an embedded identity store. Most application servers provide additional ones of their own, which are often configured outside the application (e.g., via an admin console, CLI, or XML configuration file that's stored inside the server).

Setting and configuring the Jakarta EE Security-provided identity stores and the one provided by the RI happens in a similar fashion as the authentication mechanisms: via an IdentityStoreAnnotation. Just like the authentication mechanism version, this will cause the container to add an enabled CDI bean to the system, this time one implementing the IdentityStore interface.

The following shows an example together with our earlier definition of the authentication mechanism:

```
@CustomFormAuthenticationMechanismDefinition(
    loginToContinue = @LoginToContinue(
        loginPage = "/login.xhtml",
        useForwardToLogin = false,
        errorPage = ""
    )
)
@EmbeddedIdentityStoreDefinition({
    @Credentials(
        callerName = "admin@example.com",
        password = "secret1",
        groups = { "VIEW_USER_PAGES", "VIEW_ADMIN_PAGES" }
    ),
    @Credentials(
        callerName = "user@example.com",
        password = "secret2",
        groups = { "VIEW_USER_PAGES" })
```

```
    )
})
@FacesConfig @ApplicationScoped
public class ApplicationConfig {
    // ...
}
```

The aforementioned causes an embedded (in-memory) store to be created, with two callers (users), the first one being in the groups "VIEW_USER_PAGES" and "VIEW_ADMIN_PAGES" and the second one only in the group "VIEW_USER_PAGES". The authentication mechanism will use this identity store to validate that the credentials (caller name and password) match and, if they do, to get the correct groups from the identity store.

The observant reader may notice that the terminology has changed. Before, we were talking about "roles," while all of a sudden this has changed to "groups." Is this a mistake? Well, not really. Groups and roles are subtly different. Both are just opaque strings to the container, but groups can be *optionally* mapped to roles. We won't elaborate on this process further here, but suffice it to say that by default, Jakarta EE mandates a so-called 1:1 group-to-role mapping, which simply means groups and roles are the same.

To better understand identity stores, we'll give two more examples here. For the first example, we'll look at one of the identity stores that's provided by the Jakarta EE Security API—the database identity store. This store is activated and configured using the @DatabaseIdentityStoreDefinition annotation. The three most important attributes to configure are the data source (which represents the SQL database), the SQL query to obtain the (hashed!) password given a caller name, and the SQL query to identify which groups a caller is in given the caller name. The following gives an example:

```
@CustomFormAuthenticationMechanismDefinition(
    loginToContinue = @LoginToContinue(
        loginPage = "/login.xhtml",
        errorPage = ""
    )
)
@DatabaseIdentityStoreDefinition(
    dataSourceLookup = "java:app/MyDataSource",
    callerQuery = "SELECT password FROM caller WHERE name = ?",
    groupsQuery = "SELECT name FROM groups WHERE caller_name = ?"
)
```

```
@DataSourceDefinition(
    name = "java:app/MyDataSource",
    className = "org.h2.jdbcx.JdbcDataSource",
    url="jdbc:h2:~/test;MODE=LEGACY;DB_CLOSE_ON_EXIT=FALSE"
)
@FacesConfig @ApplicationScoped
public class ApplicationConfig {
    // ...
}
```

In this example, a data source is defined for the H2 database using the `org.h2.jdbcx.JdbcDataSource` driver. Naturally, this can be done in a similar way for any other database that has a JDBC driver. Alternatively, the data source can be defined externally to the application. The caller query that we used is "`select password from caller where name = ?`", which means we assume a table with at least two columns—one holding the caller name and the other the hashed password. Such table could be created by, for example, the following SQL statement:

```
CREATE TABLE caller(
    name VARCHAR(32) PRIMARY KEY,
    password VARCHAR(255)
)
```

The query that we used for the groups is "`select name from groups where caller_name = ?`", which assumes a table with at least two columns—the caller name and the group name, with one row for each group the caller is in. Such a table could be created by, for example, the following SQL statement:

```
CREATE TABLE caller_groups(
    caller_name VARCHAR(32),
    name VARCHAR(32)
)
```

When populating the caller table, it must be noted that a default hash algorithm is assumed for the password column, namely, `PBKDF2WithHmacSHA256`. This algorithm can (should) be customized by setting the number of iterations, the key size, and the salt size.

Instead of using an identity store that's provided by the Jakarta EE Security API, we also have the option of providing our own custom one. A common use case for that is using the application's own services to load the application-specific user data.

The following shows an example of such an identity store:

```
@ApplicationScoped
public class UserServiceIdentityStore implements IdentityStore {

    @Inject
    private UserService userService;

    @Override
    public CredentialValidationResult validate(Credential credential) {
        UsernamePasswordCredential login =
            (UserNamePasswordCredential) credential;
        String email = login.getCaller();
        String password = login.getPasswordAsString();
        Optional<User> optionalUser =
            userService.findByEmailAndPassword(email, password);

        if (optionalUser.isPresent()) {
            User user = optionalUser.get();

            return new CredentialValidationResult(
                user.getEmail(),
                user.getRolesAsStrings()
            );
        }
        else {
            return CredentialValidationResult.INVALID_RESULT;
        }
    }
}
```

There is no specific registration needed; the previously given class simply needs to be present in the application (be on its classpath). With such custom identity store present, the ApplicationConfig class therefore doesn't need any config for the identity store.

```
@CustomFormAuthenticationMechanismDefinition(
    loginToContinue = @LoginToContinue(
```

```
        loginPage = "/login.xhtml",
        errorPage = ""
    )
)
@FacesConfig @ApplicationScoped
public class ApplicationConfig {
    // ...
}
```

The `UserServiceIdentityStore` as given before delegates most of the work to a `UserService`, which would be responsible for handling `User` entities in the application. Fully discussing such service is outside the scope of this book, but we can imagine it could use, for example, Jakarta Persistence to persist and load `User` entities. Our custom identity store uses the service to try to find a `User` based on the username and the password that's being passed in via the credentials. If a `User` instance is returned, it means the name referred to an existing user, and the password was the correct one. In that case, the identity store in turn returns `CredentialValidationResult` that does two things: it indicates that authentication was successful, and it provides the container with the data that will eventually be used to set the authenticated identity for the current request. If the service couldn't find the user, then either the name or the password was wrong. In that case, the store returns `INVALID_RESULT` to indicate that authentication was not successful.

Providing Our Custom Jakarta Faces Code

In the preceding sections, we first defined our security constraints (which views are protected), then we set up the authentication mechanism (how do our callers interact with our application in order to authenticate), and finally we set up the identity store (where the caller data resides).

It's now time to plug our own custom code into the authentication process. This primarily happens by providing the view that the authentication mechanism directs to when it needs to collect the caller's credentials (email and password in this case).

The login page can be kept relatively simple—a standard form page, with two inputs bound to our backing bean, and a button to submit.

```
<!DOCTYPE html>
<html lang="en"
    xmlns:h="jakarta.faces.html"
>
    <h:head>
        <title>Log In</title>
    </h:head>
    <h:body>
        <h1>Log In</h1>
        <h:form>
            <h:outputLabel for="email" value="Email" />
            <h:inputText id="email" value="#{login.email}" />
            <br />
            <h:outputLabel for="password" value="Password" />
            <h:inputSecret id="password" value="#{login.password}" />
            <br />
            <h:commandButton value="Login" action="#{login.submit}" />
            <h:messages />
        </h:form>
    </h:body>
</html>
```

The preceding page is a totally normal Jakarta Faces view. This specifically means that contrary to classical HTML <form method="post" action="j_security_check"> of FORM authentication, the authentication mechanism does not monitor the postback URL in any way and therefore there aren't any constraints being placed on the input elements that collect the credentials.

Instead, the Jakarta Faces backing bean has to collect these credentials and then programmatically pass these along and signal the authentication mechanism to continue the dialog. Before passing the credentials along, Jakarta Faces is free to do its own validation and engage in its own dialog with the caller without the authentication mechanism having to be involved with this. Note that the command button explicitly doesn't use Ajax to submit. You can do so, but then the average web browser won't suggest the end user to remember the login credentials on its behalf.

The following shows a full example of the backing bean handling the login call. We'll discuss the parts individually below.

```java
@Named @RequestScoped
public class Login {

    @NotNull
    @Email
    private String email;

    @NotNull
    @Size(min = 8, message = "Password must be at least 8 characters")
    private String password;

    @Inject
    private SecurityContext securityContext;

    @Inject
    private ExternalContext externalContext;

    @Inject
    private FacesContext facesContext;

    public void submit() {
        switch (continueAuthentication()) {
            case SEND_CONTINUE:
                facesContext.responseComplete();
                break;
            case SEND_FAILURE:
                facesContext.addMessage(null, new FacesMessage(
                    FacesMessage.SEVERITY_ERROR, "Login failed", null));
                break;
            case SUCCESS:
                facesContext.addMessage(null, new FacesMessage(
                    FacesMessage.SEVERITY_INFO, "Login succeed", null));
                break;
            case NOT_DONE:
                // Doesn't happen here
        }
    }
```

```
    private AuthenticationStatus continueAuthentication() {
        return securityContext.authenticate(
            (HttpServletRequest) externalContext.getRequest(),
            (HttpServletResponse) externalContext.getResponse(),
            AuthenticationParameters.withParams().credential(
                new UsernamePasswordCredential(email, password))
        );
    }

    public String getEmail() {
        return email;
    }

    public void setEmail(String email) {
        this.email = email;
    }

    public String getPassword() {
        return password;
    }

    public void setPassword(String password) {
        this.password = password;
    }
}
```

We start the backing bean with two instance variables corresponding with the credentials we collect.

```
@NotNull
@Email
private String email;

@NotNull
@Size(min = 8, message = "Password must be at least 8 characters")
private String password;
```

This clearly shows the advantage over the FORM authentication mechanism in that we can easily prevalidate the user's input using Jakarta Bean Validation. Because of Jakarta Faces built-in integration with Jakarta Bean Validation, a standard faces message will be made available for rendering should the input not pass validation.

Next, we defined injecting the contextual objects it needs. These are

```
@Inject
private SecurityContext securityContext;

@Inject
private ExternalContext externalContext;

@Inject
private FacesContext facesContext;
```

The observant reader will recognize ExternalContext and FacesContext as being two well-known native Jakarta Faces classes, with the SecurityContext being the odd one out. This class is from Jakarta EE Security, and we'll use that here to communicate with the authentication mechanism.

Continuing the dialog happens in the continueAuthentication() method as follows:

```
private AuthenticationStatus continueAuthentication() {
    return securityContext.authenticate(
        (HttpServletRequest) externalContext.getRequest(),
        (HttpServletResponse) externalContext.getResponse(),
        AuthenticationParameters.withParams().credential(
            new UsernamePasswordCredential(email, password))
    );
}
```

The call to SecurityContext#authenticate() will trigger the authentication mechanism again. Since that mechanism will be a state where it waits for credentials to be passed, it will indeed look for the credentials we pass in and use those to continue. As we'll later see, we can also request that any potentially existing state is discarded and a new dialog is started. Note that we have to cast the request and response objects to HttpServletRequest and HttpServletResponse. Unfortunately, this is needed since ExternalContext abstracts over Servlet and Portlet requests and only returns Object for those two.

The `SecurityContext#authenticate()` method returns a status that indicates in broad lines what the authentication mechanism did. The action method of our Jakarta Faces backing bean has to handle the following:

```
switch (continueAuthentication()) {
    case SEND_CONTINUE:
        facesContext.responseComplete();
        break;
    case SEND_FAILURE:
        facesContext.addMessage(null, new FacesMessage(
            FacesMessage.SEVERITY_ERROR, "Login failed", null));
        break;
    case SUCCESS:
        facesContext.addMessage(null, new FacesMessage(
            FacesMessage.SEVERITY_INFO, "Login succeed", null));
        break;
    case NOT_DONE:
        // Doesn't happen here
}
```

As can be seen, there are four possible outcomes.

The first one is `SEND_CONTINUE`, which basically means "authentication in progress." The authentication mechanism returned that status when it took over the dialog again (e.g., by rendering its own response or, more likely, by redirecting the caller to a new location). A Jakarta Faces backing bean should make sure the Jakarta Faces life cycle is ended by calling `FacesContext#responseComplete()` and furthermore refrain from interacting with the response itself in any way.

The second one is `SEND_FAILURE`, which basically means "authentication failed." This status is returned when the authentication mechanism wasn't able to validate the credentials that were provided. In most cases, this is when the caller provided the wrong credentials. A Jakarta Faces backing bean can respond to this by setting a faces message and redisplay the login form.

The third status is `SUCCESS`, which means "authentication succeeded." This is returned when the authentication mechanism successfully validated the credentials provided. It's only after this status is returned that `HttpServletRequest#getUserPri ncipal()`, `SecurityContext#getCallerPrincipal()`, etc., return non-null values to indicate the current caller is authenticated. A Jakarta Faces backing bean can respond to this in various ways (e.g., by setting a faces message and continuing to render the view, or issuing a redirect of itself).

The fourth and final status is NOT_DONE, which is returned when the authentication mechanism chooses to not authenticate at all. This happens, for instance, when the authentication mechanism is preemptively called but authentication appeared not to be necessary. Typically, a Jakarta Faces backing bean would not need to take any special action here.

Caller-Initiated Authentication

The previous code discussed the situation where an unauthenticated caller tries to access a protected resource (URL/page) and the authentication dialog is automatically started. Since this authentication dialog is started by the container, we call this "container-initiated authentication."

Another case is where a caller explicitly starts the authentication dialog (e.g., by clicking on a "login" button). Because the caller starts this dialog, we call it "caller-initiated authentication."

In case of caller-initiated authentication, the core authentication mechanism is effectively directly invoked, and the platform-provided login-to-continue functionality is skipped. This means that if an authentication mechanism depends on login-to-continue to redirect to a login page and after authentication to redirect back to the protected resource, neither of these two actions will happen when the application programmatically triggers authentication.

The CustomFormAuthenticationMechanism that we defined earlier via an annotation is indeed a mechanism that uses the platform's login-to-continue service, so we'll start the authentication dialog by directing to the same login view we used before. To indicate this is a new login, an extra request parameter is provided. The view from which we start looks as follows:

```
<!DOCTYPE html>
<html lang="en"
    xmlns:f="jakarta.faces.core"
    xmlns:h="jakarta.faces.html"
    xmlns:c="jakarta.tags.core"
>
```

```
<h:head>
    <title>Welcome</title>
<h:head>
<h:body>
    <c:if test="#{not empty request.userPrincipal}">
        <p>Logged-in as #{request.userPrincipal}</p>
    </c:if>
    <c:if test="#{empty request.userPrincipal}">
        <h:form>
            <h:button value="Login" outcome="/login">
                <f:param name="new" value="true" />
            </h:button>
        </h:form>
    </c:if>
</h:body>
</html>
```

In the backing bean, we'll inject two additional objects: an instance to obtain and store the mentioned request parameter and a reference to the Flash, which we'll use later.

```
@Inject
private Flash flash;

@Inject @ManagedProperty("#{param.new}")
private boolean isNew;
```

The managed bean's scope needs to be changed to @ViewScoped, so we can retain the value of the isNew instance variable after the login form's postback.

An important addition is to the SecurityContext#authenticate() method where we'll now provide an extra parameter: newAuthentication. The authentication mechanism does not strictly need this though, and it's just smart enough to distinguish between an initial new authentication and continuing an authentication dialog that's in progress. However, things get more difficult when a caller is in the midst of an authentication dialog and then navigates away, only to explicitly click a login button later. If the state associated with said dialog hasn't expired at that point, the authentication mechanism doesn't know a new authentication is required and will likely continue the aborted but still valid dialog.

To prevent this, we can force a new authentication by setting newAuthentication to true. This will discard all existing states. The modified continueAuthentication() method looks as follows:

```
private AuthenticationStatus continueAuthentication() {
    return securityContext.authenticate(
        (HttpServletRequest) externalContext.getRequest(),
        (HttpServletResponse) externalContext.getResponse(),
        AuthenticationParameters.withParams()
            .newAuthentication(isNew).credential(
                new UsernamePasswordCredential(email, password))
    );
}
```

Note that this version can be used for the case where we continue the dialog as well as to start a new one. When we continue the dialog, isNew will simply be false, which also happens to be the default when the parameter is not specified at all.

When using the CustomFormAuthenticationMechanism, we know there will not be any redirects or other writes to the response after we provide the credentials in caller-initiated authentication, so that gives us a convenient location to handle the redirect to a landing page after the caller authenticates: the SUCCESS case.

```
case SUCCESS:
    flash.setKeepMessages(true);
    facesContext.addMessage(null, new FacesMessage(
        FacesMessage.SEVERITY_INFO, "Login succeed", null));
    externalContext.redirect(
        externalContext.getRequestContextPath() + "/index.xhtml");
    break;
```

We're redirecting the caller here to the index.xhtml landing page. Note that this is also the view where the caller initiated the authentication dialog, but that's just a coincidence in this example. In general, the view or even URL where we redirect the caller to is completely free for the application developer to choose. Typically, a landing page of some sort is chosen, which could be the index of the application or a dashboard corresponding to the main role the caller is in. As we mentioned before, when SUCCESS is returned, the caller is fully authenticated. This means we can query the caller's roles and use these in our decision where to redirect to.

Outlook: A future version of Jakarta EE Security may introduce a hybrid option where caller-initiated authentication can still start with the same redirect as container-initiated authentication and allows for the redirect-back URL to be provided by the application.

Remember Me

Once a caller has been authenticated for a Jakarta Faces (web) application, we naturally don't want to ask the caller to reauthenticate with every request. To prevent this, the result of a successful authentication is typically coupled in some way to the caller's HTTP session. In fact, the `CustomFormAuthenticationMechanism` internally uses the Jakarta EE Security's provided "auto-apply-session" service to do just this. This service stores the data associated with said successful authentication (at least the caller name plus any groups the caller is in). Although implementation ultimately depends on where this data exactly lives and with what lifetime, in practice, it's typically in a special section of the server's memory associated with the HTTP session. This section is special in the way that it's typically session scoped, but the data is not accessible via `HttpSession#getAttribute()`.

In order to not exhaust the server's memory, an HTTP session expires after a certain amount of time. Typical expiration times are between 10 minutes and an hour. If the caller accesses the application after this time, authentication is required to be performed again.

Often though, even reauthenticating after a period of inactivity as long as an hour is undesirable. But extending the HTTP session to a longer period is undoable for the aforementioned reasons of server resource exhaustion.

Here's where "Remember Me" (remember-me) comes in. Remember-me is a somewhat playful term for a process where the caller's credentials are exchanged for a token and where this token is typically stored in a cookie that's distinct from the HTTP session cookie and has a longer time to live.

A remember-me token effectively functions as a new credential for the caller, without exposing the caller's original password. A remember-me token can basically be vended multiple times, for instance, once per device or IP (Internet protocol) that the caller uses to connect to the application. Care must be taken that while the token does not expose the caller's original credentials, it still functions as the key to a caller's account and therefore should be treated with the same precautions as one would apply to any other type of credential. Specifically, cookies containing the remember-me token should be sent over HTTPS/SSL only, and applications should not store the actual token verbatim but a strong hash of it.

As the primary reason for having remember-me is to not exhaust server memory and to be long-lived, the remember-me token is almost always stored in stable storage (e.g., a database). As such, a lookup from such storage is costlier than a lookup from the server's memory, and this could seriously affect performance when required to be done for every request, especially when many Ajax requests are being done all the time.

For this reason, remember-me is almost always used in combination with some kind of cache. The modular nature of the services that the CustomFormAuthenticationMechanism uses makes it possible for remember-me to be inserted between the auto-apply-session service mentioned before and the actual authentication mechanism. That way, we effectively get a kind of memory hierarchy; the authentication data is first attempted to be found in the HTTP session storage; if it's not there, the remember-me service is attempted; and if that one doesn't contain the data, then finally the authentication mechanism is tried.

To make use of remember-me, two things have to be done:

1. Activating the remember-me service for the installed authentication mechanism

2. Providing a special identity store that's capable of vending and validating the remember-me token

Activating Remember-Me Service

The remember-me service in Jakarta EE Security is represented by an interceptor. Via the interceptor binding annotation, @RememberMe (the remember-me service) is easily applied to our own custom authentication mechanism, one for which we have the source code. Unfortunately, it isn't as easy when these have to be applied to a bean for which we don't have the source code and in fact for which we don't even know the exact implementation type.

As the CustomFormAuthenticationMechanism that we've been using for the examples before is indeed of the latter type, there's a bit more work to do. Essentially, we need to obtain a reference of the actual CustomFormAuthenticationMechanism implementation that the container makes available and then use the CDI 2.0 InterceptionFactory to programmatically add the @RememberMe annotation. The result is then to be returned from an alternative producer method.

This is demonstrated in the following code via the new method produceAuthenticationMechanism() in the ApplicationConfig bean which we showed before:

```
@CustomFormAuthenticationMechanismDefinition(
    loginToContinue = @LoginToContinue(
        loginPage = "/login.xhtml",
        useForwardToLogin = false,
        errorPage = ""
    )
)
@FacesConfig @ApplicationScoped
@Alternative @Priority(500)
public class ApplicationConfig {

    @Produces
    public HttpAuthenticationMechanism produceAuthenticationMechanism(
        InterceptionFactory<HttpAuthenticationMechanismWrapper>
        interceptionFactory, BeanManager beanManager
    ) {
        @RememberMe
        class RememberMeClass {};
        interceptionFactory.configure().add(
            RememberMeClass.class.getAnnotation(RememberMe.class));
        return interceptionFactory.createInterceptedInstance(
            new HttpAuthenticationMechanismWrapper(
                (HttpAuthenticationMechanism) beanManager
                .getReference(beanManager
                .resolve(beanManager
                .getBeans((HttpAuthenticationMechanism.class).stream()
                .filter(b -> b.getBeanClass() != ApplicationConfig.class)
                .collect(Collectors.toSet())),
                    HttpAuthenticationMechanism.class,
                    beanManager.createCreationalContext(null))));
    }
}
```

451

The `ApplicationConfig` bean is annotated with the `@Alternative` and `@Priority` annotations. `@Alternative` is used here to indicate that the producer is not just any regular producer but one that should be called instead of any existing producer or bean. That is, the bean we are producing here is an alternative for the bean with the same type that would otherwise be selected by CDI for injection. `@Priority` is used to enable (activate) our alternative producer. Without this annotation, the producer is present but not enabled, meaning that CDI won't call it. Another way of enabling an alternative is using `beans.xml`. The number 500 here is used to select between various alternatives if multiple alternatives are enabled. In that case, the one with the highest number is selected.

The code shown before uses the somewhat well-known CDI pattern `BeanManager#getBeans()/resolve()/getReference()` to obtain the `CustomFormAuthenticationMechanism` that the container makes available. This pattern is more verbose than the simpler `CDI.current().select(...)` variant, but it allows us to filter out the `Bean<T>` that represents the producer method. Getting a reference from that `Bean<T>` from within the producer method would invoke that same producer method again and thus would cause a recursive series of calls eventually leading to a stack overflow. It goes without saying this is unwanted, hence the reason we filter that particular `Bean<T>` out.

The bean instance that is returned from the `BeanManager#getReference()` is almost certainly a proxy; `CustomFormAuthenticationMechanism` is specified to be application scoped, and it implicitly makes use of an interceptor. Due to the technical difficulty of proxying an existing proxy (think of generated proxies often being final and proxy caches being used), CDI 2.0 imposes a limitation on what types of objects it can create an intercepted instance from. To work around this limitation, we have little choice but to insert an extra manually created "pass-through wrapper" `HttpAuthenticationMechanismWrapper` instance as shown in the code before. The code of this wrapper is as follows:

```
public class HttpAuthenticationMechanismWrapper
    implements HttpAuthenticationMechanism
{
    private HttpAuthenticationMechanism wrapped;

    public HttpAuthenticationMechanismWrapper() {
        //
    }
```

```java
    public HttpAuthenticationMechanismWrapper
        (HttpAuthenticationMechanism httpAuthenticationMechanism)
    {
        this.wrapped = httpAuthenticationMechanism;
    }

    public HttpAuthenticationMechanism getWrapped() {
        return wrapped;
    }

    @Override
    public AuthenticationStatus validateRequest(
        HttpServletRequest request,
        HttpServletResponse response,
        HttpMessageContext context) throws AuthenticationException
    {
        return getWrapped().validateRequest(request, response, context);
    }

    @Override
    public AuthenticationStatus secureResponse(
        HttpServletRequest request,
        HttpServletResponse response,
        HttpMessageContext context) throws AuthenticationException
    {
        return getWrapped().secureResponse(request, response, context);
    }

    @Override
    public void cleanSubject(
        HttpServletRequest request,
        HttpServletResponse response,
        HttpMessageContext context)
    {
        getWrapped().cleanSubject(request, response, context);
    }
}
```

Outlook: It's expected that a convenience method for the aforementioned task will be added to a future version of Jakarta EE Security, thereby greatly simplifying this task.

Logging Out

Regardless of which method to log in has been used, at some point, the caller may wish to explicitly log out. A normal login (authentication) in Jakarta EE is always primarily valid per request only, but various authentication mechanisms or the services they're using (such as @AutoApplySession and @RememberMe) may keep the state beyond a single request and automatically reauthenticate the caller at every next request.

This state may be kept at various places: in cookies, in the HTTP session, in client storage, etc. In order to log out, we have to make sure all this state is cleared. In Jakarta Faces, we can do this simply by calling the HttpServletRequest#logout() method. This will immediately remove the authenticated identity from the current request and call the cleanSubject() method of the authentication mechanism, which in turn will remove any session data, cookies, etc., that it used.

The following gives an example:

```
@Named @RequestScoped
public class Logout {

    @Inject
    private HttpServletRequest request;

    public void submit() throws ServletException {
        request.logout();
        request.getSession().invalidate();
    }
}
```

Note that for a full logout, it's typically good practice to invalidate the session as well. The call to HttpServletRequest#logout() should only remove the session state used by the authentication mechanism (if any), while after a full logout, we often don't want any other session state lingering around either. Depending on the application design, it's typical to redirect the caller to the home page of the application after a logout as well.

Custom Principals

The default principal that we can obtain from the security context contains very little other than just the name or, more exactly, the caller principal name (also known as the user principal name). This is typically a unique name and often, but not necessarily, the name the caller used to authenticate with.

In practice, a web application almost always needs more information than just this name, and a richer application-specific model object representing the user is often desired. The lifetime of this model object does need to be very tightly coupled to that of the principal. For example, if the caller is logged out mid-request, the associated model object must disappear right away, and if the caller is logged in again right after (possibly still in the same request), a new model object must become available.

There are various patterns to realize this, some of them including Servlet filters and others containing CDI producers. The pattern we're going to show here, though, involves a custom principal.

A custom principal means that a specific `Principal` type is returned from the identity store, instead of just providing a `String` and letting the container decide the type. This specific `Principal` type can then either *contain* our model object (aggregation) or *be* the model object (inheritance). We'll give an example of the aggregation approach here.

First, consider the following custom `Principal`:

```
public class UserPrincipal extends CallerPrincipal {

    private final User user;

    public UserPrincipal(User user) {
        super(user.getEmail());
        this.user = user;
    }

    public User getUser() {
        return user;
    }
}
```

This principal extends from jakarta.security.enterprise.CallerPrincipal that is the Jakarta EE Security API–specific caller principal representation.

With this Principal implementation, we can now adjust the identity store that we presented earlier to return our custom principal instead.

```
@ApplicationScoped
public class UserServiceIdentityStore implements IdentityStore {

    @Inject
    private UserService userService;

    @Override
    public CredentialValidationResult validate(Credential credential) {
        UsernamePasswordCredential login =
            (UserNamePasswordCredential) credential;
        String email = login.getCaller();
        String password = login.getPasswordAsString();
        Optional<User> optionalUser =
            userService.findByEmailAndPassword(email, password);

        if (optionalUser.isPresent()) {
            User user = optionalUser.get();

            return new CredentialValidationResult(
                new UserPrincipal(user), // Principal instead of String.
                user.getRolesAsStrings()
            );
        }
        else {
            return CredentialValidationResult.INVALID_RESULT;
        }
    }
}
```

Subsequently, we can access our model object again from an injected security context.

```
@Inject
private SecurityContext securityContext;
```

```
[...]

Optional<User> OptionalUser =
        securityContext.getPrincipalsByType(UserPrincipal.class)
                          .stream()
                          .map(e -> e.getUser())
                          .findAny();
```

Conditionally Rendering Based on Access

In web applications, one often wants to render parts of a view differently based on whether a caller is authenticated or not and if so based on what roles this caller is in.

Jakarta Faces component tags don't really need special attributes for this, as the existing implicit objects combined with expression language are powerful enough to do most of the checks needed for this.

One of the most common checks is determining whether the user is authenticated. This was briefly shown in the index.xhtml view earlier:

```
<c:if test="#{not empty request.userPrincipal}">
    <p>Logged-in as #{request.userPrincipal}</p>
</c:if>
```

You can, of course, also use the rendered attribute of any Jakarta Faces component here.

```
<ui:fragment rendered="#{not empty request.userPrincipal}">
    <p>Logged-in as #{request.userPrincipal}</p>
</ui:fragment>
```

However, as you learned in the section "Jakarta Tags" in Chapter 3, this will only end up in a slightly more verbose component tree. Moreover, the rendered attribute checks will be done throughout the Jakarta Faces life cycle over and over, while Jakarta Tags are executed only once during view build time.

Note that we're using the implicit object #{request} here instead of the more general SecurityContext. This is because in Jakarta EE 8, there's no implicit EL object available corresponding to this SecurityContext. In Jakarta EE Security, as well as in the Jakarta Servlet API (from which the request, which is of type HttpServletRequest, originates), it's defined that a `null` return from `getUserPrincipal()` means the user is not authenticated. A better alignment between Jakarta EE Security and Expression Language is planned for a future version of Jakarta EE.

Another common check as mentioned is to test for the caller being in a specific role. Here too we can use the implicit object #{request}, as shown in the following:

```
<c:if test="#{request.isUserInRole('foo')}">
    <!-- foo specific things here -->
</c:if>
```

It's good to remember that as explained in the beginning of this chapter, the role "foo" doesn't have to be something that we would call a role in our normal usage of the word. That is, it doesn't have to be something like "admin", or "manager". In fact, for such very local usage as in a fragment on a view, it's often preferred to use a finer-grained name (e.g., "CAN_UPDATE_SALARY"). A common technique is to map fine-grained roles to more coarse-grained roles, such as, indeed, "ADMIN". Via this technique, a user is given these more coarse-grained roles, and the data store that stores the authentication data then only contains these coarse-grained roles as well. When an identity store such as the one we saw earlier retrieves this authentication data for a certain caller and sees "ADMIN", it would return a collection of roles to which "ADMIN" is mapped (e.g., { "CAN_UPDATE_SALARY", "CAN_ADJUST_MARGINS", ...}).

A special role that we can test for is the "**" role that is an alternative for the #{not empty request.userPrincipal} check. This role is implicitly assigned to any authenticated caller, but with the caveat that the application has not declared this in any way. If it has done so, "**" loses its special meaning and is just another opaque string for which the security system explicitly tests. Using the "**" check, the first fragment that we showed in this section looks as follows:

```
<c:if test="#{request.isUserInRole('**')}">
    <p>Logged-in as #{request.userPrincipal}</p>
</c:if>
```

In the standard Jakarta EE programmatic APIs, there are no methods available to test whether the caller is in any of two or more roles, or in all of two or more roles. If this is required, utility methods such as shown in the following code can be used:

```
public static boolean isInAnyRole
    (HttpServletRequest request, String... roles)
```

```
{
    for (String roles : roles) {
        if (request.isUserInRole(role)) {
            return true;
        }
    }

    return false;
}

public static boolean isInAllRoles
    (HttpServletRequest request, String... roles)
{
    for (String roles : roles) {
        if (!request.isUserInRole(role)) {
            return false;
        }
    }

    return true;
}
```

Sometimes, it's necessary not only to render content on a view differently, depending on what roles a caller is in, but also to take into account what other views (web resources) a caller is allowed to access. This comes into play, for instance, when rendering navigation menus (omitting the entries for views a caller does not have access to), or rendering links or buttons that navigate to views to which the caller does not have access in a special way (e.g., in red or with a lock icon next to it).

A traditional way to implement this is to test for the roles that the programmer knows give access to the given view. While this may seem to work well, it's often brittle in practice as it lets the code work under the assumption of a specific role/view relationship without any strong guarantees that this relationship actually holds.

A more stable way to test whether a caller has access to a given view is quite simply to test directly for exactly that; "does the caller have access to this view (web resource)?". The SecurityContext has a method that can be used for almost exactly this: Security Context#hasAccessToWebResource(). Since the SecurityContext is not a named bean or implicit object, we have to create a small helper bean in order to use this in EL. This is shown as follows:

```
@Named @ApplicationScoped
public class Security {

    @Inject
    private SecurityContext securityContext;

    public boolean hasAccessToWebResource(String resource) {
        return securityContext.hasAccessToWebResource(resource, "GET");
    }
}
```

There are two things to be aware of here.

First, the hasAccessToWebResource() method takes a web resource pattern, which is the same pattern as used for the url-pattern in the web.xml fragment we looked at earlier. This is close to, but not exactly the same as, the Jakarta Faces view. The Jakarta Faces view is often specified in a mapping independent way (e.g., /foo instead of /faces/foo or /foo.xhtml). The web resource pattern, however, has to be the URL itself, with the mapping included.

Second, hasAccessToWebResource() requires us to specify the HTTP method for which we test the access. This is required since in Jakarta EE Security, constraints actually apply per URL and per HTTP method. For instance, a caller can have access to POST to /foo.xhtml but not to GET /foo.xhtml. As we're going to use our utility method for navigation tests, GET is typically the right HTTP method to use, but we should be aware that sometimes we may need to test for another HTTP method.

With the helper bean in place, we can now easily check for access to a target resource on a view and alter the rendering based on that. To demonstrate this, we'll first define three new web resource constraints in web.xml.

```
<security-constraint>
    <web-resource-collection>
        <web-resource-name>Bar</web-resource-name>
        <url-pattern>/bar.xhtml</url-pattern>
    </web-resource-collection>
    <auth-constraint>
        <role-name>bar</role-name>
```

```
            </auth-constraint>
    </security-constraint>
    <security-constraint>
        <web-resource-collection>
            <web-resource-name>Foo</web-resource-name>
            <url-pattern>/foo.xhtml</url-pattern>
        </web-resource-collection>
        <auth-constraint>
            <role-name>foo</role-name>
        </auth-constraint>
    </security-constraint>
    <security-constraint>
        <web-resource-collection>
            <web-resource-name>Baz</web-resource-name>
            <url-pattern>/baz.xhtml</url-pattern>
        </web-resource-collection>
        <auth-constraint>
            <role-name>baz</role-name>
        </auth-constraint>
    </security-constraint>
```

After these constraints have been defined, we can render links to them with access checks on the enabled attribute.

```
<h:link value="Go to Bar" outcome="/bar"
    disabled="#{not security.hasAccessToWebResource('/bar.xhtml')}" />
<h:link value="Go to Foo" outcome="/foo"
    disabled="#{not security.hasAccessToWebResource('/foo.xhtml')}" />
<h:link value="Go to Baz" outcome="/baz"
    disabled="#{not security.hasAccessToWebResource('/baz.xhtml')}" />
```

Authenticating with a caller having, for instance, the roles "bar" and "foo", but not "baz", will result in the link to /baz being rendered as disabled.

Cross-Site Request Forgery Protection

Cross-site request forgery (CSRF) is an attack that lets users without their consent or even knowledge do a request to a site where they may possibly be logged in. Such request then has some side effect that in some particular way may be beneficial to the attacker.

For instance, suppose your bank has a URL of the form `https:/example.com/transferAmount=4000&targetAccount=7836` that means "transfer 4000 euros from my account to the account with ID 7836." In this statement, the "my account" is being determined via the logged-in session (typically a cookie) that you have with your bank. Now an attacker might not be able to capture your session cookie, but that's not necessary in this example if only your browser can be tricked into sending the `https:/example.com/transferAmount=4000&targetAccount=7836` request from any other website that you visit while you're logged in to your bank in another tab or window, with the `targetAccount` parameter set to an ID of an account that the attacker controls. Note that in practice, a GET request and request parameters would not likely be used, but POST and POST parameters would be used instead. However, for both, the same basic vulnerability holds.

If we want to protect our application against receiving such malicious requests, then one of the ways to do so is including "something" (i.e., a token) in the request that is:

1. Specific to a certain caller

2. Expires after some time

3. Can't be easily guessed

As it happens, Jakarta Faces already has something that fulfills all these three requirements, and that's the `jakarta.faces.ViewState` hidden parameter that one finds within Jakarta Faces forms.

Caution   There's a caveat though, and that's that this parameter only fully fulfills those requirements when using postbacks, state saving on server is used, and the view in question is not stateless. Only in that case is the value of `jakarta.faces.ViewState` effectively a token. Since this is the default, Jakarta Faces is relatively safe out of the box here, but this protection is compromised as soon as we deviate from these defaults, for instance, by using stateless views. See also the section "Stateless Forms" in Chapter 4.

Next to this implicit CSRF protection, Jakarta Faces also has explicit CSRF protection. This explicit CSRF protection adds a token for all cases and additionally adds checks for the "referer" and "origin" HTTP headers. Note that HTTP headers should normally not be trusted for incoming requests, as they can be very easily spoofed. However, for this particular attack, we're not trying to defend against just any random HTTP request but specifically against requests sent from a trusted browser. The header checks are also in addition to the token check, and the token check must always pass first.

Defining which views should be protected by a CSRF token and the additional header checks happens in a way that's somewhat similar to how we defined roles for views: a collection of URL patterns in a deployment descriptor. This time the deployment descriptor is `faces-config.xml` instead of `web.xml` though. The following gives an example for these entries in `faces-config.xml`:

```
<protected-views>
    <url-pattern>/bar.xhtml</url-pattern>
    <url-pattern>/foo.xhtml</url-pattern>
    <url-pattern>/baz.xhtml</url-pattern>
</protected-views>
```

Note that the `url-pattern` here is the exact same pattern that is used in `web.xml`. One thing to be aware of here is that despite `faces-config.xml` being a Jakarta Faces–specific deployment descriptor, the `url-pattern` here is again for the full URL relative to the application root which means it has to include all mappings used such as `/faces/` and `.xhtml`.

Adding a `faces-config.xml` with the previously shown `protected-views` fragment to the example application code we've been working on in this chapter will render the link on `index.xhtml` to, for example, `/bar.xhtml` in the following way:

```
/bar.xhtml?jakarta.faces.Token=gdMoNbfOycv2v8Ogr
```

As can be seen, the `jakarta.faces.Token` request parameter has been added by Jakarta Faces. The token is tied to the user's HTTP session, so if the HTTP session expires, the token also expires. The token is cryptographically strong, meaning that it fulfills all three requirements for a CSRF protection token as stated earlier.

If the token is tampered (e.g., we use xxMoNbfOycv2v80gr instead of gdMoNbfOycv2v80gr) or is missing altogether (i.e., we request /bar.xhtml), then Jakarta Faces will throw a `jakarta.faces.application.ProtectedViewException`. In case the link originated from a stateless page, Jakarta Faces applications can handle this exception by notifying the user and allowing to re-render the original page again. In the preceding example, that would mean re-rendering `index.xhtml`. The genuine user would get a new CSRF protection token then, while an attacker will not get the expected side effect from the original request.

As mentioned, there's a `referer` and `origin` header check as well. For this check, Jakarta Faces checks whether the `referer` header, if available, is set to a URL that originates from the same application. To demonstrate this, consider a second Jakarta Faces application with only an empty `faces-config.xml` and the following view:

```
<!DOCTYPE html>
<html lang="en"
    xmlns:h="jakarta.faces.html"
>
    <h:head />
    <h:body>

<h:outputLink value="http://localhost:8080/project/bar.xhtml?jakarta.faces.
Token=gdMhNbfOycv2v80gr">
            test
        </h:outputLink>
    </h:body>
</html>
```

Assuming our first application with the CSRF-protected `bar.xhtml` is deployed to `http://localhost:8080/project`, clicking the output link from this second application will cause the `jakarta.faces.application.ProtectedViewException` to be thrown again in the first application. Note that the `referer` is an optional check that's only done when the `referer` header is actually present, as is the case with the link in the second application.

If we enter `http://localhost:8080/project/bar.xhtml?jakarta.faces.Token=gdMhNbfOycv2v80gr` directly into the address bar of a browser or request it directly via a command-line utility such as `wget` or `curl`, there won't be a `referer`, and the request will be accepted.

In practice, a GET request has less value of being protected against CSRF attacks since these actually *should* be idempotent (should not have side effects and should only display data). Instead of shielding GET requests with CSRF protection tokens, it's probably a far better idea to refactor an application to not have non-idempotent GET requests.

For postbacks, the CSRF protection token works in much the same way though. To demonstrate, consider changing the /bar.xhtml view into the following:

```
<!DOCTYPE html>
<html lang="en"
    xmlns:h="jakarta.faces.html"
>
    <h:head />
    <h:body>
        <h:form>
            <h:commandButton value="Test" action="#{bar.submit}" />
        </h:form>
    </h:body>
</html>
```

Rendering this page will result in the form target URL having the CSRF protection token applied to it in the same way as we saw for the GET requests, for example:

```
<form method="post"
    action="/project/bar.xhtml?jakarta.faces.Token=gdMhNbfOycv2v80gr" ...>
```

This is thus another difference with the implicit jakarta.faces.ViewState token, which is always a POST parameter.

Web Parameter Tampering Protection

Web parameter tampering is an attack against an application where an attacker modifies parameter values that are sent (back) to the server hosting the application. If the application doesn't validate those values correctly, an attacker could gain more benefits than entitled to or may get the opportunity to carry out additional attacks.

For example, suppose a web application renders a list of roles that can be assigned to another user, say, "user," "manager," and "sales." An attacker could attempt to modify the data posted back and change the selection of "user" into "admin." If the server blindly accepts the input and "admin" is an existing value, this allows the attacker to give another user the "admin" role, even when the attacker is not privileged to do that.

Jakarta Faces has an implicit protection against a subset of this attack, namely, against values being posted back from a selection (specifically, from UISelectOne- and UISelectMany-based components). This works by Jakarta Faces either restoring the view from jakarta.faces.ViewState after a postback (when full state saving is used) or re-creating it (when partial state saving is used). Only values that were also rendered are accepted. The usual caveat applies though, and that's that with partial state saving, the data bound to the component needs to be identical before and after the postback. This, however, can easily be accomplished by using the view scope.

To demonstrate, consider the following view:

```
<!DOCTYPE html>
<html lang="en"
    xmlns:h="jakarta.faces.html"
    xmlns:f="jakarta.faces.core"
>
    <h:head />
    <h:body>
        <h:form id="form">
            <h:selectOneMenu id="selected" value="#{bean.selected}">
                <f:selectItems value="#{bean.available}" />
            </h:selectOneMenu>
            <h:commandButton id="select" value="Select" />
        </h:form>
        <p>Chosen value: #{bean.selected}</p>
    </h:body>
</html>
```

and the following backing bean:

```
@Named @RequestScoped
public class Bean {
```

```
    private List<String> available = Arrays.asList("foo", "bar", "kaz");
    private String selected;

    public List<String> getAvailable() {
        return available;
    }

    public String getSelected() {
        return selected;
    }

    public void setSelected (String selected) {
        this.selected = selected;
    }
}
```

Choosing, for example, "bar" and clicking "select" will render "Chosen value: bar," as expected. Changing the value being sent can be done in various ways, for instance, via an intercepting proxy like Burp Proxy or by editing the live source via the developer tools from a browser such as Chrome.

Selecting the "foo" entry after the change as shown in Figure 13-1 and clicking the select button again will cause the "foox" value to be sent to the application. This value will be rejected by Jakarta Faces, and as a result, "Chosen value:" will be rendered, indicating that our tampered value indeed has not been accepted.

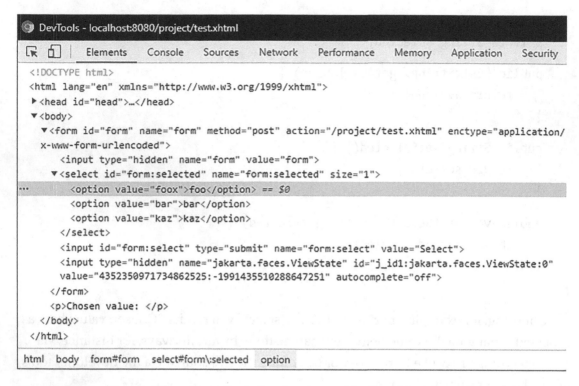

Figure 13-1. Tampering the selected value from "foo" to "foox" in HTML source code via Chrome's DOM inspector

Cross-Site Scripting Protection

Cross-site scripting or XSS is an attack that has a couple of variations, but practically it boils down to a web application rendering data that it got from (other) users directly as part of the markup sent to the client. If this data itself contains scripting code (typically JavaScript), the browser may execute it blindly, allowing the attacker to read, for example, cookie data and to send that over to a server controlled by the attacker.

Jakarta Faces provides protection against this type of attack by having contextual output escaping enabled for many common contexts. The most common context is writing out HTML, where all Jakarta Faces output writers by default XML escape their output.

To demonstrate, consider the following backing bean:

```
@Named @RequestScoped
public class Bean {
```

```
    private String value = "<script>alert('hi')</script>";

    public String getValue() {
        return value;
    }
}
```

The value instance variable contains a script that we don't want the browser to execute. In this example, it's hard-coded, but in practice, it could come from stored data in, for example, a database.

Now we'll render this value using two simple default constructs of Jakarta Faces: a direct expression language expression on a Facelet and the <h:outputText> component.

```
<!DOCTYPE html>
<html lang="en"
    xmlns:h="jakarta.faces.html"
    xmlns:f="jakarta.faces.core"
>
    <h:head />
    <h:body>
        <p>#{bean.value}</p>
        <p><h:outputText value="#{bean.value}" /></p>
    </h:body>
</html>
```

When requesting this view and looking at the HTML source, we'll see that both times the value has been rendered as "<script>alert('hi')</script>" (i.e., in an escaped form that the browser won't execute).

In case we explicitly don't want this escaping to be done, the escape attribute of <h:outputText> can be set to false. For example:

```
<h:outputText value="#{bean.value}" escape="false" />
```

Requesting the view again with the preceding component on it will cause a JavaScript alert to appear to be saying "hi." Had this been malicious code being input by an attacker, the security of the client's system would have been compromised. The escape attribute should therefore only be used with the utmost care.

Output for usage in URLs is escaped as well, but there it's escaped differently, since it's a different context. To demonstrate, consider adding the following component to the view:

```
<h:link outcome="/foo">
    Go to foo
    <f:param name="param" value="#{bean.value}" />
</h:link>
```

After requesting this view, we'll see the link has been rendered as

```
<a href="/project/foo.xhtml?param=%3Cscript%3Ealert%28%27hi%27%29%3C%2F
script%3E">
    Go to foo
</a>
```

What has happened here is that our original value has been escaped for usage as a URL parameter using URL encoding, which, as can be seen, is different from XML escaping, hence the term "contextual output escaping."

Related to XSS protection, sensitive cookies that the application uses should be set to HttpOnly, meaning they'll be sent to the server with each request but can't be read by scripts on the client. For the session ID cookie, this can be done in web.xml as follows:

```
<session-config>
    <cookie-config>
        <http-only>true</http-only>
        <secure>true</secure>
    </cookie-config>
</session-config>
```

Note that the cookie is set to "secure" as well here. This is not related to XSS but sets that the cookie is to be sent only when HTTPS/SSL is used. This protects the cookie from being eavesdropped (e.g., on a shared Wi-Fi network). Since development often happens over HTTP using localhost, such a setting may be problematic for development purposes. If this is the case, then alternatively the cookie can be set to secure or not using ServletContext#getSessionCookieConfig() in a ServletContextListener:

```
@WebListener
public class ApplicationConfig implements ServletContextListener {

    @Override
    public void contextInitialized(ServletContextEvent event) {
        if (...) {
            event.getServletContext()
                .getSessionCookieConfig()
                .setSecure(false);
        }
    }
}
```

where ".." is an application-specific check to see if it's running in "dev mode." You could even use Jakarta Faces own `Application#getProjectStage()` for this.

Source Exposure Protection

Source exposure in the context of server-side web applications refers to the unwanted disclosure of parts of the web application's source. This is a security risk, not only because of the exposure of the source itself (which may be a trade secret) but also because it may give an attacker insight on which to base follow-up attacks (the source may contain references to other systems, beans, or even comments with passwords, although those kinds of comments should of course not be there to begin with).

Due to a number of somewhat perhaps unfortunate design choices in the past, Jakarta Faces has some specific vulnerabilities here, which mostly concern how URL mapping is done but also concern the location of resource files. To understand this vulnerability, we first explain how Jakarta Faces mapping and the `FacesServlet` work.

The main entry into every Jakarta Faces application is the `FacesServlet`. This is a Servlet provided by the Jakarta Faces framework that acts as a so-called front controller through which all Jakarta Faces requests are routed.

A request to a Jakarta Faces view such as `foo.jsf` will thus first need to go through this Servlet, which will then in some way locate the definition of the tree of components that represent the view `foo.jsf`. We'll call this actual definition the "physical resource." Out of the box, Jakarta Faces supports one type of physical resources: Facelets files with the extension `.xhtml`.

In order for the FacesServlet to be able to handle all these requests, it has to be mapped to one or more URL patterns that capture them. To be able to do this, Jakarta Faces supports prefix, suffix, and exact mapping.

If no explicit mapping in web.xml is specified and a recognized Jakarta Faces artifact is found in the application (such as an empty faces-config,xml or the @FacesConfig annotation), then the FacesServlet is automatically mapped. Since Jakarta Faces 2.1 and Servlet 3.0, this automatic mapping is to the following patterns:

- /faces/* (prefix mapping)

- *.jsf (suffix mapping)

- *.faces (suffix mapping)

Since Jakarta Faces 2.3, this also includes the following:

- *.xhtml (suffix mapping)

Especially older (existing) Jakarta Faces applications still explicitly map the FacesServlet in web.xml, which then looks, for example, as follows:

```
<servlet>
    <servlet-name>facesServlet</servlet-name>
    <servlet-class>jakarta.faces.webapp.FacesServlet</servlet-class>
</servlet>
<servlet-mapping>
    <servlet-name>facesServlet</servlet-name>
    <url-pattern>/faces/*</url-pattern>
    <url-pattern>*.jsf</url-pattern>
</servlet-mapping>
```

In suffix mapping and when using Facelets, the FacesServlet will first try to locate the physical resource with the same path and name as the requested resource, but with the suffix replaced by .xhtml. For example, a request for /path/foo.jsf will result in a lookup for the file /path/foo.xhtml.

With prefix mapping, the FacesServlet will try to locate the physical resource with the same name and path as the requested resource, but minus the prefix path. For example, a request for /faces/path/foo.xhtml will result in a lookup for the file /path/foo.xhtml.

This, however, may introduce a security issue that will result in exposure of the Facelet source code. Namely, the lookup for /path/foo.xhtml is done in the web root of the WAR in which the FacesServlet resides. Unless otherwise (implicitly) mapped, every file in the web root is directly accessible for download. In this case, if /path/foo.xhtml is directly requested instead of /path/foo.jsf or /faces/path/foo.xhtml, this request will not go through the FacesServlet and returns the bare Facelets source code of that page instead of the rendered markup.

There are two ways to prevent this exposure of source code:

1.   Map the FacesServlet directly to *.xhtml.

2.   Add a security constraint to web.xml.

Mapping the FacesServlet directly to *.xhtml may be the most natural solution. With this mapping, the requested resource is identical to the physical resource. If /path/foo.xhtml is requested, then the FacesServlet will try to locate /path/foo.xhtml. Via this mapping, there is no second path to reach the Facelets source and hence no risk of exposing it.

Side note: Being able to use *.xhtml mapping was a new feature in Jakarta Faces 2.0. Doing this in Jakarta Faces 1.x resulted in an infinite loop on RequestDispatcher#forward().

To map the FacesServlet to *.xhtml, the easiest way is to rely on the default mapping of Jakarta Faces 2.3 as explained earlier. If this is not possible for some reason, add the mapping to the FacesServlet mapping in web.xml as shown in the following code:

```
<servlet-mapping>
    <servlet-name>facesServlet</servlet-name>
    <url-pattern>/faces/*</url-pattern>
    <url-pattern>*.jsf</url-pattern>
    <url-pattern>*.xhtml</url-pattern>
</servlet-mapping>
```

As an alternative, a security constraint can be defined that prevents access to *.xhtml resources. There is rarely a good reason to prefer this over the simpler *.xhtml to *.xhtml mapping, but for completeness, this can be done as follows:

```
<security-constraint>
    <display-name>No access to Facelets source</display-name>
```

473

```
    <web-resource-collection>
        <web-resource-name>XHTML</web-resource-name>
        <url-pattern>*.xhtml</url-pattern>
    </web-resource-collection>
    <auth-constraint />
</security-constraint>
```

A special case of exposing Facelets source code happens with composite components. Composite components are components that are implemented via a Facelet instead of a Java class. By convention, they have to be placed in a subdirectory of the directory named /resources that resides in the web root, for instance, /resources/ bar/foo.xhtml. This will make a component "foo" available in the namespace "jakarta.faces.composite/bar".

Components are of course not views, and the user should not be able to request those directly. Unfortunately, /resources is not in any way a special directory to Jakarta EE. Jakarta Faces assigns a special meaning to it by convention, but to the Servlet container, it's a directory like any other. This specifically means there's no protection applied to this and any user can directly request resources from it. In other words, this directory is "world readable." Even with an *.xhtml mapping, this not only allows the user to guess which components we have but lets the user attempt to execute those as well. Clearly, this is not what we want.

There are again two solutions for this:

1. Configure another directory to be the Jakarta Faces resources directory.

2. Add a security constraint to web.xml.

In Jakarta Faces 2.2, a method was introduced to address this security vulnerability. Namely, via the jakarta.faces.WEBAPP_RESOURCES_DIRECTORY context parameter, another directory can be configured to be the Jakarta Faces resources directory instead of /resources. For example:

```
<context-param>
    <param-name>jakarta.faces.WEBAPP_RESOURCES_DIRECTORY</param-name>
    <param-value>WEB-INF/resources</param-value>
</context-param>
```

Note that the path is relative to the web root and may not begin with a "/".

Alternatively, or for Jakarta Faces 2.0/2.1, a security constraint can be configured in web.xml again that prohibits caller access to /resources. This can be done in a similar way as protecting for *.xhtml access.

```
<security-constraint>
    <web-resource-collection>
        <web-resource-name>resources</web-resource-name>
        <description>The resources directory</description>
        <url-pattern>/resources/*</url-pattern>
    </web-resource-collection>
    <auth-constraint />
</security-constraint>
```

CHAPTER 14

Localization

Jakarta Faces has always had decent internationalization support. Since Jakarta Faces 1.0, you can supply `java.util.ResourceBundle`-based bundle files in different locales, which in turn get dynamically included as text in the web page at the declared places. Also, all Jakarta Faces converters and validators have their own set of localized default messages which you can easily customize via a message bundle or, since Jakarta Faces 1.2, via new `requiredMessage`, `converterMessage`, and `validatorMessage` attributes. Jakarta Faces 2.0 adds, via the new `jakarta.faces.application.ResourceHandler`, API (application programing interface) support for localizable assets such as stylesheets, scripts, and images.

The act of internationalization, "I18N," is distinct from the act of localization, "L10N." The internationalization part is basically already done by Jakarta Faces itself as being an MVC (model-view-controller) framework. All you need to do is to take care of the localization part. Basically, you need to specify the "active locale" in the view, supply the desired resource bundle files, if necessary translated with the help of a third-party translation service, and declare references to the bundle file in your Jakarta Faces page.

In this chapter, you will learn how to prepare a Jakarta Faces web application for different languages and how to develop it in order to make localization easier for yourself as to maintenance.

Hello World, Olá mundo, नमस्ते दुनिया

To start off, create a bunch of new bundle files in `main/java/resources` folder of the project. The `main/java/resources` folder of a Maven WAR project is intended for nonclass files that are supposed to end up in the `/WEB-INF/classes` folder of the final build. The bundle files can be in `java.util.Properties` format, with the `.properties` extension.

© Bauke Scholtz and Arjan Tijms 2022
B. Scholtz and A. Tijms, *The Definitive Guide to Jakarta Faces in Jakarta EE 10*,
https://doi.org/10.1007/978-1-4842-7310-4_14

477

The file name of those files must have a common prefix (e.g., "text"), followed by an underscore and the two-letter ISO 639-1-Alpha-2[1] language code (e.g., "en" for English, "pt" for Portuguese, and "hi" for Hindi). It can optionally be followed by another underscore and the two-letter ISO 3166-1-Alpha-2[2] country code (e.g., "GB" for Great Britain, "US" for United States, "BR" for Brazil, "PT" for Portugal).

main/java/resources/com/example/project/i18n/text.properties
```
title = Localization example
heading = Hello World
paragraph = Welcome to my website!
```

main/java/resources/com/example/project/i18n/text_pt_BR.properties
```
title = Exemplo de localização
heading = Olá mundo
paragraph = Bem-vindo ao meu site!
```

main/java/resources/com/example/project/i18n/text_hi.properties
```
title = स्थानीयकरण उदाहरण
heading = नमस्ते दुनिया
paragraph = मेरी वेबसाइट पर स्वागत है!
```

Do note that all those bundle files have common keys "title", "heading", and "paragraph", which are usually in English. It's basically the lingua franca of the Internet and web developers. It's considered the best practice to keep the source code entirely in English, particularly if it is open source.

Also note that the English bundle file doesn't have the "en" language code in the file name as in text_en.properties but is just text.properties. Basically, it has become the fallback bundle file that is supposed to contain every single bundle key used in the entire web application. This way, when a bundle file with a specific language code doesn't contain the desired bundle entry, then the value will be looked up from the fallback bundle file. This is useful for situations wherein you'd like to gradually upgrade the bundle files, or when you have certain sections in the web application which don't necessarily need to be localized, such as back-end admin pages.

[1] https://en.wikipedia.org/wiki/List_of_ISO_639-1_codes
[2] https://en.wikipedia.org/wiki/ISO_3166-1_alpha-2

Configuration

In order to familiarize the Jakarta Faces application with those bundle files and the desired locales, we need to edit its `faces-config.xml` file to add the following entries to the `<application>` element:

```
<application>
    <locale-config>
        <default-locale>en</default-locale>
        <supported-locale>pt_BR</supported-locale>
        <supported-locale>hi</supported-locale>
    </locale-config>
    <resource-bundle>
        <base-name>com.example.project.i18n.text</base-name>
        <var>text</var>
    </resource-bundle>
</application>
```

The `<base-name>` must specify the fully qualified name (FQN) following the same convention as for Java classes and that it doesn't include the file extension. The `<var>` basically declares the EL (Expression Language) variable name of the bundle file. This will make the currently loaded resource bundle available as a Map-like object in EL via `#{text}`. To avoid conflicts, you only need to make sure that this name isn't already possessed by any managed bean or any implicit EL objects.

Referencing Bundle in Jakarta Faces Page

It's relatively simple, just treat `#{text}` as a Map with the bundle keys as map keys.

```
<!DOCTYPE html>
<html lang="#{view.locale.toLanguageTag()}"
    xmlns:h="jakarta.faces.html">
    <h:head>
        <title>#{text['title']}</title>
    </h:head>
```

```
<h:body>
    <h1>#{text['heading']}</h1>
    <p>#{text['paragraph']}</p>
</h:body>
</html>
```

Jakarta Faces will already automatically determine the closest matching active locale based on the HTTP `Accept-Language` header[3] and set it as `locale` property of `UIViewRoot`. The `Accept-Language` header is configurable in browser's settings. In, for example, Chrome, you can configure it via `chrome://settings/languages`. If you play around with it, for example, by switching between English, Portuguese, and Hindi as the top-ranked language setting in browser and refresh the Jakarta Faces page, then you'll notice that it changes the text to conform the browser-specified language setting. If you check the browser's developer tools, usually accessible by pressing F12, and inspect the HTTP request headers in the network monitor, then you'll also notice that the `Accept-Language` header changes accordingly.

You might have noticed in the previously shown code example that the `lang` attribute of the `<html>` tag references `#{view.locale.toLanguageTag()}`. Basically, this will print the IETF BCP 47 language tag[4] of the `locale` property of the current `UIViewRoot`, which is in turn available as an implicit EL object `#{view}`. The `locale` property is an instance of `java.util.Locale` that has actually no getter method for the language tag such as `getLanguageTag()`, but only a `toLanguageTag()` method, hence the direct method reference in EL instead of the expected property reference.

The `lang` attribute of the `<html>` tag is not mandatory for the functioning of Jakarta Faces localization feature. Moreover, Jakarta Faces treats it as template text and does nothing special with it. You can safely leave out it. It is, however, important for search engines. This way, a search engine like Google will be informed which language the page's copy is in. This is not only important in order to end up correctly in localized search results but also important in case you serve the very same page in different languages. This would otherwise by the average search engine algorithm be penalized as "duplicate content," which is thus bad for SEO (search engine optimization) ranking.

---

[3] https://www.w3.org/Protocols/rfc2616/rfc2616-sec14.html#sec14.4
[4] https://en.wikipedia.org/wiki/IETF_language_tag

You'll also have noticed that the bundle keys are specified in the so-called brace notation #{text['...']}. The string between single quotes basically represents the bundle key. In this specific case, you could also have used #{text.title}, #{text. heading}, and #{text.paragraph} instead. This is, however, not the common practice. Using the brace notation not only gives a generally clear meaning to what the EL variable represents (a resource bundle), but it also allows you to use dots in the bundle key name such as #{text['meta.description']}. The EL expression #{text.meta.description} has, namely, an entirely different meaning, "get the description property of the nested meta property of the text object," and acts thus like text.getMeta().getDescription(), which is incorrect.

Changing the Active Locale

You can also change the active locale on the server side. This is best to be done in a single place in a site-wide master template that contains the <f:view> tag. The active locale can be set in the locale attribute of the <f:view> that can accept either a static string representing the language tag or a concrete java.util.Locale instance. The locale attribute accepts an EL expression and can be changed programmatically via a managed bean. This offers you the opportunity to let the user change it via the web page without fiddling around in the browser's language settings. You could present the available language options to the user in a Jakarta Faces page and let each selection change the active locale. This can be achieved with the following Jakarta Faces page:

```
<!DOCTYPE html>
<html lang="#{activeLocale.languageTag}"
    xmlns:f="jakarta.faces.core"
    xmlns:h="jakarta.faces.html">
    <f:view locale="#{activeLocale.current}">
        <h:head>
            <title>#{text['title']}</title>
        </h:head>
        <h:body>
            <h1>#{text['heading']}</h1>
            <p>#{text['paragraph']}</p>
```

```
            <h:form>
                <h:selectOneMenu value="#{activeLocale.languageTag}">
                    <f:selectItems
                        value="#{activeLocale.available}" var="l"
                        itemValue="#{l.toLanguageTag()}"
                        itemLabel="#{l.getDisplayLanguage(l)}">
                    </f:selectItems>
                    <f:ajax listener="#{activeLocale.reload()}" />
                </h:selectOneMenu>
            </h:form>
        </h:body>
    </f:view>
</html>
```

It is slightly adjusted from the previous example; there is now <f:view> around
<h:head> and <h:body>. The locale attribute of <f:view> references the currently active
locale via the #{activeLocale} managed bean, which is as follows:

```
@Named @SessionScoped
public class ActiveLocale implements Serializable {

    private Locale current;
    private List<Locale> available;

    @Inject
    private FacesContext context;

    @PostConstruct
    public void init() {
        Application app = context.getApplication();
        current = app.getViewHandler().calculateLocale(context);
        available = new ArrayList<>();
        available.add(app.getDefaultLocale());
        app.getSupportedLocales().forEachRemaining(available::add);
    }
```

```
public void reload() {
    context.getPartialViewContext().getEvalScripts()
        .add("location.replace(location)");
}

public Locale getCurrent() {
    return current;
}

public String getLanguageTag() {
    return current.toLanguageTag();
}

public void setLanguageTag(String languageTag) {
    current = Locale.forLanguageTag(languageTag);
}

public List<Locale> getAvailable() {
    return available;
}
}
```

In @PostConstruct, ViewHandler#calculateLocale() is used to calculate the current locale based on Accept-Language header and the default and supported locales as configured in faces-config.xml. This follows exactly the same Jakarta Faces–internal behavior as if when there's no <f:view locale> defined. Finally, the available locales are collected based on the configured default and supported locales.

The available locales are, via <f:selectItems> of <h:selectOneMenu>, presented to the user as drop-down options (see Figure 14-1). The nested <f:ajax> makes sure that the selected option is set in the managed bean as soon as the user changes the option.

Figure 14-1. *Changing the active locale*

The #{activeLocale.languageTag} property delegates internally to the current java.util.Locale instance. This is basically done for convenience so that we don't necessarily need to add a converter for #{activeLocale.current} in case we want to use it in <h:selectOneMenu>.

<f:ajax listener> basically performs a full page reload with the help of a piece of JavaScript that is executed on completion of the Ajax request. This is done by adding a script to the PartialViewContext#getEvalScripts() method, which is new since Jakarta Faces 2.3. Any added script will end up ordered in the <eval> section of the Jakarta Faces Ajax response, which in turn gets executed after Jakarta Faces Ajax engine has updated the HTML DOM (Document Object Model) tree.

The script itself, location.replace(location), basically instructs JavaScript to reload the current document without keeping the previous document in history. This means that the back button won't redisplay the same page. You can also use location.reload(true) instead, but this won't work nicely if a synchronous (non-Ajax) POST request has been fired on the same document beforehand. It would be reexecuted and cause a double submit. And it unnecessarily remembers the previous page in the history. This may end up in confusing behavior because the back button would then seem to have no effect as it would redisplay exactly the same page as the active locale is stored in the session, not in the request.

Alternatively, instead of invoking `<f:ajax listener>`, you can in this specific use case also use just `<f:ajax render="@all">` without any listener. It has at least one disadvantage: the document's title won't be updated. In any case, using `@all` is generally considered a bad practice. There's only one legitimate real-world use case for it: displaying a full error page on an Ajax request.

As a completely different alternative, you could make the active locale request scoped instead of session scoped by including the language tag in the URL as in `http://example.com/en/page.xhtml`, `http://example.com/pt/page.xhtml`, and `http://example.com/hi/page.xhtml`. This way, you can change the active locale by simply following a link. This only involves a servlet filter that extracts the `java.util.Locale` instance from the URL and forwards it to the desired Jakarta Faces page and a custom view handler that includes the language tag in the generated URL of any `<h:form>`, `<h:link>`, and `<h:button>` component.

Organizing Bundle Keys

When the web application grows, you may notice that bundle files start to become unmaintainable. The key is to organize the bundle keys following a very strict convention. Reusable site-wide entries, usually those used as input labels, button labels, link labels, table header labels, etc., should be keyed using a general prefix (e.g., "`label.save=Save`"). Page-specific entries should be keyed using a page-specific prefix (e.g., "`foldername_pagename.title=Some Page Title`"). The following is an elaborate example of a localized Facelets template, `/WEB-INF/templates/page.xhtml`:

```
<!DOCTYPE html>
<html lang="#{activeLocale.language}"
    xmlns:f="jakarta.faces.core"
    xmlns:h="jakarta.faces.html"
    xmlns:ui="jakarta.faces.facelets"
    xmlns:c="jakarta.tags.core"
    xmlns:fn="jakarta.tags.functions"
>
    <c:set var="page" value="page#{fn:replace(
        fn:split(view.viewId, '.')[0], '/', '_')}" scope="view" />
    <f:view locale="#{activeLocale.current}">
```

```
    <h:head>
        <title>#{text[page += '.title']}</title>
        <meta name="description"
            content="#{text[page += '.meta.description']}" />
    </h:head>
    <h:body id="#{page}">
        <header>
            <nav>
                <h:link outcome="/home"
                    value="#{text['label.home']}" />
                <h:link outcome="/login"
                    value="#{text['label.login']}" />
                <h:link outcome="/signup"
                    value="#{text['label.signup']}" />
            </nav>
            <h:form>
                <h:selectOneMenu
                        value="#{activeLocale.languageTag}">
                    <f:selectItems
                        value="#{activeLocale.available}" var="l"
                        itemValue="#{l.toLanguageTag()}"
                        itemLabel="#{l.getDisplayLanguage(l)}">
                    </f:selectItems>
                    <f:ajax listener="#{activeLocale.reload()}" />
                </h:selectOneMenu>
            </h:form>
        </header>
        <main>
            <h1>#{text[page += '.title']}</h1>
            <ui:insert name="content" />
        </main>
        <footer>
            © #{text['page_home.title']}
        </footer>
    </h:body>
    </f:view>
</html>
```

The Jakarta Tags `<c:set>` basically converts the `UIViewRoot#getViewId()` to a string that is suitable as a page-specific prefix. The Jakarta Faces view ID basically represents the absolute server-side path to the physical file representing the Jakarta Faces page (e.g., "/user/account.xhtml"). This needs to be manipulated to a format suitable as a resource bundle key. The `fn:split()` call extracts the part "/user/account" from it, and the `fn:replace()` call converts the forward slash to underscore so that it becomes "_user_account". Finally, `<c:set>` stores it as "page_user_account" in the view scope under the name "page" so that it's available as `#{page}` elsewhere in the same view.

You'll notice that `#{page}` is in turn being used as, among others, the ID of `<h:body>`. This makes it easier to select a specific page from a general CSS (Cascading Style Sheets) file just in case that's needed. `#{page}` is also being used in several resource bundle references, such as `#{text[page += '.title']}` that ultimately references, in case of "/home.xhtml", the key "page_home.title". With such a template, you can have the following page-specific resource bundle entries:

```
page_home.title = My Website
page_home.meta.description = A Hello World Faces application.
page_login.title = Log In
page_login.meta.description = Log in to My Website.
page_signup.title = Sign Up
page_signup.meta.description = Sign up to My Website.
```

The following is an example of a template client that utilizes the previously shown template /WEB-INF/templates/page.xhtml, the /login.xhtml:

```
<ui:composition template="/WEB-INF/templates/page.xhtml"
    xmlns:f="jakarta.faces.core"
    xmlns:h="jakarta.faces.html"
    xmlns:ui="jakarta.faces.facelets"
>
    <ui:define name="content">
        <h:form id="login">
            <fieldset>
                <h:outputLabel for="email"
                    value="#{text['label.email']}" />
                <h:inputText id="email" required="true"
                    value="#{login.email}" />
```

```
                <h:message for="email" styleClass="message" />
                <h:outputLabel for="password"
                    value="#{text['label.password']}" />
                <h:inputSecret id="password" required="true"
                    value="#{login.password}" />
                <h:message for="password" styleClass="message" />
                <h:commandButton id="submit" action="#{login.submit}"
                    value="#{text['label.login']}" />
                <h:message for="login" styleClass="message" />
            </fieldset>
        </h:form>
    </ui:define>
</ui:composition>
```

The following is what the associated resource bundle entries look like:

```
label.email = Email
label.password = Password
label.login = Log In
```

Note: In case you find that the page looks crippled, simply add a CSS file with the following rule to start with:

```
nav a, fieldset label, fieldset input {
    display: block;
}
```

Localizing Conversion/Validation Messages

In case you have prepared a simple backing bean class Login with two string properties, email and password, and a method submit() and submit the previously shown login page without filling out the email input field, then you'll face a validation error in the following format:

```
login:email: Validation Error: Value is required.
```

When you switch the language to Portuguese and resubmit the empty form, then you'll see that it's also localized. However, when you switch the language further to Hindi, then you'll notice that there's no standard Hindi message bundle in the standard Jakarta Faces implementation. You'd need to provide your own. There are several ways to achieve this.

First, Jakarta Faces input and select components support three attributes to override the default message: `requiredMessage`, `validatorMessage`, and `converterMessage`. The following example shows how to override the default required message:

```
<h:inputText ... requiredMessage="#{text['message.required']}" />
```

This is arguably the easiest approach. The major caveat is that you have to copy/paste it everywhere in case you haven't wrapped it in a reusable tag file like `<my:inputText>`. This is not DRY.[5]

Another way is to supply a custom message bundle that overrides all predefined bundle keys specific for Jakarta Faces conversion/validation messages and register it as `<message-bundle>` in `faces-config.xml`. You can find all predefined bundle keys in Chapter 2.5.2.4, "Localized Application Messages," of the Jakarta Faces specification. The bundle key of the default required message "Validation Error: Value is Required" is thus `jakarta.faces.component.UIInput.REQUIRED`. We can adjust it in new message bundle files as follows:

main/java/resources/com/example/project/i18n/messages.properties
```
jakarta.faces.component.UIInput.REQUIRED = {0} is required.
```

main/java/resources/com/example/project/i18n/messages_pt_BR.properties
```
jakarta.faces.component.UIInput.REQUIRED = {0} é obrigatório.
```

main/java/resources/com/example/project/i18n/messages_hi.properties
```
jakarta.faces.component.UIInput.REQUIRED = {0} आवश्यक है.
```

Finally, configure it in the `<application>` element of the `faces-config.xml` file:

```
<application>
    ...
    <message-bundle>com.example.project.i18n.messages</message-bundle>
</application>
```

---
[5] https://en.wikipedia.org/wiki/Don%27t_repeat_yourself

You'll perhaps have noticed the {0} placeholders in the messages. They represent the labels of the associated input and select components. The labels default to the component's client ID, which is basically the ID of the Jakarta Faces–generated HTML element as you can find in the browser's page source. You can override it by explicitly setting the label attribute of the component.

```
<h:inputText id="email" ... label="#{text['label.email']}" />
<h:inputSecret id="password" ... label="#{text['label.password']}" />
```

Note that putting the message bundle in a different file than the resource bundle is not strictly necessary. You can also just put the message bundle entries in text. properties files and adjust the <message-bundle> entry in faces-config.xml to point to the same FQN as <resource-bundle>.

Obtaining Localized Message in a Custom Converter/Validator

The value of the <message-bundle> entry can be obtained programmatically via Application#getMessageBundle(). You can in turn use it to obtain the actual bundle via the java.util.ResourceBundle API, along with UIViewRoot#getLocale(). This allows you to obtain a localized message in a custom converter and validator. The following is an example of such a validator, which checks if the specified email address is already in use:

```
@FacesValidator(value = "duplicateEmailValidator", managed = true)
public class DuplicateEmailValidator implements Validator<String> {

    @Inject
    private UserService userService;

    @Override
    public void validate
        (FacesContext context, UIComponent component, String value)
            throws ValidatorException
    {
        if (value == null) {
            return;
        }
```

```
    Optional<User> user = userService.findByEmail(value);

    if (user.isPresent()) {
        throw new ValidatorException(new FacesMessage(getMessage(
            context, "message.duplicateEmailValidator")));
    }
}

public static String getMessage(FacesContext context, String key) {
    return ResourceBundle.getBundle(
        context.getApplication().getMessageBundle(),
        context.getViewRoot().getLocale()).getString(key);
}
}
```

Note the managed attribute of the @FacesValidator annotation. This will basically turn on CDI support on the validator instance and hence allow you to inject a business service into a validator. The same attribute is also available for @FacesConverter.

The shown validator example assumes that the following entry is present in the resource bundle files as identified by <message-bundle>:

```
message.duplicateEmailValidator = Email is already in use.
```

Localizing Enums

The cleanest approach to localize enums is to simply use their own identity as a bundle key. This keeps the enum class free of potential UI-specific clutter such as hard-coded bundle keys. Generally, the combination of the enum's simple name and the enum value should suffice to represent a site-wide unique identifier. Given the following com.example.project.model.Group enum representing a user group:

```
public enum Group {
    USER,
    MANAGER,
    ADMINISTRATOR,
    DEVELOPER;
}
```

and the following resource bundle entries in `text.properties`:

```
Group.USER = User
Group.MANAGER = Manager
Group.ADMINISTRATOR = Administrator
Group.DEVELOPER = Developer
```

you can easily localize them as follows:

```
<f:metadata>
    <f:importConstants type="com.example.project.model.Group" />
</f:metadata>
...
<h:selectManyCheckbox value="#{editUserBacking.user.groups}">
    <f:selectItems value="#{Group.values()}" var="group"
        itemLabel="#{text['Group.' += group]}" />
</h:selectManyCheckbox>
```

Note that the `<f:importConstants>` is required to be placed inside `<f:metadata>`. Its type attribute must represent the fully qualified name of the enum or any class or interface that contains public constants in flavor of `public static final` fields. The `<f:importConstants>` will automatically import them into the EL scope as a `Map<String, Object>` wherein the map key represents the name of the constant as string and the map value represents the actual value of the constant.

With `#{Group.values()}` you can thus obtain a collection of all constant values, and each value is then localized in `itemLabel`. Also note that `itemValue` is omitted as it defaults to the value of the `var` attribute that is already sufficient.

Parameterized Resource Bundle Values

You can also parameterize your resource bundle entries using the `{0}` placeholders of the `java.text.MessageFormat` API.[6] They can on the Jakarta Faces side only be substituted with `<h:outputFormat>` whereby the parameters are provided as `<f:param>` children, in the same order as the placeholders. Given the following entry:

---

[6]https://docs.oracle.com/en/java/javase/17/docs/api/java.base/java/text/MessageFormat.html

```
page_products.table.header = There {0, choice, 0#are no products
                                          | 1#is one product
                                          | 1<are {0} products}.
```

it can be substituted using <h:outputFormat> as follows:

```
<h:outputFormat value="#{text['page_products.table.header']}">
    <f:param value="#{bean.products.size()}" />
</h:outputFormat>
```

Database-Based ResourceBundle

Jakarta Faces also supports specifying a custom ResourceBundle implementation as <base-name>. This allows you to programmatically fill and supply the desired bundles, for example, from multiple bundle files, or even from a database. In this example, we'll replace the default properties file-based resource bundle by one which loads the entries from a database. This takes us a step further as to organizing the resource bundle keys. This way, you can even edit them via a web-based interface. The following is what the Jakarta Persistence entity looks like:

```
@Entity
@Table(uniqueConstraints = {
    @UniqueConstraint(columnNames = { "locale", "key" })
})
public class Translation {

    @Id @GeneratedValue(strategy = GenerationType.IDENTITY)
    private Long id;

    @Column(length = 5, nullable = false)
    private @NotNull Locale locale;

    @Column(length = 255, nullable = false)
    private @NotNull String key;

    @Lob @Column(nullable = false)
    private @NotNull String value;

    // Add/generate getters and setters here.
}
```

Note that the Jakarta Persistence annotations provide sufficient hints as to what the DDL (Data Definition Language) of the table should look like. When having the property `jakarta.persistence.schema-generation.database.action` set to `create` or `drop-and-create` in `persistence.xml`, then it will automatically generate the proper DDL. For the sake of completeness, here it is in HSQL/pgSQL flavor.

```
CREATE TABLE Translation (
    id BIGINT GENERATED BY DEFAULT AS IDENTITY PRIMARY KEY,
    locale VARCHAR(5) NOT NULL,
    key VARCHAR(255) NOT NULL,
    value CLOB NOT NULL
);

ALTER TABLE Translation
    ADD CONSTRAINT UK_Translation_locale_key
    UNIQUE (locale, key);
```

And here's what the Jakarta Enterprise Beans service looks like.

```
@Stateless
public class TranslationService {

    @PersistenceContext
    private EntityManager entityManager;

    @TransactionAttribute(value = REQUIRES_NEW)
    @SuppressWarnings("unchecked")
    public Object[][] getContent
        (Locale locale, Locale fallback)
    {
        List<Object[]> resultList = entityManager.createQuery(
            "SELECT t1.key, COALESCE(t2.value, t1.value)"
                + " FROM Translation t1"
                + " LEFT OUTER JOIN Translation t2"
                    + " ON t2.key = t1.key"
                    + " AND t2.locale = :locale"
                + " WHERE t1.locale = :fallback")
            .setParameter("locale", locale)
            .setParameter("fallback", fallback)
```

```
        .getResultList();
    return resultList.toArray(new Object[resultList.size()][]);
    }
}
```

For Jakarta Persistence, we only need an additional converter that converts between java.util.Locale in the model and VARCHAR in the database, which is represented by java.lang.String. You can use the AttributeConverter for this. It's much like a Jakarta Faces converter but then for Jakarta Persistence entities. It's relatively simple; there's no additional configuration necessary. See the following:

```
public class LocaleConverter
    implements AttributeConverter<Locale, String>
{
    @Override
    public String convertToDatabaseColumn(Locale locale) {
        return locale.toLanguageTag();
    }

    @Override
    public Locale convertToEntityAttribute(String languageTag) {
        return Locale.forLanguageTag(languageTag);
    }
}
```

Now we have the custom ResourceBundle; it's called DatabaseResourceBundle. Put it in the package com.example.project.i18n.

```
public class DatabaseResourceBundle extends ResourceBundle {

    private static final Control CONTROL = new DatabaseControl();

    @Override
    public Object handleGetObject(String key) {
        return getCurrentInstance().getObject(key);
    }
```

```
    @Override
    public Enumeration<String> getKeys() {
        return getCurrentInstance().getKeys();
    }

    private ResourceBundle getCurrentInstance() {
        FacesContext context = FacesContext.getCurrentInstance();
        String key = CONTROL.getClass().getName();

        return (ResourceBundle) context.getAttributes()
            .computeIfAbsent(key, k -> ResourceBundle.getBundle(key,
                context.getViewRoot().getLocale(),
                Thread.currentThread().getContextClassLoader(),
                CONTROL));
    }

    private static class DatabaseControl extends Control {

        @Override
        public ResourceBundle newBundle
            (String baseName, Locale locale, String format,
                ClassLoader loader, boolean reload)
            throws IllegalAccessException, InstantiationException,
                IOException
        {
            FacesContext context = FacesContext.getCurrentInstance();
            final Object[][] contents = CDI.current()
                .select(TranslationService.class).get()
                .getContent(
                    locale,
                    context.getApplication().getDefaultLocale());

            return new ListResourceBundle() {
                @Override
                protected Object[][] getContents() {
                    return contents;
                }
            };
```

```
        }
    }
}
```

Finally, adjust the `<resource-bundle><base-name>` entry in `faces-config.xml` to specify the fully qualified name of the custom `ResourceBundle` as follows:

`<base-name>com.example.project.i18n.DatabaseResourceBundle</base-name>`

The actual implementation of this `ResourceBundle` is frankly somewhat hacky, only and only because of the following limitations:

1. Jakarta Faces doesn't allow defining a custom `ResourceBundle.Control` via `faces-config.xml`.

2. Providing a custom `ResourceBundle.Control` via SPI (Serial Peripheral Interface) as `java.util.spi.ResourceBundleControlProvider` doesn't work from WAR on.

3. Creating multiple separate `DatabaseResourceBundle` subclasses for each single locale registered in `faces-config.xml`, such as `DatabaseResourceBundle_en`, `DatabaseResourceBundle_pt_BR`, and `DataBaseResourceBundle_hi`, in order to satisfy the default `ResourceBundle.Control` behavior, is not maintenance friendly in the long term.

An additional advantage of this approach is that it allows you to programmatically clear out any database bundles in the cache by simply calling `ResourceBundle#clearCache()`. Namely, the Jakarta Faces implementation may in turn cache it in its `Application` implementation, causing the `ResourceBundle#clearCache()` to seem to have no effect at all. Mojarra is known to do that.[7]

---

[7] https://stackoverflow.com/q/4325164/157882

HTML in ResourceBundle

This is a bad practice. It adds a maintenance burden. For large sections of content, you'd better pick a more lightweight markup language than HTML, such as Markdown.[8] This is not only safer as to XSS (cross-site scripting) risks but also easier for the user to edit via a text area in some Content Management System (CMS) screens. This is best to implement in combination with a database-based resource bundle. You could add an extra boolean flag to the `Translation` model indicating whether the value should be parsed as Markdown.

```
@Column(nullable = false)
private boolean markdown;
```

Then, inside `TranslationService#getContents()`, select it as the third column.

```
"SELECT t1.key, COALESCE(t2.value, t1.value), t1.markdown"
```

And, finally, in the `DatabaseControl#newBundle()` method, after retrieving the contents, you could postprocess them based on the boolean. You could use any Java-based Markdown library for this, such as CommonMark.[9]

```
static final Parser PARSER = Parser.builder().build();
static final HtmlRenderer RENDERER = HtmlRenderer.builder().build();
...
for (Object[] translation : contents) {
    if ((boolean) translation[2]) {
        translation[1] = RENDERER.render(PARSER.parse(translation[1]));
    }
}
```

---

[8] https://en.wikipedia.org/wiki/Markdown
[9] https://github.com/atlassian/commonmark-java

CHAPTER 15

Extensions

If there is one single element or virtue of Jakarta Faces to which we can attribute its lasting for so long, it's probably its ability to be extended in a large variety of ways. From the onset, Jakarta Faces made it possible to have most of its core elements replaced, decorated, or augmented.

This gave rise to a large number of extension libraries and projects. In the very early days, these were A4J (Ajax4JSF), Tomahawk, RichFaces, the stand-alone Facelets project, PrettyFaces, and many, many more. A4J was merged into RichFaces, and RichFaces itself was eventually sunset in 2016. Facelets was incorporated into Jakarta Faces itself, while PrettyFaces became part of the Rewrite framework. These days well-known and active extension libraries are PrimeFaces, OmniFaces, and BootsFaces, among others. While individual libraries have come and gone, the main constant is the extensibility of Jakarta Faces from its first days until the present.

It's sometimes said that all those libraries address defects or omissions in Jakarta Faces, but this is not entirely accurate. In fact, Jakarta Faces was explicitly designed to make such extensions possible and therefore to allow, even stimulate, such extension libraries to appear. For instance, a contemporary peer technology of Jakarta Faces, Jakarta Enterprise Beans (formerly known as Jakarta Enterprise Beans, Enterprise JavaBeans), had few to no extension points, and thus, despite its many shortcomings, we never saw much of an ecosystem flourish around it.

Extension Types

There are a couple of different ways by which to use the various extension points in Jakarta Faces. A major distinction is between the "classical" approach and the "CDI-centric approach."

499

© Bauke Scholtz and Arjan Tijms 2022
B. Scholtz and A. Tijms, *The Definitive Guide to Jakarta Faces in Jakarta EE 10*,
https://doi.org/10.1007/978-1-4842-7310-4_15

In the latter approach, there's very little to nothing that Jakarta Faces has to explicitly support extensibility, as CDI has a number of mechanisms built in to support extending or replacing CDI artifacts. Table 8-1 in Chapter 8 showed these artifacts.

Extending CDI Artifacts

One of the ways CDI augments or replaces a type fully is to provide an alternative producer. We already saw this technique being used in Chapter 13, albeit for a slightly different use case.

The easiest way is if you need to fully replace the type. If augmenting is needed, some code is necessary to obtain the previous type, which, with the current version of CDI (4.0), is slightly verbose.

The following shows an example where we replace the request parameter map with a new map that has all the values of the original map, plus an additional value that we add ourselves:

```
@Dependent @Alternative @Priority(APPLICATION)
public class RequestParameterMapProducer {

    @Produces @RequestScoped @RequestParameterMap
    public Map<String, String> producer(BeanManager beanManager) {
        Map<String, String> previousMap = getPreviousMap(beanManager);
        Map<String, String> newMap = new HashMap<>(previousMap);
        newMap.put("test", "myTestValue");
        return newMap;
    }
}
```

The getPreviousMap() method is, as mentioned, somewhat verbose. It's defined as follows:

```
private Map<String, String> getPreviousMap(BeanManager beanManager) {
    class RequestParameterMapAnnotationLiteral
        extends AnnotationLiteral<RequestParameterMap>
        implements RequestParameterMap
    {
```

```java
        private static final long serialVersionUID = 1L;
    }

    Type MAP_TYPE = new ParameterizedType() {

        @Override
        public Type getRawType() {
            return Map.class;
        }

        @Override
        public Type[] getActualTypeArguments() {
            return new Type[] {String.class, String.class};
        }

        @Override
        public Type getOwnerType() {
            return null;
        }
    };

    return (Map<String, String>) beanManager
        .getReference(beanManager
        .resolve(beanManager
        .getBeans(MAP_TYPE, new RequestParameterMapAnnotationLiteral())
        .stream()
        .filter(bean -> bean
            .getBeanClass() != RequestParameterMapProducer.class)
        .collect(Collectors.toSet())),
            MAP_TYPE,
            beanManager.createCreationalContext(null));
    }
}
```

It's expected that the task of obtaining this "previous" or "original" type will be made easier in a future revision of any of the specs involved. For instance, a future version of Jakarta Faces will likely introduce ready-to-use annotation literals for its (CDI) annotations, such as the RequestParameterMapAnnotationLiteral shown here.

In order to test that this alternative producer works, consider the following backing bean:

```
@Named @RequestScoped
public class TestBean {

    @Inject @RequestParameterMap
    private Map<String, String> requestParameterMap;

    public String getTest() {
        return requestParameterMap.get("test");
    }

    public String getFoo() {
        return requestParameterMap.get("foo");
    }
}
```

and the following Facelet:

```
<!DOCTYPE html>
<html lang="en"
    xmlns:h="jakarta.faces.html"
>
    <h:head/>
    <h:body>
        <p>Test: #{testBean.test}</p>
        <p>Foo: #{testBean.foo}</p>
    </h:body>
</html>
```

Deploying an application containing these artifacts with a request parameter of, say, "foo=bar" will reveal that the new map indeed contains the original request parameters as well as the value that we added ourselves.

Extending Classical Artifacts

The classical approach to augment or fully replace a type in Jakarta Faces is by installing a factory for that type. The basic way such a factory works is in broad lines identical to the CDI approach demonstrated earlier; the factory returns an implementation of the requested type and obtains a reference to the "previous" or "original" type.

Being classical in Jakarta EE typically means XML, and indeed the classical factory involves XML. Specifically, registering a factory entails using the `<factory>` element in `faces-config.xml` and a specific element per type for which a factory is to be provided. As of Jakarta Faces 4.0, the following factories are supported:

- `<application-factory>`

- `<exception-handler-factory>`

- `<external-context-factory>`

- `<faces-context-factory>`

- `<facelet-cache-factory>`

- `<partial-view-context-factory>`

- `<lifecycle-factory>`

- `<view-declaration-language-factory>`

- `<tag-handler-delegate-factory>`

- `<render-kit-factory>`

- `<visit-context-factory>`

- `<flash-factory>`

- `<flow-handler-factory>`

- `<client-window-factory>`

- `<search-expression-context-factory>`

Next to these, there are another number of artifacts that can be replaced/augmented in a somewhat similar but still different way; here, there's no factory returning the type, but an implementation of the type is specified directly. This variant is specified using the `<application>` element in `faces-config.xml`. As of Jakarta Faces 4.0, the following types can be replaced/augmented directly:

- `<navigation-handler>`

- `<view-handler>`

- `<resource-handler>`

- `<search-expression-handler>`

- `<flow-handler>`

- `<state-manager>`

- `<action-listener>`

Note that all of these are singletons. From the Jakarta Faces runtime point of view, there's only one of each, but multiple implementations each adding something are supported by means of wrapping, which therefore forms a chain (implementation A wrapping implementation B, wrapping implementation C, etc.).

The aforementioned specific elements used for each type immediately highlight an issue with the classical approach; Jakarta Faces *has* to provide explicit support for each specific type to be replaced/augmented in this way. By contrast, the CDI approach allows us to pretty much replace/augment any type without requiring any special support from Jakarta Faces other than that Jakarta Faces uses CDI for that artifact.

On the bright side, the factory implementation is currently somewhat simpler compared to the Jakarta Faces version, as the "previous" or "original" type is simply being passed to it in its constructor instead of having to be looked up using verbose code.

As an example, we'll show how to augment the external context factory. For this, we start with the mentioned registration in `faces-config.xml`.

```
<factory>
    <external-context-factory>
        com.example.project.ExternalContextProducer
    </external-context-factory>
</factory>
```

The implementation then looks as follows:

```
public class ExternalContextProducer extends ExternalContextFactory {

    public ExternalContextProducer(ExternalContextFactory wrapped) {
        super(wrapped);
    }
```

```
@Override
public ExternalContext getExternalContext
    (Object context, Object request, Object response)
{
    ExternalContext previousExternalContext =
        getWrapped().getExternalContext(context, request, response);
    ExternalContext newExternalContext =
        new ExternalContextWrapper(previousExternalContext) {
            @Override
            public String getAuthType() {
                return "OurOwnAuthType";
            }
        };
    return newExternalContext;
}
}
```

There are a few things to observe here. First of all, every factory of this kind has to inherit from a predescribed parent factory, which in this case is ExternalContextFactory. Second, there's an implicit contract that must be followed, and that's implementing the constructor exactly as shown in the example. That is, add a public constructor with a single parameter the exact same type as the superclass, and pass this parameter on to the super constructor. This instance is then available in other methods using the getWrapped() method.

Testing that this indeed works is relatively easy. We use a similar backing bean as with the CDI version:

```
@Named @RequestScoped
public class TestBean {

    @Inject
    private ExternalContext externalContext;

    public String getAuth() {
        return externalContext.getAuthType();
    }
}
```

and the following Facelet:

```
<!DOCTYPE html>
<html lang="en"
    xmlns:h="jakarta.faces.html"
>
    <h:head />
    <h:body>
        <p>Test: #{testBean.auth}</p>
    </h:body>
</html>
```

As the external context is also a type that's injectable via CDI, the observant reader may wonder what happens when both a CDI alternative producer and a classic factory are provided for that type. The answer is that this is strictly speaking not specified (thus undefined behavior), yet in practice, it's strongly implied that the classic factory is used as the source to ultimately get the external context from. This means that an alternative producer for ExternalContext will only affect the direct injection of ExternalContext, and not any situation when this type is obtained in any other way, for instance, by calling FacesContext#getExternalContext(). This is something users should clearly be aware of. The expectation is, though, that a future revision of the spec will make a CDI producer the initial source.

Plug-ins

A different type of extending that Jakarta Faces offers next to the alternative producers and factories is what's essentially a plug-in. Here, no core Jakarta Faces type is replaced or augmented, but an additional functionality is added to some part of the runtime. Most of these additions, therefore, have to declare in some way what it is they are exactly adding, which is different from the factories which just provided an implementation of type X or Y.

Plug-ins are added as elements of the <application> element in faces-config.xml, just as some of the factory-like types mentioned earlier. The following are supported:

- <el-resolver>

- <search-keyword-resolver>

We already saw an example of the Search Keyword Resolver in the section "Custom Search Keywords" in Chapter 12. Characteristic for that one being a plug-in was the method isResolverForKeyWord(), by which the plug-in could indicate for which keyword, or keyword pattern, it would operate.

We'll take a look at one other example here, namely, the EL resolver. The EL resolver itself is not a Jakarta Faces–specific type but originates from the Expression Language (EL) spec. This spec does, however, have important parts of its origins in Jakarta Faces.

The EL resolver allows us to interpret the so-called base and property of an expression in a custom way. Considering the expression #{foo.bar.kaz}, then "foo" is the base and "bar" is the property when resolving "bar", while "bar" is the base and "kaz" is the property when resolving "kaz". Perhaps somewhat surprising at first is that when "foo" is being resolved, the base is null and "foo" is the property.

In practice, adding a custom EL resolver is not often needed, and we can often get by with simply defining a named CDI bean that does what we require. Custom EL resolvers could come into play when Jakarta Faces is integrated in a completely different environment though, one where we'd like expressions to resolve to a completely different (managed) bean system. Even so, a CDI-to-other-beans-bridge might be a better option even there, but it's perhaps good to know a custom EL resolver is one other tool we have in our arsenal.

Anyway, to demonstrate what an EL resolver can do, we'll show an example where the base of an EL expression is interpreted as a pattern, something we can't do directly with a named CDI bean.

The following shows an example EL resolver:

```
public class CustomELResolver extends ELResolver {

    protected boolean isResolverFor(Object base, Object property) {
        return base == null
            && property instanceof String
            && ((String) property).startsWith("dev");
    }

    @Override
    public Object getValue
        (ELContext context, Object base, Object property)
    {
```

```
        if (isResolverFor(base, property)) {
            context.setPropertyResolved(true);
            return property.toString().substring(3);
        }

        return null;
    }

    @Override
    public Class<?> getType
        (ELContext context, Object base, Object property)
    {
        if (isResolverFor(base, property)) {
            context.setPropertyResolved(true);
            return String.class;
        }

        return null;
    }

    @Override
    public Class<?> getCommonPropertyType
        (ELContext context, Object base)
    {
        return base == null ? getType(context, base, null) : null;
    }

    @Override
    public boolean isReadOnly
        (ELContext context, Object base, Object property)
    {
        return true;
    }

    @Override
    public void setValue
        (ELContext context, Object base, Object property, Object value)
    {
```

```
        // NOOP
    }

    @Override
    public Iterator<FeatureDescriptor> getFeatureDescriptors
        (ELContext context, Object base)
    {
        return null;
    }
}
```

If we now use the following Facelet:

```
<!DOCTYPE html>
<html lang="en"
    xmlns:h="jakarta.faces.html"
>
    <h:head />
    <h:body>
        <p>Test: #{devThisIsDev}</p>
    </h:body>
</html>
```

we'll see "Test: ThisIsDev" being printed when requesting it. What's happening here is that the custom EL resolver handles every name that starts with "dev."

Dynamic Extensions

The previous examples were mostly about registering the extensions that we needed statically, for example, by registering a factory or the type directly in `faces-config.xml`. Factories give us an opportunity for some dynamic behavior. That is, at the point the factory is called, we can decide what new type (if any) to return.

For even more dynamic behavior, it's frequently required to be able to dynamically add the factories, or in CDI to dynamically add the producers. CDI has an elaborate SPI (service provider interface) for this (simply called "CDI Extensions"), which is, however, somewhat outside the scope of this book.

For classic factories and actually everything that's in `faces-config.xml`, there's a somewhat low-level method to add these dynamically: the Application Configuration Populator, which we'll discuss next.

Application Configuration Populator

The Application Configuration Populator is a mechanism to programmatically provide an additional `faces-config.xml` file, albeit by using the XML DOM (Document Object Model) API (application programming interface). This DOM API can be slightly obscure to use, and the power of the Application Configuration Populator is limited by its ability to only configure. There's no SPI in Jakarta Faces to directly modify other `faces-config.xml` at this level.

The mechanism works by implementing the abstract class `jakarta.faces.application.ApplicationConfigurationPopulator` and putting the fully qualified class name of this in a `META-INF/services/jakarta.faces.application.ApplicationConfigurationPopulator` file of a JAR library.

To demonstrate this, we'll create another version of the `ExternalContextProducer` that we demonstrated earlier, this time using the mentioned `ApplicationConfigurationPopulator`. For this, we take the same code, remove the `faces-config.xml` file, and add the `META-INF/services` entry as well as the following Java class:

```
public class ConfigurationProvider
    extends ApplicationConfigurationPopulator
{
    @Override
    public void populateApplicationConfiguration(Document document) {
        String ns = document.getDocumentElement().getNamespaceURI();
        Element factory = document.createElementNS(ns, "factory");
        Element externalContextFactory =
            document.createElementNS(ns, "external-context-factory");
            externalContextFactory.appendChild(
            document.createTextNode(
                ExternalContextProducer.class.getName()));
        factory.appendChild(externalContextFactory);
```

```
    document.getDocumentElement().appendChild(factory);
  }
}
```

A caveat is that since this uses the `java.util.ServiceLoader` under the hood, it really only works when `ConfigurationProvider` and `ExternalContextProducer` are packaged together in an actual JAR library placed in the `/WEB-INF/lib` of the WAR, instead of just being put directly in the WAR.

The Application Main Class

Earlier we discussed the Application Configuration Populator, which, as we saw, is actually a `faces-config.xml` provider of sorts. This means it works with fully qualified class names and elements that are still text in nature.

Jakarta Faces features a variety of somewhat more traditional programmatic APIs as well, with perhaps the most well-known of them being the `jakarta.faces.application.Application` main class, which is among others a holder for the same singletons that we mentioned previously in the section "Extending Classical Artifacts." For completeness, we'll repeat this list here.

- `jakarta.faces.application.NavigationHandler`

- `jakarta.faces.application.ViewHandler`

- `jakarta.faces.application.ResourceHandler`

- `jakarta.faces.component.search.SearchExpressionHandler`

- `jakarta.faces.flow.FlowHandler`

- `jakarta.faces.application.StateManager`

- `jakarta.faces.event.ActionListener`

All of these have corresponding setters on the `Application` class. For instance, the following shows the Javadoc and method declaration for `ActionListener`:

```
/**
 * <p>
 * Set the default {@link ActionListener} to be registered for all
 * {@link jakarta.faces.component.ActionSource} components.
 * </p>
```

```
 *
 * @param listener The new default {@link ActionListener}
 *
 * @throws NullPointerException
 *                if <code>listener</code> is <code>null</code>
 */
public abstract void setActionListener(ActionListener listener);
```

Likewise, the `Application` class also has "add" methods for the plug-in types we mentioned in the section "Plug-ins."

- `jakarta.el.ELResolver`

- `jakarta.faces.el.PropertyResolver` (deprecated)

- `jakarta.faces.el.VariableResolver` (deprecated)

- `jakarta.faces.component.serarch.SearchKeywordResolver`

A difficulty with using the `Application` class to set these singletons is, first of all, that it's timing sensitive. This means we can only set such classes from a certain point, which is obviously not before the point that the `Application` itself is available, and for some singletons not until the first request is serviced. This first request is a somewhat difficult point to track.

Specifically, the resource handler, view handler, flow handler, and state handler, uhhh, state *manager*, can't be set anymore after the first request, while the EL resolver and search keyword resolver can't be added either after said first request.

To demonstrate this, we'll add the custom EL resolver again that we demonstrated earlier, but in a more dynamic way now. To do this, we remove the EL resolver from our `faces-config.xml` file and add a system listener instead. Our `faces-config.xml` file then looks as follows:

```
<application>
    <system-event-listener>
        <system-event-listener-class>
            com.example.project.ELResolverInstaller
        </system-event-listener-class>
        <system-event-class>
            jakarta.faces.event.PostConstructApplicationEvent
```

```
        </system-event-class>
    </system-event-listener>
</application>
```

Indeed, this doesn't get rid of the XML and, in fact, it's even more XML, but reducing or getting rid of XML is not the main point here, which is the ability to register the EL resolver in a more dynamic way.

The system event listener that we just registered here looks as follows:

```
public class ELResolverInstaller implements SystemEventListener {
    @Override
    public boolean isListenerForSource(Object source) {
        return source instanceof Application;
    }
    @Override
    public void processEvent(SystemEvent event) {
        Application application = (Application) event.getSource();
        application.addELResolver(new CustomELResolver());
    }
}
```

What we have here is a system event listener that listens to the PostConstructApplicationEvent. This is generally a good moment to add plug-ins like the EL resolver. The Application instance is guaranteed to be available at this point, and request processing hasn't started yet, so we're surely in time before the first request has been handled.

Local Extension and Wrapping

In some cases, we don't want to override, say, a view handler globally, but only for a local invocation of, typically, a method in a component. Jakarta Faces gathers for this by passing on the FacesContext, which components to use as the main entry point from which to get pretty much all other things. Components are for Jakarta Faces not CDI artifacts or otherwise injectable, so the CDI approach for the moment doesn't hold for them.

Local extension can then be done by wrapping the FacesContext using FacesContextWrapper and passing that to the next layer. Note that the Servlet spec uses the same pattern where the HttpServletRequest and HttpServletResponse

can be wrapped by a filter using `HttpServletRequestWrapper` and
`HttpServletResponseWrapper` and passed on to the next filter, which can wrap it again
and pass it to its next filter, etc.

To illustrate this, suppose that for a certain component we'd like to augment the
action URL generation used by, among others, form components in such a way that
"`?foo=bar`" is added to this URL. If we do this by globally overriding the view handler, all
components and other code using the view handler would get to see this URL, while here
we'd only want this for this very specific component.

To achieve just this, we use wrapping here as illustrated in the following component:

```
@FacesComponent(createTag = true)
public class CustomForm extends HtmlForm {

    @Override
    public void encodeBegin(FacesContext context) throws IOException {
        super.encodeBegin(new ActionURLDecorator(context));
    }
}
```

Implementing the wrapper without support from Jakarta Faces would be a somewhat
tedious task, to say the least, as the path from `FacesContext` to `ViewHandler` is a few calls
deep and the classes involved have a large amount of methods. Luckily, Jakarta Faces
greatly eases this task by providing wrappers for most of its important artifacts, with an
easy-to-use constructor.

The pattern used here is that the top-level class (`ActionURLDecorator` from
the example earlier) extends from `FacesContextWrapper` and pushes the original
`FacesContext` to its superclass. Then the path of intermediate objects is implemented
by overriding the initial method in the chain (`getApplication()` here) and returning a
wrapper for the return type of that method, with the super version of it passed into its
constructor. This wrapper then does the same thing for the next method in the chain,
until the final method is reached for which custom behavior is required.

The following gives an example of this:

```
public class ActionURLDecorator extends FacesContextWrapper {

    public ActionURLDecorator(FacesContext context) {
        super(context);
    }
```

```
@Override
public Application getApplication() {
    return new ApplicationWrapper(super.getApplication()) {
        @Override
        public ViewHandler getViewHandler() {
            return new ViewHandlerWrapper(super.getViewHandler()) {
                @Override
                public String getActionURL
                    (FacesContext context, String viewId)
                {
                    String url = super.getActionURL(context, viewId);
                    return url + "?foo=bar";
                }
            };
        }
    };
}
}
```

With these two classes present in the Jakarta Faces application, now consider the following Facelet that makes use of our custom form component:

```
<!DOCTYPE html>
<html lang="en"
    xmlns:h="jakarta.faces.html"
    xmlns:test="jakarta.faces.component"
>
    <h:head />
    <h:body>
        <test:customForm action="index">
            <h:commandButton action="index" value="Go Index" />
        </test:customForm>
    </h:body>
</html>
```

Remember that no XML registration is needed for the custom component when it's annotated with @FacesComponent(createTag=true) and that its XML namespace defaults to jakarta.faces.component and its component tag name to the simple class name; see also Chapter 11.

If we request the view corresponding to this Facelet and press the button, then we'd indeed see "?foo=bar" appearing after the URL, meaning that our local extension of the view handler via a chain of wrappers has worked correctly.

Introspection

An important aspect of being able to extend a framework correctly is not only to be able to utilize extension points but also to be able to introspect the framework and query it for what artifacts or resources it has available.

One of the places where Jakarta Faces provides support for introspection is its ability to reveal which view resources are present in the system. Remember that in Jakarta Faces, views like, for example, Facelets are abstracted behind the view handler, which in turn manages one or more view declaration language (VDL) instances. A VDL, also called a templating engine, has the ability to read its views via the resource handler. As we've seen in this chapter, all these things can be augmented or even fully replaced.

This specifically means that views can come from anywhere (e.g., from the filesystem (most typical)) but can also be generated in memory, be loaded from a database or fetched over the network, and much more. Also, the simple physical file to logically view name mapping such as that used by Facelets doesn't have to hold for other view declaration languages at all.

Together this means that without an explicit introspection mechanism where the view handler, VDL, and resource handler can be asked which views/resources they have available, we would not be able to reliably obtain a full list of views.

Such list of views is needed, for example, when we want to utilize so-called extensionless URLs, which are URLs without any extension such as .xhtml or .jsf and without any extra path mapping present such as /faces/*. Lacking any hint inside the URL itself, the Servlet container on top of which Jakarta Faces works has to have some other way of knowing that a certain request has to be routed to the faces servlet.

A particularly elegant way to do this is by utilizing Servlet's "exact mapping" feature, which is a variant of URL mapping where an exact name instead of a pattern is mapped to a given servlet, which in this case would be the faces servlet. Since the Servlet spec has an API for dynamically adding Servlet mappings, and Jakarta Faces has an API to dynamical introspect which views are available, we pretty much only have to combine these two to implement extensionless URLs.

The following shows an example of how to do this:

```
@WebListener
public class ExtensionLessURLs implements ServletContextListener {

    @Override
    public void contextInitialized(ServletContextEvent event) {
        FacesContext facesContext = FacesContext.getCurrentInstance();
        event.getServletContext()
            .getServletRegistrations()
            .values()
            .stream()
            .filter(servlet -> servlet
                .getClassName().equals(FacesServlet.class.getName()))
            .findAny()
            .ifPresent(facesServlet -> facesContext
                .getApplication()
                .getViewHandler()
                .getViews(facesContext, "/",
                    ViewVisitOption.RETURN_AS_MINIMAL_IMPLICIT_OUTCOME)
                .forEach(view -> facesServlet.addMapping(view)));
    }
}
```

What happens here is that we first try to find the faces servlet, which incidentally is another example of introspection, this time in the Servlet spec. If found, we ask the view handler for all views. As mentioned earlier, this will internally introspect all the available view declaration instances, which in turn may introspect the resource handler. The "RETURN_AS_MINIMAL_IMPLICIT_OUTCOME" parameter is used to make sure all views are returned in their minimal form without any file extensions or other markers appended. This is the same form that can be returned from, for example, action methods or used with the action attribute of command components.

Having obtained the stream of views in the right format, we directly add each of them as exact mapping to the faces servlet that we found earlier.

For example, suppose we have a Facelet view in the web root in a folder /foo named bar.xhtml. Then getViews() will return a stream with the string "/foo/bar". When the faces servlet is mapped to this "/foo/bar", and assuming the Jakarta Faces application is deployed to the context path /test on domain localhost port 8080, we can request http://localhost:8080/test/foo/bar to see the rendered response of that Facelet.

Note that even though it's relatively simple to achieve extensionless URLs in Jakarta Faces this way, it's still somewhat tedious to have to do this for every application. It's expected that a next revision of Jakarta Faces will support this via a single setting.

Index

A

accept attribute, 395, 396
Accept-Language header, 483
actionListener attribute, 120
ActionSource interface, 74
Active locale, 484
addPhaseListener() and
      removePhaseListener()
      methods, 85
Alexander Smirnov's Telamon
      framework, 5
@Alternative and @Priority
      annotations, 452
Application programming interface (API),
      1, 175, 361, 477
Application-scoped data, 318
Application-scoped managed beans, 294
@Asynchronous annotation, 363
AuthenticationMechanismDefinition
      annotation, 434
autorun attribute, 141

B

Backing bean, 287
    binding attribute, 288
    duplication and unreusability, 290
    faces developer, 289
    FacesServlet, 291
    Jakarta Faces phases, 269
    layers, 328–330
    methods, 269
    MVC, 288
    service layer, 287
    value attribute, 288
Backing component, 269
BeanManager#fireEvent()method, 367
beforePhase()and afterPhase()
      methods, 84
binding attribute, 133, 134
Brace notation, 481
Browser-specified language, 480
Bundle files, 489
Bundle keys, 485

C

Cache busting, 236
Cascading Style Sheets (CSS), 487
CDI-injectable Jakarta Faces, 324
CDI.resolveItSomehow()method, 316
cleanSubject()method, 454
Client-window-scoped managed
      bean, 298
Component Search Expression
      Framework, 421
Component tree
    Ajax lifecycle, 79
    custom component system
      events, 91, 92
    definition, 63
    HTML components, 66, 67, 70
    HTTP, 63–66

519